Unitive Philosophy

By the Same Author

The Bhagavad Gita — translation and commentary.

Experiencing One-World.

An Integrated Science of the Absolute: based on the Darśana Mālā (Garland of Visions) of Narayana Guru, 2 Vcls.

Wisdom — The Absolute is Adorable.

The Word of the Guru: The Life and Teaching of Guru Nārāyaṇa.

Anthology of the Poems of Narayana Guru.

Autobiography of an Absolutist.

World Education Manifesto.

Towards a One World Economics.

Dialectical Methodology.

Wisdom's Frame of Reference.

Nataraja Guru

February 11, 1895 — March 19, 1973

Unitive Philosophy

by

Nataraja Guru

PRINTWORLD

Publishers of Indian Traditions

Cataloging in Publication Data — DK

[Courtesy: D.K. Agencies (P) Ltd. <docinfo@dkagencies.com>]

Nataraja Guru, 1895-1973, **author.**
Unitive philosophy / by Nataraja Guru.
pages cm
"First published in combined format, 2005" – Title page verso.
Copyright: Narayana Gurukula, Varkala, Kerala.
Includes index.
ISBN 9788124603390 (HB)

1. Vedanta. 2. Hindu philosophy. I. Narayana Gurukula. II. Title.

LCC B132.V3N38 2024 | DDC 181.48 23

ISBN 978-81-246-0339-0
First serialized in Values Magazine, 1963-66
First individual publication, 1986
First published in combined format, 2005
Reprinted in 2024

Website: www.geocities.com/islandgurukula
E-mail: tapovana@hevanet.com
Author: Nataraja Guru (1895-1973)

Printed and published by:
D.K. Printworld (P) Ltd.
Regd. Office: "Vedaśrī", F-395, Sudarshan Park
ESI Hospital Metro Station, New Delhi - 110015
Phones: (011) 4172 2626, 98713 94815
e-mail: indology@dkprintworld.com
Website: www.dkprintworld.com

Foreword

Nataraja Guru, formerly Dr. P. Natarajan M.A., L.T., D. Lit. (Paris), M.R.S.T. (London), was a product of modern Western education while simultaneously being a close disciple of Narayana Guru, a philosopher-saint of the East. His philosophy is thus a perfect blend of modern scientific thought and the perennial nondual mysticism of Advaitins (nondualists). Perceiving science with the intuitive eye of a philosopher-mystic enabled him to interpret philosophy in terms understandable and agreeable to modern scientists.

Scientists explore the reality underlying all natural phenomena, and try to explain the world in terms of that reality. Mystical philosophers, on the other hand, expound this one reality, realizing their own oneness with it. These two trends of thought harmoniously merge in the philosophy of Nataraja Guru.

One of the basic concepts of Indian mystical philosophers is that the apparent world is comprised of names and forms (*nama* and *rupa*), and they seek the one Reality behind such a world. Any exposition of such a vision necessarily has to rely on language as a medium. The linguistic exposition of the Ultimate Reality thus naturally finds expression through two facets: a name-based or word-based language and a form-based language. The former linguistic expression is referred to as metalanguage by Nataraja Guru, while the latter is called protolanguage. The vision being expounded and explained attains finality only when these two linguistic facets meet in the neutral ground of the reality searched for and the resulting unity is intuitively visualized. This insight is the keynote of Nataraja Guru's philosophical vision.

Metalanguage being a common everyday experience that all are familiar with, its application as a linguistic device in the philosophical representation of reality should come as no surprise. Conversely, protolanguage, or picture language, is best exemplified in communication by hand gestures. Iconography is another form of it. The most popular and mathematically precise protolanguage, however, is that of the Cartesian Correlates. Nataraja Guru displays no hesitation in employing this latter device to complement his otherwise metalinguistic philosophical exposition.

Cartesian Correlates admit the use of two axes of reference, one vertical and the other horizontal. Nataraja Guru, in his originally devised philosophical methodology, uses the vertical axis to stand for the eternal reality that exists absolutely and changelessly through time, and the horizontal axis to represent the spatially spread out transient world of multiplicity. The nonduality of these two conceivable realms of reality is represented by the central, neutral point where the two axes meet.

Nataraja Guru gave final shape to his philosophy in *An Integrated Science of the Absolute*, which is in fact a thoroughgoing exploration of reality through Narayana Guru's final work, *Darsanamala* (Garland of Visions). As a preliminary to it, he wrote a commentary on the *Atmopadesa Satakam* (One Hundred Verses of Self-Instruction) of Narayana Guru. This commentary was written mainly from the Western point of view, while the task of a commentary from an Eastern point of view was left to his disciples. As an exhaustive introduction to his *Atmopadesa Satakam* commentary, the Guru also wrote three series of articles, namely *Vedanta Revalued and Restated*, *The Philosophy of a Guru*, and *A Search for a Norm in Western Thought*.

In the first series of articles, Nataraja Guru examines the traditional background of Vedanta, which Narayana Guru restated and revalued in his philosophy, both metalanguage-wise and protolanguage-wise. The second series evaluates Narayana Guru's philosophy, as expounded in the *Atmopadesa Satakam*, as the perfect philosophy of an ideal Guru belonging to the Age of Science, at the same time highlighting his original contributions. The main features of the entire range of Western thought are brought under scrutiny in the third series in a penetrating attempt to uncover a universal norm, which in Vedanta is served by *brahman* (the Absolute) or *atman* (the Self). The study indeed unveils such a norm, which is woven throughout the entire fabric of Western thought.

The present volume is a compilation of these three series of articles, edited by Scott Teitsworth of the Portland Gurukula, U.S.A. *The One Hundred Verses of Self-Instruction*, to which these series form an introduction, has been published as a separate volume by Narayana Gurukula.

Swami Muni Narayana Prasad

Narayana Gurukula,
Srinivasapuram P.O.
Varkala, Kerala

Contents

Part II
The Philosophy of a Guru

Part III
The Search for a Norm in Western Thought

When I remember the days with Nataraja Guru, words hardly come to my mind although he used to orchestrate words in a super symphonic manner from early morning till late at night. The dearest memories I have of him are kept in that secret casquet within my soul which is mainly filled with silence.

Then, if I become a little more attentive to the details, these memories become mostly visual and Guru's silhouette fills my mind. . .

So human, so graceful,
So beautiful, Indeed a great dancer, Guru Nataraja
Salutations to him, again and again.

J. Letschert 7/8/83

Introduction

Science and philosophy both seek certitude. Each in its own way attempts to interpret the world in undeniable terms.

The history of European or Western science and philosophy is of a roughly linear progression from ignorance or doubt toward more clearly defined states. By contrast, Indian thought has followed a cyclic or circular pattern. Various systems of complete visions or darshanas have existed from very early on, but over time most of those systems degenerated into agglomerations of faith, confusion or superstition. Periodically, great thinkers have been able to restore the meaning of some of those systems by restating them in terms of their own era. Such a process is known as revaluation, by which value is restored to a vision from which all meaning has been leached out.

Narayana Guru was one of the great revaluators of India's Vedantic wisdom of the twentieth century. His disciple Nataraja Guru, with an extensive grounding in both Western and Eastern science and philosophy, became his expositor, enthusiastically applying the Guru's wisdom to the modern world, where it can be seen as encompassing numerous lines of thought.

The modern mind has been weaned on wisdom presented in simplified and easily digested language, which is fine as far as it goes. Nataraja Guru is not part of that movement, however. His aim was to complete and fulfill the historical trends in philosophy, and the vision he imbibed from Narayana Guru does not comfortably fit into simple terminology. It requires substantial effort on the part of the reader. Nataraja Guru leaves it up to the individual whether to appreciate what he says or not, refusing to draw attention to conclusions he considers obvious. Guru and disciple are to him equal partners in the learning process, the former striving to express truth in ever more perfect terms, while the latter works equally diligently to bring the words to life in his or her own mind.

Since many people wonder why they should bother with such a taxing philosophy, let's turn first to the Guru's defense of it:

> The question that a modern man will naturally ask about this taking refuge in such subtleties like "the meaning of meaning" for proving the reality of the Absolute would be: Why take so much trouble when the visible, demonstrable, practical world in which we live is sufficient for man for all ordinary purposes?
>
> This would be quite germane, if bread here was all that we needed for life. Man, however, does not live by bread alone. He craves for freedom too, and as *Homo sapiens* he is a thinking animal. This means that he must solve problems big or small to fulfill his life's purpose. Speculation inevitably steps into the breach.
>
> Philosophy would be superfluous if building bridges or developing the land for gaining bread were all that man needed. Man wants to live in security, free from fear. Fear of calamities, avoidable or inevitable, comes from various sources. Doubts from within cause discontent in each person. The mystery of life itself causes alternate fear or wonder in all normal men who do not willfully live in a fool's paradise, whether they are considered primitive or civilized, however much the latter may deny it in their pride. Wars and pestilences, famines and genocides due to fanaticisms or idolatries, need effective remedies which wisdom alone can give. Truth must make man free. (pp. 56-57)

Nataraja Guru was a master wordsmith, his speech a whirling symphony of interwoven ideas. It takes more than a little patience to learn to follow the music of it, but the vast terrain that opens up to view amply rewards the effort made. For his is that rarest of creatures: a fully formed philosophy.

Nataraja Guru scorned what he called half-baked philosophy. He felt that most people made do with unquestioned beliefs that would not stand up to unbiased scrutiny. Such poorly understood opinions are the seedbed of unhappiness, often leading to violence. He never lost sight of the idea that philosophy must bring happiness or it had no value whatsoever. He felt that Vedanta properly understood produces peace and joy without limit, as should any full-fledged system of thought.

One might initially be tempted to give up the inquiry altogether when confronted with Nataraja Guru's welter of words, unless convinced in advance of the superlative importance of their content. His insights provide access to the heart of any and all matters, leading to wholesale liberation from the bondage of incomplete or partial perspectives. To put it in a nutshell, the Guru's philosophy reveals a structural key to apprehending the absolute norm in any situation. His complex thought-structures are actually an integral part of his yogic wisdom discipline. As he sums up in the very last chapter, "The practical or beneficial service to which the scheme could be put by thinkers or writers is finally the only criterion of its validity."

Despite appearances, all (or nearly all) of Nataraja Guru's sentences can be decoded on a careful second or third reading. Often there is an initial sense of bafflement as the train of thought appears to have wandered out of sight. But it's still there, clothed in the dazzling verbal cloak of many colors of the Guru's inimitable style. By taking the time to sort out the clauses and catch the rhythm, the reader will begin to be amused rather than baffled, and will eventually find the style extremely precise and revealing. As an editor, I can attest that it is nearly impossible to change even a single word without disrupting the meaning.

Since all is provisional within maya or manifestation, Nataraja Guru is relentless in his use of conditional tenses, usually using "would be" or "might be" when the rest of us would say "is." His reversal of clauses may initially cause consternation, but the point is to counteract the habitual linear tendency of ordinary word usage. The flow of thought is reversed, twisted and ornamented like the development of a theme in music. It's a dynamic part of the presentation, dialectics in action. The reader must keep in mind the exhortation of the I Ching: perseverance furthers.

Like the crosshairs in a spotting scope, a structurally valid norm provides a reference to which all aspects of the situation can be referred. An accurately determined normative notion therefore allows the objective to be seen *as it is*, and not merely from one or another relative perspective. Lacking those crosshairs, a relativistic outlook displaces what is under consideration in the direction of the prejudice with which it is applied, and so misses the mark. Understood in this way, a normative notion of the Absolute is the most essential element in a scientifically balanced point of view.

The Absolute is the ultimate meaning contained in any system. Such meaning imparts value to all relative levels in respect to it, in the same way the trunk of a tree supports and nourishes the branches. In Chapter 6 of *Philosophy of a Guru,* Nataraja Guru describes the comparative value of the Absolute and the relative:

> A mathematically understandable schematic universe where thoughts and their linguistic expression overlap or coincide, as when names and forms converge when we say "rose" and visualize it, is at the core of the notion of the Absolute, when everything gross or inert and in reality extraneous to the Absolute, compromising or

hiding it through degrees of opacity or ignorance, is shorn from its pure, luminous and transparent nature. The veil can be thickly or thinly laid on but it is the degree of veiling that makes for all the gradations of apparent manifestation which are, in fact, extraneous to the notion of the Absolute as such.

The Guru spoke passionately of structuralism, in part because he strongly believed a pictorial approach to spirituality or reality could free humans from the veiling generated by wordy religion or philosophy. Not just any picture, certainly, but a well-organized, balanced pictorial structure with the potential to incorporate everything is the means to transcend the bondage of partial understanding.

The fault of descriptive verbiage is that its linear approach can never quite arrive at totality. The infinite is not reached by numerical increments, but by an all-encompassing, intuitive comprehension. The Absolute must be grasped as a whole.

A key idea to keep in mind here is that any standpoint that has an opposite cannot be the Absolute. Structuralism helps to identify opposing factors, which can then be discarded. In other words, structuralism is a method to envision the incomprehensible.

Every interpretation posits a particular static framework by which the non-static Absolute is viewed at that particular moment. All frames are necessarily limited in this way; oddly, the mathematical measurement of this limitation is well known and is expressed in Heisenberg's uncertainty principle. Henri Bergson attempted to overcome this seemingly insuperable barrier through an act of intuition that leaves all frames of reference behind. "The true mystic just opens his heart to the onrushing wave," is his instruction, providing a link between the highest expressions of Western philosophy and Vedantic wisdom. The Guru elaborates on this same realization by saying:

> The Absolute has to have a living content, without which it is nothing more than a word without meaning in life. The content is the resultant of the meeting, from two opposing sides, as it were, of physical and metaphysical factors, both reducible in terms of *intuition* into a common homogeneity. When so reduced into unitive terms there will be a mutual transparency and participation between matter and mind in a neutral matrix with a constant osmotic interchange, like respiration mentioned in many of the Upanishads.
>
> Action and inaction meet in such an alternating osmotic interchange that is both inter-subjective and trans-physical. This grand osmosis, which includes the macro- and microcosms at once within consciousness, collective or individual, yields peace and joy without limit. Such are some of the high claims of Vedanta. (p. 164)

The Guru adds that the process "involves neither positive effort nor negative passivity to attain."

Nataraja Guru occasionally gets sidetracked by his desire for the beauty and harmony of Vedanta to be recognized by modern scientists and philosophers. There is an element almost of defensiveness, as if he is acutely aware of the disinterest of the thinkers of his day. Since these books were written, philosophy has largely removed its blinders in respect to pure Vedanta, and the Guru would find a much more receptive audience today.

Be that as it may, his point is well taken that skepticism is as much an a priori belief as is faith, and a fair-minded scientist must strike a balance between them. It is very difficult to prove something is impossible; our doubts most often spring from simple assumptions rather than rigorous proof. Referring to the impact of the wonder experienced in arriving at a valid norm of mental orientation, the Guru says:

> The correct focus is the one that knocks down and stuns the onlooker to an utter forgetfulness of his individuality,

> He then experiences union with the Absolute — an experience "beyond all thought or word" as the Upanishads prefer to put it in the mildest of terms. There is nothing humanly impossible here, as moderns empirically-minded or conditioned might seem to think. If such a vision is the prejudice of the believer, the rejection of the same is open to a similar charge of scepticism from the opposite pole of the same knowledge situation. To keep the middle or neutral ground is what lends scientific status to such matters. A scientist holds the balance between scepticism and belief. (p. 82)

Nataraja Guru's contention that the West bears a bias against the idea of the Absolute held over from the days of the Inquisition is well taken. He adroitly identifies the absolute element in a broad segment of western philosophy, much of which styles itself anti-absolutist or relativist because of this bias.

The term relativity is itself misleading. By incorporating all relative factors into one overarching perspective the aim is to arrive at the Absolute via a unified field. Thus relativity embraces the Absolute, while absolutist attitudes paradoxically tend to become mired in parochialism, as the various totalitarian systems of the past and present attest all too eloquently.

Actually, being "scientific" is no guarantee of a normative or balanced orientation to life. Examples abound of prejudicially biased experimentation, to the point where science itself has for a long time been aware of the pervasive effects of pre-established expectations, and takes steps for their elimination. Bias is relatively easy to detect when we look back in history, but is more elusive when dealing with the present. The deconstruction movement is aimed at unearthing this built-in bias, with the discomfiting discovery that in most cases after subtracting prejudice from a field there is not much of anything of substance left in it.

While even more elusive to uncover than prejudice, any integral philosophy will have at its core an assumption of irrefutable truth on which the rest hinges. Although named differently by different thinkers, this bedrock assumption is none other than the ubiquitous Absolute itself. Thus the Guru feels it is high time to abandon the bias against the Absolute as a last clinging tendril of the Inquisition.

The danger inherent in latent bias is well expressed by the Guru when speaking of Hegel, whose philosophy he highly admired:

> Here his pan-Germanic "will to power" becomes already evident. This is the factor that warped and distorted his approach to absolutism, as we have already said. His approach needs axiological reorientation so that the pure creativity of the Absolute may not give justification for partial egoistic distortions of the will and its miscarriage into undesirable and disastrous channels, which it did, as later history records. The ego in man is an ever-present danger which will distort any normative notion and bend it to its own prejudices. Only on the soil of absolute detachment and dispassionateness can the right kind of absolutism flourish, as history and individual lives have amply shown. (p. 394)

There are a few ideas peculiar to the Guru it will be helpful to be familiar with ahead of time.

Often the Guru would begin a discourse by drawing a vertical and a horizontal line within a diamond lozenge and labeling their intercept with an O. This was the most basic version of his structural scheme of correlation. Under the heading The Absolute Independent of all Relative Reference in Chapter 6 of *Vedanta Revalued and Restated* there is an explanation of Nataraja Guru's use of the Cartesian coordinates to express truth, mentation and values. This may well be considered his most important single contribution to philosophy.

Briefly, the horizontal and vertical axes are used as a schematic representation of dialectical polarities such as physical and metaphysical, concrete and abstract, observables and calculables, space and time, name and form, and so on. Near the end of *Search for a Norm in Western Thought,* Nataraja Guru provides a broad definition: "What is given to the senses objectively is the horizontal, and what is given to the self as 'I' or 'my' or 'mine' belongs to the vertical." He further points out:

> Each such pair can be said to belong together to a psychophysical grade or order of its own. Contrast, contradiction or contrariety belong to each ambivalent, reciprocal or dichotomous couple or set of poles in the total knowledge situation, with degrees of duality regulating their bipolarity. When there is full accentuation of the differentiating principle, we live in a horizontal world of values, with plus and minus separating each pair of the same grade. When, on the other hand, the polarity is less accentuated, contradiction tends to cancel differences between pairs of counterparts by one term canceling out the other. The former has a horizontal or arithmetical status, while the latter has a vertical or geometrical status. (p. 132)

By viewing polarities as being united by an axis of relative values, a harmony may be struck between them. Such equipoise does nothing less than reveal the Absolute.

Much of this thought structure springs from dialectics, equivalent to the Yoga of the Bhagavad Gita. The Guru quotes Hegel in Chapter 9 of *The Search for a Norm in Western Thought*: "Every concept is rational, is absolutely opposed to another, and is united in comprehension together with its opposites. *This is the definition of dialectic.*" Further, in Nataraja Guru's words, dialectics consists of "equating counterparts, which give us certitude by revealing that one set of facts, truths or realities are the same as another, thus disclosing some fundamental relational aspect having significance in human life."

Dialectics has a specific place in the overall scheme:

> This kind of reasoning, the dialectical, which takes us to the threshold of higher idealistic values in life is the third and the last step in philosophical methodology taken as a whole. The laws of nature refer to the world of existence. Rules of thought, whether axiomatic or based on postulates, refer to the world of subsistence. The third step of reasoning lives and has its being in the pure domain of human values, those referring to the True, the Good or the Beautiful, which are values in life and thus belong to the domain of axiology.
>
> The experimental method suits existential aspects of the Absolute, the logical suits the subsistential and the dialectical suits the value aspects of the Absolute. Interest in the physical world gives place in the second stage of ascent to logical psychology or phenomenology, where ratiocination plays its part. Finally we ascend higher into the third aspect of the Absolute where value relations hold good and the instrument or methodology used is that of dialectics. (pp. 379-80)

The overwhelming experience of wonder or beauty literally springs from a normalized attitude of mind, often called *samadhi* or sameness. How this plays out in real life is the story of the spiritual search itself:

> If we add that higher and higher bipolar interests which bind the Self with the non-Self can be imagined, some having proportionately more horizontal values implied in them than others, and which can rise vertically to the limits of purity in the Absolute itself with fully conscious affiliation to absolutist values, then the modus of spiritual progress will be fully outlined. (p. 234)

Nataraja Guru uses methodology, epistemology and axiology as English equivalents to sat, chit and ananda, or existence, knowledge, and the parameters of value. While he is trying to find equivalents in western terminology here, for most readers the Sanskrit terms are actually more familiar.

Polyvalence refers to the many-sidedness of possible meanings that can arise through exploding previous understandings.

The modern trend is to dispense with the cumbersome 19th century diacritic marks outside of scholarly works on the Sanskrit language itself. This trend is followed in the present work.

And lastly, the reader should try not to miss the sly humor with which the Guru expresses many of his ideas. Speaking of how the world of horizontal necessity interferes with the quest for truth, he says:

> Utilitarian interests in social life are many at any given time. From the refrigerator to the television set, we can think of various utilities or luxuries between which a pragmatist can be torn every minute of his life by rival and multiple attractions and repulsions. (p. 276)

The ecstatic wonder and quiet humor of the vision Nataraja Guru consistently strove to impart is beautifully expressed by Long Chen Pa in his Natural Freedom of Mind: "Since everything is but an apparition, perfect in being what it is, having nothing to do with good or bad, acceptance or rejection, one may well burst out in laughter."

Scott Teitsworth
Portland, Oregon, 2005

Particulars

Values Magazine, begun in 1955, was the precursor of the still-extant Gurukulam Magazine. The three works combined here as *Unitive Philosophy* appeared in sequence in Values as follows:

Vedanta Revalued and Restated
— Nov. 1963 – Nov. 1964.

The Philosophy of a Guru
— Jan. 1965 – Nov. 1965.

Search for a Norm in Western Thought
— Jan. 1966 – Nov. 1966.

The writing of Nataraja Guru's magnum opus, *An Integrated Science of the Absolute,* began in tandem with his work on *The Search for a Norm in Western Science.*

Having come to believe that a true unified field theory would not merely unite gravitation and electromagnetism, but physics and metaphysics, and that integrating those aspects of reality was an essential problem facing civilization, Nataraja Guru wrestled with the issue through most of the nineteen-sixties. Thus *Unitive Philosophy* can serve as an introduction to the Guru's ultimate contribution to global thought in his *Science of the Absolute.*

The unifying thread of the Absolute runs through all three books in this compilation. *Vedanta Revalued and Restated* presents the Indian notion of the Absolute, often overlooked in the popular interpretations, and introduces Nataraja Guru's scientific structural analysis. *Philosophy of a Guru* surveys the Absolute as found in Narayana Guru's philosophy, which Nataraja Guru considered to be among the finest expressions of wisdom anywhere. The third book, *The Search for a Norm in Western Thought*, traces the often-invisible presence of the Absolute through the history of Western Philosophy, including rationalism and skepticism.

Each individual book features a summary in the last chapter, which might well be read first, and *Vedanta Revalued and Restated* also has a explication of the scope of Vedanta in Chapter 8 that would be a good overall starting point for readers unfamiliar with the subject matter.

Taken as a whole the books reveal the profound wisdom of one of the great thinkers of our age, who is able to encompass the entire panoply of human endeavor at a glance. The reader is invited to try such a cosmic perspective on for size.

Part I
Vedanta Revalued and Restated

1

The Background, Origin and a New Approach

India is a land of enigmas and wonders. Besides its mountains, rivers and seas, its people present such a variety of types, dress and language, and such a wide range of beliefs and behaviour patterns as to puzzle the newcomer.

Prevailing cults, doctrines and dogmas present a confused tangle. Their time-honoured customs and manners challenge and baffle the researches of the most penetrating of inquirers. The Indian subcontinent may thus be said to present the aspect of a veritable museum, with an endless variety of interesting features.

Exaggerations and superlatives are normal in this land of rolling plains and snow-capped mountain peaks. Pitch-dark nights alternate with days when sunshine manifests more colourfully what was absorbed within the womb of Nature. Enjoying comparative isolation by natural frontiers, this land has preserved something of its ancient personality, surviving the cross-breezes of time that have more easily ruffled the atmosphere of neighbouring regions.

The Historical-Cultural Background

More like a weed than a well-tended garden plant, humanity in South Asia exhibits striking contrasts as between high and low, rich and poor, Brahmin and Pariah, who segregate themselves in toil or in leisure, assorted into groups with distinct traits in an almost amorphous matrix or mixture. The major portion of the submerged masses are inarticulate or even dumb, driven by the stark necessities of life. Castes and tribes have thus persisted, with their distinguishing names and special outer marks, graded between static and closed groupings and more open and dynamic ones.

Since the Indian mind is accentuated toward subjectivity, the historical sense in respect of actual dates of facts is poorly developed. This is due to the at least 2500 and possibly as many as 7000 years to which memory has to be stretched backwards to find the sources of secular or spiritual life. Uncertainties have to be allowed in terms of centuries and not in decades, and sometimes even in terms of millennia in respect of many important events, or in the dates of important books.

Speculation has gone on unbridled through the ages on the Indian soil. Specific and generic personalities, half real and half mythological, abound, such as a Brihaspati vying with a Dakshinamurti, a Vishvamitra with a Vasishtha, and a Vyasa with a Valmiki. We are offered a gallery of figures about whose lives we know next to nothing. Often, too, a contemplative geography takes the place of one in which longitude is valid. India is spoken of as Jambu-Dvipa, the Island of Berries, in certain Sanskrit books, and there is a vast submerged continent called Tamilakam to which it belonged, spoken of in ancient Tamil literature. Epochs are referred to in terms of *yuga*s, each of them having a duration of a million years.

Scepticism and belief, reason and sentiment, have crossed over from one side to the other, changing between what was considered orthodox at one time into heterodox at another, and so on, many times over, during the long history of Indian thought. It is like a rope with many bright and dark strands, whose individual fibres took up the continuity one after another.

Such are some of the background aspects into which we have to fit our study of Vedanta, which is a revaluation of the Veda that went before it. We can think of this situation as a tree of Wisdom which has put forth its best blossoms through a period of about five thousand years, as Dr. Paul Deussen has compared it. We have to think of this cultural expression as a process of dialectical revaluation and restatement, taking place imperceptibly and in infinitesimal gradations through decades, centuries, even millennia, resulting in what is now recognized as present-day Vedanta. Alive even to this day, Vedanta may be said to be the culminating expression of Indian wisdom.

Much of present day Vedanta, however, having become overcovered with the debris of latter-day Indian scholasticism, stands in need of restatement, after being correctly revalued in the light of a correct Vedantic methodology, epistemology and axiology, in order to give it a normalized scientific status, balancing both scepticism and belief, and applying the instruments of reason, criticism and intuition to the total knowledge situation implicit in it.

Empty "Lord-Lord"-ism, harsh exclusiveness, wrong loyalty to the dead letter rather than to the spirit, partial preferences and the lack of a resultant firm justice, a misplaced sense of value, and errors of judgement which spell disasters, big or small, are some of the evils sought to be mitigated by our present inquiry. This is the task we shall undertake in the pages that follow.

Pre-Vedic India

India was already civilized before the Aryans came with their Vedic religion. Until the significance of the Indus Valley civilization was recognized, Indian historians invariably began their first chapters with reference to the Vedas as the source of Indian spiritual life. But the excavations at Mohenjo-Daro and Harappa in the Indus Valley and at sites such as Lothal in Gujarat, have opened a backward vista of a couple of millennia more in which a pre-Aryan civilization existed. When the Aryans came they had to face the challenge of an order of things that existed before, and to respond to the new situation.

The Vedas, which began by reflecting a simple, natural and fully human sense of wonder about the phenomenal aspects of life, based on a vague belief in the Absolute, had to be subjected to several revisions, revaluations, and restatements, after this contact with the previous civilization.

The result is discernible in the various grades of wisdom literature, of which the three Vedas, the Rik, Sama and Yajus stand apart as a group in themselves by the primitive purity of their style and subject matter. They are filled with a sense of the numinous. They represent the first outpourings of the awakened self of man at the dawn of Indian history.

If prose is suited to practical purposes and poetry to purer or spiritual purposes, the language of the Vedas may be said to excel in the latter. Whatever reference there might be to action in the hymns, chants and liturgies of the Vedas, refers to the context of burnt sacrifices to propitiate the pantheon of personifications of cosmological and phenomenal aspects of the Absolute. Their exact status in theology or psychology may be questioned, but the high protolinguistic and poetic value in the context of the wonder of the adorable Absolute is beyond question. They must be subjected to their own innate standards of criticism, as has been done by Jaimini, and then they become a body of wisdom which can hold its own against any philosophy in the world, including even the Vedanta, which itself, in many respects, has to presuppose the anterior and the more antique of the two disciplines, the Veda.

The Revaluation Process

The challenge and the response, or the blast and the counterblast aspects as they prevailed in India when the Aryans came into contact with the pre-Aryans, by whatever name known, has to be visualized somewhat as follows.

The green pastures and fields attracted the invaders in small groups as they penetrated inward from the northwest through a period of centuries or a millennia between the limits of 2500 to 1500 years ago, roughly speaking, if we are permitted to guess between controversial dates. They had cattle and horses and were formed somewhat like a city-state, with three groups within, which tended to segregate themselves by their natural functions as priests, soldiers and traders, and to which they added a fourth group, which was not within the fold, but could come and go as servants. The Aryans seem to have brought neither servants, nor enough women, judging from cases such as that of Dronacharya, who was a preceptor of archery to the Pandavas and who took Kripi for wife.

The origins of Vyasa and his father Parashara reveal sufficiently the state of intercourse prevailing as between the originals and the newcomers. The story of the Pandavas and the circumstances of their birth and parentage show some complexity, promiscuity and polyandry as normal in those days, as with many prehistoric peoples the world over.

Vyasa, otherwise called Veda-Vyasa, the central figure of Indian spirituality looked at from any angle or point of view, had a fisher damsel for mother, and his father Parashara was born of a Pariah woman, as stated in the beginning of the Mahabharata itself.

The settlers soon created for themselves pockets of influence, and as between those who joined the side of the newcomers and those who were of the original group. Whether by loyalty or blood, two blocs developed in and around Hastinapura or Ayodhya (modern Delhi and Oudh respectively), not necessarily at the same epoch. The story of the clan of Raghu (or Rama) had the latter city for its epicentre, and the Pandavas under Krishna, who were of the Mahabharata context, had the former.

About the activities of both of these groupings we have ample literature on which to base our broad guesswork, in the two great epics of India, the Ramayana and the Mahabharata. The Ramayana has a story that moves from the north to the south, bringing a revalued culture, not necessarily all Aryan, to instill law and order and some refinement in the peoples of the south. This may be recognized as an expression of the "blast" side of the situation in which challenge and response must be distinguished if we are to place Veda and Vedanta in their proper perspectives.

The Mahabharata episode moves from the prehistoric pre-Aryan context to an Aryan heaven which the eldest of the Pandavas refuses to enter if his dog is not admitted, and where his enemies are already fully accepted persons holding responsible offices. The Bhagavad Gita episode itself states the way in which Vedic relativism and Samkhya dualism are revalued and restated in terms in keeping with Vedantism. Elsewhere[1] we have given to these matters fuller space already, and we are only referring to this aspect here in passing, to show that Veda and Vedanta are to be looked upon as counterparts, Vedanta being the revaluation of the Veda.

From Non-Brahmin Sources

If Veda belongs to the orthodoxy of the brahmin priest, Vedanta was in the possession mainly of kings like Janaka, or men of lowly social status like Raikva, the cart driver with itches on his body, who as custodian of Vedantic wisdom would not readily impart it even to superior people such as the brahmins. Similar references which are not at all few, elsewhere in the Upanishads, point in the same direction.

Vedanta is the result of the interaction of primitive and crude Vedism — which latter was vitiated by the acceptance of cruel and unclean animal sacrifices and a harsh, exclusive priesthood, who would not allow a Shudra (the servant who

1. See *The Word of the Guru*; *The Bhagavad Gita*; *An Integrated Science of the Absolute*; *Wisdom's Frame of Reference* and *Dialectical Methodology* by the present author.

necessarily belonged to the rival group) to study the secrets of his wisdom — with a form of higher Wisdom of the Absolute, which grew up from the meeting of the twin philosophical and critically revalued spiritual traditions called the two *mimamsas* (critiques), the *purva* (former) and the *uttara* (latter), this last being closer to Vedanta proper.

The subtle dialectical relation between these two critical schools will be examined by us later. Suffice it to say here that Vedanta combines and reconciles Veda with the critical and philosophical aspect of wisdom into *brahmavidya*, the Science of the Absolute. How this is made an accomplished fact is what we have to explain.

Within the limits of belief in the Vedas and a full-fledged agnosticism, having scepticism and even atheism at its core, the tree of Indian wisdom presents us with many problems, requiring a large treatise to do it justice. In this present study we shall content ourselves with the revision, restatement and revaluation of some aspects of Vedanta that interest us particularly, in the light of modern developments in scientific and philosophical thought, and pertaining also to the philosophy of Narayana Guru, which may be said to mark the culmination of revalued Vedantism in the India of recent time. As we shall see, the structural, subjective and selective features pertaining to the notion of the Absolute evidenced in the writings of Narayana Guru are shared by Vedantic thought also, and it is exactly these aspects that are of interest to us.

How to Distinguish Veda from Vedanta

Strictly speaking, the distinction between what is known as the Veda and its dialectical revaluation into Vedanta is one of the most central and difficult problems to be faced.

For this purpose, we have to draw first the preliminary distinction between Vedism as it manifested itself in its primitive form as a natural and actual historical occurrence and critical Vedism, as it was subjected to later additions and amendments. Mere elaboration of the raw material of the Veda is one thing, and its subjection to dialectical revaluation is another. Both have gone on abreast in respect of the Veda, as it passed through the stages of *Agama*s (traditions), *Brahmana*s (commentaries) and *Aranyaka*s (forest teachings), forming various *shakha*s (branches) tending to be more critical, rational or philosophical, from mere ritualistic beginnings, supplemented by hymns, chants or mantras (evocative sound-spells).

The four stages of life may be said to correspond to the stages of the historical development of Vedic thought itself, as it passed through simple sacrificial acts with their connected gestures and chants, into more elaborated forms of ritual and mutterings, suited for various occasions and circumstances, and on to non-ritualistic pure wisdom.

Various rishis (seers), gurus (wisdom preceptors) or *muni*s (quietists), who lived in the forests away from society, had their own favourite or particular Vedic traditions and chants, each with a form of ritual belonging to it, which made them into distinct units of Vedic schools, some of which specialized in Vedic exegetics, semantics or grammar. In this way a complex situation arose in which Vedism underwent a drastic modification of context as well as content.

Thus, if Veda is the tail end of a knowledge situation, we have to think of Vedanta as belonging to the front pole where it gets more finalized by ever greater dialectical revaluations.

The intermediate literature presents a region where speculation thrives both ways as in a no-man's land between two contending armies. Each of the eighteen chapters of the Bhagavad Gita represents one of the various permutations and combinations possible in this dialectical revaluation pertaining to the categories of Existence, Subsistence and Value in Vedanta philosophy. (As we have devoted a volume to the unraveling of the intricacies of the Bhagavad Gita it is not necessary to linger here on this subject any longer.)

The two *mimamsas* (critiques) called the *pracina* (antique) or the *purva* (anterior) and the *uttara* (posterior or more finalized), have between them a subtle dialectical affinity, based on an apparent opposition, and it is to explain this affinity that the subtlest polemical, logical, exegetic and semantic powers of great teachers like Jaimini and Badarayana have been lavishly expended in their writings. When one is understood in terms of the other, reciprocally both ways, with all their subtle epistemological and axiological implications, cosmologically, psychologically and eschatologically, we can consider ourselves to have touched the core of our subject.

There are three canonical texts which have been accepted for this purpose in Vedanta, namely the Upanishads, the Brahma Sutras, and the Bhagavad Gita. Between these three we can reasonably expect all Vedantic doctrines to have been touched upon in one context or another. When these texts are treated together with the *mahavakya*s (the great dicta of the Vedanta), and if they are properly explained and understood with their significance and position in the body of knowledge, we can rest satisfied that we have given some definiteness of content to the complex and multi-apartmented mansion of what is vaguely referred to as Vedantic wisdom.

The Two Conventional Divisions

It is already conventionally accepted that the totality of Indian spirituality of the Vedic context may be divided broadly into the *jnana-kanda* (section on pure reason) and *karma-kanda* (section on practical, ritualistic or other action). When both of these exist together they enter into conflict with each other if not handled dialectically; but if treated dialectically they are absorbed without contradiction into a middle ground which is inclusive of both, where both contradiction and paradox are transcended.

There are thus two methods and two distinct epistemological positions possible: the one that admits the principle of contradiction and the other that does not do so.

Advaita (non-duality), Visishtadvaita (non-duality admitting some difference between quality and the qualified Absolute) and Dvaita (accepting the duality of ambivalent poles within the structure of the Absolute) are all possible varieties of Vedanta, each of which finds justification in the three canonical texts referred to above, and without violating the requirements of the great dicta and the spirit of Vedanta as a whole. They represent grades in which the Absolute Idea or Norm can transcend paradox or bypass the principle of contradiction and excluded middle in giving differing accentuations to the value-factor of the content of the idea from the theological, psychological or purely epistemological angles.

Ritualism and gnosis, which are rival factors involved in Vedanta, either enter into conflict horizontally, or absorb one another when vertically treated. Herein is a secret of Vedanta, on which the author of the Gita has put his finger with precision and certitude when he says:

> On what is action and what is inaction, even intelligent men here are confused. I shall indicate to you that action, on knowing which you will be emancipated from evil.
>
> One has to understand about action and understand about wrong action. Again one has to have a proper notion of non-action. The way of action is elusively subtle (indeed).
>
> The one who is able to see action in inaction, and inaction in action, he among men is intelligent, he is one of unitive attitude (*yogi*) while still engaged in every (possible) kind of work. (IV, 16-18)

In the last of these verses we have the paradox of action and inaction most squarely faced and the dialectical solution suggested without contradiction of their rival claims. Dialectically treated the paradox is resolved; but when treated from the point of view of ordinary logic which excludes the middle ground and accepts the principle of contradiction, the conflict stares us in the face, and so to treat *jnana* and *karma* together would be unjustified. We shall have more to say on this kind of dialectical methodology of the Vedanta as occasions present themselves.

Meanwhile, these citations from the Bhagavad Gita, which is perhaps the most central authority for Vedanta, being repeatedly cited in the Brahma Sutras of Badarayana, which latter is perhaps its only possible rival if any, suffice to show that the gnostic and the ritualistic traditions in Vedanta need not divide wisdom into two watertight compartments (as popular opinion might want us to believe) when viewed in the context of the higher wisdom that Vedanta is meant to represent.

What Shankara refers to as the evil of promiscuously mixing up wisdom with action (*jnana-karma-samuchchaya*) can thus be avoided when the dialectical methodology proper to Vedanta is fully explained and understood, since *samanvaya* (dialectical agreement or "harmony" as often translated) can replace the *samuchchaya* (mixing up) which would spell wrong Vedantism.

At the core of Vedantic wisdom there is lodged a paradox which we have approached frontally here, to get started on our subject. As we go along, some of the points or aspects still left obscure in the Vedanta philosophy will perhaps be cleared up. Vedanta transcends paradox by the postulation of an overall normative notion of the Absolute as an Existent-Subsistent-Value.

2

The Three Categories of Reality

All philosophy and science stand for certitude through thinking. Logic and mathematics lay down the methods by which certitudes are reached when mere thought, unsupported by methods or calculations, involves varying degrees of doubt about the steps of thinking or research.

Vedanta philosophy, or *brahmavidya* (Science of the Absolute) as it is more correctly named, is no exception to the rule. It seeks certitude about absolute Existence, Subsistence, or Value, comprised in one notion called *brahman*. (Brahman should not be confused with Brahma, the four-headed god of the Hindu pantheon. It represents the Absolute when used as a neuter and not as a masculine.)

Texts and the Great Dicta

To reveal the nature of the Absolute in poetic, figurative, or other convincingly authorized or valid language, is what the Upanishads, the most important body of literature of canonical status for Vedanta, has as its principal task.

The Absolute, being by nature a mystery and a wonder, means that the teaching of the Upanishads refers to a kind of philosophy that tends to be esoteric; but when it has been subjected to more critical, rational and intuitive treatment in the Brahma Sutras of Badarayana (which is universally recognized as the second canonical text of Vedanta), and in the third similar canonical text called the Bhagavad Gita (which, though, is sometimes referred to as a *smriti*, a code of obligatory duties of secondary importance), the subject matter of these three authoritative texts attains to a fully philosophical status both from esoteric and exoteric norms of thought.

Both a priori and a posteriori means of valid reasonings are employed in Vedanta to arrive at the four great dicta (or *mahavakya*s) which define the finalized finds (or *lakshya*) of the Vedantic research or inquiry. Expressed in the first, second or third personal or impersonal pronouns as referring to the Self or ultimate Reality, they read: "Pure consciousness is the Absolute," "That existent is the Absolute," "This Self is Absolute," and "That thou art." In whatever grammatical or syntactical form they may be put, they represent an equation between two aspects of the Absolute, one which is visible and the other which is intelligible whether in the context of the cosmological, the psychological or the theological orders of reality.

The great dicta may be said to be answers to the two most generalized problems of all philosophical inquiry; two grand questions arising ever and everywhere in the human understanding: Who am I? And how came this world? These two questions are fundamental and basic to all philosophical inquiry on the part of anyone endowed with natural curiosity to know about his environment and himself as together making a sensible whole in the Absolute.

Vedanta follows such wholesale lines of inquiry and boldly claims to hold the answer to these questions, which is more than the most intrepid of modern analytic philosophers dare to claim.

There are modern philosophers who tend to believe that wholesale answers to globally or totally conceived problems are no longer justified, and that the scientific spirit pertains to piecemeal annexation of one fact after another to the total store of human knowledge by demonstrable steps of trial and error. They are thus sceptical empiricists or pragmatists, confined to the instrumental or the operational world of probabilities with a partial epistemology, methodology and axiology.

Vedanta, on the other hand, is rather a bold, wholesale, frontal and a priori approach to ultimate realities of the most generalized order; and its natural starting point is belief rather than scepticism.

Valid Means of Certitude

The other valid means of certitude such as what is demonstrable and given to the senses, such as the eyes, etc. (pratyaksha), are not omitted, but given a revised epistemological and subjective status in Vedanta. They are fitted into an overall scheme with a transparency or homogeneity in the common medium of participation, which is neither mind or matter, but something with a neutral status in the Absolute.

Vedanta is thus a complete philosophy of the Absolute, with a rather subjectively biased epistemological status, with a methodology which admits of all valid means of certitude, from empiricism through rationalism, criticism and intuitionism, with an importance also attached to semantic considerations, and referring to a high human value or goal to be reached for all mankind.

Although often mistaken for pantheism, pessimism, solipsism, eclecticism, idealism or syncretism, none of these terms can be considered sufficient to cover the character of Vedanta, which is an integrated philosophy, a psychology, a cosmology, and a theology by its own right at one and the same time. It is often legitimately or illegitimately used as a surrogate of religion.

Although some aspects of Vedanta stand in need of revision or clarification in the light of modern norms and standards in philosophy, there is no gainsaying the verity that it represents a monument of the heights to which speculation in the human mind can attain. Progress in modern times tends rather to confirm Vedanta rather than discredit it or put it into cold storage. When properly restated, it can even offer the basis for a one world philosophy or a unified science of tomorrow.

The much misunderstood Purva Mimamsa will be seen, on closer study, to be nothing but semantics, offering the frame of reference for a language of unified science. Schematicism, structuralism, subjectivism and a selective epistemology all lie at the basis of Vedanta, in which not only the Vedas but the six systems of Indian philosophy, all of which have gone into disuse and mistrust at the present day, have been successfully integrated already into one body of unified wisdom. The normative notion of the Absolute is the factor giving unity and organic coherence to the various elements of philosophy or science, logic or mathematical discipline that have contributed, or should legitimately be taken to have contributed to this body of unitive wisdom called Advaita Vedanta, of which the other varieties, such as Dvaita (duality) and Vishishtadvaita (non-duality with Value), are only as corollaries to axioms.

Vedanta and Modern Thought

There are both points of contact and difference between Vedanta and modern Western philosophy. Having reviewed some of the significant aspects of such thought in another study,[1] we have here to keep in mind the matter again, to enable us to see Vedanta in its revised perspective, noticing agreements and disagreements between the two, widely separated as they are, between the extremes of Eastern and Western ways of thinking.

We have already seen how the official or academic philosophers of Europe, even up to the time of Hegel, treated Eastern philosophy and Indian speculation generally as unworthy of any notice. Exceptions to the rule, such as Schopenhauer, Schelling, Schlegel and others, besides Max Müller and Paul Deussen, as we have seen, admired it almost as partisans in its favour.

It is the mean between the two attitudes of disadoption and adoption that we have to strike, to arrive at the normal

1. See *The Search for a Norm in Western Thought* by the author.

view in this matter. The sceptical, empirical standpoint is at present having great credit in modern Western thought. This is due partly to the reaction against the extreme dogmatism of the Middle Ages and the rise of the scientific spirit after the Dark Ages passed into the Age of Enlightenment and Reason.

From the paradoxes of the Eleatic philosophers and the hylozoism of the pre-Socratic animists and nature philosophers who speculated about the reality of the elements of water or fire in a scheme of existent realities, to the extreme idealism of a Hegel, we have one sweep of the story of human speculation in the West, which we can keep in mind in order to see the highlights and contributions of each new development insofar as these are likely to be of interest to us in placing Vedantic thought and the lines of its speculation in its proper perspective in the context of human understanding, as natural to man any time and anywhere.

A perennial and world background in which normal human speculation naturally thrives, when once properly visualized, will help us to rid ourselves of parochial or mental barriers of language or customs of different regions or times. We can then seek that central scientific notion common to both philosophy and science and clarify it for the thought of the one world of tomorrow, in which the idea of one language too would have full relevancy, as helping to avoid confusion of tongues, which a scientific language alone can be expected to solve, as it has to some extent already done. A Russian and an American scientist can now communicate in the language of formulae and equations, with letters of the Greek alphabet, and so it becomes possible to pass on any information in such a language from within one frontier to another.

Philosophy too, when rid of linguistic or cultural frontiers, will tend to bring humanity together in a more real sense than in the case of the Tower of Babel, which left the question of a common language outside its scope.

Integrated wisdom must accommodate existential laws, logical rules, critical methods, and give full scope to intuition. Modern phenomenology and existentialism too, have their contributions, which we have to notice so that we get a total or global view of speculation as a whole, as normal to man anywhere and at any time.

What is often referred to as perennial philosophy at present tends to come nearer to mysticism rather than to the philosophies of the present time, which are referred to as analytic. This distinction itself will be seen to be arbitrary, when we have examined the whole field of speculation and understanding in the light of a normative notion of the Absolute. We cannot here attempt a thorough or systematic study of these aspects, but only a summary review of the whole position in a sweeping and general way.

Three Broad Divisions of Philosophy

Vedanta examines absolute reality under the three categories of *sat* (Existence) which is philosophically the domain of ontology; *chit* (Subsistence) which results from abstract reasoning, and which is the domain of the ratiocinative or rational aspect of philosophical inquiry; and *ananda* (which refers to the world of Value, whether moral, aesthetic or of higher contemplation), with the good and the beautiful coming under this division, which has recently been named axiology.

Ontology, epistemology and axiology may be said to cover roughly these three zones or degrees of speculation. Often these divisions overlap or presuppose each other till they become merged into the one central, neutral, normative notion, called the Absolute. The actual, the logically true and the beautiful or the good as summum bonum, may be said, in a more popular way, to cover the same divisions.

The cosmological, psychological and theological versions of the same have been recognized in Vedanta as the *adhibhautika*, the *adhidaivika* and the *adhyatma* aspects of the Absolute, which is yet another way of dividing up the total field of speculation, based on the subject matter or object matter to which it refers. Sometimes too, both subject and object matters are treated together, more unitively, as in keeping with the nonduality of approach.

Although, strictly speaking, Vedanta adheres to *ajata-vada* (theory of non-creation) yet there is, in popular Vedantic works, under a chapter known as *utpatti prakarana* (chapter on genesis), some reference to how, in the beginning, the world originated. Thus some aspects of genesis are included in Vedanta as also its inevitable counterpart, eschatology, which treats of matters pertaining to the soul after its departure from here, or refers to the end as *pralaya* (general finality). Theories of reincarnation and the survival of the soul in various regions have occasionally been worked out in Vedantic texts. When the story of creation and the survival of the soul, with its progress in the spiritual world are brought into the scope of philosophy it begins to resemble theology or religion.

A total subjective and absolutist way of approach, giving primacy to the mind rather than to matter, which is of the essence of spirituality, as against mere one-sided materialism, characterizes Vedanta on the whole, although the rejection of the materialist standpoint from its scope is not altogether intended. Mind and matter in Vedanta may be said to be treated as counterparts, with equal claims, as in the standpoint of neutral monism postulated by William James and approved by Bertrand Russell. As a result, empirical evidence (*pratyaksha*) occupies a respectable position side by side with *shabda* (a priori validity based on authoritative texts) in Vedantic methodology.

Religion and Philosophy

Indians have had no reason to divorce religion from philosophy to the extent Europeans had to due to the extremes and excesses of the dogmatism of the Middle Ages. The horrors of the Inquisition were a nightmare that haunted the conscience of the West, which can vie only with the cruelty and injustice of the caste system that has persisted in India. Both have tended to drive a wedge between aspects of spiritual life which, without them, should have belonged together as one discipline or expression of aspiration for Truth or Freedom. As a perennial philosophy, Vedanta tries to steer clear of historical and other considerations, and thus has a global, integral and unitively comprehensive character of its own, though with its own necessary methodological, axiological and epistemological peculiarities.

Though coloured somewhat by Vedism, it is not to be thought of in terms of any genetic fallacy stemming from its origin and growth on the Indian soil. Advaita Vedanta or more simply Advaita philosophy, when revalued and restated, can give us the norm and reference, both theoretical and practical, of a way of life and certitude that can claim a fully scientific status, while being a complete philosophy in its own right.

Partial philosophical growths or expressions which have gained the foreground in various epochs in the history of the world, can all be given their proper places as aspects of such a philosophy of philosophies, or science, that Vedanta has claimed to represent, even from the Upanishadic times.

How far the various philosophies of the Western world can, by their light, confirm and not discredit some of Vedanta's primary methodological, epistemological or axiological postulates in yielding more certitude to it as a complete philosophy in itself, is what we shall try to show in the pages that follow. For purposes of orderliness, we shall adopt the Vedantic categories of *sat*, *chit* and *ananda* (Existence, Subsistence and Value) as aspects of the Absolute, to establish points of contact or contrast between Western philosophy and Eastern philosophy as represented by the Advaita philosophy of India.

The Absolute as Existent

We have the experience of existing things. This experience is the natural starting point of all inquiry of truth, whether scientific or philosophical. The mysterious universe of Jeans, or the "all things wonderful" that the Lord God made, of the children's hymn book, refer to the existential order of things.

What is observed by the naked eye, or even the eye aided by instruments like the microscope or the telescope, refers to this aspect of reality. Particle physics or bacteriology reveal one side of the existing universe, while the galaxies of the expanding universe represent the other pole. These are known as the microcosm and macrocosm respectively.

We have to distinguish, however, the metaphysically existent from the ontologically existent. There is existence as opposed to essence in Scholastic philosophy, which has also to be noted. Brute actuality based on sensation is called the sensum, and when removed one degree subjectively or secondarily, has more of the status of a percept, rather than that of a sensum. Conceptual and nominal abstractions of the existent are also possible to abstract from the given actuality of a situation.

Significant existences have to be separated, as coloured by degrees of interest in things that exist. Epistemological realism and idealism are both possible in modern philosophy. Materialism itself has no definite meaning, especially in modern days where matter and energy are becoming interchangeable terms.

All-encompassing Character of 'Sat'

Sat (ontological reality) as understood in Vedanta has no metaphysical limits put on it as in the West, where ontology is excluded from the purview of epistemology. Physical *sat*, ontological *sat*, axiological *sat* are all comprised in Vedanta within an overall epistemology. All these have metaphysical presuppositions implicit in them, so that, when Vedanta speaks of something as *sat*, it is to be a significant aspect of reality, rationally, critically or intuitively understood, and also good, morally and aesthetically too, in the context of the Absolute, which is the highest of significant values in the Self.

An actuality that exists in the most primary sense has to be accorded to the senses, especially to the senses of sight and touch. Lightning and thunder, though related as cause and effect, are not as actual as a stone that we can see and touch, although the former, too, enter our consciousness directly though separately through hearing and sight. Weight is a reality that is not so directly given to the senses as colour. The outside colour of the room in which we might be sitting at night, as it was seen during the day, is not an actuality, to the extent that memory has to support perception. Thus, when closely examined, empirical ontology referring to material existence, which is treated as if it had apodictic certitude, has no such simple status. The position of neutral monism, which treats of reality as consisting of neither mind nor matter, comes very near to the concept of *sat* as used in Vedanta.

Sat is one of the three possible categories under which the Absolute can be viewed. It comprises the truth of the dictum *cogito ergo sum* of Cartesianism and the *esse est percipi* of Berkeley, and holds them both together by means of the ultimate notion of the Absolute, which is the basis of them both, and which could not be conceived by the human understanding if it did not exist in the pure sense of *sat* as used in Vedanta.

A verse in the Bhagavad Gita stresses this all-encompassing philosophical character of the notion of *sat* sufficiently to bring out the three grades in which existence is to be understood:

> This (term) *sat* (the real) is used in the sense of existence and also of goodness, and likewise O Partha (Arjuna), to

> all laudable actions, the expression *sat* is usually applied. (XVII, 26)

Immanent, empirical, transcendental, and even value aspects are comprised in the notion of *sat* in Vedanta. How this is made possible will become clearer as we proceed. It is an inter-subjective and trans-physical value factor in the Absolute Self.

Western Philosophical Affinities

When we look for support in the history of Western thought in fixing the connotation of what exists, we have to hearken back to the pre-Socratic hylozoists to find any firm philosophically valid ground. It is here that we find anything near to the notion of *sat* in Western philosophy.

Thales of Miletus gave to water the status of the source of all things; and Anaximander spoke of the original material substance as the "principle" of all things. He is said to have described the soul as aeriform.

Heraclitus assumes ethereal fire as the substantial principle of all things, which he at once identifies with the divine spirit that knows and directs all things. The process with him is twofold, involving the transformation of all things into fire and then of fire into all things. This latter movement is styled the "way downward" which leads from fire (identical with the finest air), to water, earth, and so to death. The former movement is the "way upward" from earth and water to fire and life. Both movements are everywhere intertwined with each other, all identical and not identical. We step down a second time into the same stream and yet not into the same stream, for example.

Lonian philosophy must have been influenced by Egyptian thought and Egypt might have had affinities with India. Whichever might have been the earlier, it is here in the hylozoist absolutism which speaks in terms of flux and of ascent and descent of the substance treated as a pure principle, that we must establish, if at all, a point of contact between existential aspects of the Absolute in Eastern or Western philosophy.

Modern phenomenology has borrowed this way of looking at the world of things or elementals from the pre-Socratics. The Phenomenological *Epoche*, which as an entity, non-theoretical in status but still referring to no single predicable thing in the world, arrived at by a "bracketting" and "disconnecting" from the natural "world about one" which Husserl tries to distinguish, comes near to the notion of *sat* of the Vedanta.

In Bergson the flux or process of becoming of matter that is non-mechanically conceived, under a *schema moteur*, as a cross-section of fluid reality, also has points of similarly with the notion of *sat* in Vedanta.

The quantum mechanics of modern physics, which tends to make matter a mere wrinkle in space, vectorially conceived, would also suggest the pure notion of *sat* as understood in Indian philosophy. Plato's reference to "the mobile image of eternity" and Aristotle's idea of the mind that "becomes all things" touch the same entity of notion that *sat* represents.

In Vedanta *sat* is an extreme philosophical abstraction, and we shall not enter more elaborately into its epistemological validity here. For the present, we must content ourselves by indicating where the points of contact lie in the Western world of speculation for the notion of *sat* to be understood in its proper philosophical perspective.

Value Gives Stable Content to Existence and Vice Versa

Brahman or the Absolute is the highest of human values in Vedanta, and if existence is to be thought of as belonging to the context of the Absolute, the notion of existence must, by implication, indirectly at least, have reference to this high value. Anything non-significant and inconsistent with the highest aims of man, having no reference to the Absolute, becomes *ipso facto* nonexistent in principle, although it might be an actuality in the merely empirical context.

This way of interpreting the meaning of existence is supported by the theory of indirect meaning that Shankara accepts and adopts, when explaining the three attributes of *satyam*, *jnanam*, *anantam brahma* (the Absolute is existent, knowing and infinite). The connotation of any one of these is to be looked upon as modifying the others, till they refer to the Absolute in a total meaning-content. This semantic principle of indirect meanings (*lakshanartha*) applied to one Absolute, without any contradiction between component terms, is one of the secrets of Vedantic exegesis. This same way of giving significance of reality of *sat* (existence) is seen employed and explained in the Bhagavad Gita:

> Whatever is sacrificed, given or done, and whatever austerity is gone through, without faith, it is called *asat* (non-existent, no good) O Partha (Arjuna): it is not (of value) here or hereafter. (XVII, 28)

All truth, reality, or fact must satisfy the three tests of (1) being a significant value in human life here or hereafter; (2) being valid according to reason; and (3) being conceivable as existent, at one and the same time. This will apply equally to actions, gifts, things or properties dealt with in transactions between man and man. Vedantic methodology, epistemology and axiology have thus to be treated together in order to yield the integrated unitive wisdom which it is meant to represent.

3

The Problem of Transition from Existence to Subsistence

How the mind is inserted into matter, how the body is articulated to the mind, and how there is participation between the subjective and the objective aspects of reality, are questions pertaining to one and the same problem. This problem has puzzled and eluded philosophers, theologians, as well as scientists everywhere up to the present.

Whichever viewpoint is used, the link which enables psychophysical interaction can be conceived only by what the terminology of Vedanta describes as *samana-adhikaranatva* (homogeneity of ground, context, or medium).

When different metals are to be soldiered, there has to be a special medium or flux to hold them together effectively, intimately and strongly. Water or air can each mix with their own kind most intimately without any difficulty. Sounds and colours can each blend imperceptibly with degrees of clashing or lack of harmony. It is not hard to infer, from common experience as also from the syntactical and semantic requirements of the grammar of any language, that the law of homogeneity is a common matrix in a fully intimate blending, where there is perfect harmony.

When participation itself is possible, it is thus legitimate to infer the presence of a common medium or a matrix in which that possibility exists. Conversely, consciousness, which is homogeneous and absolute without any internal contradiction or conflict within itself, provides for participation between any apparently heterogeneous factors or elements, whether they are concrete or abstract.

The notion of the nondual Absolute can be taken here as an a priori postulate; or we can arrive at this common ground as an inductive hypothetical inference where mind and matter stand on neutral ground. Thus we see that the law of homogeneity holds good, not only in physics, but also in logic, language, mathematics or metaphysics.

The Laws of Contradiction and Homogeneity

How can the two laws of contradiction and of homogeneity both be accommodated within the Absolute as the common ground of reality, truth or value, on which basis alone these laws can even be conceivable? This is the next problem that we come up against.

This problem has been the source of much difference of opinion in the rival philosophies of nonduality, qualified nonduality and duality, each of which has held its ground successively in the Vedanta. Duality can be accepted mildly, or in a stronger sense within the heart of the notion of the homogeneity of the matrix of reality, which is none other than the Absolute.

In the transition from the world of existence to that of subsistence (which depends for its reality on the mind and its power of reasoning) we have to face the implicit paradox of having to think of the possibility of these laws as being together in one and the same medium, matrix or basis.

Philosophers attempt usually to get over this difficulty like performers on the flying trapeze. At a certain stage in their argument, they let go their hold on existence and catch on to a reality of a different order. Theologians also skip over this same difficulty when they pass from the reality of the world to that of God. Scientists confront this same problem by trying to distinguish between the relativistic and the absolutist approaches, and end up dwelling on speculative subtleties as puzzling as those of the Scholastic metaphysicians they look down upon.

The law of homogeneity cannot be accommodated alongside this inner contradiction in reality without transcending the implied paradox. In order to transcend this paradox, each philosopher resorts to some favourite pairs of expression such as the distinction between the immanent and the transcendent, the practical and the pure, or the visible and the intelligible. Modern scientific philosophers may prefer the terms observables and calculables. Whichever the terms used, we always find there are two of them having a polarity, an ambivalence, a dichotomy or an antinomy implied between them. The phenomenal and the noumenal, the worlds of appearance and reality, the relatively and the absolutely real are other twin terms implying contrast, contrariety, or contradiction of various degrees in different philosophies whether of the East or West. Transcending paradox is the main difficulty that the magic of words is meant to accomplish.

Up and Down Movements in the Search for Certitude

Thought circulates in an existent, subsistent and value world, whether in science, logic or philosophy. The thinking mind is guided by interests, and each life interest gives some satisfaction to the self. Like a bird lighting on the branch of a tree, subjective interests settle for a moment on the ramifications of rival interests claiming attention at a given time and place in the subjective-objective world. The subjective and objective counterparts of the existent-subsistent-value factor tally for a moment and attain the real, but they are soon dissolved, like a bubble that bursts in rainwater.

According to the alternating inner dispositions and urges, such as those of appetite or sex, there can be imagined an alternating circulation in the global consciousness of every man and of all men treated together. When value attaches itself to Platonic intelligibles, culminating in the summum bonum, we have what might be visualized as ascending dialectics. And when the reverse process takes place, thought lingers on values that are earth earthy, on the prime matter in the unmoved mover, where pure acts reside and where Aristotelian entelechies become possible.

In between these ambivalent poles of the supreme good and the essentially actual, in the circulatory amplitude of thought, we have other possibilities too numerous to classify. This is the domain of maya's uncertainty of value in the context of absolute reality. We should think of this intermediate negative zone differently from its positive counterpart. The transcendent and the immanent change sides here. Cause or effect, subject or object, the specific or the generic prevail in interest or significance alternately. There can be no rule of thumb to determine which has real value significance, and therefore has existence or reality. So it is in between the plus and minus factors that all becomes upredicable in this zone, which is both intermediate and negative in its content. The Sanskrit word *anirvachaniya* (unpredicable) refers thus to the overall maya, the most generalized category of error possible in the fullest context of absolutism.

When maya is eliminated, all uncertainty finally vanishes; and then by double assertion prevailing over what is discarded by double negation, the Sun of truth-value dawns. This notion of maya thus corresponds to the *negativitat* of Hegel. But Hegel's positive Absolute lost its way in pan-Germanic enthusiasms of which Vedanta was innocent. The bright sun of the high value that is fully absolutist reached by double positive assertion is given its due importance in Vedanta. It is here that Vedanta scores over Hegelian absolutism, indicating a clear and normative philosophy as well as a correct way of life.

Three Zones of Reasoning

To complete the methodology of the Vedantic Absolute, we have therefore to recognize three distinct zones, each having its own kind of reasoning. Because thought is, as it were, refracted as it passes through a transparent prism, certain structural peculiarities prevail here which give a complicated innate structure to the total field of Vedantic inquiry.

The level of existence is the bottom stratum where human inquiry begins. From natural curiosity about actual single objects of interest, the understanding penetrates into more generalized and abstracted situations, with memories and anticipations of past or future possibilities or probabilities colouring the relation. Sense data assume an ontological compactness, and directed by life interests, there is ascent or decent in the scale of possible human values. The object prevails and looms large at one moment, and then at another moment the subject is the centre of interest. Life tendencies give to these relational interests both content and direction as they move in a time or space field within normalized consciousness which is neither inside nor outside.

After existent aspects have been sublimated, the bipolarity passes into the indeterminate zone of maya's domain where a confusion of indeterminate values attract and repel in alternation or together at a given moment.

On rising above this level there is a steady betterment in the world of values which are free of sensual, perceptual, or even of conceptual content. All are of a purely nominal significance. Even naming is finally abandoned when descending dialectics is used to remove the over-positive tones of values which do not refer fully to the Self or the Existent.

Thus existent, subsistent and value factors correct the exaggerations of each other and of one another. Finally, pure being attains to self-awareness in the Absolute.

An Alternating Process

It will suffice here to indicate that, in this dynamic structure of the circulation of thought, there is an upward and downward movement between the a priori and the a posteriori, between the synthetic and the analytic aspects of thought, as it circulates between the plus and minus poles, within whose amplitude of dialectical reasoning or intuition Vedantic reasoning lives and moves.

In order to show that such structuralism is present and fully recognized in Vedanta, we give here two references from *L'Absolu Selon le Vedanta* by Prof. O. Lacombe. He writes:

> One sees also that the aspect of abundance of being, so dear to a *Bhartriprapancha*, who sacrificed in it the first and most fundamental of strictly ontological requirements, the principle of contradiction as not less dear to Sankara. It decomposes, however, in traversing the prism of non-being, into two coupled notions, one of which is altered in relation of the other.[1]

The reference to the prism of non-being through which ontological abundance passes, indicates in complicated language that structuralism which we have already examined.

Writing about the alternation of immanence and transcendence, the same author not only deals with this kind of structuralism but even of a kind of osmotic process that takes place between these aspects of the self. After saying that the "order of emanation" has priority over the "order of return to the absolute principle" when viewed from the side of the relative, Lacombe describes the circulation as follows:

> On arrival as on departure, at the very core of the dizzy unevenness marked by the opposition transcendence-immanence, where the osmosis that is infinitely subtle and gentle of their correlation plays, there reigns the infrangibility of their equalizing movement.[2]

These extracts will suffice to show the outlines of a structuralism and a process which have to be imagined as

---

1. Our translation (Geuthner, Paris, 1937), p. 69.

2. Ibid., p. 65

abiding at the core of the notion of the Absolute as viewed from the side of the relative.

Such ideas are not fancifully conceived by the professor but are fully justified in Vedantic texts. In the *Gaudapada Karika* of the Mandukya Upanishad, whose authority is by no means negligible, there is the analogy of the fire-brand that is moving, a comparison intended to bring out the relationship between the thing in itself as the Absolute and its own relativistic aspect:

> A fire-brand, when set in motion, appears as straight, crooked, etc. So also consciousness, when set in motion, appears as perceiver, the perceived and the like.[3]

In the writings of Narayana Guru we find that this circulation in consciousness is referred to more pointedly and clearly in his *Atmopadesa Satakam:*

> Awareness in order to know its proper state
> Itself the earth and other manifestations became;
> And in inverted state, now mounting, now changing,
> Like a circulating faggot of fire, it keeps turning round.
> (Verse 33)[4]

The Bhagavad Gita too has this idea of circulation and alternation:

> The Lord dwells in the heart-region
> of all beings, O Arjuna,
> causing all beings to revolve through the principle of
> appearance (*maya*) (as if) mounted on a machine.
> (XVIII, 61)

The alternating process is more expressly indicated by Professor Lacombe later in the same paragraph already quoted:

---

3. *Mandukya Upanishad* with *Gaudapada Karika*, Nikhilananda, (Mysore, 1955), p. 264.

4. See comment in the *One Hundred Verses of Self-Instruction*, by the present author.

> At the time of manifestation, the accent weighs more and more on immanence; at the time of reabsorption it refers more and more to transcendence. Never, however, is either the one or other term ever sacrificed.[5]

If we were to put the matter of a circulation taking place within a dialectical ascent and descent in our own words, we would describe the process as follows:

The chain of associations flits from one object of interest to another and is regulated by value considerations. Between cognition and connation, as psychologists would put it, there is an analytic and synthetic alternation in the phases of reasoning, which can be ratiocinative at a given moment and emotionally coloured at another. Circulation of thought normally takes place in the mind's search for certitude. Each certitude has a corresponding element of interest on which it rests, before passing on to the next element where it can find satisfaction momentarily or more enduringly as the case may be. Absolute happiness is the highest of satisfactions, where the movement of the circulating fire faggot is quenched, to put it in the language of the *Mandukya Karika*. Happiness would thus result from a form of finalized certitude, which Vedanta promises.

When value factors predominate, experimental and formed reasonings give place to more intuitive and dialectical reasonings. Existential aspects alone demand experimental demonstrations. These are based on the a posteriori approach. Full a priorism prevails when dialectical intuition comes to be employed, where value factors are more significant. Intermediate between these we have syllogistic forms of reasoning which depend on the universal or the particular alternately, yielding certitude and the satisfaction that goes with it. Thus descent and ascent, in the circulation of thought based on interest, alternating with intelligence, takes place all the time within human understanding, as it seeks greater

5. *Op. cit.* p. 65.

and more significant certitude in life's problems and interests, great or small.

The Immanent to Transcendent Leap

Between existence (*sat*) and reason (*chit*) in the contemplative and absolutist context of Vedanta, there is a deep chasm where brute actuality is left behind and pure nature or substance, both immanent and transcendent at once, is attained.

If we can imagine the process of human inquiry along the lines outlined above, with the gift of some intuition added to merely mechanistic reasoning, there is a feat like that of the leap of the trapeze athlete involved in the transition as it proceeds normally in graded order from one subject of interest-significance to another. This transit is necessary if we are to follow further along the path of contemplative philosophy that Vedanta really represents.

The participation of the existent with the subsistent does not take place on even ground. When one has been left behind, the other is attained by human understanding after consciousness itself attains to a certain degree of lucidity in the awareness of the Self, however dim it might have been in the beginning.

Transcendence belongs more intimately to the absolutist context, while immanence leads directly to the world of multiple relativistic values. The localized and pluralistic items that demand our attention minute by minute, which have been compared by Narayana Guru to a group of fancy-feathered small birds pecking at fruits and changefully moving within the branches of a tree,[6] have to be subdued so that, in the bright self-awareness of general human

6. Enjoying the five fruits, such as beauty, mounted on a foul-smelling gun and evasively flying back and forth are five birds; having brought them down, through an inversion, that radiant inner awareness should fill one's entire being. — Narayana Guru, *Atmopadesa Satakam,* verse 8.

understanding in purer consciousness, they are abolished and absorbed.

Mechanistic and Intuitive Thought

The case of absolute truth has suffered from ancient times, and still suffers, because three steps of thought remain undistinguished and promiscuously mixed up.

When we formulate a law such as "action and reaction are equal and opposite" as in the mechanics of the Euclidean and Newtonian order, we have an epistemology and methodology that go together with such a statement. On the other hand, when we say that "the entropy of the universe is tending towards zero" we generalize and state a more subtle universal law where observables enter weakly, and calculables are treated in a purer or higher mathematical fashion.

Although both statements are capable of being expressed by equations, one refers to the mechanistic and the other to the purer world given to mathematical intuition. When we pass on higher still into the domain of pure value and try to equate items such as "pure reason" with the summum bonum, intuition comes into play more strongly, and thought proves itself by its axiomatic content.

The laws of physics, the truths of logic, and higher and purer equations of the value world require different treatment for verification or demonstration. In actual practice it has been taken for granted till recently that science relies on the first kind of reasoning only. This, however, has now definitely been abandoned. In order to mark the latest position in this all important question of the relation between the "mind and the machine" let us examine an extract from an authority on the subject. Writing in *The Listener*, London, of October 17, 1963, P.G.M. Dawe of Oxford University, says:

> To interpret the results of elementary mind-body experiments in vocabularies appropriate to the engineer, such as those of the information theory, entropy, or computer technology or in terms of models, may

> sometimes be theoretically interesting and even elegant, but has had limited psychological significance. . . . It is now clear that the discoveries and theories of the scientists always directly involve developments of their imagination or mind and otherwise of the story of their subject. . . . The concepts of physics, or the invention of a machine are therefore to be fully understood only in terms of a story relating to the lives of individual men and women, and not vice-versa.

The latest tendency in scientific psychology is thus in favour of considering thought-processes as non-mechanistic and as coming nearer to living intuitionism rather than being empirically rational. We have to let go our hold on brute facts and even of the language appropriate to mechanics to describe or understand the inner workings of the mind, even in everyday matters of utilitarian values. When more idealistic or spiritual values are involved in individual or collective human behaviour, the accent has to be placed on the fully transcendental aspects. Between the poles of what Kant has called the a priori synthetic in transcendentalism and the analytic or aesthetic, there is a subtle movement which, as we have seen above, has been compared in Vedanta to an osmosis between two aspects of the Absolute.

What interests us directly here is the fact of the transition from the existent (*sat*) to the subsistent (*chit*). The subject on which we shall focus our attention next is how the value factor, named *ananda*, enters subtly into *sat* and *chit*, and how they fuse or combine by subtle osmosis, and thus help to give content or significance to the Absolute as understood in Vedanta.

4

The Absolute as Word-Value Significance

Fact, truth or reality must have some significant value content. If this is absent it becomes empty and cannot do any good for anyone who might have mere intellectual curiosity about it. Man is the measure of all things, and the self which seeks certitude through science or metaphysics must have a resting place in utility or a final good that works and makes them happier and better in one sense or another.

Thus the value factor is an inseparable counterpart of what is merely true mathematically or logically. A tautology is a statement of truth which leaves the one who believes in it unaffected; while a mere contradiction when discovered helps only to reject wrong but not to accept any truth or value.

The charge against metaphysics by positivists of the present day holds good insofar as metaphysics exults in mere verbosity, relying on mere tautological a priorisms of synthetic transcendentalism, without relating truth operationally to the working or living world of human significance, whether at the utilitarian or real level. In short, the truth must make man free and supply the bread along with the freedom for which man hungers at one and the same time.

Thus it is that the third category of Absolute Reality called *ananda* (value interest) enters into a complete philosophy such as Vedanta claims to be. *Ananda* is often translated "bliss" which would suggest the trance of a yogi. It is to be understood, however, in revised and restated terms as that axiological factor which, side by side with existence and subsistence, is an integral part of all true philosophizing when it is not limited merely to abstract metaphysical speculation.

The three categories of Existence, Subsistence and Value have to fuse together by a sort of osmosis or interaction between them, cancelling one-sided exaggerations possible at each level, before a significant notion of the Absolute can emerge to view. Thus it is that the Self and the non-Self cancel out into a high value in oneself which becomes fully significant.

A Complete Philosophy of Life

The value element has to enter into the composition of the two other categories of existence (*sat*) and reason or subsistence (*chit*) in a very intimate manner of inherence or *samavaya* before the alchemy of the absolute Value can emerge at every level of life. Just as a mechanical mixture and a chemical compound are distinguished in science, so the intimate manner whereby existence is modified by attributes to substance in terms of *chit* requires the exercise of the subtlest form of intuition to grasp.

The Substance and other attributes of Spinoza's philosophy have natures which make for "thinking substances." There is nature which is still in the process of *becoming* something else by attributes (*natura naturans*), and there is nature that has *become* an existent thing in a more actual sense (*natura naturata*). This is a philosophical subtlety which, like the paradox of the participation of mind and matter, is a major one that philosophy has had to face whether in the East or the West. Metaphysical speculation has lingered long on this subtle distinction between material evolution (*parinama*) and purer change or becoming (*vivarta*) in a more vital sense as intuitively and non-mechanistically understood, as in Bergson.

Pure becoming is referred to as change in *prakara* or mode of expression by Ramanuja, while Shankara would call it a mere eidetic phenomenon, *vivarta* (specific cognizable aspect of the same absolute substance), in which both kinds of change, horizontal and vertical, have to inhere.

Samyoga and *samavaya* are two relations in absolute Substance, the former based on mere contiguity in space, and the latter in continuity in mental associations. Potassium nitrate, sulphur and carbon placed contiguously in space do not enter into intimate contact with each other as when gunpowder actually explodes. Being and becoming have to be conceived as twin aspects of the same relationship, one vertical and the other horizontal. The "blue lotus" inheres in the class "lotus" understood without its specific colour, and vice versa, very intimately, while a "blue" lotus in wood painted blue has its substance and attribute merely horizontally associated by *samyoga,* which is accidental or incidental. Thus there are vertical and horizontal specifications to which existent and subsistent realities are subject in the context of Absolute Reality as understood in a complete philosophy of life.

The Three Categories Inhere and Specify One Another

The Absolute of Vedanta is given a priori and then confirmed a posteriori.

Axioms and postulates are valid at one end, and, at the other pole of the knowledge situation, visual or experimental demonstration has its place, though only inductively. If we admit now that any truth that has no value significance to the Self or to man cannot be taken seriously by any philosophy worthy of the name, we come to the position that a thing of no value is equivalent to being false or nonexistent.

Existence, Subsistence and Value have to fall in a vertical line, giving to each object, truth or interest its place in an absolute scheme under the aegis of an overall normative notion of the Absolute. The Absolute is the highest of value references available to philosophical speculation, and when the Absolute, Self and Value are all thought of together as each giving meaning to the others and thereby abolishing possible unilateral error or exaggeration, we succeed in giving content to the otherwise empty word called the Absolute.

The *sat*, the *chit* and the *ananda* aspects or categories have all to be fitted into a common scheme as comprised in the notion of the Absolute as the reality of highest significance to life. Metaphysics otherwise would be verbose nonsense.

In order that this may not be so, philosophers of both East and West have depended on the magic of words as a means to clarify the situation. Cause and effect, the generic and the specific, and the analogically understandable relationship of semantics to higher mathematics, algebraic as well as geometrical, have all been already explored to find a proper frame of reference, where speculation could cohere and make sense. Syntactics and semiotic processes have not been omitted, either in India or in Europe, by ancients as well as moderns. We can enter only very cautiously into this domain, where stalwarts like Shankara, Panini and others have trodden the ground with confidence and ease. All we can say generally here is that the magic of words has been freely employed by Shankara and others.

Modern thinkers too give increasing importance to such questions as "the meaning of meaning." It is here that Vedanta stands on common ground with the most advanced of modern thought. Works like *Vedanta Paribhasha, Bhasha Parichheda, Vakya Vritti* and other advanced texts of Vedanta and allied disciplines, cry out for greater recognition in order to show that words have a central place in revealing the final nature of the Absolute.

If Shankara, the greatest of Vedantins, gives primacy to the word and its direct and indirect meanings (calling them *vachyartha* and *lakshanartha* respectively) in revealing the final nature of Truth as the highest Good, the reason is that *shabda* or word is our final epistemological reference for ultimate certitude.

Thus, ranging from *pratyaksha* (given to the senses) through *anumana* (inference), *arthapatti* (hypothetical postulation), *anupalabdhi* (negative certitude), and *shabda* (word), the valid means of knowledge all become acceptable to the Vedantin at one and the same time.

At one pole we have verification of existence by means of *pratyaksha* (observable demonstration), and at the other extreme, we have *shabda* (word) which is fully a priori and synthetic in status. *Pratyaksha* is empirical, analytic, positive and a posteriori, while *shabda* is the other pole where axiomatic validity prevails.

The structure of the relation between these means of testing truth is complex and needs reduction to simplicity by Vedantic thought. The net result is that we can arrive at final simplification by a process where *sat, chit* and *ananda* inhere and specify each other to result in the full notion of the Absolute of Vedanta. What is too vague and generalized here can only be explained step by step as we examine items of method, epistemology or value, one after another.

The Ultimate Structure of Thought and Word

The question that a modern man will naturally ask about this taking refuge in such subtleties like "the meaning of meaning" for proving the reality of the Absolute would be: Why take so much trouble when the visible, demonstrable, practical world in which we live is sufficient for man for all ordinary purposes?

This would be quite germane, if bread here was all that we needed for life. Man, however, does not live by bread alone. He craves for freedom too, and as *Homo sapiens* he is a thinking animal. This means that he must solve problems big or small to fulfill his life's purpose. Speculation inevitably steps into the breach.

Philosophy would be superfluous if building bridges or developing the land for gaining bread were all that man needed. Man wants to live in security, free from fear. Fear of calamities, avoidable or inevitable, comes from various sources. Doubts from within cause discontent in each person. The mystery of life itself causes alternate fear or wonder in all normal men who do not willfully live in a fool's paradise, whether they are considered primitive or civilized, however much the latter may deny it in their pride. Wars and pestilences, famines and genocides due to fanaticisms or idolatries, need effective remedies which wisdom alone can give. Truth must make man free.

Such are some of the implications of a full philosophy which tend to get overcovered by extraneous considerations brought about by man's technological triumphs in modern times. Vice and crime cannot be corrected merely by technical skill or the conquest of space. Problems of divorce and delinquency cannot be overcome by a mechanistic approach. The problem of evil or suffering is as much within human nature as it is in nature outside. As even Russell would admit, there are realities, both mental and physical, which belong to the domains of two distinct dictionaries, the empirical and the mental, at least as Berkeley saw it. The form of logic, the structure of thought and language, conceptualism, subjectivism, structuralism, and other aspects of what is ultimately real, occupied and are occupying the minds of fully qualified scientists such as Eddington and Schrodinger even in this age of science. Vedanta, though an ancient discipline, is no exception here.

Vedantic Methodology, Epistemology and Axiology

The three categories of Existence, Subsistence and Value have to be approached with methods and theories of knowledge proper to each, so that their dynamism and interrelationships within the core of the Absolute can be understood.

On the Indian soil, philosophical speculation has gone on unbridled through the ages, and different points of view of the Absolute have taken shape, all having some common basis of method or value significance. India has had its sceptics and empiricists in the Charvakas and the Lokayatikas before Vedantic thought began to evaluate them in more absolutist terms. In European thought scepticism came late and persists with force even to the present.

Belief and scepticism are in reality two poles of the same knowledge situation, when understood globally, completely, and in the light of the structure of thought as a whole. There is no physics without mathematics, and there is no proof without reliance on axioms. Observables and calculables have to go hand in hand to yield worthwhile or workable certitudes.

When the total structure of the absolute knowledge situation is taken in by the mind, we can clearly visualize the subtle dynamism, the osmosis, and the semiotic processes or apperceptions taking place within consciousness when viewed in its proper epistemological perspective. There are thoughts or truths that are transparent to some, and others which have an ambivalent polarity between them, repelling one another. There are thoughts more essential than others, and relationships that are more eminent.

Full-flooded generosity prevails at the core of the Absolute. Thoughts are reflected and refracted at certain planes or levels and, in the insertion, participation or articulation of certain aspects of thought elements, there is an osmotic interchange of plus or minus existence or essence. There is neutralization of existence and essence.

Finally, thought processes circulate, making figures of eight within consciousness, changing interphysically and trans-subjectively, as when two people converse. There is changeover from synthetic to analytic, from the a priori to the a posteriori, from the positive to the negative, at different ontological or teleological levels, where phenomenological *epoches* take place. We are only using here terms current in modern philosophical literature to indicate that Vedanta too has its time honoured methodology and axiology in its dynamically, though perhaps tacitly, understood schematic representation of Absolute consciousness in which all philosophy has to live and move.

Schematism and structuralism of a subjective status, in which mental events are isolated and studied, to be put together into a global whole, are notions that are all becoming more and more acceptable to modern thinkers, who are philosophers of science, or scientific philosophers. Some of them tend to be classed as sceptics while others are believers. Whether classified as one or the other, they have necessarily to belong together as seekers of truth, fact or high value, if they are to be called philosophers at all.

It is here that Vedanta steps in with its contributions which, when reexamined and restated, would help a global philosophy or an integrated science to evolve. It is in the structure of thought, which itself lies at the basis of the spoken word, that the details of thought processes can best be studied. Linguistic usage, semantics, syntactical peculiarities and the pragmatics of language are looked upon more and more to give up the secrets that have remained closed to speculation till recently.

Logistic, vectorial and projective geometry, and quantum mechanics are all making their contributions. Vedanta too, in the days of Shankara, entered into subjects such as the semantic polyvalency of words to reveal the final nature of the Absolute which, instead of being a mere tautological verity, or a contradiction within itself, would help to relate fruitfully for thinking man, the two limbs which pertain to it—the world on the one hand and the self of man on the other. When Vedanta is revalued and restated in the light of modern knowledge, especially of the physical world, as seen by modern philosophers of science, a Science of the Absolute may reasonably be expected to emerge.

Shankara's Use of Semantics

The notion of the Absolute in Vedanta recedes from the

concrete actual facts of the pluralistic, phenomenal world presented to the senses, by distinct stages of perceptualism, conceptualism and nominalism, into the core where it can meet its own counterpart of the pure noumenal aspect on common homogeneous ground.

Thus when negatively focused through these stages, it reaches the world of the word and its meaning, where "the meaning of meaning" gains full reality. And so, when we take the leap from the empirical to the transcendental, we cross a deep chasm separating aspects of word meaning to where the neutral notion of Absolute Reality abides as the common ground of the physical and mental worlds.

The semantic polyvalency of words thus gains primacy when we begin to analyse the notion at this inner subtle core, where the Absolute thinking substance, with its accidents and attributes, make existence and essence meet eminently in its status of pure philosophical relationship.

After reaching the core by this kind of negative abstraction and generalization, we can travel along a deflected direction of the same light that has taken us to the core of the substance, and follow up positively and analytically the conceptual and nominalistic attributes of the thinking substance in its process of *becoming* and not merely *being*.

That ascending and descending dialectics are possible in this circulation is evident in many parts of Shankara's commentaries on the Gita, the Brahma Sutras and the Upanishads. Taking refuge in semantics when speculation along rational lines fails, is not a new method whose originality goes to Shankara's credit. Jaimini, the author of the *Purva-Mimamsa-Sutras,* relied on semantics to serve his philosophy based on the exegetics of Vedism to a fuller extent. Shankara, having to establish his conclusions on the anterior position taken by Jaimini, had necessarily to refute them using similar weapons.

Thus it is in the semantic analysis of word content that Vedantism gains full validity. Not only are the scriptures relied on unquestionably by Shankara, but even popular usages belonging to the pragmatics of language rather than to pure semiotic processes are relied on to refute a successive range of sometimes as many as five *purva pakshins*, or graded opponents, set up by himself as representing invalid positions, each one of whose opinions he first states in his own words, before refuting them beginning with his retort *iti-chet-na* (If you say that, no).

On final analysis of his own position, when all others who seem sufficiently intelligent are refuted in succession, is some preciously subtle stuff which is like foam picked up on the seashore, leaving almost nothing but an absolute meaning-content notion, either bitter or sweet, as a residue. Before the last bubbles burst, we find that it is on semantics that his Vedanta largely relies.

We cannot do better here than to give an instance of how all is viewed finally in semantic terms by Shankara, following the *purva mimamsa* (anterior critique) which showed him the way in this matter.

Shankara's Vedanta Rests Finally on Semantics

Veda means wisdom, and its reference to the four Vedas of the Aryan tribes as they entered India is only its secondary meaning. The Vedas are distinguished as *shruti* or that which is heard from a rishi or fully qualified authority in teaching wisdom.

Wisdom is largely a collection of axiomatic a priori verities, and, like the axioms and postulates of algebra and geometry, these are infallible in the certitude quality they contain. There are other Vedas equal to the Indian Vedas, such as the Pentateuch of the Jews. When wisdom is said to be revealed it only means that it is not the work of any single individual, like a chariot made by a chariot builder. A priori truths exist by themselves, mathematically valid as it were, in the sky or something corresponding to the sky, in vectorial space or pure space, understood as the basis of both algebra and geometry.

The truth of Pythagoras' Theorem is not in actual space nor in theoretical space, but in both.

Language lives and moves in a space where all descriptions become valid, whether treated as perceptual or conceptual. Thus the ultimate notion of the Absolute, when understood in most general and abstracted terms as a thing-in-itself, can belong only to the world of the word.

"The Word was in God and it was God," — such biblical statements refer to the Absolute as the Logos, which is nothing new, and when Vedanta reduces all into the syllable AUM, as in the Mandukya Upanishad, it only recognizes the same verity.

It is in this sense that Shankara reduces the Absolute to its purest form by a semantic analysis which is at least as valid as a logical or mathematical proof. The practical proof and the theoretical proof join in the Pythagorean Theorem as a central verity combining both into one certitude in knowledge. Similarly, the Absolute of Shankara is neither empty of all content nor filled with the multiple entities of the phenomenal world.

As genus and species can be made to refer to one unique genus in universal terms, it is possible to reduce by a semantic negative process and reach the unique class of all classes in the Absolute. Shankara avoids both leaning on the side of pantheistic pluralism or favouring the theory of emptiness (*shunya*) in arriving at the Absolute of the Upanishads masterfully by his approach through semantic analysis of a text in the Taittiriya Upanishad, which deserves careful scrutiny on our part. Shankara excels here, and succeeds in making his several rivals in polemical duels thoroughly vanquished and silenced before his sledgehammer arguments.

An Example of Shankara's Method

Taking the text, *satyam jnanam brahma* (*Brahman*, the Absolute, is Reality, Knowledge and Infinity) of the

Brahmananda Valli of the Taittiriya Upanishad (II.1), Shankara first makes it clear that these attributes have to be treated as "indirectly" and not "directly" applicable. The latter, which would be literal, treating the words as they are understood ordinarily, he distinguishes as *vachyartha;* while the former, which is based on analogy and has the notion of the universal and unique genus of the Absolute to reveal, he calls *lakshanartha,* where the attribute refers backward to help us to see the unique nature of the Absolute, distinguishing it *negatively* from any other specified object in the universe. In his own words in his *Bhashya*, we read:

> "Brahman is Reality, Knowledge and Infinity" is a sentence which indirectly distinguishes the Absolute (*brahman*). Reality and others are verily three terms qualifying Brahman, which is the qualified.
>
> (If it be said) that because of being specified by attributes, indirectly they refer (positively) to the qualified aspects, there is no such defect. Why? Because the attributes give primacy to the indirectly qualified (subject), rather than giving primacy to the attributes themselves. (If it be asked) where there is the specification as between sign and thing signified, quality and thing qualified, we say it is to distinguish between objects of the same genus that attributes are used, but the indirectly qualified (subject) however, is as in the definition of space as that which gives its room to every other thing, to be distinguished from everything else in the universe. It is (this kind of) indirect meaning that has to be given (to the text in question).

Answering further, in the same commentary, to the objection whether by applying the negative method of "not this, not this," (*neti-neti*) the Absolute would not itself vanish into nothingness, Shankara again relies on a semantic argument, and says that the words Reality, etc., would not have any function at all if they referred to nothing. Since grammatically they are meant to have a function in the scriptures, they must at least specify the subject *Brahman*, by excluding negatively those which are in conflict with the attribute mentioned, thus delimiting the function of each attribute such as Reality, etc.

Shankara's own sentence on this last point of saving the notion of the Absolute from falling into the nothingness (*shunya*) of the Buddhists reads:

> Meaning of Reality etc., in effect, however, would (still) delimit the meaning of Brahman, the qualified, by excluding those attributes whose function would be in conflict with what is proper to it.

The word content of the Absolute is finally underlined in the third part of the same comment, as follows:

> The word Brahman, by its proper meaning, has force of "signification," (*brahma shabdo'pi svarthena arthavan eva*).

Existence, Subsistence and Value thus inhere in the notion of the Absolute, giving it content and significant value all together and each by each, negatively and indirectly, by analogy. These discussions above have necessarily to remain complex and subtle at present. We have to bring in the structure of thought schematically in order to simplify and clarify the position here. This we shall tackle presently.

5

Semantic Polyvalence in Vedantic Thought

The history of Indian philosophic thought is related to the Upanishads either by agreement or by difference. Rationalism and ritualism have played rival roles. Scepticism and belief have alternated, as also the primacy of existential or subsistential aspects, which have invited attention alternately.

The course of this alternation has been referred to as the "white and black" onward paths in the Gita (VIII.26), giving such an alternation a perennial status in the context of the progress of thought in the world anywhere. When the a priori is stressed and the scripture respected by a believer, the white pole of abstract ideas is touched, and, on the other hand, when the pendulum swings to the other end of the scale of values, we have rank scepticism, empiricism, stress on the visible at the expense of the invisible world, and, naturally, too, an a posteriori approach to where demonstrably and operationally valid verity takes the field as a high pragmatic or utilitarian value, in the world of the conquest of factors such as space. Time and eternity do not belong to this pole, and tend to have decreased significance.

The absolute knowledge situation has to be clearly visualized before we can see Vedanta in its proper perspective and context. It is neither orthodox nor heterodox, sceptical nor believing, immanent nor transcendent, ontological nor teleological, pure nor practical, but combines both matter and mind on its own neutral ground. Vedanta, when it gives importance to the validity of what is given to the senses (*pratyaksha*), tends to keep company with the heterodox, and when it gives primacy to the word or validity of scripture (*shabda*), it tends to be uncompromisingly and even harshly orthodox.

An examination of the further implications of the semantic polyvalence which we have begun, side by side with structural implications of Vedantic thought, supported by Shankara or the Upanishads, would therefore, help us very much to clarify our position. In the first instance, it will help us to see clearly that Vedanta is neither a rival philosophy nor a religion, but a correct attempt to integrate all Indian thought under one methodological, epistemological and axiological discipline.

Semantic Analysis of "That thou art"

Another semantic analysis of the great dictum (*maha-vakya*) of the Vedanta, *tat-tvam-asi* (That thou art) will give us a clearer perspective, which will serve as a stepping-stone for us to see the schematic or structural features of thought as an integrated global unity or whole, where word and meaning cling together in the central context of the notion of the Absolute.

We have already scrutinized the semantic subtleties implied in the three attributes of *Brahman* (the Absolute) in the words *satyam* (existent), *jnanam* (rationally subsistent) and *anantam* (infinite) (which last attribute was meant to cover *anandam*, "bliss or value factor"[1]) where we noted the distinction between *vachyartha* (literal or direct meaning) and *lakshanartha* (indirect meaning by analogy). The negative specification has also been noted.

The indirect meanings possible in any context have been divided into *jahat* (losing its original meaning) and *ajahat* (not losing) as a further subdivision of the indirect. In modern

1. On this point see *The Religion and Philosophy of India: The Upanishads*, Deussen, (Clark, Edinburgh, 1906), p. 127,

language we can distinguish these subdivisions as being based on a metonymy: *ajahat* can be called quantitative or analytic, and *jahat* qualitative and synthetic. The familiar examples, used by Shankara in his *Sarva-darshana-siddhanta-sara-samgraha* (verses 733-51), to bring out this subtle semantic distinction, are two in the first instance: (1) "A milk-village in the Ganges" (*gangayam-ghoshah*) and (2) "The piebald runs" (*shono-dhavati*).

In the first case the defect of meaning is corrected by treating it as a metonymy with an inner logical relation, while in the latter example the figure of speech to be employed is a synecdoche. When the two instances are thus understood figuratively still and not literally in two different ways, we can paraphrase them as (1) "The village *where milkmen live is on the border* of Ganges," and (2) "The piebald *horse* is running."

In the first instance the defect to be corrected is of a mere relational nature in description, while in the second instance quantitative ideas of part and whole enter. This distinction in the two semantic or meaning-worlds is a fundamental one, and if we decide to label the second quantitative significance as "horizontal" we would be justified in calling the relational one "vertical." The horizontal is near to the pragmatics of language while the vertical would correspond to a purer semantic process.

The Third Example: "He is this Devadatta"

Shankara resorts to a third example before he comes to the "That thou art" formula to which he wishes to lead us. This example is the phrase *so-ayam-devadattah* (He is this Devadatta). Here a combination of vertical and horizontal factors is required to make sense. One of the words, "he" or "this", has to shed part of its vertical or horizontal significance in order to avoid any inner contradiction standing in the way of the phrase making full sense.

Shankara himself, following the precedent of more ancient linguistic experts before him, calls this third way of making sense out of indirect figurative language *bhaga-lakshaana* (partial indirect usage). The relevant verse[2] translated as it stands, reads: "When that part which is opposed, having been rejected, non contradiction is indicated; That is called partial indirect usage (*bhaga lakshana*) by those experts who understand signs."

This last or third variety of figurative or indirect meaning is what Shankara recommends when analysing the dictum "That thou art." The scriptures that repeat this formula cannot be wrong and have to make sense somehow. This being a given position for Shankara, by this partial indirectness (*bhaga lakshana*) resulting in the rejection of what is not agreeable in the two expressions "that" and "thou" as referring to God and man respectively in ordinary non-figurative language, we have to understand that they must be neutralized or cancelled out reciprocally.

One expression is thus made to correct the asymmetry of the other, and this corrected meaning is sometimes spoken of as the *bhaga-tyaga-lakshnartha* (meaning arrived at by the rejection of the part that is incongruous).

Thus we see that for giving significant content to the Upanishadic formula referring to the Absolute, and saving it from the danger of nihilism, Shankara is so hard put to it as to resort to subtleties of grammar, rhetoric, syntactics, semiotic processes and pragmatics in the structure and mechanics of language and usage, in reasserting the validity of the Vedantic position. Vedanta thus becomes a complex affair, and but for the life of the sannyasins in India who conform to the Vedantic way of life, the whole school must have killed itself off by now, and, like European Scholastic hair-splitting, must have died a natural death by over-specialization.

---

2. Ibid. Verse 735.

Fortunately we find however, that in modern India, teachers of Vedanta like the Guru Narayana, whose writings we have examined elsewhere, are able to simplify the position again, and thus keep Vedantism still alive in the land of its birth. Modern mathematics, logic and semantics only help to give it a further lease of life instead of letting it get outmoded.

Two Axes of Reference

To simplify the position, which as we have seen is too complicated for the ordinary man, and even for an expert in any one aspect, Narayana Guru has reduced the whole problem, in his *Atmopadesha Satakam* (Verses 36-42 inclusive), and, side by side with the examination of the structure of thought processes as such, he also makes use of semantics to clarify the powers of thought, by taking two typical propositions: (1) "This is a pot" and (2) "This is knowledge."

Both these move semiotically from the general and virtual to the particular and specific, one in the domain of the practical and the other in the domain of the pure world of meanings. If one is distinguishable as a horizontal movement towards the plus side, the other may be said to be a vertical movement to the plus side, which could be also thought of as a negative specification of a pure notion such as that of the Absolute Self.

Reduced to two such axes of reference, and making them cross at right angles, so as to indicate the principle of contradiction or contrariety implied as between a mediate and immediate process of semiosis, treated together as a unitive whole, with a subtle osmotic reciprocity at the point where they participate with each other on homogeneous ground, we have for our use a schematic and structural plan of the interaction of the two sets of processes.

The content of the sentence "This is a pot" being given immediately to the senses, and the movement resulting in positive specification of the pot as against any other object in the visible world, is an *exclusive* one that rejects many possibilities in favour of a single specific fact. The content of the sentence "This is knowledge" has to be understood through the mediation of many examples which have to be thought together as coming under the category of knowledge *inclusively*, and the synthetic process is further to be accentuated negatively or in a priori fashion to arrive at the certitude that the pure self of man alone can offer as a firm ground. Negative inclusion leads to certitudes of the unique Self which is no other than the Absolute.

The Implied Paradox between References

The Bhagavad Gita (II.16) states the nature of the implied paradox between two aspects of the absolute Reality in the following words:

na'sato vidyate bhavo
na'bhavo vidyate satah
ubhayorapi drshtontastv-
anayos tattvadarshibhih

> What is unreal cannot have being and non-being cannot be real; the conclusion in regard to both these has been known to philosophers.

The osmosis of the subtle thought process takes place in the semantic world of the meaning of meaning of words. Within this paradoxical core of the knowledge situation understood unitively, globally and integrally is the context of the normative notion of the Absolute. The whole of this has to be understood intuitively as belonging structurally, schematically and subjectively to the background aspect of human understanding, where thoughts circulate and trace their courses. Some attempt to justify this view has been made in our examination of modern thought elsewhere. Here it is our object to give evidence in passing only, for the present, that even in Vedanta the same peculiarities are valid in its methodology and epistemology.

The Schematic Status of Existence in Shankara's Epistemology

We have already seen how the ontology of Vedanta has a notion of Existence (*sat*) which has neither an immanent nor transcendental, empirical nor idealist, material nor mental, status, epistemologically understood. It has a subjective status of its own.

We shall try to fix more definitely here the ontology of Vedanta, where Existence (*sat*) is to be understood schematically and intuitively in the context of absolute Self-consciousness.

If we can think of space philosophically as a generalized abstracted notion, both existing and subsisting, as Kant recommends, we shall have got near to the schematic status that is meant here. Shankara himself, as we have seen at the end of the last section, relies on the definition of space as that which is not a thing itself, but gives room to all things within it. He defines it, like Aristotle would himself have done, when he says it is *avakasha datr* (that which gives room), which is the same as Aristotle's definition, which says space is "that without which bodies could not exist, but itself (space) continuing to exist when bodies cease to exist."[3] When space exists horizontally as static and fixed space in extension, it can be called *space spatialized*, and when vertically conceived as successively capable of giving room for other bodies to occupy it, we have *space spatializing*.

Space Mentally Analysed

Thus space, when intuitively scrutinized, yields two axes of reference: one in which bodies refuse to give room to others, as in the property of impenetrability of matter known to physics textbooks, and the other in which space is still in the dynamic flux of becoming (*bhava rupa*).

3. Aristotle, *Physics,* Book IV.

Aristotle explains this aspect of space further, in the same context of his definition given above: "for in case it (space) were a body, then two bodies would exist in the same place."

Thus we can think of inclusive space and exclusive space, the former vertical and the other horizontal. As many vessels of graded sizes can be telescopically fitted into one another, many objects can occupy the same space, but the same vessels arranged on the table horizontally, would each represent a space exclusive of every other. Space can thus be of two kinds: that which rejects another or that which includes all at different times or at once. Space can thus be negatively or positively, vertically or horizontally, specified. We have seen how Shankara himself makes use of such a frame of reference for bringing out the negative specification of the Absolute in defining it by attributes.

To bring out more clearly than hitherto that it is such a schematically conceived factor that Shankara has in mind when he thinks of absolute Existence (*sat*), we shall give an example here of his way of refuting a series of anterior questioners, in the following quotations:[4]

> (The questioner argues: If causes as well as effects such as clay and pot, being transitory, are to be considered unreal, would not such a procedure in reasoning abolish everything? To this Shankara answers):
>
> "No; for we are conscious that all our experience consists of a double notion: the notion of being, the real, and the notion of non-being, the unreal."
>
> (Here Shankara pauses a moment to explain the bipolar relation in terms of thought between what is said to exist (*sadbuddhi*) and its object in thought (*sadbuddhi vishaya*). They have their reality established on functional coordination (*samanadhikaranatva*). On the

4. From *Bhagavad-Gita Bhashya of Shankara on* II.16. I have been guided by Prof. Lacombe's French translation (L'*Absolu selon le Vedanta* pp. 41-43) of which this is a near rendering.

homogeneous ground as between them, Shankara explains that the attribute, as object, being transitory, is alone abolished, but not "that of being, and consequently, the object of the pot is unreal, by reason of the transitory character of that thought, but not the object of the thought (*sad-buddhi-vishaya*), because this latter does not pass").

Shankara: No. For one perceives the thought of being in respect of cloth also. It is the thought of being which has the object for its attribute.

Q: Like the thought of being, the thought of pot also is conceived by relation with another pot.

S: No. Because it is not conceived in respect of a cloth, etc.

Q: But the thought of being also, when the pot has disappeared, is not known either.

S: This is not valid, because there is no corresponding subject. The thought of being is related to the attribute, because it cannot, in the absence of the subject, have any attribute; how could it have anything to refer to at all in such a case? But this is not because there is no objective reality corresponding to the thought of being.

Q: If the subject — the pot for example — is not real, the unity of the functional reference of the two notions is not justified.

S: The objection is not valid. Because in the case of mirages and the like, we judge "this is water." Although one of the two terms is not real, we recognize this coordination.

In consequence, from the unreal — body, etc., coupled with their contraries, and their causes — there is no passage to being; and, similarly, from the Real — the Self — there is no cessation of being, of in existence, for at no time does the thought of the Real pass away, as we have said.

We have expressly indulged in this fairly long quotation from Shankara, the greatest perhaps of the representatives of Vedantic thought, as he, with his characteristic insistence, presents here in fully critically philosophical form, acceptable even to moderns, a point of view which will reveal itself to be schematic in status.

The distinction between a pot as a single object actually sensed, and the "thought of a pot" as an subjective counterpart of something that has being, is a point vital to his argument. The latter is an abstraction and a generalization which the mind makes so that in the homogeneous ground of the Absolute both the pot as such and the being as such can meet on common ground. Horizontal attributes can be substituted, but both the pure subject and the object of being subsist eternally, at least schematically and structurally, within the very core of the notion of the Absolute. The Absolute is thus saved from nihilism on one side and from pluralism on the other.

6

Two Certitudes for the Same Truth

The truth of the Pythagorean theorem is one, while the certitude in regard to it is derived in two different ways.

In the lower classes of high school, pupils are asked to cut out of paper the squares on the two sides of a right-angled triangle, and to divide them into convenient bits so as to fit them correctly into the square on the hypotenuse. When the bits fit the latter correctly without overlapping we arrive at a form of certitude which we call a practical proof.

The same certitude or proof can be approached by descending from mathematical axioms of algebra, irrespective of all quantitative or visible implications, as when the teacher of the higher classes of the high school proves the theorem on the blackboard. Thus two different approaches lead to the same neutral or central truth, which is neither merely practical nor merely theoretical. The visibles and the calculables come together to yield a unitive certitude in the heart of the Absolute itself.

The two approaches to one certitude thus envisaged has been at the basis of much polemics in Vedanta, giving rise to different schools, some tending to accept contradiction and others passing beyond it. If we think of the Buddhist Nihilists as taking a very extreme leftist position in this matter, and those like Bhartriprapancha who incline towards the other extreme of pantheism, we can fit in the intermediate schools in graded fashion between them, putting Shankara as the one next and nearest to the Nagarjuna school of Madhyamika

Buddhists, so called Nihilists, and Nimbarka or Madhva at the other extreme.

We have to remember, however, even here that a duality in the name of epistemology is not the same as a duality in the name of axiology. Ramanuja and Madhva, thinking as they do in the name of one adorable Absolute, belong to the context of axiology in their Absolutism. Shankara's position is more tenable epistemologically than axiologically.

As in the case of photographic prints, some of which might have more contrast or more faintness of outline, these possible gradations do not intrinsically affect the absolutist content of any of them. A magic lantern might show structural details when focused in a certain way, which might get faint or effaced when over-focused or under-focused. The circle of white light could represent a neutral state between what shows structure and what is merely understood theoretically in terms of axiomatic truth.

Vedantic literature abounds in such terms as *saguna brahman* (the Absolute still within the scope of the three qualities) and *nirguna brahman* (unqualified Absolute) which are the *apara* and *para*, and sometimes distinguished also as the lower or the higher *brahman* respectively. Whatever its implications, the lower *brahman* is supposed by philosophers like Shankara or Ramanuja to lead to different grades of salvation. Others think that one implies the other, and still others say that, judged by the effect on the votary or contemplative, both are the same. G. Thibaut, in his Introduction to the *Brahma-sutra Bhashya of Shankara*, gives a complete account of the possible prevailing differences:

> Among the passages where diverging views of those teachers are recorded and contrasted, three are of particular importance: firstly a passage in the Fourth Pada of the Fourth Adhyaya (Sutras 5-7) where the opinions of various teachers concerning the characteristics of the released soul are given and where the important discrepancy is noted that, according to

Audulomi, its only characteristic is thought (*chaitanya*), while Jaimini maintains that it possesses a number of exalted qualities and Badarayana declares himself in favour of a combination of these two views.

The second passage occurs in the Third Pada of the First Adhyaya (Sutras 20-22) where the question is discussed, why in a certain passage of the Brihadaranyaka, Brahman is referred to in terms which are strictly applicable to the individual soul only. In connection therewith the Sutras quote the views of three ancient teachers about the relation in which the individual soul stands to Brahman. According to Asmarathya (if we accept the interpretation of the views given by Shankara and Shankara's commentators) the soul stands to Brahman in the *bhedabheda* relation, i.e., it is neither absolutely different nor absolutely non-different from it, as sparks are from fire. Audulomi, on the other hand, teaches that the soul is altogether different from Brahman up to the time when obtaining final release it is merged in it: and Kasakritsna finally upholds the doctrine that the soul is absolutely non-different from Brahman, which in some way or other presents itself as the individual soul.[1]

Within the span of a compact paragraph the above quotation, when carefully re-read and scrutinized, will help to show us where, in the methodology, epistemology or the axiology of Vedanta, is to be located the divergence of views in respect of the notion of the Absolute that all claim to derive from the common source of the Upanishads.

To this list of ancient Vedantins or philosophers of allied disciplines who are mentioned in the Brahma Sutras such as Atreya, Asmarathya, Audulomi, Kasakritsna, Jaimini, and Badari, we could add Shankara, Ramanuja, Madhva, Vallabha and Nimbarka, whose versions of the final doctrine

---

1. G. Thibaut, *Brahma-sutra Bhashya of Shankara*, p. xix, vol. XXXIV. (S.B.E. London, 1896).

of the Upanishads have been recorded as different. Prof. Max Müller aptly compares this common Upanishadic source of ancient Indian thought to the Himalayas, and the various schools or systems, more correctly called *darshanas* (visions of the Absolute) in the context of Indian thought, to the great rivers that have their common source in the snowy heights but flow in divergent directions. Though poetically sublime, this analogy does not reconcile the contradictions which, if viewed rather in an overall context of the Absolute, might perhaps be better reconciled and resolved unitively, as we shall presently show.

The Absolute Independent of all Relative Reference

If the word *brahman* is meant to refer to the Absolute, as is evidently intended, then it goes without saying that it cannot refer to any notion outside itself for its meaning. If there are two absolutes one must contradict the other, and, if so, either or both fail to be absolutes, or else the relation between them must be merely tautological in status.

Thus, strictly speaking, terms like the lower or the higher *brahman* or Absolute cannot be epistemologically justified, although for methodological or axiological considerations such could find legitimate use. There would then be at least four different notions of the Absolute, one that is positive and another that is only negative within both the higher and lower. Tautologically speaking, we could have one Absolute really so and another only virtually so or falsely so, when viewed admitting the contradiction of ordinary logic that excludes the middle ground. An Absolute other than its relative counterpart will thus result, implying an Absolute more positive than the other, the former with an outer contradiction excluding the middle ground, and the latter which includes all within its middle ground though still nominally distinguishable as more positive or negative. A vertico-horizontal frame of reference is implied here. The neutral Absolute would find its place at the point of intersection of these two references on a ground common to both in which the two aspects participate. A complex of possible Absolutes would thus lead to much confusion.

If mathematics reflects logic, as modern symbolic algebra and logistic imply, if language admits the principle that a double negation is an assertion, if algebraic convention accepts two minuses multiplied making a plus, two pluses remaining the more so, etc., and if an arithmetical quantitative negative and positive are different from a qualitative positive or negative in terms of the vertical and horizontal correlates of Descartes, it would not be totally unwarranted for us here to think of a neutral Absolute which is the Absolute of all absolutes, and a pair of quantitatively or arithmetically conceived relatives, one with a plus and a minus horizontally, and the other consisting of a pair of unitively or qualitatively conceived absolutes on the vertical axis of reference, the negative of which could be called a relative Absolute and the other a positive Absolute. The Absolute of absolutes would be the normative one whose two sets of certitudes meet in a central conviction of all.

Another way of visualizing degrees or kinds in the context of absolutism would be to view it semantically or through linguistic usage, reflecting the thinking process that must be supposed to underlie all language, as when we say, "I do not deny that the statement is false," which can only confirm the untenability of the statement in question all the more. Something could be "more so" qualitatively or quantitatively. A fully absolute notion of the Absolute could either fall on the other side of the horse as with an over-zealous rider, or not reach the saddle at all. The notion of the Absolute has to emerge in its full absolutist status by transcending its horizontal alternatives as well as its own inner contradictions with its full import of Absolutism itself. The notion of the Absolute has somehow to transcend all paradox, and even vestiges suggestive of it. This is an utterly necessary position, epistemologically speaking. Ultimate truth cannot be thought of as having a rival or be ranged against itself. That Vedanta does recognize this ultimate absolutist status for its Reality, Truth or Value is evident from the seventh verse of the Mandukya Upanishad, which reads:

> Not inwardly cognitive (*anta-prajna*), not outwardly cognitive (*bahih-prajna*), not both-wise cognitive (*ubhayatah-prajna*), not a cognition mass (*prajnana-ghana*) not cognitive (*prajna*), not non-cognitive (*a-vyavaharya*) ungraspable (*a-graha*), having no distinctive mark (*a-lakshana*), non-thinkable (*a-chintya*), that cannot be designated (*a-vyapadesha*), the essence of the assurance of which is the state of being one with the Self (*ekatma-pratyaya-sara*) the cessation of development (*prapamcjopashama*), tranquil (*shanta*), benign (*shiva*), without a second (*a-dvaita*) — such they think is the fourth. He is the Self (*Atman*). He should be discerned.[2]

Here, except that there is an implied equation between the Self and the notion of the Absolute and that it is calm, benign and non-dual in content, no specific positive qualities are attributed to it. Vedanta attains to a status as near to that of the *shunya-vada* of the Buddhist philosophy of the Middle Way (*Madhyamika*) as possible here. The other extreme position may be represented by the so-called dualists, such as Madhva.

The Problem of Accommodating Different Visions of the Absolute

An electric light might burn bright or dim and still have the same light involved. Between its limits, the function of electrical energy can vary, giving us innumerable intermediate gradations. What the infinitesimal calculus recognizes is just this variability, not in quantitative arithmetical terms but in integral or differential terms, sometimes expressible in rationally denumerable numbers.

---

2. R.E. Hume, *The Thirteen Principal Upanisads*, (Oxford, London, ed. 1951), p. 392.

When a bulb is supplied with weak light, the filaments inside it are visible, but as the intensity is increased we pass through intermediate stages where duality between light and darkness fuse and absorb each other till mere light, stunning and all-inclusive, remains. The vertical stages of the same light might permit degrees of duality till full unity prevails. Between the *vijnanavada* (idealism) of the Buddhists, through the *saguna Brahman* (conditioned Absolute) of Vedanta, we have to allow for an epistemology which recognizes dualities of various degrees, till double negation makes the vision fully positive and nondual. Overfocused, our own images can intervene as mediators into the picture, and when underfocused, relativistic networks of ramified entities, perceptual or conceptual in status, can fill the field of vision. Laws, logical necessities and intuitive certitudes can be seen to occupy the gamut of visions of the absolute Value, the subjective capacity for the vision being neutralized at each level by the counterpart that meets it, as it were, descending from above.

Several grades of hypostasies and hierophanies can be accommodated within the scale of values thus visualized, the plus always cancelling and neutralizing the minus, to yield a vision in terms of a neutralized Absolute. Variability, viewed within such a purely mathematically conceived function, and moving between pure fundamental variables of the human spirit, may rise or fall or trace figures of eight that alternate within the four limbs of the complex quaternion of the Absolute.

From the radiant Vishnu to the humble tulasi plant (the Indian basil), the amplitude of the range of possible values is sometimes spoken of by Vaishnava schools of thought as *taratamya* (a graded scale of values), covering the vertical range within which sacred values can oscillate. Sometimes stabilized at one level, sometimes at another, according to corresponding human capacities, the living vision of the

Absolute reigns like the eternal cosmic dance of Nataraja. The correct focus is the one that knocks down and stuns the onlooker to an utter forgetfulness of his individuality. He then experiences union with the Absolute — an experience "beyond all thought or word" as the Upanishads prefer to put it in the mildest of terms. There is nothing humanly impossible here, as moderns empirically-minded or conditioned might seem to think. If such a vision is the prejudice of the believer, the rejection of the same is open to a similar charge of scepticism from the opposite pole of the same knowledge situation. To keep the middle or neutral ground is what lends scientific status to such matters. A scientist holds the balance between scepticism and belief.

The Plus-Minus Quaternion Structure Implied in Vedanta

Significant certitudes in such a contemplative approach to Truth will at first be experienced as an alternation and changing over within the complex of actualities or virtualities in reference either to the vertical or horizontal axes.

Like a fire-faggot making figures of eight in darkness, when turned round in that way, without having fixed content at any point, we have to imagine significant values in life emerging at different levels of positive or negative actuality or virtuality. The totality spells out in terms of a phenomenological *epoche,* of which the substratum is always the same neutral Absolute. Vedantic methodology and epistemology have retained a trace of this graphic plotting of the points of value reality as implicitly outlined on the basis of the Brahma Sutras by master-minds such as Shankara.

Much of what Shankara said has now become un-understandable even to his nearest disciples — interpreters such as Padmapada and Vachaspati Mishra who in the *Panchapadika* and the *Chatussutri* respectively, have tried to interpret the great Shankara. A careful scrutiny of such comments as theirs — especially as they refer to the last three verses of the *Shankara-Bhashya* on the four first *sutras* treated as a unit, as do these two, the *Vivarana* and the *Bhamati* respectively — reveals to the modern student differences of interpretation and innate structural discrepancies, which become the fecund causes of further possible schisms in the subsequent schools that have grown round Shankara's first great exposition.

It would be highly worthwhile for us to slow down our pace of discussion, so as to take a closer look at the implication of the three concluding verses with which Shankara chooses to sum up his position.

Epistemologically and methodologically these three verses, which are not Shankara's own, but come down from well-known Vedantic tradition anterior to him, give us a peek into the structure of thought adopted by philosophers of those days. They yield for us a sort of master key to all Indian thought generally, beginning from the *Syadvada* of the Jainas and culminating in the semantic implications of Vedanta itself in its latest form.

Semantics and Structuralism Help Certitude

Vedantic methodology and epistemology must yield scientific certitude. If it fails here, Vedanta can at best be considered merely as an appendage to theology and to the mythology that goes with it. Apodictic or dialectical certitudes must conspire in Vedanta to give it philosophic validity. How this is guaranteed by protagonists of Vedanta as a full-fledged philosophy or even science as Shankara intended it to be, is revealed to us in his three concluding verses, summing up his position as follows:

gauṇa mithyātmano 'satve putra dehādi bādhanāt
sadbrahmāham ityevam bodhikaryam katham bhavet;
anveshṭavyam ātmavijñānāt prāk pramātrivam ātmanāh,
anvishṭah yād pramātaiva pāpma doshādi vaṛijitah

> *dehātma pratyayo yavat pramāṇatvena kalpitah*
> *laukikam tadvad evedam pramāṇam in ātmaniśhchayāt*
>
> As son and body, etc., are nullified, being relative or non-valid, how can the knowledge result such as I am the existent Absolute?
>
> Before what is to be inquired into as Self-knowledge, there is inquirerhood for the Self; even when inquired into, this inquiring agent itself is free from all sin or evil.
>
> Just as in worldly matters the terms 'body', 'soul', etc. are used for purposes of certitude, so too is this a valid instrument of reasoning for certitude regarding the Self.[3]

The reader should concentrate his attention here for a while and, if possible, try to be guided alternately by the *Bhamati* and the *Panchapadika*, closely following the Sanskrit explanations, if he is to discover if there is a structural pattern in the mind of Shankara, without which no precise meaning can be gathered from the actual words of the comment. There is a subtle interplay between the measurer and the measured aspects of the Absolute in terms of the Self. The *pramana* or instruments of valid reasoning are the measuring instruments, and the absolute Self within the subject is the object to be determined by measurement by the valid measuring of *pramana*. The immanent and the transcendent selves change places from one side of the knowledge situation to the other, as between subject and object, and, as a result, the sense eludes the common reader, however penetrating his merely analytic scrutiny of the text may be.

One feels like a dog chasing its own tail in following the guiding thought process underlying the line of argument adopted by Shankara here. One is tempted to give up the inquiry altogether if one is not oneself armed with the same schematic notion that Shankara must have had in his mind.

3. Shankara's conclusion of comment on *Brahma-Sutra*, 1-4.

To resort to structuralism is as good as a semantic device serving as a master key for the clarification of the subtle intricacies of Vedantic thought.

The Protolinguistic and the Metalinguistic Approaches

The above text can be read and re-read, yet different commentators will give diverging interpretations in striving to make the meaning clear and final. Some will necessarily have a frame of reference different from others, and when they elaborate or try to make more explicit what is implicitly suggested in the text, the *arthavada* or exegetics employed might carry them too much in one direction or the other, depending on their own innate predilections, tastes or past conditionings. The result is the plethora of meanings diverging between the *Vivarana* and the *Bhamati* schools with their various sub-schools, each laying stress on one aspect as against its rival ones. Such ramifications prove endless in their possibilities, leaving us no wiser than when we started with the text itself.

Is there a way out of such an impasse? What we have always suggested here and elsewhere in our writings is the way of bringing the protolinguistic approach into close juxtaposition with the metalinguistic one. The distinction between the two approaches has first to be clearly visualized. There is a primitive and pure structure of thought implicit in all wisdom literature, especially of the Vedas. The thought and language of Purva Mimamsa, which rely much on semantics, participate in the same underlying structural elements of absolute consciousness, as it were, from two opposite poles of the total knowledge situation.

Vedanta treats of this global or total situation, without an idea of which, like a book that has lost its binding strings, the thoughts that should give it unity fail to hang by the same peg. Analysis and synthesis, the a priori and the a posteriori, have to find in the Self the unifying factor. When thus correlated with the notion of the Self and equated with the non-Self, its own dialectical counterpart, we attain, by tallying one with the other, a degree of certitude that achieves an apodictic status.

Axiomatic certitude meets experimental or observable certitude, and when both these fuse the resultant certitude gains a fully scientific status. Just as the verity of the Pythagorean theorem can be confirmed in two ways, through blackboard explanations by the teacher as well as by actually cutting and pasting squares on triangles by the students themselves, and the two approaches lend weight to the resultant certitude; similarly here, the clarifications of Shankara's disciples can be verified in both of the two possible ways, either protolinguistically and structurally or by the more theoretical approach which we can call metalinguistic.

The Structural Analysis of the Given Vedanta Text

In analysing the content and import of the three verses, let us divide this up into three parts as represented by each verse as it stands.

The first verse has in its very first line four items put in relation. There is on one side the reference to (a) "son" and to one's own (a^1) "body." As applicable to each of these respectively we have the terms (x) *gauna* (a relative value) and the body as (x^1) *mithya* (false). When we give the symbols to the four items as (a) and (a^1) for the first pair, and (x) and (x^1) for those qualifying them, it is possible to arrange all four in a horizontal line, as in figure A below.

In the second verse there is reference backward to the Self or subject which is here treated as the measuring subject of truth. Instead of the inquiry pointing its arrow forward towards the non-Self, as usual with ordinary scientific inquiry in the empirical world of relations or values, the reversal in the process of research is indicated.

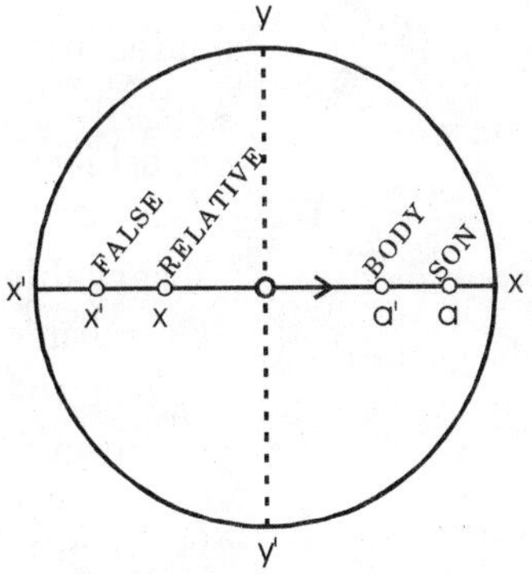

Fig. A Horizontal Values Interrelated

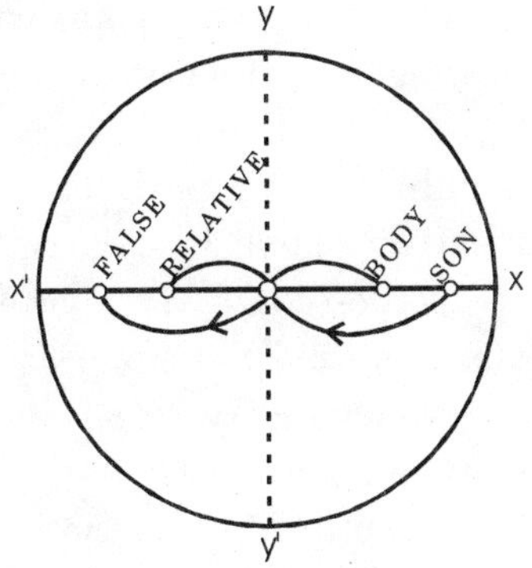

Fig. B. The Correlates of Cancellation

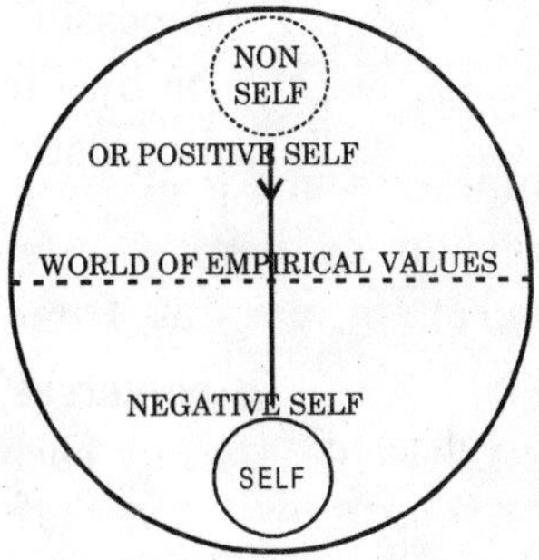

Fig. C. Negative Research

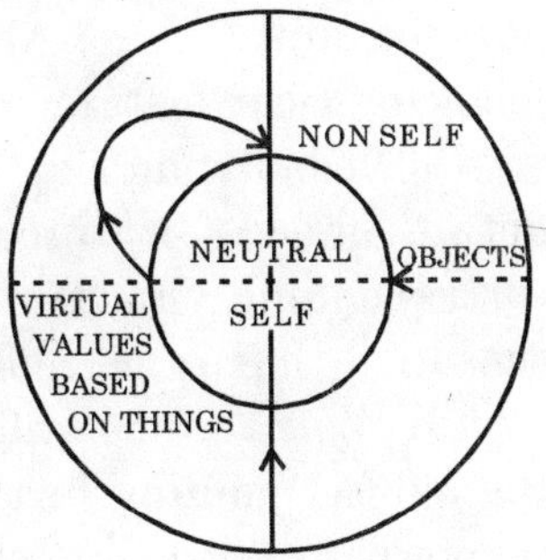

Fig. D. The Neutral Self

In the third verse the transcendental status of the observer or researcher of the absolute Self is brought out. The Self is taken to be already endowed with attributes of sinlessness and purity. The Self and its counterpart in the non-Self are here brought into dialectical relation for purposes of certitude through research.

By an analogy established between the *laukikam* (earthy, empirical) approach and that of the transcendental, in Verse 3 the distinction between a positive and negative line of research into the true content of the Self is established. The steps of reasoning can be graphically explained in the diagrams shown here.

The first verse asserts in schematic mathematical language that relativistic and false values existing objectively are abolished when a backward reference is made in terms of value to the Self. The very cancelling of counterparts effectively abolishes them.

In the second verse, after reversing the inquiring process, it passes from the empirical (horizontal) order of value to the transcendental (vertical) by pointing out a subject free from all evil or sin.

In the third verse the Self and its counterpart are brought together and neutralized one by the other, thus pushing the same process of negative reasoning to its utmost limit, when finally the subjective and objective traits are absorbed in the nondual unity of the Absolute. It is easier now to see the following clear features emerging out of the three verses:

(1) Vedantic inquiry is a negative process and goes from actual objects of interest such as son or body to its corresponding virtual neutral counterparts, passing from sensation thus to perception.

(2) When we go still deeper into consciousness we find the subject gaining further primacy over its own non-Self counterpart. What we seek as a thing to be measured becomes itself a measuring rod that is already perfect and free. This reversal of direction and catching up with the transcendental while letting the empirical go, is all-important for the methodology of Vedanta, which thus differs from its own twin school of Purva Mimamsa, which comes closest to it.

(3) The *measure measured* which is the non-Self and the *measure-measuring* which is the Self, give certitude to each other till they merge into absolute unity, and no question of measurement then arises at all.

Thus we see that when structurally reviewed, the three verses attain a degree of certitude that remained elusive for us in mere metalinguistic language. We can see now how Shankara followed strict lines of thought not only in the choice of examples, but in the progressive *via negationis* that he maintained till all positive and negative values were finally neutralized in terms of the Absolute Self.

Just as the two possible proofs of the Pythagorean theorem each have their contribution to the scientific certitude arrived at, so we can make use of the structure of thought reflected in protolinguistic semantics to arrive at apodictic clarity in Vedantic matters. Shankara must have had in his mind this semantic structural scheme, taking account of the total knowledge-situation, when he wrote his great comments and which therefore make them stand out as unique both for theoretical and practical veracity and value.

7

The Integrated Knowledge Situation of Vedanta

Vedanta uses both logic and dialectic according to the existent, subsistent or value aspects of the reality under discussion, passing from the syllogistic way to the higher way in which thesis and antithesis are absorbed into a synthesis, as known in Hegel. Even the Aristotelian syllogisms are employed in Vedanta in the light of the absolute value, to whose determination all Vedantic reasoning is always directed. The transition between the logic that accepts the principle of contradiction and the one that includes the middle ground without contradiction is gentle, and may be said to take place with differential and infinitesimal principles between the counterparts. To use the terminology developed by us and already employed at the end of the last section, we can say there are two sets of counterparts, one the horizontal which refers to the empirical values in life of the workaday world, and the other the vertical which is transcendental in status, where the counterparts are more fully absorbed and cancelled out synthetically at a higher value level.

Even in the empirical world of values the more negative includes and absorbs the less negative as we proceed following the *via negationis* of *neti neti,* which the Upanishads recognize as the method proper to Vedantic thought as a whole. To arrive at the full notion of the Absolute the paradox that life presents as between appearance and reality has somehow to be transcended by any philosophy that seeks final truth. Vedanta faces the total knowledge situation with

Freedom or Emancipation as its goal for man. The methodological and epistemological peculiarities of Vedanta are therefore its own, and have to be studied for their own sake.

No less an authority of Vedanta than the great Shankara himself clearly had a methodological approach in mind which was both rational in the ordinary sense of accepting contradictions, and fully dialectical in its more final stages, with counterparts to be cancelled in favour of a central and neutral notion of the Self as a high human value in the context of the Absolute. The principle of contradiction gave place to a higher form of dialectical reasoning which synthetically absorbed its counterparts without an excluded middle ground between the two limbs or terms of the reasoning process. In addition, we have developed our own protolinguistic or schematic pictorial language which we have found very useful in bringing out into clear relief the structural aspects of the reasoning process.

Subjectivism, Schematism and Dynamic Process Visualized Together

Vedanta treats of *Ananda* (Value), *Atma* (psychological Self) and *Brahman* (the Absolute) as interchangeable terms in the context of full Absolutism. In other words, epistemologically a certain degree of subjectivism is its basic starting point. Without being open to the charge of solipsism or syncretism, or of degenerating into mere eclecticism, Vedanta attempts to integrate and hold together unitively, different branches of knowledge such as the psychological, the cosmological and the theological, with a scheme of reference of its own. The dynamic aspects, which are inevitable components of Truth understood in living terms, are fitted into one picture with process and reality — being and becoming — envisaged as a total dynamic knowledge situation.

When philosophy generalizes items of reality into categories the philosopher employs a selective process. When as with Kant these selected categories are fitted organically into a scheme, we have a static picture of reality. When Bergson speaks of improving on the *scheme* of Kant or of a *schema moteur* in terms of the *elan vital* as involved in a process of becoming, we have a more living dynamic picture of reality. When each dynamic unit in a system of units is conceived as partaking of a pre-established harmony, with both plurality and atomic simplicity irrespective of size, we have the monadological version of the same, which supplements the partial picture we have been able to build up without the principles of "sufficient reason," *petites perceptions,* and "the best of all possible worlds," being added to complete the vision of truth.

All this has to live and move in the Self. The Self itself has, epistemologically at least, its own non-Self aspect, and between the two there is a subtle osmotic interaction. Fichte and Hegel have developed their philosophy on these lines. These notions when formed in Vedanta should not therefore be considered utterly strange. Modern phenomenology also has its contribution, giving its touches to complete the knowledge situation as a whole, which Vedanta always keeps in mind, implicitly or explicitly.

The colourful world of effects, having simple physical causes like the colours of the spectrum, is a peripheral epiphenomenon merely, which Vedanta deprecates in favour of some value it calls *nitya* (lasting). Although mountains and waves are in a sense *anadi* (without beginning), when they enter the world of human values the pleasures they yield have no firm or stable basis, depending on moods that alternate from period to period and between people of different ages or sexes. The changeless and lasting values lie deep in the Self of man. Introspection therefore reveals the world that belongs to Vedanta, which proposes to put an end to suffering. Mere pleasures are therefore discountenanced in

Vedanta, and affiliation to the Absolute as the *summum bonum* is recommended.

Seven Questions Answered Together in the Gita

A philosophical treatise normally develops its subject item by item in a certain order. If the order is based on logic, we call the treatise systematic in presenting a certain overall viewpoint in philosophy, which it examines with all its implied pros and cons. Indian philosophical systems, so-called, are not so much dependent on logical sequence as on the total vision of the knowledge situation, on whose basis it derived its degree of clarity or certitude. Such global or total visions of truth are called *Darshanas*, and the logical reasoning element that enters into the fabric of the system would seem from Western standards to be deficient or weak. Analogies based on common knowledge often take the place of experimental demonstrations, and at the other pole of the knowledge situation, where axiomatic a priorism is justified, speculation in Vedanta relies on what is called *shabda pramana* (a priori validity of the reliable heritage of human knowledge called scripture). Although the Vedas are normally considered in India as constituting such authoritative scriptures, we need not, in our time, with our freer outlook, limit ourselves to any one body of scripture, Eastern or Western. When both poles of the knowledge situation are treated together, and when the highest of human values called final emancipation is kept in view, the resultant philosophy might resemble theology. Psychology, cosmology, eschatology, science and religious practices, all come within the purview of an integrated or complete concept of philosophy, which uses experience, reason and intuition as means for arriving at total certitude. The truth thus revealed is, or should be for Vedanta at least, worthwhile or significant to man in all places and for all times.

In this connection, let us pause again for a moment to scrutinize an accepted Vedantic text, to make sure that in this matter we are not straying away from data available in recognized canonical texts of Vedanta.

The two opening verses of the eighth chapter of the Bhagavad Gita, devoted to what it calls *Akshara Brahma Yoga*, consist of seven questions put together by Arjuna, for reasons of his own, to Krishna for a total or wholesale answer to all of them, which he gives without circumlocution as directly as possible in the three verses immediately following.

The seven questions and their answers by Krishna are:

> What is that Absolute? What is the principle of the Self? What is action? What is said to be principle of existence? And what is spoken of as the principle of divinity?
>
> Here in the body what and how is to be understood the principle of sacrifice? Again how are you to be known by self-controlled persons at the time of going forth from this body?

The answers come like a sledgehammer as directly as the questions themselves:

> Unexpendable, the Absolute Supreme; its own nature the principle of the Self is called; the creative urge, the cause of the origin of existent beings is designated action.
>
> The principle of existence is the transient aspect, and spirit is the principle of divinity; what pertains to sacrifice is myself here in the body, O most superior among bearers of the body.
>
> He who goes forth, thinking of Me alone, attains my being. (VIII.1-5)

The questions have an inner structural unity of their own to which the answers are meant to tally in a one-to-one relationship. Without reading more into these words, either of the questioner or the answerer, let us try to match the corresponding counterparts in each of the questions.

Reference to the Body

One should note, in the first place, the repeated mention

of the body, not only with reference to Krishna but in reference to Arjuna. It is not the gross and inert mass of flesh or matter which is here understood, but the inhabitant of the body, something more purely existential, subsistential, and of high value. It is a concrete universal which is under reference.

In this sense the body-bearer called Arjuna is the dialectical counterpart of the body of Krishna as representing the essence of the Absolute. In the second verse one notices a reference to the body that is qualified by two requirements. It has to be the body of a man of self-control and again it must be that of one who is about to pass from the present life to the life beyond. If the questioner's body represents the thesis aspect of the dialectical situation, Krishna as the embodied Absolute principle is its counterpart representing the antithesis. The synthesis of these two counterparts will result in the *akshara brahman* (the Absolute that is unexpended, that knows no change).

The next natural question to be asked is where do the elemental existences that are components of the two bodies, whether of Krishna or of Arjuna, fit into the scheme? This question occurs in the words "What is the principle of existence?" of the first verse, to which the answer is given in the fourth verse as follows: "The principle of existence is the transitory aspect as opposed to the enduring." These two are at the basis of the paradox that life presents consisting of the permanent and the passing aspects of ultimate value.

The word karma (action) is given the most central of positions in the scheme as being creative and implying the urge of *elan vital* at the very core of the life of an organism. As *pure act* this creative urge has a vertical aspect and a horizontal one, the former referring to the purer process of becoming where the past and the future meet in abstract and general terms. Although the transient aspects are not outside the Absolute, it is in the pure sense that action could refer to becoming in the context of fuller absolutism. The pure becoming is thus to be thought of as being traced along the vertical axis, while the creation of existence may be said to be its horizontal concomitant.

Krishna is both divine and the Absolute, to which any idea of sacrifice known to religions in the world may be said to refer. The Vedic religionist would think in terms of divinity while the rational Samkhyan would use the word *purusha* (Spirit) in its place. Both of these tend to fall on the plus side of the vertical axis.

All these factors implied in the seven questions are comprised in the nature of the Self (*svabhava*), which is the ground of all the other items. The Self and Nature are here meant to be interchangeable terms. The self of Arjuna would be nearer to Nature and the Self of Krishna to the Spirit or *Purusha*, which is the receiver of all sacrifices. The two differ in that their centres are at different levels in the vertical axis. The divine Self is an extrapolated version of the lower self. The values that the higher Self is attached to are nobler and brighter than those of the lower, which is steeped in necessary and dark levels of life here on earth. The neutralized and normalized Absolute occupies a central position in the total knowledge situation, of which these are symmetrical expressions, each with a penchant or slant of its own. As between the normalized and centralized Absolute and its other versions, there are different degrees of participation, some being more transparent than others.

When there is perfect homogeneity between the lower and higher selves, there is perfect participation on a fully transparent basis. Other degrees of participation between opaque and transparent aspects of the Self can be imagined as being implied between any two of the endless gradations of possible selves, all having their centres in the vertical axis. A refraction and reflection of tendencies can also be added to the general scheme, thus being built up where existential and nominal values meet from opposite poles, implying the counterparts of Self and non-Self. Verbose speculation would fail us here because the possible gradations are infinite.

The active consciousness in its centre is the richest part of the whole knowledge situation and is the seat of pure apperceptions between the Self and non-Self aspects which are ever taking place. Such are some of the further implications of the picture that this chapter of the Gita tries to present, whose structural implications it will be profitable for us to examine next.

Structural Interpretation of the Problems and Answers

The volley of seven problems raised together by the disciple and answered equally together by short phrases has the purpose of showing how these problems and their answers hang together in the total absolutist knowledge situation. It is the innate structure at the core of the notion of the neutral Absolute that makes even such an interpretation possible. That the author of this Vedantic text had such a structure in mind when he made Arjuna frame his questions in such a form that they could be conveniently answered by the teacher Krishna is evident and will become more evident when we have examined more closely the details of the structural implications. We shall take one question after another as they have been put and answered, and indicate marginally the structural implications, taking care that we do not read more into it than was actually meant by the author himself.

1. Q. What is that *Brahman*?

A. Unexpendable (*aksharam*) is Brahman Supreme (the Absolute Most high).

Problem 1

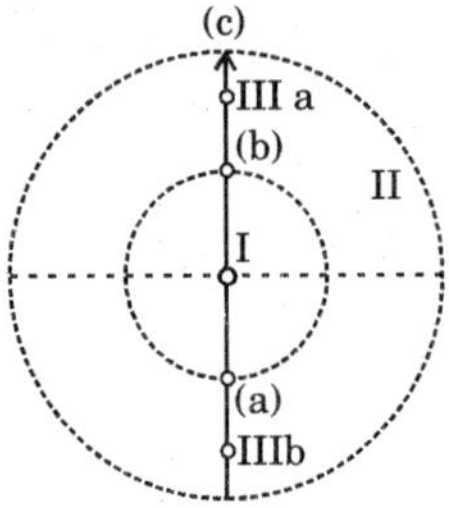

NOTES AND LEGEND

The Absolute is one and eternal and has its own cosmological, psychological, and theological implications. It is a neutral and abstracted notion covering existential, subsistential and value aspects of total reality in terms of knowledge.

The total situation comprised by the Absolute with an arrow that is vertical and pointing upward represents the unexpended, enduring positive notion of the Absolute with three limits, (a) (b) and (c), marking the existential, subsistential and value levels. The inner zones "I" are the psychological while the larger zone "II" comprises the cosmological and theological, with "IIIa" "IIIb" as hypostatic and hierophantic values of religion.

2. Q. What is *adhyatma* (that which pertains to the Self)?
   A. *Svabhava* (one's proper nature).

Problem 2

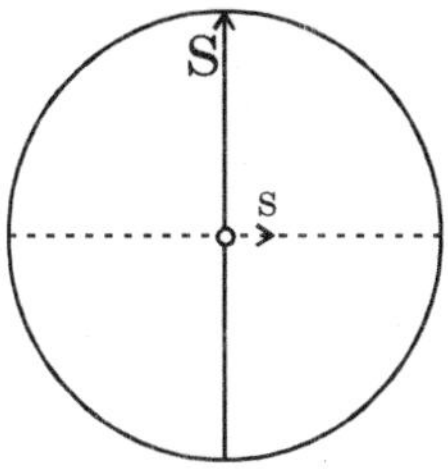

NOTES AND LEGEND

As Value, Self and the Absolute are treated as interchangeable terms in Vedanta, this question becomes relevant. It is put next in importance as the second problem. The larger cosmological aspect is omitted and the Absolute is viewed in terms of Self-consciousness. The individual self, when contemplatively tuned, takes a central place. The *jiva* (living self), small "s," and the collective Self, capital "S," of humanity are both comprised in the *adhyatma* here. The upward arrow indicates the verticalized positive orientation of the spirit as conducive to spiritual progress. The horizontal tendencies are not abolished in "S" but remain secondary and incidental. Nothing is really omitted from it, but everything is retained in the form of an intuition of actuality more mentally or in terms of subjective consciousness. The non-contemplative *jiva* has a horizontal orientation.

3. Q. What is *karma* (action)?

A. The creative urge that originates in the past and refers to the future as a process of becoming.

Problem 3

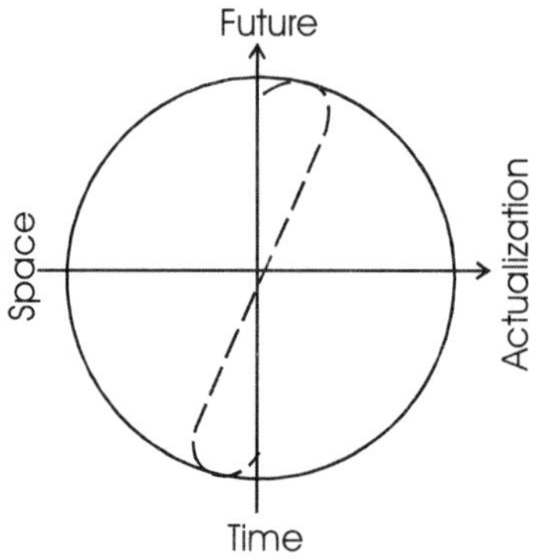

NOTES AND LEGEND

Karma (action) is the eternal flux and becoming by which, as life pulsates at every moment, the future becomes creatively transformed in terms of the past. This force, ever moving or active in a pure or practical sense, alternating and participating in both these aspects in cycles, is referred to as action, as coming within the scope of the most comprehensive definition of action or motion in the core of life or in the Absolute. Its psychological implications as a perception and its cosmological dynamism in the general process of becoming have to be understood intuitively along the lines which Bergson's philosophy has elaborated.

The ambivalent alternation of activity in the core of a living organism has a spatial aspect and a time aspect referring to the past and the future. The space involved here is not actual space measured by a yardstick but an intuition of space schematically understood irrespective of big or small. The pulsation which takes the form of a figure of eight has been elaborately justified elsewhere in our writings. The line indicates the psychophysical motor dynamism at the basis of all activity, participating both in the vertical and the horizontal aspects at once.

4. Q. What is *abhibhutam* (what pertains to the elementals?)

A. It is the transient aspect.

Problem 4

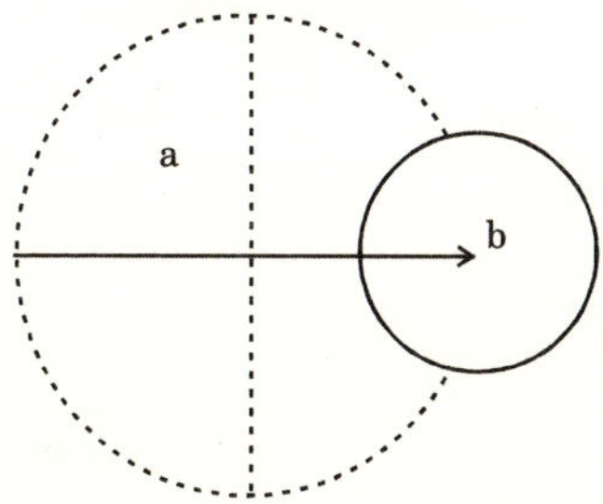

NOTES AND LEGEND

The elementals are the basis of the material manifestations of the physical universe. They are not lasting values because they do not hold the field of human interests uniformly, independently of time or place. Although the concrete universals implied in the physical world may be considered lasting (*anadi*) or beginningless in the world of interests or value, axiologically, they change and pass according to particular conditions. The more lasting is the more real. All values that are subject to change are thus absorbed and included in the more universal and eternal values of life and thus nullified (*badhita*).

When a man is attached to his body and thinks of being fat or strong, or when he treats his son as a high value for the guidance of his life, the tendencies in the Self are said to refer to the horizontalized world of elemental or material values here. The contemplative of Vedanta minimizes such values but fixes his mind on perennial values in the vertical, whether a divinity or the Absolute. In the figure the vertical is secondary and the horizontal gains primacy. The smaller circle "b" shows in aggregate a unit value, like a son or a body.

5. Q. What is the theological or divine object?
   A. *Purusha* (Spirit) is the divine object.

Problem 5

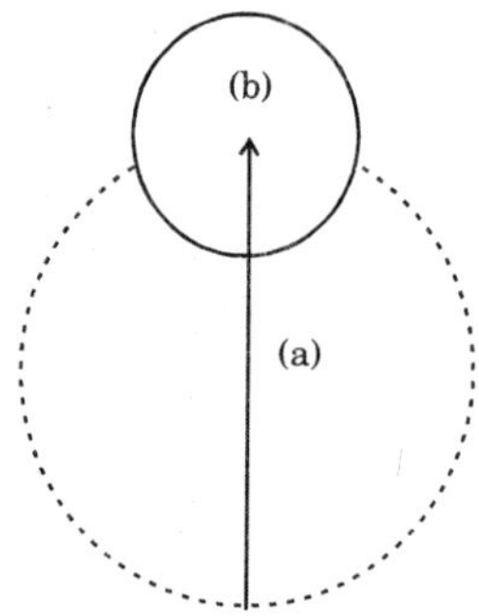

NOTES AND LEGEND

This question is relevant because there are religious minded people who are not fully affiliated to absolutist values but belong to the same general context, with some positive aims that are good as far as they go. The particular case of someone devoted to a divinity is acceptable to an absolutist votary only as far as the value comes within the scope of the more universal and eternal aegis of the Absolute. The lesser and more relativistically understood gods are covered by the greater, as a well within a lake or flood as the Gita puts it in II, 46.

The concept of the *Purusha* of the Samkhyas is a rational philosophical version of the verticalized positive value open to the same objection as the divinity of the believer. Thus three values in life, viz., worship of divinities, dualistically treating the spirit as real, and full-fledged absolutism, are stages in verticalized tendencies. *Pitriyana* (ancestor worship) is altogether discountenanced as falling on the negative side, with only regret for reward. The rational goal as well as heaven are covered by the smaller circle as value (b). Horizontal values do not figure here.

6. Q. In the body, how and who is the factor of sacrifices?

A. I myself am the factor of sacrifice in the body.

Problem 6

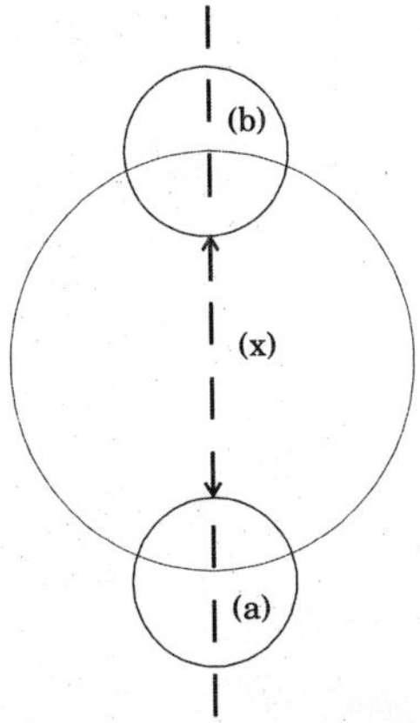

NOTES AND LEGEND

The Vedic sacrifices are directed to the propitiation of gods like Indra and Varuna. In Vedanta or in the Gita however, it is Krishna as the Absolute Value factor who is the acceptor of all sacrifices. Sacrifice can be treated as an attitude or as a principle. The "how" and the "who" in the text cover both the body (as a universal concrete) as well as an *attitude* or *aspiration* more abstractedly understood. The question side has further the condition of a man of self-control as the subject (see question 7 below). Such a man would alone be fit to have absolute emancipation as the result of his sacrifice. Others might reach relativistic intermediate goals.

A bipolarity between the sacrificer (a) and the acceptor of all sacrifices (b) is the condition required for the abolition of the duality in the neutral Absolute. It is here a two-way process of osmosis between (a) and (b) resulting in the normalized neutrality of the Absolute in (x), which is the final goal envisaged in Vedanta. The double arrowheads show this two-way osmosis.

7. Q. How are you to be known by self-controlled persons at the time of going forth?

A. He who at the time of death thinking of Me alone leaves the body and goes forth, reaches My being, etc.

Problem 7

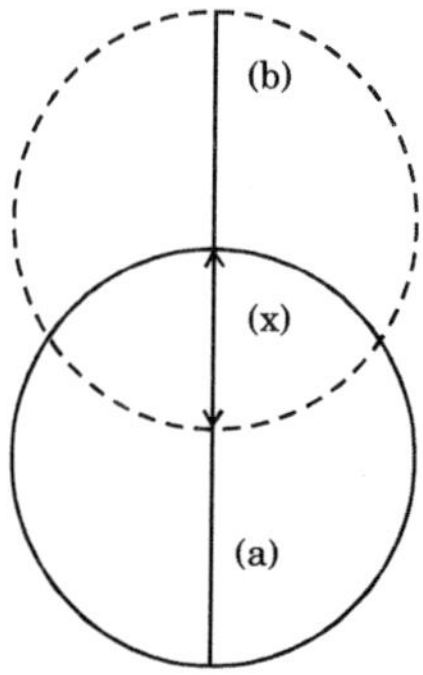

NOTES AND LEGEND

This refers to the final abolition of duality between subjective and objective selves in the Absolute, setting the limit to the spiritual progress understood in Vedanta, for which the clarifications above were preparatory.

The total knowledge situation and the limit of spiritual progress on the part of a contemplative are schematically summed up and the various stages involved marked out in a graphic form succinctly for the guidance of seekers. Here wisdom is to be understood as a means as well as an end in itself.

The heterogeneous collection of questions purposefully put with an integrated scheme in Arjuna's own mind, makes it possible here for the wisdom teacher Krishna to answer a plethora of secondary problems which otherwise would have made the answers unnecessarily verbose and complicated.

The sacrifices to the Absolute Value, and Absolute Value as the personal or impersonal principle to which (or to whom) the sacrifices refer, tend to merge here into one. The principle of sacrifice itself is covered by an intuitive or mystically contemplative attitude of yoga (union) which establishes a bipolar relation between the subjective and the objective aspects of the same Self. When the osmosis is complete there is full transparency on both sides, of (a) the subjective aspirant, purified by self-control and ready to understand the wisdom implications of the situation, and (b) the counterpart of the same Self, on the side of the knowable (*jneya*). The spiritual status of one or the other becomes one of non-difference as the bipolarity is more firmly established. They attain *tadatmya* (that same-selfhood) or *sayujya* (union). The vertical line itself is the sacrificial principle here.

The reference to leaving the body by a self-controlled man is to raise his status vertically by aspiration to that of the aspired One in terms of knowledge of the Absolute (x).

The Bane of Verbosity in Metaphysics

The modern revolt against metaphysics is based on the objection that is too verbose. This is justified to some extent. When teaching a magical sleight of hand trick it is far easier to be guided by watching someone doing it than to learn it from a book which describes the index finger and thumb in such and such positions, dorsal, ventral, etc. The latitudes and longitudes on a map help to place the position of a location such as Cape Comorin, which ancient maps for many centuries situated somewhere near the place where Korea ought to be. Still, used correctly, latitudes and longitudes as schematic versions of visible landmarks help to eliminate verbosity and all its ambiguities. A nurse can read the graph of a fever more easily than a statistically presented version which the doctor, perhaps, could more easily read. As in the Pythagorean theorem, one way lends certitude to the other. The central reality of the Absolute is neither here nor in the Self or the non-Self, neither there nor in this or that, but in the Absolute itself, which has a status in reality all its own. The possibilities of graphic representation in philosophy is a field that has so far been only poorly explored or utilized to avoid the bane of verbosity. Vedantists have been aware of its possibilities, as indicated in the Upanishads, the *Jaimini Sutras*, the *Vasishtha*, and even the *Panchadasi,* to which we shall direct our attention in one of the sections to follow.

8

The Double Domain of the Word

Let us think as before of sitting facing the white circle of light shed on a white screen by an optical projector. The projector could be over-focused and would then shed a blurred image of anything on a slide interposed between the light and the screen. The same result happens when under-focused. There are thus different perspectives possible.

The notion of the Absolute, when correctly focused, is represented by the white light, and when slightly out of focus whether on the plus (objective) or minus (subjective) side, it will reveal the structure of the object or the subject respectively. The neutral Absolute is independent of either perspective, whether objective or subjective, and it is therefore said to transcend duality either from the side of the phenomenal or the noumenal aspects. Such is the Advaitic (nondual) view of the Absolute, which necessarily resembles the position of those who think in terms of vacuity, the *shunyavadin*s of Madhyamika Buddhism represented by the school of Nagarjuna.

Shankara, however, fills this seeming vacuity with the content of an absolute Substance such as Spinoza defines. The absolute Substance is where thought and matter meet as if from opposite poles, to cancel themselves out in favour of the central neutral notion of the Absolute. In other words, at such a neutral point, where names and forms meet without being distinguished as one or the other, subject and object coalesce in the homogeneous matrix of pure word content.

That there cannot be two absolute truths without contradiction or tautology involved, and that varying grades of perspective are possible of the same truth, is the justification for the above assumptions. Further, the neutral point, where nonduality must reside, while participating in both plus and minus overtones or undertones of the same truth, must remain homogeneous to both. These aspects have been elaborated elsewhere.

The Thin Line Separating Perceptual and Conceptual

Having fixed the white circle of light as representing the Absolute, one has to go one step further in order to distinguish the double domain implicit schematically and structurally at a certain zero degree of subjectivity in consciousness. We have to imagine a thin horizontal line cutting the circle into two halves, the top half having a more conceptual or nominal status, and the bottom half a more perceptual, actual or epistemological status.

We thus arrive at the domain of the Word, consisting of two distinct dictionaries such as Bertrand Russell would distinguish. The line separating the two domains of the Word is of a semantic order only, like the mesh of lines that Spinoza would place before a circle, or like the schematic version of space and time of which Kant would speak.

In Vedantic parlance, the line of demarcation, which is real only as a reference, is the line that would separate *nama* (name) from *rupa* (form). The visibles and the intelligibles of Plato and the matter and form of Aristotle imply the same thin line of demarcation at the core of Absolute Reality, which is independent of all differences, internal or external, and free from all contradictions or relationships of part-whole big-small, one-many, etc.

The perceptual side would loom large when the projector sheds its light under-focused and the nominal when over-focused. Between the plus and the minus, the Word resides both as the *symbol* of the thing or as the *thing* of the symbol. Perfect reversibility and interchangeability of the two aspects should be granted. The former would represent the words of the dictionary conceived by Bishop Berkeley's philosophy and the latter would correspond to the empiricism of Locke's secondary qualities. Both are to be schematically understood as participating homogeneously in one and the same word matrix, where the word units of both dictionaries range the two domains in cryptocrystallized or amorphous forms, before being fully actualized in crystalline forms. Such a domain of the Word was meant by the word *logoi* of the Greeks as used by Philo the Jew of the Neo-Platonic Alexandrian context, and is also found in the pre-Vedantic context as we shall presently see.

The Dynamism of Word Osmosis

The above *schema* of the domain of the Word, with its two compartments, has to be given a living dynamic status if the picture we have drawn is to be understood without static fixation. There is an alternating semantic exchange of content in a process of semiosis which, like osmosis between cells, goes on in the mutually transparent double domain of the Word that we have distinguished above. Thought breathes and circulates with the life itself.

The following might sound overstated to persons unfamiliar with the full implications of Vedantic thought. Vedanta recognizes that the whole of reality is covered by *nama* (name) and *rupa* (form). This is the same as saying that the universe of reality is none other than relations or relata which are either nameable as concepts or visible as forms, as percepts.

Nama and *rupa* can both become merged into the absolute Substance that *brahman* represents. When interest and action are introduced into such a relation-relata complex of concepts and percepts, thought circulates analytically or synthetically or culminates horizontally in some action. Like the beating of the heart, action and will, both pure and practical, circulate and pass over from one side to the other of the two worlds of the Word that we have distinguished. The psycho-static picture becomes changed into a psycho-dynamic one, in which there is an osmotic ebb and flow between the poles of thought, which is always solving problems for some desirable action of flight or attack. One has to supply by imagination and intuition, this living picture of the ambivalent, alternatingly rotating process taking place within orbits of interest of greater or lesser time duration. Bergson's philosophy would greatly help here.

Having devoted other works to the elaboration of such a dynamism in thought we need not linger here long. That Vedantic thought too runs along these lines, is what we would like to stress here. In this matter we cannot appeal to a better authority than Prof. Max Müller who was a full-fledged Western philosopher in his own right, and one of the best authorities on Vedanta combined, and who at least cannot be charged with saying something he knew nothing about. In his third lecture delivered before the Royal Institute of London in 1894 on "Vedanta Philosophy" he said:

> The word is the manifestation of thought; every word, we must remember, expresses a concept, not a percept. Tree is not meant for this or that tree; it is the general concept of all trees, and if every individual thing is the realization of an ideal type of thought or word, if every man for instance is the realization of the divine thought or word of man or of mankind, we need not be startled when we find in India as well as in Greece a belief that God created the world by the Logos, or by the word, or by the many words, the *logi*, the ideas of Plato, the species or types of modern science.[1]

Although the dynamic aspects of semantic word circulation and the two distinct domains of the Word are still only vaguely conceived by Prof. Müller in this quotation, it

1. F. Max Müller, *Vedanta Philosophy*, (Susil Gupta, Calcutta, 1950), p. 84.

contains sufficient evidence to show that the related theories of the Logos, and that of *nama-rupa* which Vedanta accepts, had early beginnings in divergent geographical and cultural contexts in the human speculative history of thought.

Both in the Vedic and in the Greek or Hebrew contexts, it is necessary for us to rid the theory of its mythological implications and view each in terms of simple semantic processes understandable in the light of the modern science of semantics. We should further think in terms of the schematization based on subjective structuralism, so that implications of *form* as against *name* may not be omitted. Prof. Müller himself refers to the three contexts in which the theory of the Word was developed by the ancients, from which we glean the following:

The Word in the Vedic Context

We read, in Max Müller's words:

> Thus we find in the Rigveda, 3.6.8 a hymn placed in the mouth of *Vach* or speech had become not only one of the many deities, but a kind of power even beyond gods, a kind of Logos or primeval wisdom. There speech says of herself:
>
> I move along with Rudra, the God of storm and thunder, with the Vasus, with the Adityas, with the Viswedevas. I support both Mitra and Varuna, the two Aswins, Indra and Agni.
>
> I am the Queen, the gatherer of treasures. I am intelligent, the first of those who deserve sacrifice; the gods have made me manifold, standing in my places, entering into many things.
>
> I stretch the bow for Rudra to kill the enemy of Brahman, I cause war for men. I stretch out heaven and earth.
>
> I breathe like the wind, holding to all things, beyond the sky, beyond this earth. Such a one am I by my power.

Continuing, Prof. Müller says: "Such expressions seem to me to presuppose in the distant past the conception of Speech or the Word as a creative power, though possibly in the vague character of the Jewish Wisdom (Sophia) rather than in the more definite form of the Greek Logos."[2]

The Word in the Old Testament

In Proverbs VIII, as Max Müller again points out, wisdom personified speaks as follows:

23. I was set up from everlasting, from the beginning, or even the earth was.
25. Before the mountains were settled, before the hills was I brought forth.
27. When he prepared the heavens, I was there; when he set a compass upon the face of the depth.
30. Then I was by him, as one brought up with him; and I was daily his delight, rejoicing always before him.

The opening verses of the Gospel of St. John are highly reminiscent of the above words of the Old Testament Proverbs, and give the Word a central place prior and more fundamental than creation or even God.

The Greek Logos and Later Upanishadic Versions of the Status of the Word

The Maitri Upanishad (VI.22) reads: "Two Brahmans have to be meditated on, the word and the non-word. By the word alone is the non-word revealed." Prof. Max Müller has this to say on the double aspect here under reference:

> Here we have again the exact counterpart of the Logos of the Alexandrian schools. There is, according to the Alexandrian philosopher, the Divine Essence which is revealed by the Word, and the Word which alone reveals it. In its unrevealed state it is unknown, and was by

2. Ibid. pp. 84-85.

> some Christian philosophers called the Father; in its revealed state it was the Divine Logos or the Son. . . .
>
> From all this it seems to me that we are driven to admit that the same line of thought which after a long preparation found its expression in Philo and later on in Clement of Alexandria, was worked out in India at a much earlier time, starting from very similar beginnings and arriving at very similar results. But there is nothing to indicate borrowing on one side or the other.[3]

Interchangeability of Word with Brahman

We have lingered expressly here somewhat at length, relying largely moreover on the speculations connected with Word wisdom in Vedanta stated by no less an authority than Prof. Max Müller, with the object of showing that the semantic and schematic approach to the notion of the Absolute in Vedantic thought is nothing strange, nor a novelty originating in ourselves here. Widely divergent contexts in philosophical speculation have dealt with the same or almost the same fundamental idea. From Vedic, Greek and Hebrew antiquities the Word and the Absolute have been thought of together and often treated as interchangeable terms.

"The Word was God," etc., of St. John is a startling statement by itself, treated casually and taken for granted by the Christian devotee and bypassed by the common man. When understood in the context of Word wisdom, where the word and the non-word cancel each other out into the neutral Absolute, we shall begin to see the same in the light of the analysis of Vedantic dicta like "That thou art" etc., as masterfully accomplished by Shankara and other Vedantins in books such as the *Vakya Vritti*, which are wholly devoted to the analysis of semiotic processes both direct and indirect, or syntactical and semiotical as modern semantic experts would distinguish them. By cancelling the plus and minus

3. Ibid. p. 90.

indirect meanings of the expressions "That" and "Thou," the neutral notion of the Absolute is arrived at. Even the word *brahman* as used in the Vedantic context from most ancient times goes to justify this interchangeability.

The *Shatapatha Brahmana* (XI. 2.3) which is second only to the Vedas in antiquity and in canonical status, is nearer to Vedanta than to the Vedas, and further elaborates the role of the Word in relation to the notion of the Absolute more vividly than in the Vedas. We read:

> Brahman was all this in the beginning. It sent forth (created) the Gods, and having sent them forth, it established them over the worlds, Agni (fire) over the earth, Vayu (wind) over the air and Surya (Sun) over the sky. . . . As to the worlds above these, Brahman established over them the deities who are above the former deities. And as these worlds are manifest and their deities, these worlds and their deities are manifest where he established them. . . . Then Brahman went to the half (which was not manifest) beyond and having gone there he thought 'How can I get into these worlds?' and Brahman got into these worlds by two, by forms (*rupa*) and words (*nama*).[4]

The double domain of the Word is unmistakably clear in the above quotation, which we could hardly resist from quoting, especially because of the schematic details it reveals, which deserve careful scrutiny. Further, what is more important for us here is to note that the two branches of name and form, put together, can be interchangeably equated to *brahman* itself, as when we write:

Absolute = name + form.

Highlights from the Above Approach

Vedic, Vedantic and Purva Mimamsic speculation has relied tacitly or overtly on an approach to truth based on the recognition of the Word. Neutralized between subjectivism

4. Ibid., pp. 88-89.

and objectivism, more in favour of the former than the latter, if at all, Vedantic speculation has relied on the meaning content of the Word to arrive at the supreme synthesis of all speculative aspects.

We have quoted freely from ancient scriptures, relying on Max Müller who was the first of Vedantic exponents to put his finger on the Word content aspect of Vedantic thought and was bold enough to bring its importance to light. He pointed out that in words like *Vachaspati* (Lord of language) and *Brahmanaspati* (Lord of the World-All or Absolute), the Word (*vak*) is used interchangeably with the notion of the Absolute. Both the Chandogya Upanishad (1.2.11) and the Brihadaranyaka Upanishad (1.3.20)[5] support this view.

The semantic analysis of "That thou art" and other dicta thus comes to occupy the core of Vedantic speculation. To recognize this enables us to avoid irrelevant verbosity passing in the name of Vedantic philosophy. Let us therefore glean from the above and from what we have so far said generally the following points, so as to enable us to build on them further in the few studies of this series that remain for us.

1.0. Vedanta is concerned with a neutral normative notion of the Absolute.

1.01. Vedanta speculation is poised between subjectivism and objectivism. Actualities of the non-contemplative mechanistic world are outside its scope.

1.02. As with Bergsonian metaphysics, Vedanta speculates from inside the total knowledge situation, as it were, instead of taking disjunct outside views of it.

1.03. The dialectical approach of Zeno and Parmenides, as further elaborated by Bergson and Hegel, where counterparts are cancelled out into pure notions in the context of the Absolute, is natural to Vedanta. Bipolarity, ambivalence, alternation, and circulation between positive and negative, are normal notions to Vedantic speculation.

5. F. Max Müller, *The Six Systems of Indian Philosophy*, (Susil Gupta, Calcutta, 1952), vol. 1, p. 53.

Phenomenology and existentialism too share much speculative ground with Vedanta.

1.1. Vedanta has its own ontology and epistemology where immanent and transcendental aspects are treated unitively. It cannot be strictly called idealistic or materialistic. When the crudely empirical sense expressions of life are eliminated and consigned to the limbo of error, the remaining transcendental-cum-immanent content of consciousness is where Vedantic speculation lives and moves.

1.2. Vedantic speculation gives primacy to the material cause over the three others, instrumental, formal or final.

1.3. Vedanta follows the negative way of the *via negationis*.

1.4. For Vedanta, word and thought are related.

1.5. There is a schematism, structuralism and semantics properly recognized in Vedantic speculation.

1.6. The domain of the Word, which is at the core of the notion of the Absolute, consists of two halves, one made up of *what is revealed* and the other of *what is not*. These have a reciprocal osmosis or circulation of thought elements always taking place between them.

1.7. All genera, species, classes, sets or groups, whether of percepts or concepts, form ramifications in the two halves of the content of consciousness as relations or relata, one set appearing as a reflection of the other, forming the two dictionaries of Word content. The Tree of Porphyry is only one version of these two possible trees. (Being concerned with predicables it confines itself to concepts, and leaves out "animals" etc., as subaltern genera.)

1.8. Vedanta, which is a culmination of the Vedas and the *Brahmanas* as we shall see when we come to structuralism, schematism and subjectivism as found in the Upanishads, the Gita and Brahma Sutras, revels in revealing the correlations of cosmological, psychological and theological values or factors. What we have studied in the present section forms the background of such further elaborations of structuralism, etc., to be undertaken before we terminate these studies.

1.9. The possible varieties of speculation in Vedanta, such as those of Shankara, Ramanuja and Madhva, all thrive side by side without conflict in Indian Vedantic tradition, because they are all capable of being treated as different perspectives of the same Absolute. Some present an *over-focused* version while others provide an *under-focused* version. Some stress methodology, others epistemological correctness, while still others pin their faith on value factors such as piety, etc.

2.0. Epistemology, methodology and axiology have to be treated separately in any Vedantic revaluation that attempts to disentangle Vedantic thought in scientifically revalued and restated terms.

We shall reserve the further examination of the structural implications that have become evident already in the pre-Vedantic literature that we have cited above for later, when we come to examine the same phenomenon in Vedantic literature proper, such as the Upanishads, the Brahma Sutras and the Bhagavad Gita.

9

Varieties of Vedantism

Scientifically speaking, there cannot be more than one Vedanta, if by Vedanta we mean, as we ought to mean, the wisdom of the Absolute. In fact, however, it has become a common practice, both in the religious and philosophical contexts, to speak of kinds or schools of Vedanta or Vedantisms.

Vedanta can be so degraded and distorted as to refer to mere credos and cults, as we often see, and many kinds of deistic and theistic outlooks flourish today under Vedantic labels. Even under the names of single Vedantic teachers like Shankara, many apartments and anterooms are at present accommodated in the mansion of Vedanta, some of which, at least, have questionable claims.

Much lukewarmness and indifference passes for virtues such as tolerance or piety or generous broadness of outlook. Some call it Hindu, while others claim true Vedanta to be that or this or other orthodoxy or heterodoxy, observance or belief, giving primacy to one or another tenet, god or goddess of the Hindu pantheon, Shaivite or Vaishnavite. Vedantas thus flourish as rivals side by side with those that are based on mother worship.

Each has an accent, stress, doctrinal colouration or tint distinguishing it from its rivals, and many polemical battles are fought over subtle implications of teaching to this day, most of which makes little or no sense even to the educated Indian. One pretence hides another and silent oracles nod in knowing assent over articles of faith where close examination of claims will often reveal empty jargon. Vedism, Rationalism or Yoga change sides from the left side of heterodoxy to the right side of orthodoxy. Puerile forms of faith find place within some modern brands which, claiming to be pure, integral or non-attached, make of Vedanta a jumble like bits of paper in a wastebasket, hardly attaining to coherence even as a mosaic.

The votaries of Vedanta are so varied at the present day that it has become a blanket term to hide all that is vaguely, eclectically, syncretically or solipsistically understood, and even popular superstition is at times not effectively excluded from what the term Vedanta should strictly connote or denote. The Brahma Sutras themselves would exclude Yoga and treat Vedanta as the closed preserve of persons of certain castes alone. Even sitting or standing postures gain delimiting significance in Vedanta and rank superstitions sometimes pass muster without the scrutiny of healthy standards of criticism.

Not a Surrogate of Religion

All these are marks of decadence in Vedanta, which has become goody-goody or namby-pamby, lending itself to be used to pamper to spurious spirituality and sometimes even supporting charlatanish religions or occult growths or expressions.

We often notice too that Vedanta is used as a surrogate for closed religions and statically made to support the dead letter and hidebound attitude of orthodoxy. Like salt that has lost its savour, such Vedanta loses its fundamental quality by being compromised with relativistic values. Like pure milk carried in a dog's-leather container, there is nothing one can do about such varieties of Vedanta other than to cast them out of the window.

To be properly recognizable, Vedanta must have such a radically unmistakable ring of the Absolute and such strict norms and standards of thought, that it will not tolerate cant within its domains.

Vedanta, like mathematics, is presented in science texts or *shastra*, as the Gita claims to be at the end of each chapter. The Gita's open and dynamic character is so categorical and unequivocal as to make Krishna, as the true Vedantic Guru, declare its character by saying:

> As each chooses to approach Me, even accordingly do I have regard for them. My very path it is, O Bharata (Arjuna) that all men do tread from every (possible) approach. (IV, 11)

Such a categoric denial of any closed and static outlook, taken together with the other well-known Upanishadic dictum that "he who sees plurality wends from death to death" (Katha Upanishad, IV, 12) must be enough to dispel any vestige of doubt in the matter of the unity demanded in one voice by the canons of Vedanta. Those like even such an eminent modern authority as Dr. Radhakrishnan, who says that the Upanishads "speak with a double voice" or that it has two distinct philosophies to teach, do great injustice to this subject, which is perhaps the proudest monument of Indian wisdom. This is apt to not be fully understood in the light of modernist speculation of the West, which cannot truly penetrate deep enough to the core of unity with whose voice Vedanta has always spoken.

There might be overtones and undertones in the voice of Vedanta but to say that two voices hide within it is to detract from the essential character and value of the highest wisdom heritage of India. Absolute truth cannot ever be dualistically conceived, and if it has been apparently so construed, as with the Dvaita (Dualism) and *Vishishtadvaita* (Qualified Non-dualism) of Madhva and Ramanuja respectively, the unity of the Absolute has not really been marred, because it is the structural perspective and not the content as such that has been at the bases of those "varieties" in Vedanta, so called.

Vedanta and Vedantisms should never be mixed up in the mind.

Vedanta Attempts Integrated Wisdom

No comparison is thinkable except on the basis of a common ground on which the differences can be established. Vedanta considered as the culmination of the ritualism of the Vedas and as the integrated and finalized version of the philosophical tradition of the Indian soil, orthodox or heterodox, anterior to it, must offer a common basis justifying the philosophies of Shankara, Ramanuja and Madhva as possible varieties of Vedanta.

Both philosophy and religion, materialism and idealism, Jaina and Buddhist heterodox speculation and those that tow the orthodox line, Samkhya rationalism and Yoga discipline, find in the three canons of Vedanta — the Bhagavad Gita, the Upanishads, and the Brahma Sutras — their natural point of revalued and restated integration. Vedanta represents the integration and "the finest blossom on the tree of Indian wisdom" as Paul Deussen would say. Nothing significant is lost nor any crowning crest-jewel of doctrinal conclusiveness omitted or bypassed by Vedanta.

The Great Dicta express its doctrinal conclusion unequivocally. Theological, cosmological, psychological and eschatological values are preserved here and discussed by the various teachers with a methodology, epistemology and axiology all its own. The contributions of the six systems of visions (*shad-darshana*) as well as the content of Vedism, are together retained in Vedanta. In short, Vedanta can claim to represent an earnest attempt at formulating an integrated wisdom of the Absolute, holding out the freedom or salvation that contemplative spirituality anywhere in the world offers as the highest hope and consolation of man. These claims of Vedanta have always been recognized and hardly need reiteration here.

Genetic and Social Aspects Less Important than Content

Shankara had Buddhistic nihilism as his background,

while Ramanuja had the Bhagavata religion of the Pancharatra, and Jainism and Buddhism too played their part. With Madhva the presence of Islam as a social force and the Jaina background also determined the shape of his Vedanta.

These genetic and objectively evident social actualities, doctrinal peculiarities and practices need not concern us here primarily, because it is the core or content of Vedanta as such that will give us the surest key. A scientific comparison and contrast of these standards are of methodological import, such as the *sat-karana-vada*, the approach by giving primacy to cause over effect, while others, like the stress on escaping rebirth, etc., are axiological or eschatological in import. The intuition or logic employed by the kind of Vedanta under consideration would have to be based on epistemology.

These then form the first broad basis for a scientific classification of the varieties of Vedanta. Shankara excelled in epistemology, while Ramanuja was axiologically more sound, and Madhva on his part was strong in *tattva* (principles of reasoning) as can be judged by what is called *abhinava-anyatha-khyati-vada* (new way for accounting for error) and his *svarupananda taratamya* (graded scale of self-bliss), etc.

The total knowledge situation, the word and its structure, stemming from pure semantics, have always belonged to Vedanta as its very core. The subjective, selective, perennial, structural and schematic inherence of Vedantic speculation have to be recognized by us in comparing the varieties of Vedanta. Dialectical counterparts and antinomies have to be discovered as distinguishing features of Vedantic speculation.

At present Vedantic speculation has lost its way in the maze or tangle of Vedantic texts, commentaries, glosses, variously called *bhashyas*, *vartikas*, *vivaranas* or *tikas*, resulting in a veritable forest of speculation, in which even an expert of present day India or an adept of the West can easily lose his way.

From the seven categories (*sapta padartha*) of the Nyaya-Vaisheshika, through the duality underlying *Prakriti* (Nature) and *Purusha* (Spirit) of the Samkhya-Yoga, to the twin schools of the Mimamsas, where semantic considerations gain ground to fully give an underlying unity of schematized structure for all or any variety of Vedantic thought, the common basis must be clearly visualized. Then alone can the specific and the generic varieties of the family of Vedantic thought, its affinities and contrasting traits be scientifically discussed.

Besides these six systems that have nourished so much speculation, there are the various *shakha*s (branches) with *samhita*s (compendiums) derived from different orthodox or heterodox traditions that have flourished during several millennia on the soil of India, that help us to separate the distinguishing traits of Vedanta that existed before books like the Gita finally attempted to integrate all Vedantic thought into one body.

The Bhagavathas, the Pancharatras, centred on supreme persons of the status of demi-urges raised to Absolutism, as in the case of Purusha Narayana mentioned in the *Shatapatha Brahmana* in relation to the *Pancarata Sattra*, besides the Vedic and Upanishadic background largely relied on by Shankara, will reveal to future research valuable traits in grading and classifying all Vedanta under one integrated schematically homogeneous structural pattern. How Vedantic speculation hangs together by one and the same unifying peg can be revealed by certain features common to all of them.

Components of Madhva's Vedanta

In Chapter 7 we examined the structural unity underlying the total knowledge situation as understood in the Gita, where a volley of seven problems are raised at one stroke by Arjuna as questions to his Guru, Krishna. In order to get started with a grip on the main problems involved, we shall first examine an old Sanskrit verse in which the distinguishing traits of Madhva's variety of Vedanta are reviewed, before passing on to Ramanuja and Shankara. Nimbarka, Vallabha and Chaitanya being less familiar, we shall pass them over for the present.

> *srimad madhvamate harih partarah satyam jagat tattvatah, bhedo jivaganah hareranucharah nichochha-bhavamgatah; muktir naijasukhanubhutir bhaktistu tat sadhanam, hyakshadi trinayam pramanam sakalam naikyavedya harih.*
>
> In the doctrine of Srimat Madhva, Hari (Vishnu) is the most ultimate, the world is real in principle, differences (there are) among classes of created living beings, the devout followers of Hari (Vishnu) having attained to low or high status, salvation (consists of) one's proper (capacity) for (attaining) happiness (in the self) and devotion (bhakti) is the means thereof, the three tests of truth are the three such as perception, (and) what is given as the result of knowledge derived from all scriptures (taken together) is Hari [Vishnu or the Absolute].

From this we may conclude the following:

1. Madhva considers the world as real in principle and not as an actuality.

2. This principle or *tattva* is to be understood as of two categories, *svatantra* and *paratantra* (self-controlled or under other control), while both these are united in an eternal flux or process which is called *pravahato anadi* (beginningless as flowing).[1]

The Absolute of Madhva derives its name from the Vaishnava tradition where it is conceived as a supreme Person (*Purusha*) Hari or Krishna.

3. There is a scale of spiritual values at the core of the Absolute in relation to which all beings could be classed or

1. Dr. B.N.K. Sharma, *Philosophy of Sri Madhvacharya,* (Bharatiya Vidya Bhavan, Bombay, 1962), p. 158.

graded. This doctrine is referred to by the Sanskrit term *syarupananda taratamya* (graded stages in self-realization).

4. Salvation is the experience of the bliss of self-realization and the means for such is pure devotion (to the Ultimate).

5. Reasoning is based on three methodological principles, beginning with (a) perceptual verification, together with (b) inference and (c) reliance on the a priori, which is called *shabda pramana.*

6. The Absolute (named Hari, Krishna or Vishnu for traditional reasons) is the content of all wisdom texts. It is to be known through their study as being the content of the totality of their teachings taken together.

Under these six items all the components that go to make Madhva's variety of Vedanta distinguishable, are, in the main conclusively comprised.

Ramanuja's Frame of Reference in Vedanta

Vedanta as understood by Ramanuja is different from that of Madhva only in verbal versions of doctrine. The frame of reference in both cases remains basically the same. The former is called a *Vishishta Advaitin* (one who stands for a nonduality that admits of specific predicates of the Absolute), while the latter is popularly known as a *Dvaitin* (a dualist).

These labels are misleading to the extent that they refer to the primacy or stress given to methodological or epistemological aspects. The general frame of reference adopted by both, however, remains fundamentally the same. We shall enumerate here first the broad doctrinal peculiarities of Ramanuja's Vedanta, before trying to establish the similarity of the frame of reference common to both. The following extracts are taken from the original work of Ramanuja himself called *Vedartha Samgraha.*[2]

---

2. English translation by S.S. Raghavachar M.A., (Mysore: Ramakrishna Ashram, 1951), Paragraphs 231 to the end of the book, pp. 186 ff. Paragraphs indicated in parenthesis.

The Vedas in their totality teach us the nature of Narayana, the Supreme Brahman. (231)

When words are used in the pre-established Vedic order, they carry their original significance, otherwise they are different in significance. (233)

The Brahman knowable through the Vedas is Narayana, who is antithetical to all evil, transcendent and unique. He is an ocean of hosts of auspicious attributes. His supreme glory is beyond thought in its nature and attributes. He has as the means of his sport the entire universe, etc. (234)

Brahman himself, qualified by all entities as the modes, is signified by all terms which are applied to him by way of coordinate predication (*samanadhikaranatva*). (235)

The supreme Brahman resolved by himself to take up many modes and thought, "Let me become many." He caused the individual selves to enter them as principles of their animation. He then brought into being the whole of the gross world out of these elements animated by the conscious principles through mutual permutations and combinations (*bahuprakaram*). Then the supreme Brahman entered into all these entities as their ultimate Soul. Thus he exists in the state of effect as the supreme Self with all existence constituting his body. He exists characterized by these modes (*prakaras*). (236)

The Great elements (*mahabhutas*) in their primeval subtle condition constitute what is *Prakriti* (nature). The sum total of individual selves (*bhoktrivarga samuha*) is called *Purusha* (Spirit). Thus the *Paramatman* himself is designated by the terms *Prakriti* (nature) and *Purusha* (Spirit). Remaining the real, he became the real and the unreal (Taittiriya Upanishad 11, 6). The means for the attainment of Brahman is *para bhakti* which is of the nature of meditation which has acquired vividness of clearest perception (*vishadatma pratyakshata*). The term

> *bhakti* signifies a particular kind of love (*prīti*). Love is a particular kind of cognition. (238)
>
> But love is the same thing as joy (*sukham*). (239)
>
> The cognition of that object is itself the joy in question *tad-vishayajnanameva sukham*). (240)
>
> Entities other than Brahman can be objects of such cognitions of the nature of joy only to a finite extent and for limited duration. Since the form of cognition as joy is determined by its object, Brahman itself is joy. (241)
>
> When Brahman becomes the object of one's contemplation, he (the meditator) becomes blissful. (242)

A careful scrutiny of these two varieties of Vedanta will help us to see their common epistemological, methodological and axiological frame of reference. As for Shankara, we have already incorporated his frame of reference in many discussions of aspects of Vedanta in general. We shall complete them in due course, when we take up the examination of the structural implications of Vedanta generally at closer quarters in the next chapter.

10

Favourite Examples in Vedanta

Science seeks certitude through experiments. Mathematics relies on proofs capable of being expressed in the form of equations. The Pythagoras theorem, as we have seen, is capable of two proofs that meet to give one certitude which is neither abstract nor concrete exclusively. Vedanta too has its favourite method of arriving at certitude. When common experience vouches for truths in everyday life, experiments conducted under elaborate laboratory conditions become unnecessary. Language enshrining the common experiences of mankind in the form of proverbs or just common sense can be relied on to give us certitude on many problems of importance in life.

Parables, fables and figures of speech have taken a large place in lending support to speculation all over the world. Such a source of certitude, when properly rid of the extraneous, is not to be discredited, and should be considered as valid at least as proofs in Euclid, which derive their certitude from axiomatic a priori truths. When such mathematical truths are called postulates, theorems, riders, corollaries or lemmas, insofar as they are derived from self-evident verities acceptable to all they have the same value as demonstrations. Experience can substitute for experiment in many cases. The falling of an apple cannot be called an experiment conducted by Newton to afford a basis for his theory of universal gravitation. Even non-scientists know that bodies are attracted towards the ground and not towards the sky. The rest of Newtonian theory has the status only of calculation or speculation or both.

Therefore, if Shankara and Jaimini give a large place to *shabda pramana* (scriptural authority) to arrive at certitude in respect of overall philosophical problems such as the nature of the Absolute, it is not their weakness but rather their strength.

Vedanta Lives by Its Own Unique Examples

Language is most ordinarily used to describe objects or simple events. When intentions and interests enter into the world of events and relations between man and man, and when actions, single or in chains, further complicate the situation, the importance of the visible is slowly superseded by what is unquestionably accepted through language as representing the consensus of knowledge in respect of the experience of mankind.

Scriptures, therefore, have legitimately relied on parables, fables, analogies and simple figures of speech like metaphors and similes. Works like the Tao Teh Khing teach through simple anecdotes. The myths of nations contain secrets that the intuitive mind can grasp. The Bible lives by its parables.

Vedanta too is no exception to this general rule which applies to all scriptures anywhere, except perhaps in one respect which has specially interested us in the present series of studies, which have been primarily intended to revalue and restate the whole field of Vedanta, highlighting more especially those aspects which rely on the inner structure of thought itself.

It is here that Vedantism excels in its use of its favourite examples, analogies and pictorial language. These have more of a protolinguistic slant and have such a telling apodicticity that throughout the long history of Vedanta of two or three thousand years, they have retained tenaciously their place in its literature.

Even a modern Vedantin desiring to change the time-honoured examples of Vedanta, such as the pot and the clay, the wave and the sea, the snake and the rope, and the silver and the mother-of-pearl, would feel exasperated to do without these favourite literary devices which have struck root at the core of all Vedantic speculation.

The reason for this willful persistence of such examples as something so dear to Vedantists every time and everywhere, and which might even be said to be the distinguishing characteristic for recognizing Vedantism as it prevails even today, can be attributed only to the fact that they contain some elements inevitable to the Vedantic speculator for clinching his main issues and findings.

Certitude for the Vedantist is not to be understood as consisting of a predication about truth. The doctrines of Vedanta are not articles of faith understood as enumerable in a series, as in the case of metaphysical or religious speculation common in the West. The Vedantist prefers to call what he believes as truth "vision" rather than the components of a "system" or school of thought. Each school, if it could be so called, has a central vision or *darshana,* often cryptically and briefly expressible in the form of a dictum implying in each such case an experience of the speculator, meditator or contemplative concerned. His certitude is often referred to as *aparoksha anubhuti* (non-transcendental personal experience). Such experience has to be as compact and concrete as a *karatala amalakam* (a gooseberry held in one's palm). Verbose predications of philosophical findings are discredited by Vedantins in favour of the certitude of the yogi in whom the vision and the visionary attain to compact unity.

It is because Vedanta aims at a certitude that is felt inside as well as known to be yonder at one and the same time, that the peculiar examples, analogies and pictorial language that we are going to discuss here become all important. The Upanishads are replete with instances of picture-language, some elaborate, some more compact, which latter could be called ideograms.

Analogies are variously woven into the fabric of the Vedantic texts, and the suffix *iva* (like) is very profusely relied on, as any page of the Upanishads would reveal. More complex literary devices with scientific purposes of bringing out structural, schematic or subjective subtleties are masterfully employed by the rishis who were the authors of the Upanishads. They all tend to minimize metalinguistic verbiage.

When these fables, anecdotes or parables are somewhat elaborate, they become distinguished as *vallis*, like *Brahmananda Valli* and *Bhrigu* Valli, etc. of the Taittiriya Upanishad, or *Kanda*s as of the Chandogya Upanishad. When examined with structuralism in mind, even these anecdotes reveal to us peculiarities of composition which cannot be explained otherwise than by the theory that the rishis themselves had the same structuralism in their minds. It is when such features become evident to the student that he can rest convinced that he has himself come to some kind of sure understanding of the purpose or the gist of Vedanta as a whole.

Let us now fix our attention on some of the favourite examples of Vedanta.

Appearance and Reality

All philosophical inquiry presupposes distinction between truth and falsehood, fact and fiction, or more generally speaking, between what is apparent and what is behind appearance. Fact-finding, truth-seeking and problem-solving are all meant to avoid nuisable situations in life and to seek progress to happiness. Unhappiness is never a recognized end of philosophical inquiry. If all that glitters were gold, there would have been no need for any philosophizing at all. Thus two overall categories are implied in all philosophizing. If there are more than two, they could all at least be included under these two as classes. Absolute Truth is what can make man free. It is the value-pearl of great price, and potent in leavening the whole lump of life. Even a little of Truth or Wisdom can save man from great fear, as the Gita prefers to put the same Biblical verity.

Further, these two categories of appearance and reality, with which, as presuppositions, philosophy itself becomes possible, have between them an implied principle of paradox. The nature of this paradox is subtle and the complexion of the same can vary in degrees of possible differences between the two aspects involved, ranging from full contradiction at one extreme, and grading into non-contradiction when purer pairs of opposites or antinomies are involved.

Each such pair can be said to belong together to a psychophysical grade or order of its own. Contrast, contradiction or contrariety belong to each ambivalent, reciprocal or dichotomous couple or set of poles in the total knowledge situation, with degrees of duality regulating their bipolarity. When there is full accentuation of the differentiating principle, we live in a horizontal world of values, with plus and minus separating each pair of the same grade. When, on the other hand, the polarity is less accentuated, contradiction tends to cancel differences between pairs of counterparts by one term canceling out the other. The former has a horizontal or arithmetical status, while the latter has a vertical or geometrical status.

The three examples that we shall scrutinize, which are, by acceptance or by rejection, equally favoured by Vedanta, will reveal further the structural pattern we have just tried to trace, together with the dynamism natural to it.

The Water and the Waves

We should consider first perhaps the most common example of Vedanta, where appearance is compared to waves on the ocean and reality is compared to the material cause of each wave qualitatively understood, which is none other than the water without which waves become even unthinkable.

If the waves refer to the visible aspect of reality, water refers to its intelligible cause. The former could be called schematically the horizontal aspect of the absolute reality, and the latter its projected vertical counterpart. The quantitative multiplicity of waves on the ocean has nothing to do with the depth of the water in a purely qualitative sense. Between the qualitative and the quantitative there is an implied paradox when understood in the light of a neutral epistemological subjectivism proper to Vedantic speculation, as we have already pointed out.

Thus the wave and the water example, so dear to Vedantins, affords a frame of reference in order to correlate appearance with reality. There is a participation between these two only at a common neutral zero point of the total or absolute knowledge situation. Body and mind, spirit and matter, meet centrally and diverge peripherally.

Both wave and water, when understood as actualities, imply full contradiction, but when understood intuitively or in pure terms, they tend to merge in the common epistemological heterogeneous matrix of thought. How this can be understood has been explained by us elsewhere when treating of the *schematismos* of Kant, the *schema moteur* of Bergson, and the structuralism of Eddington.[1]

Philosophy consists of delving into the depths of the material cause of effects that are apparent and given directly to the senses. When the cause is distinguished we get to a relationship between cause and effect which will afford the first overall frame of reference for clarifying the relation between true and false values in life. Accepting the principle of contradiction fully at the initial stages of reasoning, but tending to absorb contradiction unitively in the final stages of philosophical inquiry, this two-sided example of wave with water as its real cause beneath it affords the Vedantic speculator two intersecting or correlating axes, constituting

1. See *An Integrated Science of the Absolute* by the author.

a frame of reference which can be used with great advantage in avoiding the bane of verbosity in metaphysics.

The Rope and the Snake

The second example we have selected is not used with the same purpose by all Vedantins. It is used with full favour by those who belong to the nondual (Advaita) school, which is perhaps the most important of all Vedantic Schools, to which the great name of Shankara lends its support.

This example is particularly suitable for contrasting favourable with fearful or unfavourable value-factors in respect of what is good to man in distinguishing appearance from reality. Both snake and rope are contrasted on the basis of an axiologically based epistemology. Knowledge about the real abolishes the fear implied in the world of relativistic appearances. The weak man of ignorance sees a fearful snake where there is only a harmless rope. The snake is an eidetic or phenomenological presentiment. The rope represents truth in itself or in its simplest form of existence (*sat*).

If the phenomenon of the snake is treated as a horizontal aspect, the reality of the rope would represent the vertical aspect, on which the snake is a mere supposition or superimposition (*adhyasa*). The contrast between appearance and reality here is not as strictly and symmetrically maintained as in the previous example we have analysed. Moreover, the aspect of the evil is made to loom disproportionately larger than its dialectical counterpart of reality represented by the rope.

The Charvakas, who correspond in India to the Epicureans of the West, have rightly objected that failure to appreciate the intrinsic goodness or value of the world and rejecting it totally as being of no value, as when the snake is abolished by right knowledge (as this favourite example of Vedanta would imply) means that nothing significant to human life in the remaining reality would be left over as residue. There is a subtle structural violation of symmetry here between the plus and minus value factors involved in the example.

Both Ramanuja and Madhva have protested in their own ways against this disproportionate exaggeration of the aspect of evil in the world. In doing so, however there is room to think that they themselves have fallen into an opposite error, by seeming to recognize ordinary everyday values such as decorations and embellishments with which Vishnu is represented. In their eagerness to overthrow the theory of maya, which implies the falsehood of the phenomenal world, they have permitted puerile values to enter the domain of spirituality, as it were by the back door.

Further, the comparison of reality to a rope makes it insignificant as well as insipid to the common man. A flavourless reality may not satisfy even a normal saint who would like the salt to have its own quality of savour. None can enjoy mere tastelessness.

In recent years Narayana Guru, who revalued and restated Vedanta, reconciling all the schools above, applied the corrective revision to this favourite example by substituting a flower garland for the rope. Both appearance and reality regain, by this corrective touch, a more symmetrical status, where some residual value is retained in favour of both aspects, thus bringing them under one axiological treatment.

The Pot and the Clay

The example of the pot and the clay, which we shall take next, together with the kindred examples of the thread and the cloth and the ornament and the gold, are used in Vedanta in connection with establishing the importance of *upadana karana* (the material cause) over all the other causes, which are all horizontal in their implication. These latter kinds of causes are incidental, occasional, or less important.

For Vedanta as a whole, what is most important to derive from this example consists in the primacy given to the vertical axis of reference.

Ramanuja and Madhva recognize the necessity to give primacy to the *upadana karana,* which has its reference in the vertical axis, in their analyses of causes and effects. However, they do so without fully recognizing the contradiction between appearance and reality. They try to minimize the contradiction in favour of a vertical unity in diversity, treating these two aspects with more or less internal duality, each in his own way.

A duality between plus and minus inside the vertical axis itself might be resolved by the differing dialectics employed by each of them, Ramanuja stressing the unity between *samanya* (general) and *vishesha* (specific), and Madhva bracketing each life value into subjective and objective groups in an ascending scale, culminating in Vishnu who would thus correspond to the Monad of monads of Leibniz.

We have to concede that there are two kinds of connection, firstly, a necessary and more intimate connection, *samavaya* (continuity), and secondly, mere juxtaposition, mechanistically understood, and called *samyoga sambandha* by Vedantins. The potter using lumps of clay in a vertical series, one after another, can, within some time, cover the floor with many different kinds of pots or pans. When spread out horizontally, they can be referred to as multiple effects of the potter's work. In the process of the manifestation of the universe, the potter would represent the creator and the pots would represent creation. The colour of the potter's stick is only incidentally related to his work; while he himself could change places with his wife or son without altering the total situation of the potter's shop. As against this contingent, secondary or attributive nature which is accidental or incidental to the total situation, the clay has a necessary, inner, intimate, vertical link with its effect. The relationship is more intimate. We cannot think of getting the effect by substituting it by anything other than just that kind of clay that the potter selects and prepares for the success of his art of pottery. It is both existent and unsubstitutable or non-interchangeable. We can easily see here how useful this favourite example is to bring out the distinction between vertical and horizontal cause and effect series, with one or the other of which the whole of the phenomenal or the noumenal world may be said to be filled.

Shankara makes capital out of this distinction insistently and in great detail, as we have seen. He wonders why clay alone can give rise to pot, why gold alone can give rise to gold ornaments, and milk alone can produce curds. A Western philosopher might consider this problem too simple to be worth answering. He would simply turn away, refusing to treat it as a problem of philosophy at all, muttering perhaps to himself "of course the tree is known by its fruits." Although very simple as a problem, the subtle, vertical relationship that exists between causes and effects of this particular order, changes the complexion of philosophizing altogether and tilts it in favour of Vedantic methodology. Vedanta leans largely on this simple vertical axis of reference, and to tamper with it would be to endanger the whole of its multi-storeyed superstructure. Like the mysterious letter "h" used in Max Planck's quantum mechanics, this example refers to the most fundamental key to all varieties of Vedanta, and gives us its chief distinguishing feature in one phrase.

The Mother of Pearl and Silver

Besides these highly favoured examples there is a whole range of others, some more frequently encountered. We cannot enumerate or examine all of them here, but we shall select a few more which have structural implications particularly interesting to us in our present study.

By far the most important is the example of the *shukti-rajatam* (mother of pearl and silver). The calcium carbonate of the shell is the material basis, which represents *sat* or reality, on which there is silver or silveriness established or superimposed. This silver-semblance, according to modern biology, is only an opalescent iridescence due to the polarization of light in the nacreous layer inside the shell. We are treating the example here only as meant by Vedantins, overlooking these scientific aspects.

We can glean the following structural peculiarities from this one example itself:

Appearance is supposed or superimposed on a basic existent reality separable vertically into two poles. The lower half or the minus pole is represented by the material of the shell. The silveriness belongs to the positive pole of the vertical axis whether it is treated as actual illusion, semblance, or half-truth, to be valued or to be considered valueless according to the temperament of the philosopher concerned. If other examples like that of the snake and the rope help us initially to reject outright what is evil and implied in the visible world, admitting full contradiction between good and evil, here these two cling more closely and subtly together, so as to reveal thought-contradictions or different grades of value relationships available to man in his life here.

This example, moreover, happens to be unlike the example above of the rope and the snake, and one that is equally a favourite with Shankara, Ramanuja and Madhva. The reason is that by its very structure and actual constitution this example lends itself admirably to be used to reveal subtle aspects of error and judgement about appearance and reality at one stroke, instead of having to treat them in disintegrated fashion and in separate abstruse paragraphs referring to each of these aspects, as is more usual in verbose philosophical treatises.

Many arguments get clinched together into a compactly conceivable knowledge situation by this one example.

While Ramanuja would say that the silveriness that is seen as an actuality refers to silver present here or somewhere else in the universe on the basis of *esse est percipi*, Shankara would tend to dismiss the silver-semblance as an error of judgement altogether, admitting full contradiction between good and bad, right and wrong, existent and non-existent.

Madhva, who is well known as an *anyatha khyativadin* (one who locates error elsewhere), has his own brand of the theory of error, outside the five classical ones, which is called *abhinava* (new) *anyatha-khyati.*[2]

This is not the place to enter into a full discussion of his theory of error and right judgement. Suffice it for us to state in passing that, unlike Ramanuja, Madhva looks at error as taking place between two ambivalent counterparts in one and the same vertical axis. His duality resembles duality between two monads as understood by Leibniz, where they range vertically from simple monads of the Monad of monads through the best of all possible worlds corresponding to actuality.

Horizontal values and actualities enter more into the vision of life as envisaged by Ramanuja. Madhva prefers to sink deeper into the world of *tattvas* or elemental categories where his scale of values can find full amplitude to swing between the poles of his *svarupananda taratamya* (scale of values in terms of self-bliss), by which the holy *tulsi* (basil) plant and Hari (Vishnu) as the highest Absolute, get linked vertically in living terms for the guidance of the devout seeker of wisdom of the Absolute.

We have said enough for the present to show how this example is precious to Vedanta.

All that we want to underline here is that this example yields us a structural basis for discussing different epistemological aspects by different Vedantins that no other example that we can readily think of affords. Ontology, epistemology and axiology can refer to the same content of right or wrong judgement by virtue of this example. The value of such an example is what has made it such a favourite with Vedantins.

---

2. Dr. B.N.K. Sharma, See *Philosophy of Sri Madhvacharya*, (Bombay, 1962), p. 131.

How the Examples are Used to Discuss Appearance and Reality

While we are on this subject we might profit as well by a short reference to various theories of error and right judgement prevailing in Vedanta which make maximum use of this mother-of-pearl-silver semblance. A Sanskrit verse sums up for us all the theories of locating error:

atmakhyatirasat khyatir
akhyatih khyatiranyatha
tatha anirvachaniya khyatir
ityetai khyati panchakam.

The sense of these words translated freely reads as follows:

> Self as manifested, non-existence as the base of phenomena, non-manifestation, manifestation of something else, and indeterminability of manifestation — such are the five kinds of phenomenal presentiment.

Relating these presentiments with our own example, we find that the first named, which is the position of the Buddhist idealist, locates the source of phenomena in the inner self or in the will as with Schopenhauer. The whole pearl would thus be located inside.

The second position mentioned corresponds to the so-called Buddhist nihilists, who deny the validity of existence altogether. They would refuse to take notice of both silver and mother-of-pearl.

The third position refers to that of Purva Mimamsakas who would tend to treat both appearance and reality on a par of equality, admitting no error. The silveriness would not confuse them.

The fourth position is that of the Nyaya School, which claims that though silver does not exist in the mother-of-pearl it does exist somewhere, for example in a silver mine.

And finally the fifth position is that of a Vedantin proper, like Shankara, who would postulate impredicability of truth either in the mother-of-pearl or in the silver.

To complete this list, we could here add the case of Ramanuja, who would say that the element of silver in some subtle form as present somewhere in the universe is the basis of silveriness. Thus nothing is false for him. As for Madhva, he would tend to put reality in a fluid scale of values arranged in series. Silver could thus change places with something lower of less value, or of higher value.

Other Miscellaneous Examples

The total range of examples in Vedanta, if we could collect them from the Bhagavad Gita, the Brahma Sutras or the Upanishads, even leaving out more recent works like the *Yoga Vasishtha*, could fill pages. We shall select only a few because of their particular structural implications.

A lamp steadily burning in a windless place is mentioned in the Gita as representing the state of a person enjoying the peace of yoga or samadhi. A tortoise that withdraws its limbs within its shell is compared to the verticalized attitude of a yogi in correct meditation, again in the Gita. The Upanishads refer to a large fish swimming within a river, sometimes knocking at one bank and at other times the other bank, to represent an apt example of spiritual progress. A leech that progresses caterpillar-like, letting go its hind hold only after gaining a grip at the forward end, a snake that sheds its skin season after season, or a horse that can shake mud off its skin are other examples bringing out aspects of the progress of the soul from here to hereafter. Detachment while living in the world is compared to a lotus leaf that lives in water without getting wet.

To establish the ambivalent yet unitive relationship between the plus and minus of the vertical axis, we have the example of fire and the sparks that rise from it. The sparks are both non-different vertically and different horizontally from the fire.

The foam, the wave and the bubbles of water in the ocean that pantheists would accept as all real at one and the same time, admitting an element of paradox, are abolished by Shankara by a stricter vertical treatment in which the items like foam are understood to be aspects of water.

The wind that carries ships away from their normal courses is referred to in the Gita to represent the horizontal factor of evil or an anti-spiritual factor prevailing in the world. Phenomenalism is compared to wind in other places also.

The example of the spider and its web is also very advantageously put forward to show that the gross manifested world can have its origin in a god who need not be considered heterogeneously different from it.

We could go in this manner multiplying examples, the most telling of which invariably reveal some subtle structural implications. The reader himself must stop to scrutinize them when he comes up against them in reading Vedantic texts, so as to extract from them the full benefit of their structuralism, discoverable in most cases. When this is done, Vedantic examples come to have a very telling and apodictic character. Examples help to clinch subtle speculative issues by affording an almost tangible basis for them, which, in some cases at least, are as good as experiments as far as certitude, of a degree that can be called even scientific, is concerned.

11

Schematic Protolinguism in Vedanta

Vedantic speculation thrives both on a priori definitions and apt examples taken from the world of a posteriori experience. One lends certitude to the other, and both together yield the required conviction. The use of metaphor or its principle of analogy is vital to Vedanta. We have examined the favourite examples of Vedanta in the previous chapter. It is the structural implications of the examples dear to the Vedantin that have made them inevitable to him through the ages. Similar is the case with some of Vedanta's more striking analogies, in symbolically representative picture-language or cryptic ideograms.

Here, instead of metalinguistics, it is protolinguistics that is so advantageously employed by the rishis who are the authors of the Upanishads.

Allegories, parables and anecdotes abound in metaphorical analogies, very often expressed in schematic protolinguistics or pictorial language to save them from the tribulations of mere verbosity, which is the bane of the metaphysician.

Having done with typical and favourite examples in the last chapter, let us pass on here to some of the favourite schematic picture-devices employed in Vedanta.

In the picture-language of the Upanishads, we touch the most secret aspects of Vedanta. They read like conundrums, and the riddles that they have presented have set a Ramanuja against a Shankara and a Madhva against both, without any one of them being wholly wrong.

We have already explained the implications of such terms as subjectivism, structuralism, schematism and proto-linguistics elsewhere, so that we need not linger here explaining them again. A whole monograph has been written on the linguistic aspects, which must be enough to banish vagueness as far as could be done in respect of this aspect. With deck thus cleared already, let us here go into the scrutiny of the implications of some of the pictorial enigmas found in Upanishadic literature.

The Many, Two or One of Vedanta

The polemical storm centre or trouble spot in Vedanta is round the question of one reality, two realities, or many realities in one. Under the chapter of "Varieties of Vedantism" we have examined some aspects of this question already. The three great teachers of Vedanta have all accepted the Upanishads, the Bhagavad Gita and the Brahma Sutras as their canonical sourcebooks, and agree also in the great dicta or *maha vakyas*, which state succinctly the finalized doctrine (*siddhanta*) of the Vedanta.

The sources and conclusions being thus firmly secured, it is not hard to agree that it is because of differing methodological, epistemological or axiological accentuation that these teachers differ between themselves. But the fact that the body of the Upanishads, which is the greatest of the sources for Vedanta, and perhaps the most final and also the most authoritative for any Vedantin, is the alpha, and the great dicta which sum up its conclusions is the omega of the total situation comprised by Vedanta as a whole, together makes the differences in between these two poles as necessarily of only secondary importance.

If the tree and the fruit are the same, the histological peculiarities between tree and tree need not be given an importance disproportionate to the total purpose that Vedanta is meant to serve.

To take another example, if a son sees a photograph of his father, and recognizes him as such, the main purpose of the photograph may be said to have been served, although in choosing one copy out of many prints of the photo he might prefer a lighter or a darker one, or choose between one in which recognition for him might be easy or difficult due only to unimportant secondary considerations. Even the Gita accommodates multiplicity, duality, or dichotomy within its universal unitive vision in Verse IX,15.

The Two Birds on the Same Tree

We read in the Svetasvatara Upanishad (IV.6):

> Two birds, fast-bound companions,
> Clasp close the self-same tree,
> Of these two, the one eats sweet fruit;
> The other looks on without eating.

Here we have one of those enigmas of the Upanishads. Some derive from this picture-language support for two distinct truths or realities, while there are others, like the followers of Dayananda Sarasvati, for whom this gives justification for three realities, two represented by the birds and the third by the tree. The possibilities of such differing theories are due neither to the inadequacy of the picture language employed nor to the inability of interpreters to grasp the secret or subtle implications of such a conundrum-like picture-language.

We tend to believe here that it is not the fault of the Upanishadic seers. The structurally understood protolinguism which they employed to great advantage has become a closed book to moderns who are good at mechanistic logic only and ignore the subtler world given to intuitive understanding. Just as non-Euclidean geometry is only just beginning to be recognized, so the structural, schematic and epistemologically subjective aspects of the language of ancient seers remain mostly closed to the modern mind.

The following principles, however, can be derived from the scheme presented here in pictorial form:

1. The two birds belong to the same epistemological order and have a parity between them.

2. They represent the ambivalence between the visibles and the intelligibles into which all reality can be divided as in the world of the two dictionaries spoken of elsewhere by us.

3. To differentiate these two as the higher, without qualities (*nirguna*), and the lower, with qualities (*saguna*), or even as the supreme and individual selves, are all partially true statements. They gain complete or consistent, unitive or total meaning, as belonging homogeneously together, only when schematically understood after the elimination of certain of the gross implications.

4. The bird that eats corresponds to factual or perceptual verity, while the bird that merely looks on belongs to the world of the concept or the logos. We have attempted to discuss this elsewhere under the section, "The Double Domain of the Word."

5. The notion of the Absolute understood neutrally and centrally, canceling out all ambivalent aspects, is the common ground on which, at differing focuses, as it were, the two aspects participate or are inserted into each other, and thus articulate as mind and matter do. The eating bird could be called the negative, and the bird that looks on could be placed in the plus side of the vertical vectorial space. There is a one-to-one similitude between them, not merely as between a thing and its mirror reflection, but also in a subtler form of reciprocity, as seen between the right and the left hands. There is reference in both cases to a neutral point of origin and a bilateral correspondence.

6. The feathered tribe of colourful plumage is to suggest that the homogeneity is to be understood in a manner admitting of the most concrete universalities known to the perceptual as well as to the conceptual orders at once.

The Unborn Female with Two Different Males

In the same context of the same Upanishad there are further indications given to justify the implied schematism which we tried to elaborate by extracting the principles enumerated above. The immediately previous verse (IV, 5) reads:

> With the one unborn female, red, white and black,
> Who produces many creatures like herself,
> There lies the one unborn male taking his delight.
> Another unborn male leaves her with whom he has had his delight.

Here again, hasty interpretations are possible, as when it is said that the second unborn male is the individual experiencer (as suggested in a note by Hume on p. 403 in his translation). The first unborn male would then be the supreme father or God. Read together with Verse 7 which follows after the bird picture quoted above, we can easily see that, although such explanations are all possible, it is the common structure underlying all these three different versions that the Upanishadic seer wants us to grasp at one view, with all its generalized and abstract schematic implications. As we say, the difference is like that between analytical and vectorial geometries. The latter is more schematic than the former. Here too, we can extract the following principles from the above:

1. The two unborn males represent the vertical plus and minus aspects of the Absolute, as the source of manifestation, as material as well as efficient causes. The one taking delight is the efficient while the other is the positive material cause.

2. The female is the principle of maya or becoming as representing the verticalized phenomenal aspect in the heart of the Absolute. The three colours are white (plus-vertical), black (minus-horizontal), and red, being the colour of passion, is in the middle region between these poles. Passion expresses itself as a horizontal factor of action or centripetal

differentiation.[1] The many creatures are the monadic units of the same, as we see in nature that is manifested, between the plus and the minus and in a central band of passion.

Again, if we scrutinize Verse 7, it will help us to abstract the scheme better from the particularized and more concretized details of the scheme that must have been in the mind of the author. It reads:

> On the self-same tree a person, sunken,
> Grieves for his impotence, deluded;
> When he sees the other, the Lord (*Isha*) contented,
> And his greatness, he becomes freed from sorrow.

The intention of this last verse on the self-same tree as that of the two birds of the immediately preceding verse is quite evident. The male who is still taking his delight is in the red region, while there is to be understood an even more negative zone of the vertical axis, represented here by the person sunken and in impotence. This is the negative level of *tamas* (or black darkness) which can be banished by the plus side. It is neither the plus nor the minus that finally counts, but the one that transcends all three stages in a fully unitive notion of the Absolute.

The self-same tree persists in and through the graphic imagery of the three verses. It represents, structurally and schematically speaking, the vertical axis with *Isha* or the Lord as the positive factor that can save one from the slough of despondence into which man is ordinarily sunk deep.

The Two Persons of the Chandogya, Maitri and Katha Upanishads

There are other striking references to dual persons fitted into a similar ambivalent scheme. One of these, found in the Chandogya Upanishad, is more picturesque than the others. All are algebraic and geometric in implication at one and the

---

1. White, red and black are a pictorial image of the three gunas of manifestation, sattva, rajas and tamas respectively.

same time. Let us examine them side by side to reveal the underlying common scheme. The Chandogya passage (I.VI.6) reads:

> Now *sa* is the white shining of the Sun; *ama* is the dark, the ultra-black. That makes *sama.*
>
> Now that golden Person who is within the Sun has a golden beard and golden hair. He is exceedingly brilliant, all, even to the fingernail tips.

The structural ambivalence between the two sides or aspects of the Absolute Person becomes clearer when read side by side with a similar passage in the Maitri Upanishad (VI.1) which terminates strikingly with the following:

> Now that golden Person who is within the sun, who looks down upon this earth from his golden place, is even He who dwells within the lotus of the heart and eats food.

When gold is referred to, we have to take it that it is some value factor which is under reference. Such value fills the notion of the Absolute not only in abstract terms but also in concrete universal terms too, as the reference to the fingertip above would suggest.

Another similar picture from the Katha Upanishad (III.1) avoids reference to gold, but puts the value factor more conceptually though schematically as follows:

> There are two that drink of righteousness (*rita*) in the world of good deeds.
>
> Both are entered into the secret place [of the heart] and in the highest upper sphere.
>
> Brahma-knowers speak of them as 'light' and 'shade,'
>
> And so do householders who maintain the five sacrificial fires, and those too who perform the triple Nachiketas-fire.[2]

The light and shade refer to the polarity in the structure of the Absolute where the soul lives enjoying the two-sided

2. All Upanishad quotations are from Hume.

fruit of good or bad deeds. The structuralism is not confined to the full knowers of the Absolute of the Vedanta, but also to lesser men of wisdom such as those who adhere to Vedic values, not yet fully absolutist in status. This is clearly alluded to in the last part of the quotation.

What should interest us here is the fact that there are two involved in both the high place beyond and the secret place of the here and now. The two-sided structure characterizes both the enjoyer as well as the worlds of light or shade, enjoyed where they belong together.

The world of good deeds is one of axiological import. All knowledge or truth must have some significance in the world of values, otherwise it becomes tasteless or insipid. In the one world of values, two persons drink of the joy of the ultimate bliss of Wisdom. All good deeds have this one and the same goal culminating in the Absolute, where duality becomes extinguished finally. The rest of the structural or schematic implications here must be sufficiently clear to one who has followed what we have had to say about such aspects of absolutism in this or the previous chapters.

The Structure of the Absolute in Full Axiological Terms

Structuralism is plainly revealed in full axiological terms in the Taittiriya Upanishad. The references to a colour scheme and to the anthropomorphic aspect of the Absolute are here fully shed, and one gets as nearly a neutrally focused notion of the Absolute as possible in the humanly significant world of values here. The neutral Absolute cannot be without meaningful content. If it had none such, it would not find a place in any dictionary. On the other hand, all languages have some word or other standing for the notion of the Absolute. Even the most so-called primitive peoples have some notion represented by a word in their spoken or written language. *Homo sapiens* has always had a vocabulary which found room for some such word.

As Prof. Max Müller has stated. "There is hardly a tribe, however uncivilised and barbarous, which has not a name for soul, that is, for something different from the body yet closely allied to it and hard at work within it. It was but lately that I received from the Bishop of North Caledonia a new metaphor for soul. The Zhimpshian Indians have a word which means both soul and fragrance." Müller treats this metaphor as being as good as that which Plato uses in his *Phaedo* of the lyre and its music, which together form the two inseparable aspects of the Absolute.[3]

It is not hard to recognize the vertical and horizontal aspects of the same structure that underlies all significant or meaningful human notions of the Absolute. The fragrance is the vertical component and the soul may be considered as its existent horizontal basis. In the metaphor of the lyre, the instrument is horizontal and its music vertical.

Since all notions of the Absolute must have a significant content, when all is said and done, it is in axiological terms that we can give it any meaningful content at all in the human context, to which all notions, however final, must necessarily belong. The following extract from the Taittiriya Upanishad (II,5) is a masterpiece conceived along these lines:

> Verily, other than and within that one that consists of understanding is a self that consists of bliss (*ananda-maya*). By that this is filled. That one, verily, has the form of a person. According to that one's personal form is this one with the form of a person. Pleasure (*priya*) is its head; delight (*moda*), the right side; great delight (*pra-moda*), the left side; bliss (*ananda*), the body (*atman*); Brahma, the lower part, the foundation.

In order to avoid confusion from too closely scrutinizing the text for too plain a meaning, one has to remember that in Vedanta the personal *atman*, the impersonal *brahman*, and

---

3. F. Max Müller, See *The Vedanta Philosophy*, (Susil Gupta, Calcutta, 1950), p. 3,4.

bliss as a high value, are all to be looked upon as interchangeable in the context of the Absolute. The existent, the subsistent and the value aspects are treated together in Vedanta, and cosmology, psychology and theology mix beautifully and inseparably into a confection.

Then again, we have to take note of the two-sidedness of the structure, one side that is strictly anthropomorphic and the other that is only structurally so. The one with the form of a person and its converse referred to above as "that one's personal form" to which another accords, are dialectical counterparts that can be interchanged. The foundation and the superstructure have a common pattern which is neither personal nor impersonal. They both merely share in a certain schematism which conforms to that of a person with a head, right and left sides, and a ventral or bottom side. Dorsal, lateral and ventral aspects thus complete the vertico-horizontal structuralism implied here. Which gives certitude to the other is a question that should not arise here when well understood.

The morphology of the axiological notion of the Absolute cancelled out into a neutral status, as between its own plus and minus aspects, cannot be carried any further by speculative language than what is attained in this simple Upanishadic paragraph. Whether pure *morphism* presupposes *anthropos* or other the way about, is not to be decided in the neutral light of the Absolute which is pure consciousness, neither subjective nor objective. Such is the culminating point of Vedantic speculation enshrined in all the grand conclusions of Vedanta called the *maha vakyas*.

Other Examples of Structuralism in Vedantic Literature

Besides the above instances of interesting picture-language in the Upanishads, Vedantic literature generally respects, or tacitly and sometimes even openly supports, structuralism, as found in the Bhagavad Gita and the commentaries of Shankara, as also in the post-Shankara scholastically revised and restated forms of Vedanta such as found in the *Yoga Vasishtha*, the *Panchadashi* and the *Vichara Sagara*.

The authors of these later Vedantic works are mostly anonymous, and even when known by name, factual details as are available are very poor about their life and affiliations. Structuralism, however, has persisted in characterizing pure Vedanta to this day and it would be interesting for us to follow out to its limits this protolinguistic tendency, which originated in the *Panchagni Vidya* of the Vedas.

Narayana Guru himself, as we shall see, is no exception, and goes as far as trying to provide a revised and restated scientifically valid status to this tendency, in the interests of presenting an integrated picture of the total field of wisdom under one structural scheme. Scrutinized in this light, his writings make valuable contributions of his own to this kind of language, which, in an extended sense, could be adopted as the basis for a unified language of science in general, as we have suggested elsewhere more elaborately.

Shankara in *Brahma Sutra Bhashya* under I.i.17, reveals his own schematism when he refers to "the real juggler who stands on the ground differs from the illusive juggler who holding in his hand a shield and sword, climbs up to the sky by means of a rope."[4]

The Inverted Double Tree of the Gita

The most patent evidence of structuralism in the Absolute is found in the well-known Bhagavad Gita itself, in the beginning of Chapter XV. The implications of the picture-language employed and elaborated in the first four verses occupy an important position, rhetorically understood. This picture-language is abandoned at the end of the same chapter, and repeated in more metalinguistic terms as

4. Sacred Books of the East, Thibaut's translation, (Oxford, 1890), p. 70.

referring to the perishable and imperishable aspects of *a pair of Persons,* instead of in terms of the double-sided ramifications of a tree, such as that of the Tree of Porphyry.

A protolinguistic structure is implied in the ramified double tree, and a theologically understood version of the same stated in more metalinguistic terms, is to be seen in Verses 16 to 19 inclusive. We need not go into the details of the implications here, as this has been covered in the commentary on the verses referred to in our full work on the Gita.[5] Here we are more concerned with seeing the schematic and structural implications, so as to derive out of the verses confirmation of our view that they are meant to be understood in the light of the mathematically and scientifically valid structuralism whose case we have tried to present in these studies, having even anteriorly prepared the ground, stage by stage, for its justification in all our writings. The outmoded language of parables has to give place to a fully valid scientific language for contemplative mysticism, if it is to be raised to the status of a science that Vedanta can claim to be when properly understood in the light of modern thought.

Gita Schematism Scrutinized

A close scrutiny of the two sets of verses in the Gita, namely XV,1-4 and XV,16-19, will reveal to us the emphasis on a vertical principle which abolishes horizontal factors or values in life that tend to be dual and multiple. There is a "one and the many" dialectics between them. Correlated properly in Cartesian and vectorial terms, as with space and number, the imagery of the tree turned upside down and implying hedonistic Vedic values, which are to be effaced in favour of the neutral and full-fledged Absolute given to a detached mind, gives us a supreme instance of the use of schematic language in correct speculation.

The cancellation of the two persons of equal status into the supreme person, implying and transcending both of them,

5. *The Bhagavad Gita,* commentary by the author.

as stated in Verse 18 as explicitly as could be, is a supreme instance of using picture language for passing beyond the paradox implicit in the duality of the two persons. This means the Absolute and the Relative Absolute cancel each other out into the pure Neutral Absolute, which implies both without contradiction.

Such is the secret of Advaita, which the two-sided structuralism finally culminates in, marking the final point of Vedantic speculation. The epistemological status of such a neutralized Absolute has been explained by us at length elsewhere, in *Dialectical Methodology* and also in Chapter 6 of the present study entitled "Two Certitudes for the Same Truth." What are often referred to as the lower and the higher Absolutes, the Absolute with qualities (*saguna*) and the Absolute without qualities (*nirguna*), have both to be abolished in favour of one neutral or central Absolute which is neither the higher nor the lower, but of a unique status by itself, and unrelated to anything outside it, as the meaning of the term Absolute must necessarily imply.

It is exactly here that much Vedantic scholasticism of latter days has vitiated Vedantic literature down to the present. Shankara himself, although he cannot be suspected of ignorance of this final position, still left enough room in his writings for his followers to think that one or the other of the two possible versions of the Absolute was better. The juggler's example above, though schematically conceived, leaves the juggler's real status vague. This has been the fecund cause of vain polemical duels between Shankara's followers and rival schools such as those of Ramanuja, Madhva, Vallabha and others. The *Syad-vadins* who believed in the maybe/maybe-not ambiguity, and the pantheistically inclined *Bhedabheda vadins* (Difference-nondifference believers) such as *Bhartrprapancha,* the nihilists of Buddhism who emptied the Absolute of all value-content, and the *Vijnana-vadins* who tended to stress idealism at the expense of realism, all had to be discredited or inclusively understood by a finalized doctrine of Advaita Vedanta which Shankara tried to establish above all others. His attempt can only be said to have nearly succeeded because of the either-or alternative that he still seemed to lend support to when he should have more dialectically stood for "both at once" (*ubhayam saha*). This methodological distinction is well explained in the Isha Upanishad, Verses 9 to 14.

Appearance of Uma in the Kena Upanishad

In the allegory of the Vedic gods who gazed at a certain space in which there was implied the principle of the Absolute (*brahman*), in their ignorance they at first took it to be a kind of wonderful being, a *yaksha*, a sort of mysterious spirit, unknown in their context of relative values. Each of the nature gods pitched his powers at this mysterious factor, but all were confounded and defeated by its superiority. Finally, all of them appealed to Indra, their chief, in the following words:

> "Maghavan (Liberal), find out this — what this wonderful being is."
>
> "So be it."
>
> He ran unto It. It disappeared from him.
>
> *In that very space* he came upon a woman exceedingly beautiful, Uma, daughter of the Snowy Mountain (*Himavat*).
>
> To her he said: "What is this wonderful being?"
>
> "It is Brahman," she said. "In that victory of Brahman, verily, exult ye."
>
> — (Kena Up. Verses, 24-26)[6]

The allegory terminates by saying that Indra, by this, got to know the Absolute, and next to him were *Agni* (fire), *Vayu* (wind) etc., who were raised above all other gods.

6. Hume, pp. 338-339.

These details do not interest us here so much as how the *space* that was filled with nothing more than a mystery or wonder, became filled with the beauty of a feminine form. Efforts have been made to relate Uma to the Shiva context, independent of the Vedic gods. As a feminine principle she is nearer to the visible notion of the Absolute, though more negatively than positively, as the source of the manifested world which by its negation hides the full truth about the Absolute. The gods who were on the plus side of light, like Agni, could not represent or know the Absolute in its full neutral implication. We have italicized the phrase "in that very space" in the quotation to show that it is the self-same space that can yield a neutral Absolute as well as a personified value of the same absolute status, as Uma is meant to represent.

If we understand this subtle schematism in the notion of the Absolute properly, as it ought to be, as when we understand the difference between vectorial and Euclidean space in modern mathematics, it will not be difficult for us to see the reason for accepting Vishnu as Ramanuja did, as the supreme God on the plus side, even above Indra, in more intelligible, though not in visible, terms. Vishnu is the *knowable* aspect, while Uma would be rather the *known,* or given to experience, and thus a posteriori in status.

Different versions of the Absolute can thus be understood and treated unitively together as one would recognize one's father's photograph in light or dark prints, or as implied in an indistinguishable one which would at best be a puzzle, a wonder or a mystery. Such a neutral Absolute alone, however, would enjoy a fully normative and scientific status, balanced as it is between the plus and minus sides of the total knowledge situation.

The phrase we have italicized above, "in that very space," has been so done expressly to enable us here, at this concluding stage of our discussion of the schematic language of the Vedic context, to insert an important indication about it which would give us the key to the use of protolinguism in connection with the *lingua mystica* anywhere in the world.

The Doubting Thomas of the Bible had to see before he believed. In the very end of the Gita (XVIII.75), there is reference to Sanjaya, a figure of the epic context, actually seeing with his own eyes the dialogue taking place between Krishna and Arjuna. The *Yoga Vasishtha* too speaks of a king who, under a magician's spell, imagined he was born in a low class family and died in a certain known geographical region near the Vindhya Mountains. After the trance was over, he sent his messengers to see if any such place actually existed, and found his doubts confirmed by a woman weeping in a real place answering correctly to the place envisioned in the trance.

Further, if we read the Gita VIII.18,19, we can see that this schematic approach is fully recognized by its author, where he speaks of pure space alternately filled by its own vertical or horizontal contents of night or day. Schematism is thus fully understood in Vedantic literature, and in clarifying the notion of the Absolute, it is most advantageously employed by Vedantins.

12

A Summarized Running Review

1.0 Vedanta claims to treat of the Truth of truths, the Light of lights or the Science of sciences, because it concerns itself with ultimate problems of knowledge or wisdom in the light of the Absolute. To avoid suffering in life and secure happiness that is everlasting, free from bonds of birth and the cyclic course of being and becoming, is its overall aim.

1.1 Although the name Vedanta suggests the origin of this body of speculation as belonging to the context of Vedism and its later modifications, it is an attempt to steer clear of all hedonistic and relativistic values in the name of a full-fledged Absolutist outlook. It is, in fact, the resultant of the interaction of two opposing tendencies in Indian thought represented by the Purva Mimamsa (the anterior critique) and the Uttara Mimamsa (the posterior critique), the dialectical revaluation of the two reaching in Vedanta proper its fully revalued status as the basis of a Science of the Absolute.

1.2 While the four Vedas and the six Shastras (schools of philosophical discipline) have generally been associated with Vedanta as its background, and have contributed to it elements of methodological and epistemological import which inevitably became incorporated into Vedanta, the three fully recognized sources of Vedanta are the *prasthana trayi* (the three basic sources), namely, the large body of Upanishads, the Brahma Sutras (aphorisms which try to systematize and sum up Vedantic doctrine in well-reasoned or argued terms), and the Bhagavad Gita, which presents the case of Vedanta finally in the form of a Science of the Absolute with all its dialectical implications covering existential, subsistential and axiological aspects, with a methodology, epistemology and value factor kept correctly in mind, and not omitting the requirements of theology, with a cosmology and a phenomenologically revised psychology, if we may call it so.

1.3 An eschatology proper to Vedanta is found indicated here and there in the Upanishads. The philosophical attitude of neutral monism is normal to the Vedantin. An empiricism that is ontological in its presuppositions and a full transcendentalism in which what is called idealism in the West becomes acceptable, are both comprised within the scope of Vedantism. The immanent and transcendent values, truths, or facts of life, are all inclusively and unitively comprised within the epistemology proper to Vedanta.

1.4 Mere ritualisms and works give place to non-obligatory wisdom as Vedanta gains its final status.

2.0 The correct Vedantist is neither a sceptic nor a believer, but takes a neutral position between the two, in the name of the Absolute, which can sometimes have a theological, a rational, or a purely subjective bias when stated by different Vedantic teachers. Brahma, the cosmological God of the Hindu pantheon, Vishnu, the hypostatic version of the Absolute, and Shiva who represents the idea of the Absolute with all its force of change or becoming, all fit into a total scheme without contradiction in the overall global scheme that Vedanta envisages.

2.1 Other gods such as Apollo or Dionysus can also be similarly fitted into the scheme, and the Bhagavad Gita (II, 23) states that all mankind, anywhere, does already tread the path of Krishna the Absolute, as correctly and scientifically meant to be understood.

2.2 Vedanta thus does not close its door against any religion but views all possible standpoints inclusively and unitively in an integrated fashion under the aegis of the high notion of the Absolute.

2.3 Vedanta is not meant to be a surrogate of any religion, but on the other hand could advantageously be utilized for the correction of lopsided accentuations or one-sided exaggerations that might creep into any religion owing to strains or stresses of history or necessity.

3.0 Religious orthodoxies, heterodoxies, taboos, obligations, profanity, sin, holiness or the sense of the holy or the sacred belonging to hierophantic or hypostatic contexts are all thus outside the scope of Vedanta proper. The Bhagavad Gita (V,18) indicates this unequivocally.

3.1 An open, dynamic, fully catholic attitude in the true sense of the word, free from the conditionings to which the psyche is subject, is what Vedanta inculcates.

3.2 As all beings are to be looked upon as equal in value to the Self in Vedanta, it can safely be said to be based on universal brotherhood, extending to life in general as far as practicable.

4.0 God, as the All-Maker and material source of the universe, gives rise to two sets of notions about the Most High; one of which is philosophically equivalent to the Absolute, and the other which is more theological in status as the efficient cause of the universe.

4.1 Efficient and material causes operate together in manifesting the phenomenal world, to give it multiplicity of form and name.

4.2 The Absolute of Vedanta is thus finally referred to as the unsublated and unattained efficient-cum-material cause of phenomenal name-form couplets.

4.3 A theological, cosmological and psychologically phenomenological God equated to the Absolute as the Most High is the Adorable Value of Vedanta, whether visualized in anthropomorphic terms of a personal deity, or thought of as the end or goal of all speculation or teachings of all scriptures taken together.

5.0 Vedantic cosmology, eschatology and ethics have a higher and lower limit, when meant for the most intelligent, for the middling, or for the inferior aspirant in spirituality, irrespective of his particular religious group in society. These present necessarily, therefore, many and varied pictures of the progress of the soul, its origin and destiny through good or bad acts. Scriptures like the Puranas and Tihasas, as meant for the unintelligent, give graphic pictures of creation-genesis, presenting sacred or ritual based life-values of obligatory, sin-merit, or holy-profane contexts of endless variety.

5.1 Pure Vedanta accepts no creation and adheres to the mental origin of the universe in the collective mind. When darkness or ignorance is banished, all birth, life here, gods and men, merge in the unified light of the Absolute. In this sense all evolution is only applicable to material substances, while the world has only a phenomenological reality as eidetic appearances.

5.2 Heavenly life and relativistic versions of life hereafter are all discredited in thoroughgoing Vedanta, although vestiges of such persist in lower Vedantic texts, always, however, in a mystical-cum-mythical language capable of suggesting some of the highest secrets of Vedanta proper.

5.3 The much talked-of theory of reincarnation and karma states the law of inner and outer agreements of rewards and punishments for the soul or self, understood in its progress in life between the limits of the here to that of the hereafter.

5.4 The *Yoga Vashishtha* presents perhaps the purest Vedantic version compatible with the theory developed in the Bhagavad Gita (XV, 8ff), whose further elaborations in more or less mythological form are found in the eighteen Puranas that are commonly spoken of. "As thou sowest, so shalt thou reap" would roughly correspond to this law or theory in the context of the Bible. Rebirth could be abolished in favour of the life everlasting in God, or when merged in the Absolute, which state is the final union, called *sayujya*.

5.5 Shankara, Ramanuja and Madhva can be viewed as representing grades of realism in ideas of morality, devotion or salvation; the first admitting full contradiction between good and evil, to be transcended later, and the others transcending duality in terms of a graded scale of values from the humblest to the most elevated, making due allowances for differences of types.

5.6 There is an integrated unitive or globally conceived methodology, epistemology and axiology for the Vedanta. Each one presupposes the others, and all together presuppose the neutral normative notion of the Absolute. Ontology and epistemology are not separable in Vedanta, and the distinction or duality of the immanent and the transcendental merges in an integrated unitive treatment in Vedantic speculation. This is the reason why moderns tend to think of Vedanta as religious or mystical rather than scientific.

5.7 The Self is the central unifying factor in all speculative analysis or synthesis, oscillating alternately between the a priori and the a posteriori poles of the total knowledge situation. The Self could alternatingly refer to the enjoyer (*bhokta*) or subjective aspect within, and the enjoyed (*bhogya*) or the objective aspect without, both reducible to unity in homogeneous terms (*samanadhikarana*).

5.8 A four-limbed structure of the Self (*atman*) is clearly envisaged in the Mandukya Upanishad, and it has been elaborated at length by Gaudapada, the forerunner of Shankara in Vedantic speculation. The gross, the subtle, the ontologically causal or immanent, and the fully transcendental aspects of the Absolute Self, diagnosed with reference to waking, dreaming, deep sleep and fully *contemplatively* awakened states of consciousness are studied analytically and synthetically at once, with their cosmological, psychological and theological implications, in this Upanishad.

5.9 This lays the foundation of a structural subjective selectivism of factors within the notion of the Neutral Absolute in Vedantic speculation. We could refer this structure to the correlates of Cartesian structuralism as now extended into the domain of vectorial analysis with useful results.

6.0 The Absolute has to have a living content, without which it is nothing more than a word without meaning in life. The content is the resultant of the meeting, from two opposing sides, as it were, of physical and metaphysical factors, both reducible in terms of *intuition* into a common homogeneity. When so reduced into unitive terms there will be a mutual transparency and participation between matter and mind in a neutral matrix with a constant osmotic interchange, like respiration mentioned in many of the Upanishads.

6.1 Action and inaction meet in such an alternating osmotic interchange that is both inter-subjective and trans-physical. This grand osmosis, which includes the macro- and microcosms at once within consciousness, collective or individual, yields peace and joy without limit. Such are some of the high claims of Vedanta.

7.0 There are three zones, bands or stratifications that we have to distinguish in the immanent-transcendent vertical axis, made up of the material causes and their effects in the process of absolute flux or becoming. The Bergsonian *elan vital* fits correctly into this context as representing one of the purest aspects of maya or phenomenal becoming understood in the subtlest context of Vedantic speculation. In philosophical significance this maya or becoming as a process within the Absolute is next in richness only to the finalized notion of the normative Absolute. Maya thrives on names and forms, and causes and effects blend within its flux. This grand idea of flux is one of the major contributions of Vedantic speculation at least as understood in the context of Shankara's Vedantism.

7.1 The existent or the ontological, the subsistent or the rational, and the axiological where value factors enter into the scheme, are the three vertical stratifications at the core of the notion of the Absolute, which is an empty notion otherwise. These are distinguished as the *sat*, *chit* and *ananda* zones, and these are referable to the corresponding *asti, bhati* and *priya* (existing, bright and beloved respectively), within whose scope all reality or value must be comprised, whatsoever they may be. Something has to exist, has to loom in consciousness, or be significant for any philosophy worth the name to take account of it at all.

7.2 Corresponding to these three stratifications within the notion of the Absolute, we have to fit three types of reasoning: the first resembling scientific reasoning, giving primacy to observation and to visible experimental demonstrations, coming under *pratyaksha* (given to the senses); the second stratum referring to the rational and logical domain of calculations (*pramana shastra*) with inference (*anumana*) taking the central place, with inductive and hypothetical reasoning (called *arthapatti*) coming in between. The final or the third stage or step of reasoning is intuitive or dialectical, which equates value concepts, indicating nominalistic factors of value significance according to axiological laws or general ideas given a priori. From experiment to dialectical intuition there are three main steps in the use of reasoning of which the last attains to full absolutist status. Syllogistic reasoning is only of an inferior kind compared to this final ascent or descent through dialectics, which can attain the Absolute.

7.3 Methodologically, within such a three-zone stratification of the process of reasoning, Vedanta, or at least the methodology of Shankara's system, adopts a *via negationis* of reasoning from the given empirical fact to the most implicit of virtualities within the Self, discarding or canceling out the more peripheral and positive in favour of a more internal and negative. It begins horizontally at the first instance, and then proceeds through the vertical negative entities of apperceptive intuition, such as the sapidity of water, to the positive values that are ranged as knowables in the vertical scale above the elementals, through the general conceptuals of ego (*ahamkara*), relational factor (*chittam*) to intelligence (*buddhi*) and finally to the mind, which is the most peripherally oriented factor that gets related to interests of ordinary passive life. Thus passing through sense to percepts, and then jumping to the bottom of the conceptual factors to rise to pure nominals, is the process of progressive Vedantic reasoning, by which is attained the pure ever-present witness in the Self as representing the bliss of Absolute Freedom.

7.4 Shankara's commentary on the first four sutras of the Brahma Sutras concludes with tracing how all proofs arrived at through valid reasoning get identified with the self-evident Self, which comes to view as an ever-present reality for the Vedantic contemplative, without the aid of rituals or works, and without the aid of reasonings of the usual type.

7.5 Vedanta does not discard the use of *pratyaksha* (what is given to the senses) of the empirical reality in favour of a reality based on the validity of the Upanishads or the Vedas or the texts of the first order on which Vedanta finally relies to arrive at the Absolute Fact, Truth or Value, but adopts a revised ontology by which knowledge gained through the senses is given a homogeneously revised epistemological status equal to that of the validity of the scriptures.

7.6 The Vedantic scheme or frame of reference relies on the support of the visible as well as the intelligible, the a priori and the a posteriori, as belonging to a total knowledge situation schematically understood.

7.7 Vedanta is meant to be a philosophy with a way of life not necessarily leading to any religious group with closed attitudes or cults. It is meant to be open and dynamic. Tribalistic or other closed orthodoxies, and even heterodox denominations as such, have no place in a Vedantically awakened life. Castes, classes and creeds have no place in the Vedantic scheme.

7.8 Vedanta, first and foremost, is interested in finding a reply to such questions as "Who am I?" and "How does the world come to be?" These are answered squarely by the great dicta of Vedanta (the *mahavakyas*) which state "You are That," "I am the Absolute," "Wisdom is the Absolute," "The Self is the Absolute," etc.

7.9 The one central problem for all Vedanta is to equate the visible and the intelligible realities under the aegis of the Absolute, which is normative, central or neutral, inclusive of all possible dualistic philosophical aspects, such as mind and matter, etc. The central idea of the Absolute of Vedanta has to participate on equally transparent ground with both the two limbs implied in the various great dicta.

8.0 The axiological absolute can be viewed impersonally or as a theological entity. The usual attributes of God, such as omnipresence, omniscience and omnipotence would go with such a concept of the Adorable Absolute, whether spoken of as Mother, Father or the Most High. God is referred to as generous and beneficient too, with glory or greatness attached to Him. When such a God is transferred philosophically as residing within one, He is the inner controller (*antaryamin*) or the witness (*sakshin*). More ontologically, the Absolute is the Rock-Established One (the *kutastha*). The Cave-Dweller of the Heart-Space and the *sutratma* are other notions equally capable of being accommodated within the scheme of the Vedantic notion of the Absolute. The Golden Germ (*hiranyagarbha*) and the Progenitor of People (*prajapati*) are also to be understood in the same context.

8.1 One could approach the Absolute and merge with it finally so as to attain salvation or freedom in various ways, all of which come under two heads: the way of wisdom and the way of works or action. Although the distinction between them is initially understood to be one of contradiction between the two, by treating both through the dialectical method proper to yoga, they each become understandable in terms of the other. Both finally merge in the unity of the Absolute. The various possibilities in this respect are elaborated most masterfully in the eighteen chapters of the Bhagavad Gita.

8.2 The dialectical treatment of wisdom and works, so that one or other or both yield salvation or freedom, is the secretmost doctrine of the Bhagavad Gita (IV, 18). In the light of this principle of reducing opposites into unitive terms dialectically, there are other important derived doctrines of Vedanta stated in the Gita referring to a way of life, of which that of action dedicated to the wisdom of the Absolute (*nishkama-karma*) and that of not swerving from the path of life that is fully compatible with one's own past and the future (*svadharma*), which is correctly open to each person, and that of keeping the spirit ever positively oriented to the Absolute, equalizing opposites at each stage within pure consciousness, fully verticalized in yogic contemplation, of which the key word is equanimity (*samya*), are some of the important corollaries derivable for understanding the Vedantic way of life, dedicated to the Absolute.

8.3 Vedantic speculation depends very much on the validity of the Word or the Logos, which touches reality where percepts and concepts meet in pure nominalistic terms. Semantic analysis is fundamental to both the schools of the anterior and posterior critiques (*mimamsa*s). Semiotic processes that imply a polyvalence in structure reveal a scheme shared by both the visible and the intelligible aspects of the Word, as together representing the Absolute.

8.4 The Logos and the Nous meet centrally in the double-sided domain of the Word, as we have more elaborately examined elsewhere. The Word and its meaning contain all thought processes, revealing the content of the Absolute. To know the Word with all its implications in pure form is to know the ultimate content of the notion of the Absolute.

8.5 The conceptual aspect of the Word represents the plus side of the vertical axis in the structure common to the plus and the minus aspects.

8.6 As long as we have to depend on language to express what we wish to say about the nature of the Absolute, this common structure as between the subject and the object, participating ambivalently either way, as in the syllable *AUM* that the Mandukya Upanishad glorifies, could be conveniently kept in mind as a two-sided reference for regulating Vedantic verbose speculations, which are likely otherwise to go haywire.

8.7 Just as algebra gives precision to vectorial geometry and vice versa, there is a double-sided structuralism that can save Vedantic speculation from becoming too thin and airy. The Vedantic examples and analogies show that the ancients at least were fully aware to the possibilities of such a protolinguistic schematism.

8.8 Much scholastic hairsplitting has crept into Vedanta of the present day by which it becomes a question of great importance, for example, to decide whether there is salvation for humanity as a whole at one stroke, or if people enter heaven in a file.

8.9 Salvation in Vedanta, of whichever school, is to be understood in the terms of *svarupananda*, final bliss or liberation in the realization of oneself. The minor scholastic questions such as the one instanced above, fade into insignificance when the problems of Vedanta and the solutions that it offers are viewed in their proper perspective.

9.0 *YOU ARE THE ABSOLUTE.* Such is the grand conclusion to which all Vedantic speculation leads each man or mankind. Although the world of practical workaday values is not totally abolished to make normal living, in and through such a life Vedanta reveals a world of contemplative values understood under the aegis of the normative notion of the Absolute. Life here and hereafter falls into one line of harmony when both are given their proper place in the total scheme of life. Perceptual values revealed by the senses, with their attractions and repulsions alternating in unstable equilibrium, give place successively to the world of deeper and deeper lasting interest, as grasped firstly by the mind, the intellect, and the rational consciousness, then penetrating to unseen higher values of a conceptual or nominalistic order, and culminating in the High Value of the Absolute. Vital energies support the meaning of life at different levels till sublimated instincts take us to the point where the visible and the intelligible aspects meet and fuse transparently with osmotic interchange of the finest essences from both the sides of matter and mind. Duality then becomes abolished and immortal happiness gained in the Wisdom of the Absolute. Such is the bold hope that Vedanta has attempted to hold up to view for every man, as representing in himself the Highest Absolute or the Supreme Lord.

Part II
The Philosophy of a Guru

Introduction

The phrase, "the philosophy of a Guru," quite naturally calls to mind the wisdom a teacher conveys to his or her students in person or in written philosophical texts and compositions. But if we remember the literal meaning of philosophy, "the love of wisdom," we get a much broader understanding, which especially applies in this case. It is difficult to read the word "philosophy" without automatically picturing the dust clinging to old volumes or hundreds of pages filled with dull black print. But the word "love" inevitably opens the door to the realm of feeling, of value-content, and we are drawn into the dynamism of interaction.

Nataraja Guru here introduces us to one of the major philosophical compositions of Narayana Guru, *Atmopadesha Satakam*, or One Hundred Verses of Self-Instruction. Although based on *Atmopadesha Satakam*, it presents a very different approach than that taken by Nataraja Guru in his commentary on that work. Here, the verses of the composition are used to explicate the major principles of Narayana Guru's philosophy as representative of the philosophy incorporated in the Guru principle wherever it manifests. From the outset we are made aware of the inner experience of the Guru as an ardent lover who has become intimate with the realms of knowledge. There, the truths of science and the truths of mysticism come together, revealing the wonder which is ever-capable of generating the depth of interest and height of fulfillment known as the love of wisdom.

In this work, Nataraja Guru places the Guru's philosophy in the context of modern thought. Even a few pages reveal a scope of scientific and philosophic knowledge so vast that it can initially be dizzying. But as he presents his topic step by step, dizziness is replaced with an upsurge of inner brightness and energy evoked by his clarity and steady enthusiasm. This enthusiasm is not the passion of a proselytizer nor the infatuation of a convert. Rather, it is the dynamics of the love of wisdom in action. For him, the word of the Guru is not a static entity, but a vibrant, living process which he invites and guides us to enter.

Nataraja Guru shows us how that process resolves the doubts and paradoxes which have always plagued the eternally reenacted human quest for meaning. As individuals, cultural groups, religions, societies and nations, we have again and again confronted the antinomies of life. Today, humanity seems to have reached the peak of the possibility of destruction due to conflicting ideas and experiences. We are in urgent need of an approach that can offer solid ground to those seeking to go beyond conflict without at the same time instituting totalitarian restraint. Throughout human history, lovers of wisdom have persistently sought after a guiding light, and we have been blessed with many who have been successful, who merge with it and become radiant beams, lighting the way for others.

Here Nataraja Guru very clearly and precisely outlines the fundamental principles of that search and attainment. He has thus presented us with a much-needed road map which is accurate and well defined and, at the same time, permeated with the joy of arrival.

Nancy Yeilding

1

Structural key to Guru Philosophy

A Guru is a contemplative man of Wisdom. He combines science and mysticism in the neutral value that he represents in his person. He is understandable only in the context of absolutism, his visible aspects being only incidental.

We have hitherto spoken about Narayana Guru, but now we shall be turning our attention to the understanding of such a person more definitely in terms of a generalized abstraction of the concrete universal necessarily belonging to the notion of Guruhood. What is concrete and what is abstract merge finally into a neutral notion of the Absolute where duality is absorbed and abolished. Such are some of the leading ideas we shall keep in mind in the pages that follow.

We can insist on seeing before believing, or more simply on believing before seeing. The former is the a posteriori approach of the sceptic while the latter is natural to a man willing to believe. The total knowledge situation in which both these possibilities lie, when fully and philosophically understood, reconciles both approaches through simple unitive understanding, where the gap between mysticism and science tends to be abolished by an approach of one to the other, as it were, from opposite poles.

The philosophy of a Guru corresponds or should correspond to this unitive understanding which alone can banish fear and doubt and help to bring about universal brotherhood. Such truth makes one free and is a pearl of great price for humans.

The Two Anterior Positions

Scepticism and belief are two poles of the total knowledge situation, and the philosophy that can unite or solve both these antinomies is that of a normal neutral notion of the Absolute. Such a notion would be insipid and seem contentless if not equated to the Self of man. Guruhood is the notion that gives meaning to the Absolute. A correct appraisal of Guruhood gives us that final certitude which alone is the significant value that can make life purposeful.

By whatever name called or understood, in whichever context geographical or historical, a Guru marks the meeting point reconciling two opposing positions, which are those of science and scientifically revised mysticism. Modern philosophers like Bertrand Russell stand for what they themselves call a scientific or analytic philosophy which leans on the side of scepticism rather than on the side of belief. They have no use for wholesale solutions to overall problems of life, but prefer to tackle problems piecemeal by experimental or trial and error methods rather than relying on the a priori or synthetic approach. They call themselves operationalists, pragmatists, positivists, or logical mathematicians, forgetting that science is intimately linked with mathematics, which leans very much on axiomatic thinking fully a priori in status. The observables and calculables on which science thrives are the counterparts, dialectically understood, of the same visible and intelligible aspects within which metaphysics also moves.

Guru Philosophy Reconciles the Two Rival Positions

Two anterior positions have thus to be taken account of by us in placing Narayana Guru's philosophy, viz., where he fits into the context of modern sceptical thinking and where he starts to make his own contributions to Vedantic and contemplative traditions, coloured by mysticism natural to the Wisdom of the East. We can grasp the nature of Guru philosophy better and more easily if we state here in advance that we find in it a natural culmination of both modern scientific scepticism and the mystical will-to-believe. His was an integral approach in which scepticism and belief cancelled each other out into a neutral unitive notion which was fully human and within the reach of all men.

His philosophy is a prolongation of ongoing Vedantic correction and revision of its excesses and vague one-sided accentuations, aiming to make it a unitive and universal science based on a normative notion of the Absolute. Such are some of the claims we have to justify by examples from the work we are directly concerned with here, the *One Hundred Verses of Self-Instruction*, and as also seen in the Guru's philosophy revealed elsewhere. Scientific scepticism and a revised form of mysticism were the rival positions that he was able to revise and reconcile unitively in the light of a full-fledged and normative Science of the Absolute which his philosophy in fact represents.

A Guru's Philosophy is Based on Personal Experience

Experience and experiment are complementary dialectical counterparts belonging to a totally or globally understood knowledge situation. Inner experience of Truth tends to make a mystic, while factual experiments make a scientific sceptic. Mysticism has been described as the "cultivation of the presence of God." Outside events support certitude in science, while the mystic's certitude is derived from himself. Both are resultants of a bipolar situation involving scepticism and belief. Where a priorism leaves off a posteriorism steps in to take over the conduct of the process called human enquiry or understanding, which circulates between ambivalent aspects of the total knowledge situation.

Analysis and synthesis, induction and deduction, the general and the specific, mark phases or points in the calculatory course of reason as it seeks certitude. All facts or events emerge thus from the homogeneous transparent fluid matrix of thought-stuff with a rich inner zone and poor peripheral aspects, osmotically alternating in a grand cosmo-psychological respiration in which subtle essences from opposite poles are interchanged. A Guru is a man of intuition, who is aware of such pure acts taking place within the Self as the "unmoved mover" or the "thinking substance." Phenomenal and noumenal aspects of the Self or the non-Self keep essences equalized by such a circulation.

Although such statements might sound strange, too bold or untenable to modern ears, a Guru's philosophy is able to fit all these versions or visions into one unified and integrated organic scheme with a methodology, epistemology and axiology hanging together by a central normative notion in the Absolute Self. It is experiment as well as inner experience that confirms the normal total central Absolute Truth involved here. Without any implications of vagueness associated with the term "mysticism" a Guru can be said to be such a contemplative whose inner experience tallies or does not contradict what outer experiment teaches through laboratories, observatories, telescopes or microscopes.

Guru philosophy is thus a science as precise as mathematics and as experimental as physics or biology. The kind of mystical visions that are natural to a Guru are indicated in Narayana Guru's *One Hundred Verses of Self-Instruction* (*Atmopadesha Shatakam*), which we are presenting here as broadly representative of the outlines of his philosophy. Let us, therefore, linger a moment to examine some verses whose mystical content is unmistakable before passing on to some other of the important distinguishing features of the Guru's philosophy, as correctly representing a natural culmination of Vedanta and a normalized scientific philosophy in a fully modern sense.

Reason Need not Counter Experience

One has only to read three of the most central of the *One Hundred Verses of Self-Instruction,* which we are treating here as outlining the Guru philosophy for our purposes, to be convinced that the Guru is speaking his own inner experience through them, and that they are of a fully contemplative and mystical order. At the same time, however, the critical student of philosophy on closer scrutiny finds that the thoughts do not represent just merely a passing mood, a state of emotion, agony, exaltation or trance, often attributed to mystics who cultivate the presence of God in vague, sentimental, unsystematic or unscientific terms. When the student has taken pains to examine the whole series of verses in the light of reason, supplemented by the dialectical approach where what is vaguely classed as intuition plays its part, with full play of the critical faculty natural to human reasoning or understanding as employed from Locke to Hegel in the West, he will be able to appreciate that the whole series of verses is fully consequential and conforms to the requirements of valid speculation, with a method of orderly doubting like the one introduced by Descartes.

Here we have to part company with those who claim to be uncritical mystics, whether in the West or in the East, and those interpreters of mysticism who speak in merely sentimental or emotional terms, looking upon contemplative visions as passing moods unconnected with the normal reasoning faculty in man. Bertrand Russell is one such representative modern thinker who writes:

> Belief in a reality quite different from what appears to the senses, arises with irresistible force in certain moods which are sources of most mysticism, and of most metaphysics. While such a mood is dominant the need for logic is not felt and accordingly the most thorough-going mystics do not employ logic but appeal directly to the immediate deliverance of their insight. But such fully developed mysticism is rare in the West.[1]

1. Bertrand Russell, *Mysticism and Logic,* Allen and Unwin, (London, 1959), p. 19.

We shall not stop to discuss here the merits of this statement nor the case of the "thorough-going mystics" alluded to here, especially as Russell himself admits that "fully developed mysticism is rare in the West." Both in the East and the West there are those who think vaguely of the closed domains of logic and mysticism, and hold that one has to counter, compromise or contradict the other. The Guru philosophy as presented here, at least, does not fall into such a category. Here criticism, experiment and experience all coexist integrally at the core of the Absolute, which can contain so-called "empiricism" at one pole and so-called "idealism" at the other. Both together give content to the central notion representing Existence, Subsistence and Value. The closely reasoned verses which are prior to the above-mentioned central verses have a contemplative metaphysics not far different from what Bergson has explained in his *Introduction to Metaphysics,* which differs from usual metaphysics in that it takes an inner view of the total knowledge situation, and is not satisfied with putting together snaps or clichés statically understood. This distinction is a vital key to the understanding of the Guru philosophy.

The Grand Flux of Psycho-Cosmic Becoming

The following is Verse 50 from the *One Hundred Verses of Self-Instruction:*

> With earth and water, air and fire likewise,
> Also the void, the ego, cognition and mind,
> All worlds including the waves and ocean too,
> Do all arise and into awareness change.

"All worlds do rise and into awareness change," is, it must be admitted, strange sounding to modern ears unfamiliar with Bergson, Kant, Hegel, the Upanishadic way, or with the indeterministic nature of the physical world that modern relativism has brought to the forefront of thought in recent years. The mechanistic outlook has to be discarded and the notion of a *process* included in our vision of Truth or Reality.

In our commentary under the verse in question we have tried to touch upon some of the accepted philosophical positions supporting such an apparently bold statement that this verse presents. We have also devoted many pages in *The Search for A Norm in Western Thought* to elaborate the same normative philosophical viewpoint persistently kept in mind by Western philosophers ranging from sceptics or empiricists like Hume and Locke, through rationalists like Descartes, to Kant, Hegel and their modern followers. We have even quoted philosophers of science like Eddington to find just those pre-suppositions that would lend "justification" to the apparently too mystical and sweeping statement implied here. Yet, nothing incompatible with modern thought and nothing inconsistent with Vedanta has been stated here. To recognize this would be our first step in the direction of becoming more familiar with the philosophy of a Guru fully alive to all the modern currents of thought.

We have to take note firstly of the categories mentioned in the verse in graded and methodical order as well as of the schematic or structural features respected by the Guru in writing this verse, which should be quite patent to one who is aware of such implications natural to mystical language, as has been explained by us elsewhere. The series of elementals first mentioned beginning from the most gross to the most subtle pass beyond matter with the fifth item in an ascending series of sets, groups or ensembles that belong together at each level as phenomenological existential *epoches* with a unitive consistency of monads within each, till the implication of both matter and mind merge in the homogeneous transparency of pure schematism in the reference to the waves and the ocean bracketed together. Here the waves have the horizontal implications of plurality, phenomenality or a practically manifested analytic aspect which can be called effects as opposed to causes or the cause, and the ocean understood globally as a unit comprising the knowledge situation as a whole represents the pure noumenal or vertical implications of the same situation, with both belonging together to the same structural scheme.

In a universe that is subject to expansion and contraction and under the sway of an alternating process of a grand cosmo-psychic respiration within the homogeneous matrix of transparent essences, osmotically exchanged between the plus and the minus aspects, it is not difficult to think of a dialectical ascent and an alternating descent making up together a circulation such as that of the wheel that the Bhagavad Gita alludes to in III, 16. Other verses, too, of the Guru help to confirm this living picture of what takes place at the core of Absolute Self-consciousness. Many passages in the Upanishads are also suggestive of the same interesting content, without which the notion of the Absolute would ever remain empty and insipid.

Cosmic Absorption into the Plus Side

Without further apology for taking the above view, seeing that we have specifically devoted space already to clarify most of the implications brought together under this one verse here, let us now pass on to the verse after the next, skipping Verse 51, to scrutinize for a moment its presentation of the same living picture of the cosmic-cum-psychic dynamic process viewed rather from the plus side than from the minus side as in Verse 50. Verse 52 reads as follows:

> Filled with word-content, that day the firmament shall
> radiant blaze,
> And into it shall be absorbed to extinction all the visionary
> magic,
> Then, too, that small voice completing tri-basic cognition
> Shall cease, and, lo! Self-radiance prevails.

This verse may be said to touch the high water mark attainable to speculation when it manages just to remain within the scope of philosophy proper, although to practical ears even these bare outlines might still sound strange.

It is evident that here we have a mystic's vision represented, but a closer scrutiny as with Verse 50 reveals the same process structurally understood as taking place at the core of the significant Absolute in terms of Self-consciousness. The process is one of circulation and becoming absorbed at unitive, more unitive, and universal levels, whose meanings gain more and more absolute significance or value till all truth, fact or value gets merged in the highest Value of all. This is like an "echo and a light unto eternity," as the English poet Shelley has preferred to put such a culminating experience. Reason is here not abandoned, but in the ascent of thesis and antithesis canceling each other out into a synthesis at higher and higher levels in Self-consciousness is a resultant containing the thesis aspect becoming ever purer or brighter and more significant as a value.

Thus, Existence, Subsistence and Value aspects of the Absolute remain without any taint of inner conflict between any two pairs taken in the ascending scale. Light here represents the visible and sound the intelligible, which fuse together into one ineffable and ultimate Value.

Tree-Structure Evidenced in Verse 51

Lest the student should think that these structural and other implications are being read into the verses, which are just ordinary mystical effusions known in the East and also familiar in the context of European mysticism, let us take Verse 51 situated between the two we have cited already. The subject matter of this verse might seem, at first, to have nothing at all to do with the two verses with which it is bounded before and after. The analogy of the structure of a tree with two ambivalently complementary reciprocal branches, one growing at the expense or at least depending organically on the other, is clearly seen here:

From awareness, the "I" sense first emerged,
Comes then with it "This-ness" as counterpart beside,

Like branches, these two do overcover
Hiding the whole of the Maya tree.

The tree in mystical language stands for all ramified values, conceptual as well as perceptual, that claim attention or interest in a given field of consciousness at any given time. The stream of consciousness or flux of becoming is like a tree growing and putting out fruits or flowers peripherally and horizontally. The pure process takes place, as it were, vertically in full transparence between the perceptual and conceptual entities both entering the matrix of consciousness. When correctly focused between the plus and the minus, the tree tends to cancel itself out, but when the least tinge of negativism or quality is retained, as between the dual and the nondual Absolute, the ramified set-structure becomes evident with two zones covering the plus (conceptual) and the minus (perceptual), both in terms of abstract and generalized intuitions. This takes place alternately in the framework of warp and woof of time and space categories. The whole field is filled with relation-relata complexes of infinite number, with a harmony pre-established in the overall situation. The multiplicity of monads thus formed are implied in the *monas monadum,* which is the normative notion of the Absolute. Bergsonian growth, division and becoming within the core of the eternal flux of the *elan vital,* phenomenological *epoches,* and monadological schematic and structural dualities, have all to be elaborated and fitted together integrally and unitively as living like a tree or flowing like a river of maya, the relativistic aspect of the Absolute.

Other Instances from Guru-literature Suggesting Structure

Narayana Guru has a large number of philosophical compositions, mostly in verse, where the same structural scheme is implicit and sometimes even explicitly used. As an instance of explicit reference to structuralism in the Absolute, one can readily use the fourth verse of the common prayer composed in Malayalam by the Guru, called *Daiva Dashakam* (A Prayer for Humanity):

> Like sea, wave, wind and depth
> Let us within see
> Ourselves, Maya (relativism), your glory and Thee.

The schematic implications here are unmistakable. When we attempt to paraphrase the above line using the language evolved by us, we can say that the dimension of depth of the ocean, in the analogy consisting of four quaternion factors by which the total situation is intended to be comprised, is the vertical aspect of the Absolute which is, by far, the most fundamental of all. We have elsewhere shown that, in the general context of Vedantism the material cause gains primacy over all other forms of causes which can be used for speculation. *Upadana karana,* which is its name in Vedanta, is fundamentally basic and inclusive of its horizontalized counterparts. Formal cause, as known in the context of Aristotle, is an extreme abstraction implied within the scope of this master cause of all, which is the vertical principle itself. All pure mathematical equations live within the core of this vertical axis, here compared to the depth of the sea. The water does not wet the depth nor the wind dry it. The Absolute that is at the base of all phenomenalism is thus attained in this root principle which is no more or less than a dimension in the total Absolutist situation where alone the notion of the Absolute can properly be said to belong.

In the six verses following Verse 36 of the *One Hundred Verses of Self-Instruction* which we treat here as presenting us the broad outlines of a Guru philosophy, the further implications of this total knowledge situation are seen to be fully elaborated by the Guru himself. We shall have more to say on these aspects when the proper contexts present themselves. Here what we just wish to underline is that a normative and structurally understandable notion of the Absolute is the key to Guru philosophy. Verses 50, 51 and 52 are strikingly bold and deserve full scrutiny on the part of any student who wishes to be introduced into the heart of Guru philosophy. The total knowledge situation in which the logical form of Aristotle, the dialectics of Parmenides and Zeno, the antinomies or dichotomies that Kant or Bergson alluded to, the bracketing as understood in phenomenology, and the pre-established harmony of Leibnizian Monadology, with Hegelian absorption of thesis and antithesis into a higher synthesis, will all be seen to be only particular aspects of the way of Guru-speculation when fully and properly understood.

The recognition of *abhava* (non-actuality) as a *padartha* (category) is one of the other important distinguishing features of Guru philosophy. Bergsonian flux and metaphysics that gives to becoming and process a fully open and dynamic status, is another feature of a proper Guru philosophy. The three verses considered here reveal these broad features implicitly or explicitly, and we shall have occasions to come back to each of the particular aspects as we proceed.

Structural Limits of Speculation and Experience

Experience, inner and outer, meets in the Guru's person. When speculation is based on inner experience, when no laboratory experimental arrangements are needed, we tend to have literature that resembles metaphysics. Otherwise, it comes under the scope of physics. Physics and metaphysics broadly understood, belong to the same total knowledge situation in which inner and outer experience confirm each other to give apodictic or dialectical certitudes. Pure mathematics based on equations lives and moves in this same vertical axis within the range of possible human understanding.

We have, at the end of *Vedanta Revalued and Restated,* given the instance of how in one of the Upanishads the double value factor called *ananda* (Absolute Bliss) is pictured structurally as having a head, a right side, a left side and lower part, which last is treated as the most important of all as representing the Absolute. A similar verse, 15, by the Guru in his composition entitled *Advaita Dipika* (Lamp of Non-Duality) gives us a striking instance where the unity of speculative factors belonging to inner or outer experience are brought together, juxtaposed and integrated to serve as a basis for correct scientific speculation in respect of the Absolute. The verse under reference reads as follows:

> Bliss exists, it looms (in consciousness), it is One alone;
> If thought of disjunct from Self, it exists not,
> And nothing then can attain consciousness at all;
> Then mirage-water, sky-blue would become non-existent
> and sky-flower and mirage-sky ultimate value attain.

The above is one of the most complex and complicated verses ever written by the Guru, presenting in compact form a methodological and epistemological problem set in the context of bliss or value factor. To penetrate beyond the *reductio ad absurdum* method used masterfully by the Guru in his scientifically valid speculation will require the knowledge of the same structural secret that we have tried to explain and elaborate all through our writings. Without such a key hinted at here, most of the validity of the Guru's writings are likely to remain a closed book to a majority of students of philosophy.

Hence the importance of this first chapter which when grasped will open many doors in the many-apartmented mansion which is Guru philosophy. We can do no more here, in passing, than to just indicate the nature of the *reductio ad absurdum* method implicit in the above verse. The two sets of examples are bracketed in a certain way fully respecting structuralism so as to avoid giving merely nominal or conceptual factors primacy over existential and subsistential ones.

The Common Integrated Import of All Varieties of Wisdom

Concluding his composition called *Anukampa Deshakam*

(Scriptures of Mercy) the Guru strikes an important note himself with the following verse slightly retranslated here.[2]

> High scripture — meaning antique, rare,
> Or meaning as by Guru taught,
> And what the quiet recluse conveys,
> Wisdom's varieties of every sort,
> Together they are all of one kind,
> One in essence, in substance same!

When the integrated knowledge pattern implicit in various kinds of wisdom literature is properly understood it will be found that a simple human quality such as kindliness or mercy emerging as a human value can be fitted into a context of Absolute value or significance. The Koran, the *Dhammapada*, the Upanishads not excluding the Vedas, the Pentateuch and the Bible, all have their secret contributions to make to the totality of the heritage of human wisdom. The integrative "structural element" hiding at the core of all such teachings is not different from the structuralism, selectionalism and subjectivism that modern philosophers of science like Eddington and Einstein also share and wish to communicate to humanity seeking science or wisdom.

Thus, side by side with gurus conforming to the prototypes of Guruhood understood in the Vedantic context, it would not be altogether absurd to think of certain wise men of the Western context where science holds the field as gurus also. The underlying integrative factor is what gives all of them high wisdom content, as Guru Narayana evidently wishes to express in the above lines.

---

2. Nataraja Guru, *The Word of the Guru*, for a commentary on this work, pp. 355-72.

2

The Element of Wonder

Having understood the structural key to Guru philosophy, as explained in the last chapter, we have also to discover the overall plan of the hundred-verse sequence, to be able to see clearly the scope, limits and amplitude of speculation, within whose four walls, together with the structural reference that we have pointed out, Guru philosophy is to be understood in living terms.

Then and only then will it give up its secrets and become an open book to all, instead of remaining a cryptically compact sequence of verses, each succeeding one another without any visible subsections, and seemingly without any method or critically understandable theory of knowledge being respected by the author.

It is natural to expect that *philosophy proper must be capable of being critically examined* according to recognized norms and standards of reasoning or thought in general, which instrument of human understanding should find full play in any philosophy worth the name. While Guru philosophy tackles problems wholesale instead of piecemeal, this should not detract from its fully scientific status.

Indian Philosophy More Scientific

How philosophy is to become scientific is a matter about which there could be radically different opinions, even among modern philosophers of the status of a Bertrand Russell and Max Müller. We are familiar with the views of Russell tending to discredit a wholesale approach to philosophy altogether, and thus Indian philosophy too. Prof. Müller, however, thinks that Indian philosophy is more strictly philosophical than modern Western philosophies, with both of which he can be credited as having sufficient familiarity. Comparing Indian and Western philosophies, Müller writes:

> We know what an enormous amount of labour had to be spent and is still being spent in order to ascertain the exact views of Plato and Aristotle, nay, even of Kant and Hegel, on some of the most important questions of their systems of philosophy. There are even living philosophers whose words often leave us in doubt as to what they meant, whether they are materialists or idealists, monists or nihilists, theists or atheists. Hindu philosophers seldom leave us in doubt on such important points, and they certainly never shrink from the consequences of their theories.[1]

While Hegel condemned Indian philosophy as adolescent or immature thinking, here is a scholar and a philosopher, originating from the same country not many decades later, who has taken the trouble to impartially examine both Eastern and Western philosophies. His unstinted praise helps to counteract the aspersions cast on Indian thought by some Westerners. Müller's further remarks in the same context as above are therefore worth quoting:

> What I admire in Indian philosophers is that they never try to deceive us as to their principles and the consequences of their theories. If they are idealists even to the verge of nihilism they say so, and if they hold that the objective world requires a real, though not necessarily a visible or tangible substratum they are never afraid to speak out. They are *bona fide* idealists or materialists, monists or dualists, theists or atheists because their reverence for truth is stronger than their reverence for anything else.[2]

1. Max Müller, *Six Systems of Indian Philosophy,* (Calcutta, 1952), p. x., intro. vol. I.
2. Ibid., p. xi.

A downright apodictic quality has characterized Indian thought, and the Six Systems do not err on the side of vagueness of speculation. The definitions, though cryptic in linguistic formulation, are precise and clear cut when properly understood. No doubt Prof. Müller had in mind those systems that have come down to us in succinct aphoristic formulations, when he applauds the merits of Indian philosophy as against Western philosophical speculation in general.

The Fuller Scientific Status of Shankara's Advaita

When we come to the Advaita Vedanta of Vyasa or Badarayana, and especially as restated critically by Shankara, the degree of certainty attains to a more fully scientific status. The Absolute, treated wholesale and wholeheartedly, in downright or frontally facing outright terms of intellectual attack and emotional onslaught, then becomes fully apodictic. The emotions naturally resemble those of a mystic, while the intellectual approach would correspond to the pure vision of a man of dialectical wisdom.

Closely argued ways thus can coexist in Guru philosophy without violating the codes of right speculation, although to minds conditioned by the divorce of speculation and spirituality, as in modern Western thought, such speculation, even when correct, might seem strange, vague or sentimental. The mystical vision too, on the other hand, would be too strong for them to gaze at, compared to the twilight worlds of easy or complacent speculation in which modern philosophy has had to thrive. To the modern Western student, especially in academic life, philosophy is only one of his many side-interests in life.

In the case of Guru philosophy, as is only to be expected in the present case, speculation not only becomes red hot but attains to an incandescent white heat and melting point at times, as we shall presently see. All we want to point out in advance here is that this wholesale and frontal character of the approach of Guru philosophy should not be considered by the modern reader as detracting in any way from its true status of critical and correct speculation. Its value is only enhanced when it conforms to the requirements of a normalized absolutist method, a theory of knowledge, and an axiology which does not exclude the overall human problem of minimizing suffering or bondage and of securing human happiness, individual or collective, from its scope. Lukewarm, piecemeal, trial-and-error, ratiocinative, eristic or sophistic approaches, dabbling in mere opinions and counter-opinions, do not serve the purpose of healthy, wholesale and correct speculation that Guru philosophy is meant to be.

No apology is therefore needed for the bold speculative flights found in the verses we are particularly presenting here, which at first might confuse the modern reader in respect of their normality, sobriety or critical validity, from the standpoint of the so-called man in the street.

Each Verse and Topic Fits into an Overall Plan

Besides the key of structuralism which we have to keep in mind in order to appreciate methodically and critically the contents of this sequence of verses, there is the equally important fact of the symmetrically conceived overall plan within which the speculation lives and moves.

The first verse refers to the seeker for higher Wisdom and the last verse marks the culmination of his search in the realization of the Absolute as an Existent Subsistent Value, as finally equal and non-different from the Self within each man or in human consciousness treated generally.

Between these extreme limits various topics, inclusive of ethics, religion, logic, error aspects of the soul, cosmic-psychic correlation, states of consciousness, alternation between poles, vertical and horizontal value-worlds, epistemological and methodological laws or rules, dichotomy, ambivalency or polarity between aspects of the self or the person, the principle of compensation in spiritual life or in contemplative progress to wisdom, orthodoxy and heterodoxy, adoption and disadoption, the place of the a priori, the limits of logical reasoning, semantic analysis of thought in the core of the Absolute, sublimation of action in terms of Wisdom, the circulation of thought or action, participation of mind and matter, are all brought within the scope of the discussion contained in these hundred verses, and there is an innate unity of subject matter and structure so compact as to constitute and come within the amplitude of one sweeping vision of an awakened Self.

The items are so compactly presented that they defy analytical enumeration, and, as stated in the very first verse, are meant more for meditative purposes, as in the case of a sacred song, a chant or scripture. The Vedas and the Vedanta too, in India, are conceived on similar cryptic, protolinguistic, schematic, unitively compact terms of a vision that defies critical scrutiny and verification by normal human standards of thought and reasoning.

Each verse, or sometimes a sequence of two or three verses, are seen to hang together, harping on the same or a kindred theme. Sometimes the vision given to ascending dialectics is balanced by the same vision stated soon after as seen from the point of view of descending dialectics. There is occasionally a sequence of four or five verses whose subject matter is left off, to be taken up again at a later stage in a subtler or improved form at a higher level of speculation. The changeover from topic to topic takes place in such a gentle gradation that unless the reader or student is aware himself of the methodological and epistemological unity kept in mind by the Guru, he will see no reason why a certain thought should follow rather than precede the previous one.

These sets have to be distinguished by the careful student after a first acquaintance with each of the verses separately. Then, when the sets are finally seen to be interrelated, he will be able to appreciate how the work as a whole has been strung together with a sense of symmetrical beauty when viewed megascopically as a whole.

The verses as they have been translated and commented upon[3] will be seen to be sufficiently self-explanatory. Here in these remarks our purpose is limited to seeing the connecting links and logical or critical implications as between one section and another, one set of verses that belong together and another similar set elsewhere, and to note how the structural scheme of each respects the overall message that the verses as a whole wish to convey. The verses themselves are transparent enough in content both separately and all together.

We shall travel from the apparently most mystical verses to those which are more analytically and critically conceived, as we come up against each set or counterpart in later sections. The element of wonder characterizes the former mystical verses, and the emphasis on reason or analysis characterizes the critical group. Mythological imagery belonging to the soil of South India is advantageously employed by the Guru, and sometimes an appeal is made directly to the Upanishads too. These however are done in such a way as not to detract or damage the fully critical status that the verses are meant to have as a whole. It is the exigency of language alone that makes the Guru resort to such ideograms rooted in the popular mind of India. Besides ideograms, protolinguistic devices too are seen to be freely employed by the Guru. A strict scheme, semantically correct, is adhered to even here.

The Homogeneous Matrix into which the Vision of the Self is Fitted

Psychodynamics and psychostatics are terms that are sometimes used to make a distinction between living and still pictures of the working of the Self. As in the case of the thinking substance of Spinoza, there is a paradox implied here as between *natura naturans* and *natura naturata.*

---

3. In Nataraja Guru, *One Hundred Verses of Self-Instruction.*

The very first verse puts its finger on a core (*karu*) which is the source of all activities, whether thought of in terms of an *unmoved mover* within, or, in more overt terms, of a cosmological phenomenology. Each of these is a counterpart of the other. When the first few and the last few verses are carefully examined from this standpoint of psycho-phenomenal dynamism, one is able to see how doctrinal items cling together and are set as stones in a homogeneous matrix which is neither mental nor material.

Maya itself, which is the principle of error, illusion, or false value, finds place in the most central of the verses as at the beginning and end. Maya has plus, minus and neutral aspects, according to the overall epistemology respected and kept in mind throughout the composition. The gems of doctrine have also to be fitted by us into the matrix made up of pure consciousness so that they stand out but do not stand apart or differently, in quality at least, from the matrix. Advaita or nonduality implies this rule of homogeneity (*samanadhikaranatva*) as its inevitable corollary.

The vision of the Self is revealed as meeting at a neutral point between two aspects of the Absolute, a priori and a posteriori, which are represented in each instance, as it were, by two limbs of an equation, each of which is to be understood in terms of the other. The proof of either statement is brought about naturally by the cancellation of a thesis by an antithetical aspect of the same. Analogies are thus equations in which the less familiar is understood in terms of the more familiar. The two limbs always cancel out into the synthetic unity of the homogeneous matrix of the Self and its knowledge, which are dialectical counterparts. A Hegelian methodology is clearly implicit here, though in a more complete and perfected form, perennial and not merely historical, and as understood in the wisdom texts from the time of the Upanishads through the Buddha and down to the present. The dialectical approach in our own time has become more or less overlaid and forgotten, except in certain schools such as that of Marx and Engels, who apply it only to limited socioeconomic fields. The full-fledged dialectical approach, employed to the best advantage by the Guru here, when discovered by the critical student, will afford him one of the important keys by which he can make the study of these verses most fruitful. Their critical validity will then become fully evident to him.

The Nature of Proofs

Critical speculation is best when the arguments are cut and dry without leaving room for ambiguity. The experimental method of the physical sciences answers to this purpose. When Newton says that, just as an apple falls to the ground by force of gravity, there is a law of gravitation applicable to the whole of the physical universe of all bodies, his reasoning is acceptable to scientists although it is the force rather of an analogy upon which the demonstrable proof rests. Physicists might call it induction, but scrutiny of instances shows the analogical rather than the experimental logic at the basis of the proof.

Here the experimental aspect on which the grand generalization is based is so simple and negligible that it can easily be admitted by men of common sense from their everyday experience that the proof is not different from an analogical one. The relation between the experimental aspect and the law is one only of comparison between what is familiar, and what is unfamiliar, i.e., analogy. No one can say, strictly speaking, if there are not exceptions to this law, at the central, peripheral or stratospheric limits of the universe. This law however, is today universally respected as an overall statement of something that is basically and scientifically true.

If we think in terms of equations, such as momentum equals mass times velocity ($M = mv$), which we can easily prove any time by calculation and measurement in any given case, the proof is the same one of equating less general actualities to more general concepts, and when the letters Q.E.D. are put at the end of the calculation, the physicist accepts it as proof. The Pythagorean Theorem is provable in both ways by the actual cutting out and pasting of triangles or squares, or by a blackboard sequence of propositions based on axioms of a graded order whether known as postulates, riders or lemmas. Whether the a priori is more valid than the a posteriori is not certain. Both together lend validity to the truth.

The nature of a proof has itself been called into question by no less a philosopher of science than Sir Arthur Eddington who says, "Proof is an idol before whom the pure mathematician tortures himself."[4] According to him it is a form of idolatry or superstition. If the positive sciences are so weak in their proofs how can we expect their speculation to be any better?

Proofs Here as Valid as in Science

When we look at the present series of verses we find that it consists of a number of definitions and instructions given to the aspirant in contemplative wisdom of the Self. If the proofs of the modern physicists can rest on such flimsy grounds as analogy or interchangeability of the terms of an equation, then in such a subject as contemplation of the Self, where introspective experimentation of more common and more rare experiences are alone possible and are even the rule, the validity of the proofs for each of the items of Self-instruction contained here should be less open to question by a critical student, no matter how highly developed his critical faculty might be. In fact, the more acutely it is developed in him the more he should desist from asking for the more ordinary experimental demonstrations. Whether experiments prove axioms or vice versa is the question. *The best proof is what proves itself.*

---

4. Eddington, *Nature of the Physical World,* (London, 1928), p. 49.

Wonder Has a Place

There is no need for science to be cold-blooded. Under what compulsion should it limit itself by excluding the element of wonder, mystery, or legitimate inspiration? To be happy and be in a mood to sing a ditty is as natural to the man in the street as it is to rare mystics reputed to live in the caves of the Himalayas.

If the proper study of mankind is man, and if man must know his environment fully and globally to live in it correctly, a complete philosophy of life which would help him to do so must needs take into account all his subjective traits, and match them with their counterparts in the objective world. Correlations, cosmic, psychic or both, counterparts of the Self and the non-Self, and innate correspondences, have all to be matched through analogies or equations implying one or the other aspect, or both aspects at once, so as to reveal the full mechanics as well as dynamics of life. The more fluid the resulting truth, the better it would be.

It is such an inclusive way that the Guru philosophy is expressly meant to represent, and here it is only following and keeping alive in revalued terms the Upanishadic tradition. A healthy, wholesale and wholehearted philosophy, in which dialectical counterparts are juxtaposed so as to yield a unitive vision of the Self in the light of the normative Absolute, is the task which the series of verses boldly sets before itself. How far it has accomplished this great task is the question we have to answer after detailed and critical scrutiny of the verses themselves, sometimes taken in recurring and non-recurring groups of two, three, four or five, as we shall see.

Ascent Implied in the Guru philosophy

Contemplation implies a form of ascent through intensity of thought. It takes place under high pressure, as it were. Passive and lukewarm attitudes are not conducive to yield the results of true contemplation, where the inertia, the aches and pains of the body, or even love of easy-chair comfort are to be left behind by the aspirant. There is a factor called *tapas* (burning up) which presupposes an agony of some sort, and implies intensity of research, full alertness supported by clear memory, willingness to give full attention to the subject or problem at hand, and the power to listen or will to believe on a basis of correct scepticism balanced with belief. Such are some of the known prerequisites here.

The very first verse in this series of one hundred verses, in its opening phrase, stresses just this prerequisite on the part of one who wishes to grasp the Guru philosophy. The same requirements have been enumerated by Shankara and others. Bergson says:

> But the truth is that the intelligence can follow the opposite method. It can place itself within the mobile reality and adopt its ceaselessly changing direction; in short, can grasp it by means of that *intellectual sympathy* which we call intuition. This is extremely difficult. The mind has to do violence to itself, has to reverse the direction of the operation by which it habitually thinks, has perpetually to revise or rather to recast all its categories. But in this way it will attain to fluid concepts capable of following reality in all its sinuosities and of adopting the very movement of the inward life of things.[5]

Contemplative metaphysics therefore has to be approached with a revised attitude about what is to be expected. Bergsonian philosophy comes nearest to it. There are many other features of the Guru philosophy which we can only touch upon when occasions arise. Here we shall focus our attention, in concluding this chapter, on the element of wonder as admitted into correct metaphysical speculation by the Guru in his philosophy.

---

5. Bergson, *An Introduction to Metaphysics,* (Liberal Arts Press, New York), p. 51.

Bracketting of the Wonder

The Absolute Self is an enigma and a wonder. It has been called a *mysterium tremendum* (tremendous mystery), and the Gita (II, 29) states this unequivocally:

> A certain person sees this as a wonder, likewise another speaks about this as a wonder. Another hears of it even as a wonder, but even hearing no one understands this at all.

We have in the previous section examined three of the most central verses of the series before us. The rise and circulation of elements of thought at the core of the Absolute were pictured there. How the visible world itself can be effaced in the full wonder of the Absolute in terms of meaning or sound, was also boldly touched upon in Verse 52. We shall now select two other verses where again the element of mystery or wonder is pronounced. Verses 35 and 65 are turned in opposite directions like the outer brackets in an algebraic sum. First let us scrutinize Verse 35:

> Like the dawning altogether of ten thousand suns
> Wisdom's function comes; Such verily is what
> Can tear asunder the knowledge-hiding impermanent
>   darkness of Maya here,
> And, as the primordial Sun on high, prevails.

The overwhelming and total nature of Wisdom treated as a wonder here is unmistakable. By its position in the total series, we have to take note that this wonder reaches out from the negative to the positive side of the total knowledge situation. The arrow points upwards to the glorious vision possible to the contemplative. If this verse is taken as the opening of the brackets enclosing the content of general wonder of the Absolute vision of the Self, which is the subject matter here, we can see that Verse 65 suggests the closure of the same pair of brackets. The arrow is reversed. Instead of suggesting endless possibilities for the contemplative vision, there is a limitation to be imposed here lest too much positiveness of the vision should disperse the unity of the Self that is to be located in its middle neutral ground. Verse 65 reads:

> There is nothing here that we have not already once known.
> Hidden by form, Knowledge fails us; wakefully
> To know all this there is none at all, limitless as it is;
> Oh, who can there be at all to know this Wonder dear!

Here the limitlessness of the Wonder is stressed to show that the contemplative can have only such visions as his own self can contain. The Absolute Self is enclosed as it were, between two opposite tendencies, one that is of limitless expansion to the plus side and the other that points its arrow to the core of the neutral zero point of the total knowledge situation. The position of the verse in the second half of the series, well towards the end, is what alone can justify this seeming contradiction which, it will be clear, is no contradiction when Self-knowledge and its wonder are understood as the content of the work as a whole, forming its plus and minus limiting factors.

Besides these limiting verses there are others in the body of the work which the student would do well to find, and analytically and critically scrutinize himself, according to the context of each.

3

Transcending Paradox

A philosopher does not merely dabble in information, opinions or rival theories arrived at through trial-and-error methods. He is interested in finding Reality behind appearances, distinguishing Truth from falsehood and facts from mere superstitions. He employs experimental reasoning, logic and valid general ideas for determining what is existent, subsistent or of value in life. The general and wholesale approach is more natural to him than any piecemeal one, and mere possibilities and probabilities cannot satisfy the fully human curiosity or thirst for knowing which distinguishes him as belonging to *Homo sapiens.*

It is thus that speculative literature differentiates man from the anthropoid apes. He seeks the "Truth that shall make him free" and that "pearl of great price" or "the little leaven that leaveneth the whole lump." The Bhagavad Gita states the same verity, "the slightest measure of a way of wisdom alone can save man from great fear." The "master-knot has to be cut" and "doubts sundered in his heart" to liberate or emancipate him.

Unlike the halting methods of inductive scientific disciplines, which are less ambitious in this respect, the central problem of all philosophizing anywhere or at any time by humans has had the same problem or enigma to solve. It can be said to be contained in the primary questions of all philosophy such as, "Who am I?" and "How does this phenomenal world come about?" A wholehearted and wholesale approach to such problems can alone make philosophy worthwhile.

From most ancient times the world over, bold speculation has gone on to unravel the mystery, solve the enigma, or save man from the dilemma in which he is caught. His spirit of research cannot rest satisfied till he correctly locates the problem at the core of life. How does matter interact with spirit? How are body and mind articulated? How is the mind inserted into matter? How can there be full participation of the inner and the outer factors of life?

All these refer to the same central problem of solving paradoxes. Variously labeled by philosophical schools under pairs of terms such as the phenomenal and the noumenal, the visible and the intelligible, the experimental (or observable) and the calculable, name and form, or spirit and matter, in endless variety, whether brought under the Self or the non-Self, the subjective or the objective, or under spatial or temporal dimensions in which life has its being or becoming, all the dual aspects have an implied paradox between each of the pairs of terms. Mathematically they can be comprised under the *vertical* (pure) and the *horizontal* (practical).

Facing Paradox Frontally

The primary task of a philosopher is to face this problem directly. Modern philosophers like Russell tend to bypass the central problem in the name of a scientific approach. At the same time there is to their credit such doctrines as "neutral monism," which reflects a total or wholesale doctrine or approach.

Instead of a total annexation of Truth in terms of an absolutist approach, the so-called analytic philosophers prefer, in the name of science, to annex bits of a territory at a time, by methods resembling those of experimental science. The hollowness of such a claim has been discussed by us more than once elsewhere. Relativism and absolutism are ill defined by modern philosophers. Neither of these terms can have a meaning apart from its dialectical counterpart, for one has to presuppose the other to have any meaning at all. How even the Relativism of Einstein has some Absolute notion at its core is brought out clearly in the following lines which we quote from a recent authority without entering into the discussion here at any length:

After explaining, "The consequences of the Einsteinian theory are that *distance* and *time* are relative and hence measurements of them by another observer need not agree with ours," (p. 292) and deriving further implications of a Lorentz Transformation, the writer continues; "This means that although time and space are relative, a certain *mixture* of them is absolute. It is an error to think that because Einstein's theory is called Relativity, all measurements are relative. The mathematician Whitehead chose the name 'separation' for the absolute invariant $\sqrt{t^2 - x^2}$."[1]

Further light on the status of the velocity of light as an absolute normative notion at the centre of the theory of Einsteinian so-called Relativity is afforded by another statement: "No material body can have a velocity equal to or greater than the speed of light."[2]

Thus there is a paradox hiding even at the core of the meanings of the two terms Relative and Absolute. If what is Absolute is real the Relative must be called false, because there cannot be two Truths. If there are two truths one must either contradict the other or be merely a tautology of it. In Vedantic parlance the former is an *asambhava* (impossibility as a contradiction in terms) and the latter is vitiated by the evil of *atmashraya* (begging the question).

Between accepting tautology or contradiction there hides, at the core of even the most recent of speculation, supported by the strict rules of mathematics used in modern science, a master enigma, dilemma or problem, like a Gordian knot, intricate and difficult to resolve, which has taken all the

1. Edna E. Kramer *The Main Stream of Mathematics*, (Fawcett Publication, New York, 1961), p. 295.

2. Ibid., p. 292.

intelligence of wise men of all times and climes to resolve once and for all.

Modernism mistrustingly looks upon such a solution as resembling the search for a philosopher's stone, or the search for a panacea for all ills. In spite of this modern prejudice in the name of the experimental approach of science, we can see from the above citations that even at the very core of the theory of Relativity, there is hiding a paradoxical absolute element. The Guru philosophy that we are attempting to present in these introductory chapters attempts to approach this very problem that Einsteinian theorems or theories involve. A fresh and bold approach is warranted by our times, and this is exactly what Guru philosophy as we wish to present it in the pages that follow claims to bring into view.

The "Oddness" or "Mystery" of Paradox in Mathematics and Philosophy

We have just seen how paradox hides at the core of the Relativity Theory. There are certain unresolved paradoxes which are known in mathematics. Leibniz prefers to call them contradictions while Bertrand Russell would dismiss them as mere "oddities." The way anyone prefers to describe such a paradox is one of personal temperament. The sum of the odd numbers in series must give rise to a different total than the sum of the even numbers, thus giving rise to two paradoxical values of infinity. Whether merely "oddness" or "contradiction" is recognized here, the paradoxical dilemma remains to be solved. On their solution, Runes, in his *Dictionary of Philosophy* says: "Russell's solution of paradox is embodied in what is now known as the *ramified theory of types*. . . . Because of its complication this has now been largely abandoned in favour of other solutions."[3]

No proper solution has been made acceptable, either by logicians or by mathematicians. The dialectical approach of Bradley to logic brings him up to this very problem of the

3. Cf. under "Paradoxes, Logical", p. 224.

difficulty of transcending paradox when he states: "And we seem unable to clear ourselves from the old dilemma. If you predicate what is different, you ascribe to the subject what it is *not,* and if you predicate what is *not* different, you say nothing at all."[4]

Philosophically, scientifically, logically, and mathematically we are thus finding it still very difficult to transcend paradox. Between full paradoxes, dilemmas and enigmas, ranging from mild implied paradoxes to open contradictions there can be endless grades in the type of paradox we might have to solve, but in order to transcend paradox an absolutist philosophy like neutral monism, which is neither one nor the other but unites both aspects of being or becoming, is inevitable. The Bhagavad Gita states this problem of all philosophy in the following words:

> What is unreal cannot have being and non-being cannot be real; the conclusion in regard to both these has been known to philosophers. (II, 16)

In the light of the last part of this verse, any philosopher who does not face this problem with its paradoxes squarely cannot be ranged by the side of philosophers who are fully alive to the situation. This central problem of all philosophy cannot be bypassed without detracting from the full dignity and purpose of philosophy itself. It is just because the Guru philosophy here, as we shall see, squarely faces this paradox at the heart of all serious speculation, that it might appear unusual to moderns who wish to circumvent this central question by taking refuge in verbosities or in piecemeal approaches such as Russell seems to recommend. The modern notion of a space-time continuum is an attempt to transcend the implied paradox between space-like and time-like elements.

---

4. *Appearance and Reality,* 2nd ed., p. 17.

The Place of the Paradox Fully Recognized in Guru Philosophy

The subject matter and the object matter of philosophy constitute together in Guru philosophy a master enigma or wonder which is to be understood unitively in the light of each other, and even thus only in its broad outlines and in its most generalized categories, as a totality and unity in terms of the Absolute.

We have seen already first how the secret of structure holds the key to the understanding of Guru philosophy, and how, secondly, the Absolute which underlies it is of the nature of a wonder. The reasoning man is not going to rest with the thought that Truth or Reality is merely a wonder. He wishes to critically analyse it further, and break it up, if possible, into its components, subtle or gross, to see how the various aspects hang together to give unity to Truth, without which it would be meaningless in life.

Logic, ratiocination, induction, deduction and the application of the various measures of validity to arrive at conclusions, are ways that have been open to speculation as ordinarily employed by philosophers. The negative method of first determining what aspects of realty are not valid is a more scientific approach than the inductive hypothetical empirical method of piecemeal experimentation based on experience. The a posteriori approach by itself cannot penetrate into the mystery presented by life. This is evident from the fact that the hand of God or Nature is still hidden to science. Even such simple questions as sex determination in nature elude scientific clarification.

The nature of the self and its destiny is not within the reach of usual commonsense reasoning. Intuition or dialectical methods when perfected as instruments of thought, as we can hope may be in the future, are alone adequate to penetrate behind the mystery that life presents in its totality of the subjective and the objective treated together. In such a wholesale and wholehearted philosophical approach, which is that of the Guru here, the confrontation of the most central of the problems of all philosophy, that of the paradox at the centre of life, is all important. The Guru questions its nature in the work before us, the *One Hundred Verses of Self-Instruction,* in the following pointed manner:

> As a mixture of what is the world and what is the real
> That which presents itself before us is a great iniquity indeed!
> This is what is indeterminate beyond grasp of word or mind;
> How can the course of right reason move within its domain? (Verse 94)

This verse as we notice, occurs at the end part of the series of the one hundred verses. This might give room to the question whether the paradox is still valid after all the speculation of the Guru philosophy. Such a conclusion would be both true and false at once, because as we see finally the paradox is transcended. All the preceding verses are meant only to lay the foundations for the final conclusion in fully unitive terms. The method, the theory of knowledge and the value notions, each proper to the finalized position, are clearly indicated in the last verses.

Almost all the verses contain elements of the duality at the base of the paradox, and almost all the verses or groups of them indicate too, how the paradox is to be transcended by the unitive vision given to the philosophy of the Guru. Both the a priori and the a posteriori go hand in hand in Guru philosophy. Axioms and everyday experience come together to coalesce and give certitude or conviction, as far as such is possible in such a domain of pure wisdom. Let us take another verse which suggests more clearly how the paradox is resolved in terms of a dynamic circulation of existence and essences at the core of Absolute Self-consciousness:

Knowledge in order to know itself
The Earth and other manifestations became.
In inverted manner thus, now mounting, now changing
over
Like a circulating fire-faggot, it keeps turning round.
(Verse 33)

The dynamism at the core of the unitive vision of the Absolute is thus sufficiently indicated quite early in the series, and after referring to the implications of the same vision stage by stage in a certain methodical order, the Guru refers to the same paradox again at a later stage, to confirm that a form of higher intuitive and dialectically perfected reasoning is needed to get behind appearances to the core of the reality that they hide. There are various contemplative, ethical, aesthetic, logical and commonsense findings or conclusions incorporated in the body of the work, which have each to be studied in their own context. Here we are concerned with the overall paradox involved in Guru philosophy in order to see how, in each of life's problems, the way he unitively resolves paradox is applied by him to arrive at the main guiding conclusions within the scope of contemplative Self-knowledge. It is the Self as the Absolute and as the Highest of human values that should act as the normative reference or regulative principle in all matters of import in life. Such a vision lies beyond the duality of paradox. Between tautology and full contradiction, elements of paradox can hide truth as a mere dilemma, enigma, doubt or incertitude. All these dual elements referred to under the head of maya in Vedanta, tend to indeterminism and confusion of right values. Transcending such an "either-or" or "neither-nor" situation in favour of both at once is the task that Guru philosophy boldly sets before itself.

Subtler Paradoxes Examined

The Paradoxes of Zeno and Parmenides (revalued in Plato's Socratic dialogues) have occupied a central place in

Western philosophical speculation from pre-Socratic days. The one and the many, the big and the small, the part and the whole, and the Self and the non-Self, have all been subjected to dialectical treatment, and various attempts have been made to resolve them unitively, sometimes statically, sometimes dynamically, whether in the context of being or becoming. Cosmic or General Self-Consciousness is the unified field or ground on which dialectical revaluations themselves have to live and move. The Hegelian thesis, antithesis and synthesis refers to a process of dialectical revaluation on the basis of the Absolute on which it depends. In Bergson's philosophy of the flux to which the *elan vital* is subject, we have the same pure dynamism which had been previously discussed in the Zeno paradoxes and which was given a new lease of life by him after it was nearly forgotten by rationalist speculators in Europe after Descartes. The two verses of the Guru that we quote below are highly reminiscent of the fluid reality that Bergson, based on Zeno's paradoxes, has postulated:

> At birth-time being there is none,
> And the one born at another instant cannot be;
> How ever does this exist? Death too is even likewise.
> All is but a flux and becoming of the mindstuff pure.
>
> Contraries like being and becoming, how can they
> Like creation, endurance and dissolution, in one place
>   co-exist?
> For these three to pass into, there is nothing either
> Thus viewed, the earth and other things are mere words
>   alone. (Verses 79 and 80)

From the time of Heraclitus, whose famous saying was that one cannot enter into the same river twice, this doctrine of flux has been central to many and varied schools of speculation both modern and ancient, Eastern or Western. The difference with Guru philosophy here is that the Guru is not limited to perceptualism, nominalism, conceptualism or even empiricism schematically understood, but gives due place to them all in a unified manner and even in a methodic order, based on a strict epistemology and axiology. Later chapters will perhaps amplify this and justify this claim further, as we proceed.

While we are on the subject of transcending paradox, let us refer to another verse in which the transcending of paradox is accomplished in as delicate a way as in the dialectics of the One and the Many in Plato, who refers to Zeno in his *Parmenides,* where the contention of Zeno is, "Being cannot be many, because if it were, it would be like and unlike at the same time, which is impossible."[5] Here the paradox is not transcended but only a sort of reduction *ad absurdum* or *ad impossibile* arrived at. The Guru, as seen in the verse below, tackling the same problem, merges the impossibility into the neutrality or unity of Absolute Consciousness, which is the rare "secret" clarified in his philosophy elsewhere:

> Of one thing there could be many, as in many objects
> One single meaning could reside: by such knowledge we can know
> Consciousness as comprising all, differencelessly without any remainder;
> This ultimate secret, however, is not given for all to know. (Verse 73)

Cubic crystals of common salt or an orchard of apple trees of the same variety and of the same age, when taken as examples, will easily be seen to justify the seeming puzzle of the above verse. What tends to give *specificity* overtly combines in meaning innately, and what tends to be *generic* in meaning, tends to be overtly distinguishable as separate entities. Word and meaning belong to the matrix of pure mind-stuff, where both the mechanistic and the vitalistic aspects coexist without conflict or contradiction. This is one of the ways in which the paradox that life presents is seen to be

5. *Plato's Dialogues* tr. B. Jowett, (Random House, New York), p. 88.

capable of being transcended in the philosophy of the Guru. This kind of approach which is most subtle, as the Guru himself warns, need not be the only way of transcending contradiction in life. At different levels of the total knowledge situation, different approaches, some factual, some demonstrable, some logical, intuitive or dialectical, may be seen to be employed, even within the limited range of the hundred verses before us.

Paradox is Transcended by Reconciling Opposites

If the Unified Field Theory of Einstein, where gravitational electromagnetic and geometrically understood space, or world ground with a common unified schematic basis, in which micro- and macro-cosmos participate, as it were, from opposite poles of the same homogeneous totality of a time-space continuum, has become familiar and acceptable to modern ears, the heights of Guru speculation here in the verses before us need not necessarily have a strange, outlandish or antique ring in our ears either. Its full implications have been explored and scrutinized in our book, *An Integrated Science of the Absolute.*

The daily newspaper before me today (22 March, 1965) gives, on its front page a telephotograph of how two Russians have accomplished the feat of stepping out into space 300 miles from the earth. These conquests might change the complexion of the war situation from one pole, but from the other pole too human speculation has to catch up with such outer victories with equally significant victories of the spirit of man that can attain equal depths more significant for peace.

Without going into their merits, we quote below two more verses from the Guru in order to show how his speculation at the beginning of the twentieth century echoes and complements those very generalizations to which human minds, more in touch with the physical world than the mental, have been able to attain. The sublime synthesis of opposites in transcending the paradox of life, even in the domain of concrete universals and not merely in the world of semantics, is reflected in these verses which we quote by way of conclusion, without comment. The serious student will himself scrutinize and derive out of them all their implications himself, when he comes to them in more orderly fashion in the text as developed by the Guru himself.

> The atom and the infinite, thus as being and non-being,
> Loom from either side; this experience too
> Of being as well as non-being, shall thereafter extinction
> gain,
> And devoid of any basis, shall forever cease to be!
> Within the glory of pure knowing the atom bereft of all
> parts, shall extinct become,
> And the infinite too, shall thereafter its own plenitude
> attain.
> Direct experience alone can reveal this boundless
> Stuff of Intelligence Pure, this silence-filled ocean of
> Immortal Bliss. (Verses 96 and 97)

4

Horizontal and Vertical Value Worlds

The term Absolute would be a mere word without any content significant to human life if we did not look at it from the side of the phenomenal world known to us through the senses, supported by our powers of inference, deductive or inductive.

Abstraction and generalization lead us, step by step, to categories of facts, truths or realities of value in life. The lesser values are inclusively covered by the more general and the more abstract. This is the way of speculation known as the *via negationis,* or *neti neti* of the Upanishads. When the limit of such a negative way is reached there is a residue still left in the thinking mind, which when understood globally and schematically gives us the first key to the understanding of Guru philosophy, as we have tried to explain in the first chapter.

Beyond this limit of the negative approach from the phenomenal to the noumenal, the Absolute cannot be appraised by the human understanding except as a vague wonder. The wonder or the mystery that the notion of the Absolute thus presents has been dealt with by us in the second chapter. We have further explained that when critically scrutinized at closer quarters, a paradox lurks at the very core of philosophical speculation in general. We have indicated how Guru philosophy faces frontally this problem of transcending paradox. So now the stage is set for us to consider another aspect, which will afford us further ease in following the broad outlines which speculation as understood in Guru philosophy adopts.

A strict methodology and epistemology are implied in Guru philosophy, which is for the keen student to follow up when examining the text of the hundred verses. He can also reasonably expect further clarification from our final work on the *Integrated Science of the Absolute* based on the Guru's *Darshana Mala* (Garland of Visions of the Absolute), which attempts a more scientifically systematic treatment.

Psychophysical Ambivalent Alternating Process

Like the heartbeat, psychophysical life presents an alternating ambivalent process between two poles. Guru philosophy as we are able to understand it gives full recognition to this process. We have traveled far and wide in our other expositions to lay bare the structure and dynamism of this process, and found that this same structural dynamism is seen implicitly or explicitly referred to in the efforts made by great minds from most ancient times the world over. Pairs of dialectically reciprocal counterparts are referred to wherever a subtle intuitive understanding is called for in solving the problems of life. In our chapter devoted to the problems of transcending paradoxes we have made it amply clear that there is always a dual aspect present in the basic field, on which paradoxes can thrive. This ground, whether cosmological, psychological or axiological, or all three of these combined, is lodged at the core of the Absolute.

The very fact that all words representing percepts or concepts can be arranged in two columns of synonyms or antonyms shows that there is an antinomian principle, a dichotomy or polarity, which enters into a kind of subtle mathematical intersection in which two elements participate as when *time* and *distance* participate in the notion of velocity. All phenomena are capable of graphical representation as correlated elements into which two antinomian factors enter. Matter and energy are so related that both cannot be measured together without indeterminism getting involved. The Self and the non-Self are also to be looked upon either as proper or improper elements, relation or relata, cause or effect, in respect of each other. Life is a process of such alternating ambivalent factors.

Mathematical Factors

Modern algebra and geometry have many common axioms, on the basis of which sums and products of mathematical elements with the laws of commutation, association and distribution obey or answer to fundamental axioms accepted by mathematicians. There is a modern branch of the "algebra of geometry" wherein what are called *proper* and *improper* elements enter and reveal the nature of pure space or number.

Such a new mathematical treatment of algebra and geometry together is a branch of the science which has not yet been fully explored. However great its promise, we have to remember that mathematics becomes real only to the extent that its possible applications are found to be significant in the context of human experience or solve problems in life. New conventions based on old axioms and laws of mathematics, such as referred to above, are permissible in respect of both algebra and geometry. These two branches can be made to come together to interpret for us the nature of pure space or pure number. Complex numbers as well as pure space, subjected to strict though arbitrary treatments based on axioms or laws, can yield us frames of reference to be expressed metalinguistically or protolinguistically, i.e., algebraically or geometrically. In order to show that the implications of the new branch of the "geometry of algebra" has arrived very close to the next step which will bring it to what we want to represent here, it might be helpful for the student to read the following extract translated from the book *Les Nombres et les Espaces* (Numbers and Spaces) by G. Verriest[1] even if we do not stop here to explain the full implications of the extract:

1. Collection Armand Colin, (Paris), pp. 180-81, (our translation).

> In order to give in all possible cases a signification for the sum and product of two elementals, they have introduced two new elementals; *elemental zero V* (or absence of points, lines or planes) or *universal element U* (or the totality of these elements, that is to say, space). By definition the element zero V is contained in all elements and it is conventional that it has a negative number-1 of dimensions: In the same way the *universal element U,* contains all elements, and three dimensions. These two new elements are called *improper elements,* the others are the *proper elements.* Let us suppose now that A and B represent for example two lines which do not meet in space; we would have A + B = U and A · B = V, and we can see that the sum and the product of any two elements represent always an element which would be either proper or improper.

Dichotomy is thus seen between proper and improper elements in the science of the algebra of geometry dealing with numbers and spaces. It is not difficult to see that the abstractions of space and number implied in this kind of geometry of algebra or vice versa, set limits of the improper elements V and U, the latter being more philosophical than physical, as when we say with W. de Sitters that there is pure motion in the cosmology of the universe without matter, or with Einstein that there is primacy for matter in the physical world without motion. The time-space-continuum and the Unified Field Theory have some sort of mathematical structure or scheme which is difficult to be visually represented, but which depends on an algebraic abstract language. Philosophers need not give primacy to either matter or motion, and with the attitude of neutral monism, could make an effort to build up, for their own purposes of valid or correct speculation, a mathematical frame of reference that would help in guiding thought, especially in the metaphysical rather than in the merely physical aspect of the universe.

The freedom for a correct speculator to invent if needed such a frame of reference for the use of the philosophy of science is recognized by two senior mathematicians and scientists of the eminence of O.G. Sutton F.R.S. and Albert Einstein himself. That they envisaged such a frame of reference and even encouraged it may be gathered from the following extracts from each of them respectively. Sutton writes:

> Mathematicians are no respecters of tradition; but incorrigible heretics who are prepared to change their ground and invent new systems of thought as soon as the old is seriously challenged. It must not be thought that this breaking of rules always leads to significant advances. To build a geometry on a new set of axioms demands skill but not necessarily genius. The chances are, however, that any such geometry will excite little interest. The true touch of genius appears only when the new algebra or geometry opens up fresh fields of thought and this is a very rare event.[2]

On the need for not discouraging bold speculation in the matter of bridging the gulf between observed facts and axiomatic certitudes, Einstein says:

> Here too the *observed fact is undoubtedly the supreme arbiter;* but it cannot pronounce sentence until the wide chasm separating the axioms from their verifiable consequences has been bridged by much intense hard thinking. The theorist has to set about his Herculean task in the clear consciousness that his efforts may only be destined to deal the death blow to his theory. The theorist who undertakes such a labour should not be carped as 'fanciful', on the contrary he should be encouraged to give free rein to his fancy, for there is no other way to the goal. His is no idle day-dreaming, but a

---

2. Sir O.G. Sutton, *Mathematics in Action*, (Bell, London, 1958), p. 36.

> search for the logically simplest possibilities and their consequences.[3]

The Unified Field Theory of Einstein was released to the world only in February 1950, but the freedom with which he was approaching that task is already reflected in the above citation of about 1934. That the logic of modern mathematics is not rigidly fixed is amply evident from these citations. Mathematicians like Sutton and scientists like Einstein would welcome any bold attempt to integrate all thought elements on the same lines as in the Unified Field Theory. If we now attempt below a simple scheme which respects primary axioms with some ingenuity and fancifulness, which is not only allowed but even encouraged by these authorities, in order to give to the otherwise wild speculation that often tends to be lost in verbosity at least some tangible supporting points of a visible rather than a merely intelligible order, as when the geometry of algebra is kept in mind, we hope there should not be any reason for us to be blamed.

A Tensorial Psychology and Cosmology

Scalar and vectorial spaces as represented in geometrical figures are particular instances (the former more so than the latter) of another kind of geometrical space called tensorial, in which it is easier to represent cosmological models or psychological stresses and strains which require more than three numbers for their specification. As the present writer is not an expert mathematician himself, at this stage of our discussion he proposes to be guided in mathematical questions by finding support in the writings of modern experts. It might therefore be permissible here to quote from Sutton as before:

> There exist certain important quantities such as stress in an elastic body which require more than three numbers for their specification. To deal with these quantities mathematicians have devised a very general

3. *The Philosophers of Science,* Pocket Book Inc., (New York, U.S.A), p. 479.

> algebra of tensors in which scalars and vectors appear as special cases. Tensor algebra is of prime importance in the development of world models of cosmology.[4]

The same authority further quotes Whittaker and adds:

> It also appears that one such algebra is peculiarly fitted to deal with another feature of quantum mechanics, that of indefiniteness or imperfect description, a fact which Whittaker has called 'one of the most remarkable discoveries of the present century'.[5]

There is also a modern branch of psychology which uses vectorial mathematical language, which could be improved on the same lines into tensorial terms to represent stresses and strains of a psychological order.

These significant advances in the language of modern mathematics as applied to quantum mechanics, cosmology, or psychology, are fully suggestive of great possibilities in the future even in the domain of a scientifically revised philosophical speculation. One more bold step forward in the same direction as these developments, might bring us to a common structural frame of reference in which the dynamics of life as a process need not be sacrificed but included with all its variations. The simplest desiderata for such a frame, common to all aspects of absolute speculation, are vertical and horizontal axes of reference to correlate any two antinomian elements of any philosophy whatsoever, including theology as a particular instance of it. Cosmology, psychology and theology could thereby be combined under one "unitive frame of reference."

The Space within the Heart of the Upanishads and its Structural Implications

A running appraisal of our position in respect to a process in a unitive frame of reference is called for here after all our

4. Sutton, *op. cit.*, p. 33.

5. Ibid. p. 33.

elaborations of different aspects of this problem elsewhere in our writings.

(1) Minkowski's contribution of a time-space continuum implies a homogeneity of spatial and temporal dimensions which is in essence the same as the principle of *samanadhikaranatva* (homogeneity as between mind and matter), as recognized also in the doctrine of neutral monism as well as in Vedanta.

(2) The limits that the modern algebra of geometry has fixed for the improper elements spoken of above as *V* and *U*, refers to a polarity or antinomian ambivalence at the core of Existence, Subsistence and Value. These improper elements could be referred to as belonging to a vertical axis in the domain of the pure noumenal aspect as its limiting poles. In Vedantic parlance we know it as the fourth or the *turiya* limb of the Absolute Self. It is sometimes referred to in the Upanishads figuratively as the Supreme Person entered into the cavity of the heart and hypostatically located sometimes also in the orb of the Sun.

(3) Ambivalence as known in biology is like the double aspect principle, and Ramanuja's Vedanta recognizes this more explicitly than Shankara's, where too it is found implicitly in various parts of his comments. The name in Sanskrit for this is *ubhaya-linga-adhikarana* (the section referring to the double aspect).

(4) The horizontal axis consists of all workaday values and interests in ordinary life of a practical nature, and is called *vyavaharika,* as opposed to the vertical world of values called *paramarthika*. We shall be quoting below a verse from the Guru, 81, which explicitly defines these two value references under *bhokta* (enjoyer) and *bhogya* (enjoyed).

(5) Existence, Subsistence and Value are three levels of the pure vertical reference of significant values in life. The immanent and the transcendent, the ontological, the propositional (or syllogistic), and the teleological worlds of value, have to find their places in a series both ascending

and descending at once, in the total Absolute which has the limits represented by the *improper* elements of *V* and *U* as in the geometry of algebra above. Einstein's world is slightly prejudiced in favour of a world in which matter has primacy over motion, but W. de Sitter's version gives motion primacy over matter. These two versions put together unitively will give the two limits, one concrete universal and the other abstract universal, between which all possibilities of manipulations with relation-relata causes and effects or all such elements in the thinking mind, could be inclusively comprised. All thought-values must lie either in the vertical or the horizontal reference. The former is referred to as the domain of the *kshetrajna* and the latter as the *kshetra* in the Bhagavad Gita. The Guru philosophy here will be seen to imply the same broad divisions or references.

(6) A cyclic process of progressive becoming, whether as ascent or descent in the scale of spiritual values, is implied in the notion of *samsara chakra* (the wheel of becoming) and the *pravartitam chakram* (cyclic dynamism of becoming) as in the Gita, III,14. Microcosmic cycles in orbits and alternations are found in particle physics and in quantum mechanics. Mutations in life cycles and other systolic and diastolic phases in chains of behaviour or of biological synergisms and functionings are all known. No less an authority than Erwin Schrodinger in his *What is Life?* has given recognition to this common structure underlying mutations in life and quantum pulsations in physics.

(7) When two persons are referred to, as in many Upanishadic contexts, as being in the right eye and in the orb of the Sun, we have to think of two tensorial models with a one-to-one correspondence between them, hierophantically understood.

Many other instances could be cited where a unitive, schematic, selective and structural frame of reference can be arrived at by the exercise of a certain intuitive or imaginative method which has already become acceptable and in full use in science, by way of extending or extrapolating the finds of modern higher mathematics. We have elsewhere suggested that the colour solid itself could give us the basic model for integrating all thought factors in a sort of tensorial continuum where all possible colours differing in tint, brilliance, saturation or shade could be specified by three or four symbols representing dimensions. A more detailed description of this idea will be found in chapter 6.

Such a colour solid is actually in use with international colour dealers, where the vernacular for each colour is replaced by indices of specification. This solid has a vertical axis grading from black to white with a core which is grey. All colours of the spectrum can be represented on a double cone with their apexes as poles and their bases juxtaposed. As the colour variety range is not unlike the range of other sensations or even the shades of thought which underlie them, such a way of correlating thought elements would not be merely fanciful. Whether valid or not, one thing in favour of such a schematic model is that is would help to regulate speculation and keep it within recognizable limits.

An Alternative Process in the Guru's Verses

The following verses from the Guru illustrate the possibilities of a schematic reference of the kind outlined here, which is evidently respected in the Guru's writings. The two ambivalent aspects are contrasted by the Guru in terms of the sense of duration as between pure and practical time, as follows:

> Ten-thousand years do a moment make to those favoured ones
> Suckled in the milk of the pure transcendent; when knowledge
> Is within the scope of relative immanent nature,
> Half-a-second would seem a thousand years long.
>
> (Verse 15)

The intersection of the double aspect is quite evident here.

Again, the same two aspects are brought together in a vertico-horizontal correlation:

> From awareness the "I"-sense first emerged,
> Comes then with it "this-ness", as a counterpart beside;
> Like twin branches these overcover entirely
> Hiding the whole of the *Maya* tree. (Verse 51)

The double aspect of the ambivalent factor is clear here.

The same ambivalence is again stated revealing its fully living process of alternation as follows:

> As the ego-sense enters into the snake-rope forms
> Now as knowledge, now as a limbed agent in alternating duality.
> It becomes pure now and then again profane,
> Thus should he understand, the intuitive man.
> (Verse 68)

Sacredness and profanity could alternate in the consciousness of the same contemplative when the ambivalent process asserts itself. Restated in terms of action, which is negative, and knowledge, its own dialectical counterpart, we have again:

> Now there is action, which is nescience, and again
> There is pure knowledge, which is science;
> Ordained by *maya* though these stay divided thus,
> The meta-dual attitude, the unitive *turiya* yields,
> (Verse 72)

Nature in which man's destiny is placed has a choice between two cross-purposed worlds, which enter his life-interests alternately as follows:

> Nature dividing one time as the enjoyer
> As everything outside, immanent or transcendent in glory looms,
> At another time again, by 'this-ness' expanded
> It spreads out as the enjoyable universe.
> (Verse 81)

The figure of eight progression within the ambivalent poles is under reference more evidently in the following:

> Breaking up, staying on, or rising again after a change over
> To continue, such is the course of the bodily nature here;
> Watchful of all the three from its position ultimate
> Is the one cleftless Self that free from all change remains.
> (Verse 88)

In other verses of the series this duality of reference is more unitively brought together, as in the analogy of sparks of fire which are not different from the fire itself. The underlying scheme, however, is not affected by the change in analogy.

> As out of knowledge, sparks of fire innumerable arise
> Asserting the being of non-being so as to make the world emerge.
> Know that outside of knowledge not a thing exists;
> Such knowing unitive awareness yields. (Verse 89)

Subtler analogies in which the duality between the twin aspects is further reduced are found in other verses of the series. An analogy rich and graphic in suggestive imagery of the dual process is contained in this verse:

> As with a well into which measureless sand is wafted
> By successive gusts, tier on tier, so too
> Exposed to the waftings of untruth's hierarchy,
> The inner Self, inwardly multitudinous forms it gains.
> (Verse 76)

The categorical finality with which the Guru brings strictly under the two references of the Absolute and the relative, the infinite and the finite, represented by the vertical and the horizontal references as understood here in mathematical language, all relations and relata, causes and effects, giving rise to forms, entities and elements known through names, without anything being left over as a remainder, is stated in the following verse, which we quote here by way of concluding this section:

> One that is beyond all count and the ordinary—
> Besides these two what is of other form
> In memory, in sleep nor in any city on high
> Could such have any existence, indeed! (Verse 67)

In other words, the totality of Absolute Reality is comprised completely within these two references, the vertical and the horizontal.

5

The Self and Non-Self in Spiritual Progress

The Self and the non-Self can be treated as dialectical counterparts and both placed in one unitive context of the Absolute. Fichte, among Western philosophers, viewed these in such a perspective, although the dialectical implications of his methodology and epistemology were not quite clear.

In Vedanta it is normal to speak of *atma* (Self) and *anatma* (non-Self) as *pratiyogis* (counterparts) with an intimate bipolar relation (*samavaya*) between them, and not merely a contiguous relationship (*samyoga*). These two can be looked upon as fitting into a one-to-one relationship in tensorial space, one having its locus here and the other having it in some hypostatic value-world beyond or elsewhere, such as in the orb of the sacred Sun known to the Vedas.

The non-Self can be thought of in a more workaday sense as fitting into a horizontal world of practical values, while the purer Self with its dialectical counterparts, one ontological here and the other of a teleological or transcendental order elsewhere in the beyond or above or the ultimate or infinity, referring to vertical value worlds, could represent all values possible for the Self to be affiliated to in contemplative life. We have already explained and justified the use of these references in previous studies.

The Self can be thought of as a big fish swimming in a stream, almost with the current and in its direction, and alternately avoiding the two banks, if we may take an analogy dear to the Brihadaranyaka Upanishad. The coastal sides represent its limits in the horizontal axis of reference while itself and its almost motionless motion would represent the Self, whether thought of as a sphere, ellipse or the tractrix that mathematicians like Lobachewsky have suggested for the structure of space tensorially understood and independent of size.

The Upanishads often speak of a person the size of a thumb entered into the cavity of the heart, who has his counterpart in the Sun. There is a subtle dialectical equation of these into unitive terms of thesis, antithesis and synthesis. The Self and non-Self have to be fitted into a schematic structure before what we should understand as the purpose of all such scriptures can be fulfilled or justified. Such is the scope of this chapter.

The Self Placed in Its Axiological Context

From the time of early Buddhism the one controversy that has raged in the polemical wars in the domain of Indian speculation has been over the existence of a soul or Self, called the *atman*. Early Buddhism pronounced its verdict clearly against any such substance or entity and distinguished itself from later Buddhist schools by this one feature, referred to by scholars as the *anatmavada* (the doctrine of the denial of the Self). Brahmanism and Buddhism were ranged in opposite camps based on this rivalry or contention.

Later modifications in the three main schools, each of about five hundred years duration, from the time of Ashoka to the Gupta period in Indian history, sometimes turned the tables against the position of the first five hundred years, and having done so twice over, the present position of Buddhists in this matter is a delicate balance between what is generally referred to as the *shunya-vada* (doctrine of nothingness) and the *vijnanavada* (doctrine of mind-stuff).

This latter is of the order of mere simple events like waves in consciousness understood as a flux or of moments. There are many sub-varieties even as between these two positions according to Vasubandhu, Asanga, Dignaga and Dharmakirti. These polemical battles involving subtleties, like those which raged before the age of enlightenment in the history of European thought, remain still, in our time, on a basis of thin and airy speculation. It is hard to determine what kind of content remained as a residue either in Buddhism or in Shankara's version of Vedanta, after all that was extraneous to final or Absolute Reality was subtracted from the given total in consciousness.

Logic of the subtlest kind and yogic intuition from the other pole, as it were, of the knowledge situation have to give us the understanding of the content of Absolute Truth through their combined cooperation or harmonized effort. In the matter of understanding the Self in relation to its counterpart of the non-Self, as properly belonging to its general context of value, so that we can get a correct perspective and focus our attention on what remains after all extraneous factors have been eliminated, the Guru philosophy here adopts three distinct measures:

Firstly, it devises a method of experimentation or regulation under selected conditions of common experience, to throw into proper relief the nature of the Self explicitly, and thereby that of the non-Self also, necessarily though only implicitly. Secondly, it undertakes to lay bare the axiological structure of the non-Self aspect or the environment of the Self, so as to enable us to distinguish the stages of spiritual or contemplative progress in the world of interests or values in which life hereunder is cast. And thirdly, it employs the semantic world of meaning of meanings so as to bring to light the progress of the Self through value aspects, both external and internal treated together, so that a student endowed with some intuition can visualize for himself the various value worlds or stages through which the Self has to pass before it comes to realize itself in terms of full Self-knowledge or Wisdom, as marking the point of culmination of the process of emancipation or salvation.

While these sections will be separately touched upon below, with relevant citations from the hundred verses before us, it is for the interested students also to note that the implications of these three topics, with justifications where necessary, overlap other verses in the series. Without such mutual presuppositions this idea of progress to the goal of all Self-contemplation must remain partial or otherwise truncated in total consistency or unity. The total vision alone can satisfy scientific curiosity. There is a vertical axis of reference for all spiritual progress, which consists of a dialectical descent or ascent in a scale of values, some positive and others negative, and also a horizontal axiological reference which intersects or cuts across its grain. Subtle indications or implications herein will have to be recognized by the student himself as he proceeds.

The Guru's Method of Laying Bare the Content of the Self

Experiments, examples, analogies, and even common parlance supporting common sense are pressed into the service of speculation by the Guru, whether called scientific, philosophical or both. The best experiment conducted under the strictest of selected or regulated conditions still has only a certitude of a hypothetical and inductive status. Theories which are based on degrees of "expectation" or guesswork are tentatively formulated as laws, often only to be superseded by better formulated laws of greater abstraction and generality and of more universal applicability in a wider field.

Such is the course of certitude in speculation through the history of thought anywhere in the world. For the commonsense example of an event as simple as the falling of an apple, which was Newton's basis for the formulation of the Universal Theory of Gravitation, no laboratory is needed. The experiment and the familiar example come to have a similar value in making the law valid. Analogies, parables, fables or other graphic representations serve the same purpose of grounding the hypothetical constructions of scientific or philosophical speculations more firmly in validity. If all these help in the degree of certitude, why not make use of imaginary experiments which tally with common sense or commonly known experience or facts? This question would be but legitimate, and it is therefore quite in order that the Guru employs a "supposed" experimental situation in which one human consciousness controls the other, when both are fitted into a darkroom situation as seen below, which is to ensure a certain degree of subjectivism necessary for the experiment to give the requisite certitude. We shall see at the end of this section how the Guru uses semantics also with advantage to lay bare the structure or dynamism of the Self.

Each word of the precise experimental situation, as conceived by the Guru in the following verses, is important to note. The translation has therefore intentionally erred on the side of literalness rather than on the side of the exigencies of English usage or style, so that the keen student may not miss the full import and purpose behind them.

When two persons exchange meaningful words in a bipolar situation in which the self of the one is the non-self of the other, and are unitively included in a trans-subjective and inter-physical sense, such as that of the *schema moteur* that Bergson speaks of, we have an experimental situation supposed that is most suited to examine the content of the Self. What one *says* and what the other *hears* are both meant to help certitude in respect of the Self, which stands neutral, as it were, between the subject and the object. The darkroom would eliminate the visible aspects, which interfere with pure contemplation, for the purposes of laying bare the content of the Self. We read:

> "Who is sitting in the dark? speak," says one,
> Whereupon the other, intent himself to know likewise,
> On hearing the first, he asks; "Who may you even be?"

For both of these the word of response is one alone.
(Verse 10)

The repeated 'I,I' contemplated from within
Is not many, but one; divergent egoity,
Being multiple, in the totality of such
The Self-substance too, continuity assumes.
(Verse 11)

With skin and bone and refuse and many an inner factor of evil end
Lo, wielding these, one ego looms; This which passes
Is the other; That greater Self which grows to perfection
O, grant the boon, that it may not the ego swell!
(Verse 12)

The experimental situation of an order in which both the inter-physical and the trans-subjective sensory motor factors come into interplay on a basis of parity, bipolarity or one-to-one correspondence, is sufficiently real in the first verse above. Both the persons involved ask questions with an earnest desire to know. The replies meet unitively on a ground neutral to both persons involved, in the common situation.

In the second verse the content of the common response on the part of the two concerned together is further analysed into its vertical and horizontal implications. The horizontal is multiple and the vertical is unitive in status. A warning is however sounded against the mistaking of mere megalomaniac egoism for the pure realization of one's Self.

In the third verse the vertico-horizontal implications within the structure laid bare in mathematical terms in the second verse are further made explicit so as to bring out factors that help or hinder contemplative life.

The Self as Seen within the Context of its Axiological Counterparts

When the same structure is extended beyond the limits of the psychophysical range within which tendencies operate, we reach all the numerous objects of interest, some such as colour given to the senses, and others given to deeper-seated instinctive dispositions, like sex, hunger, etc., which make the Self reach out to the external zone where interests can meet their corresponding objects of satisfaction. Hunger meets food, sex meets the mate, the eye meets light, the ear meets sound, etc. Favourite ideologies too, cluster together into systems of value dear to each person, here or hereafter. These axiological clusters that belong together, sometimes called religion or at other times associated more closely with tribal or atavistic memory factors, tending to be orthodoxies, establish a bipolarity between the Self as understood above and its object of intentions or interests.

All men seek happiness always in this way. A martyr to a religion or a martyr to science are both possible because of the full bipolarity of interest factors involved, as between such value systems on the one side and the Self, equated with them axiologically, on the other. This kind of bipolar affiliation can sometimes bind two lovers and make them enter into a suicide pact. From all these familiar instances, it should be gathered, as the verse below clearly points out, that there is a bipolar affiliation possible sometimes with horizontal values of the "enjoyable" world by the "enjoyer" which is the Self. The "enjoyer" as the Self fits into the vertical reference axis, while the "enjoyable" world of interests spreads out in multiplicity in space as the axis we have distinguished as horizontal. (Refer for this correlation to Verse 81, which we have cited in the previous chapter.) The concerned verse here is:

> The dweller within the body, from its own status in pure being
> In respect of each possible thing, treats all
> As "that is mine" or "this is mine" transcending bodily sense;
> All are in reality realized when we think of what this means. (Verse 48)

In other words, all persons in ordinary life, when they say that a certain object of interest is their own, unconsciously reveal that the pure substance of which the Self consists is capable of being related in bipolar parity of status with items of interest pertaining to the non-Self pole of the total situation implied in spiritual life. As such a bipolar link would mean a certain homogeneity or transparency between the Self and the non-Self poles represented in the situation, one has, in principle, the right to infer that the Self and the non-Self aspects have merged into unity, which is the essence of the state of Self-realization.

The Guru avers here that a rare stage of spiritual Self-realization is thus found to be familiarly present in common life around us, as when a mother will risk her own safety for the sake of the child in danger. Suicide pacts exemplify the same truth as we have already mentioned. The same lesson is intended by many of the Greek tragedies. If we add that higher and higher bipolar interests which bind the Self with the non-Self can be imagined, some having proportionately more horizontal values implied in them than others, and which can rise vertically to the limits of purity in the Absolute itself with fully conscious affiliation to absolutist values, then the modus of spiritual progress will be fully outlined.

Whether such a unitive goal is attained in principle only or whether it is real in the workaday sense is itself a question which in principle should not arise. On final analysis such a doubt would negate itself by the very principle that is being asserted here. It would be like a man asking for the time of the first train in the morning and then, having got the answer, asking if by any chance there is an earlier one. The first answer must cover the second.

The Axiological Field of Interests Analysed

There are seven verses, from 36 to 42, which belong together as pertaining to the semantic analysis of thought processes within the consciousness of the Self when related unitively and homogeneously to the non-Self. These could be subjected to analysis through the semantic world of meanings or the "meaning of meanings," the possibilities of which and its employment in Vedanta by Shankara and the Purva Mimamsakas have already been discussed by us in *Vedanta Revalued and Restated.*

Just as the elements of the algebra of geometry are divided into "proper" and "improper" elements, and all primary mathematical operations refer only to one or the other of these, as we explained in the previous chapter, all propositions in the world of interested or significant discourse in life can refer only to the worlds either of the "pure" or the "practical," which correspond to the improper or proper references respectively in the language of modern graphical mathematics where symbols and figures coalesce. The improper element here is the vertical reference and the proper the horizontal.

Verses 36 and 37 quoted below arrive at a similar generalization in respect of all possible predications, propositions or postulates. Causes and effects, relations and relata, quantitative and qualitative aspects, are all covered or meant to be covered, as so many particular instances of sets or classes or categories by the terms "same" and "other" (*sama* and *anya*) as used by the Guru and brought together into the same unified field of discourse or knowledge situation in these two verses. This is done just in the same way as time and space dimensions are brought under the same unified field in Einsteinian mathematical physics. The normalized Absolute of the wisdom context can be thought of in the same way as mathematicians abstract and generalize variables or elements, proper or improper, to cover all contingencies, necessities, probabilities or possibilities.

In the first of the seven verses the pure epistemological aspect is covered. Then, taking two familiar predications known to the world of discourse in common human life, the Guru establishes a scheme of semantic correlation. Definitions and striking examples follow. Within the scope of these seven verses the Guru accomplishes at one stroke what otherwise would have covered verbose volumes. The exposition is crystal clear and would do credit to the best of academically trained professors that I have known. We read:

> The powers of understanding are many; all of them under two sets
> Such as the "same" and the "other" inclusively can be brought;
> Merging into that form of "other-sameness" of these,
> To clarity of vision one should awake. (Verse 36)

> To subdue, even somewhat, the obduracy of the "other"
> Is hard indeed without understanding's limitless power;
> Even by such should one gain mastery over it and thus attain
> Close access to Her who is discrimination's anti-sensuous one. (Verse 37)

These verses are clothed in the language of contemplation and at the end of the second verse there is clear indication of the way of contemplation. The two aspects named, referring to the vertical "same" (*sama*) and the horizontal "other" (*anya*), are further elaborated and precisely defined with reference to familiar semantic examples as follows:

> What appraises manifold variety, the "other" that is;
> And the "same" is whatever unitively shines on:
> Thus grasping the situation above, into that state
> Which yields sameness, melt and mix and erect sit.
> (Verse 38)

Even here, a direction for the contemplative aspirant to follow in his meditations is indicated. The masterly semantic analysis is clarified more elaborately as follows:

> Following up further the said powers, a further bifurcation there is,
> One of these is an attribute of the "same" while the other

> Qualifies the harsh "other" that never detachment gains;
> Thus making two kinds of each of these. (Verse 39)

The recognition of the two axes of reference in these verses is not difficult at all to see. The dynamism by which both these axes come to have, on their plus sides, their own respective specific aspects added on, as it were, as when zero is added on to a number to enhance its value, is indicated in the next verse as follows:

> On to the "same" as on to the "other" there constantly
> alight
> Their respective specifying factors; although not
> proportionate,
> Through the spinning phase of these two in all
> All predications whatsoever there are do come to be.
> (Verse 40)

Not satisfied with the definitions of the two axes and indicating their possible respective specificatory factors, the Guru goes on in the next two verses to give concrete examples from the context of semantics. Common sense sanctions the truth of well-known expressions or vice versa, just the same as experiments or experience can support conviction. Untenable or unsound thought cannot endure through generations if it is not based on support even from language, and conversely, what language has long and generally sanctioned can be relied on to give validity to otherwise subtle realities, as the Purva Mimamsakas and Shankara in his commentaries have largely relied upon.

The Guru takes full advantage of this recognized method. Pure semiosis takes place in the vertical axis as in the sentence "This is knowledge," and practical and pragmatic meanings run between the plus and minus limits of the horizontal axis where there is a multiplicity of possible discrete interests spread out in the world of the "enjoyable." The rest of the implications of these two verses are sufficiently clear when they are read side by side with our comments on them in *One Hundred Verses of Self-Instruction.*

> In "This is a pot" the initial "this" is the harsh
> While the "pot" is what makes its specific attribute;
> For the mind with its myriad Indra magic to come,
> Understand that "this" is the basis of functioning.
> (Verse 41)

> In "This is knowledge" the initial "this" is the "same"
> While its specifying factor is the cognitive consciousness;
> For the mind and all else to be effaced for the good path
> to gain,
> "This" it is that one should contemplate. (Verse 42)

The last "this" can be seen to refer to the bottom of the vertical axis in which pure contemplative values live and move and, although negative in status like the square root of minus one in geometrical algebra, it is the richest of all poles or zones in consciousness, generally and abstractly understood. If any aspect of these discussions, which are so subtle, is still unclear, further reading of the comments in *One Hundred Verses of Self-Instruction* in the light of the mathematical structure of correlation we have developed, stage by stage in these pages, may be profitably relied upon by the serious student.

6

The Universe of Contemplative Discourse

"The word was with God and the word was God" is the way in which the central normative notion of the Absolute is referred to in the Biblical context in terms of the Universe of Discourse. The Verb, the *Logos* or the Word and its meaning thought of together semantically, marks the mathematical core of the notion of the Absolute.

The Guru's own prayer recognizes this verity when it says that, "The word we utter is even Thee," (*Daiva Dashakam,* Verse 7). The Mandukya Upanishad too gives the word *AUM* the supreme position of representing the Absolute completely without any remainder. That the notion of the Absolute and the Universe of Discourse are related to each other directly is thus a fully recognized secret in the Hebrew, Greek, Hindu and Guru contexts, all of which we are concerned with here.

Shankara's philosophical speculations also lean largely on the semantic polyvalence of words, as we have already examined elsewhere in more than one context.[1] A mathematically understandable schematic universe where thoughts and their linguistic expression overlap or coincide, as when names and forms converge when we say "rose" and visualize it, is at the core of the notion of the Absolute, when everything gross or inert and in reality extraneous to the Absolute, compromising or hiding it through degrees of opacity or ignorance, is shorn from its pure, luminous and

1. Cf. Chapters IV and V of *Vedanta Revalued and Restated.*

transparent nature. The veil can be thickly or thinly laid on but it is the degree of veiling that makes for all the gradations of apparent manifestation which are, in fact, extraneous to the notion of the Absolute as such.

The Unified Field Theory of Einstein also reduces all the elements, categories or factors of reality, whether material or mental, to one homogeneous space-time continuum. This matrix is neither mental nor material but conforms to the requirements of a neutral monism that has become acceptable even to positivists or empiricists of the present day, not to speak of pragmatists like William James. The Universe of Contemplative Discourse is only a similar attempt to find a basic ground for all significant thoughts or words.

One-Many, Part-Whole, Big-Small Are All Extraneous

The world of mechanistic discourse should first be distinguished from that of contemplative discourse. The latter is schematic, selective and subjective, and excludes all quantitative attributes belonging to the horizontal mechanistic world of brute events and inert things that are actual, gross, raw material, before any abstraction or generalization of mathematical or philosophical thinking has been applied to them. Commercial competitive values of the busy life of towns or shipyards where cranes load and unload merchandise are farthest removed from the calm contemplative world where peace is the keyword.

These aspects do exist within the scheme of the Self as the Absolute; only they do not loom into rival values of conflict or strife between man and man. Sheer necessities might reduce even a contemplative to a compromise, more or less, with the same mechanistic world in which all men are obliged by absolute necessity to live. It is the aim of the contemplative to orient his spirit in the direction of pure verticalized values where conflicts tend to become minimized till they are finally absorbed and abolished by the highest or most crowning and all inclusive of human values, which is the Wisdom of the Absolute.

To distinguish these horizontal values in life and treat them as of secondary importance thus is the only task left for the contemplative. When all that is extraneous has been detracted from the universe of discourse in general we get a residual pure world of Contemplative Discourse where thoughts can freely live and move. The possibilities of thought are thus endless in gradation or variety. All semiotics, syntactics and pragmatics of language have in this universe a possibility to live in an inner ordered fashion. The various words in the dictionary find place either in the conceptual or the perceptual half of this universe, the more positive being conceptual in status. Such a pure mathematical space, free from quantitative implications, comes nearest to the tensorial space known to modern mathematics.

When we find references to the space in the cavity of the heart or in the orb of the Sun in the Upanishads, we have to think in terms of this kind of space, which is neither big nor small, one nor many, and neither part nor whole. Cartesian analytical geometry has a notion of space, and the vectorial space that is now known to the geometry of algebra is a further abstraction and generalization of it. If we proceed in the same direction of generalization and abstraction so as to afford a frame of reference or unified field for quantum mechanics or particle physics, or even to accommodate the general or the limited theories of Einstein, we come to a tensorially conceived space. If this idea is further purified for contemplative purposes, we come to a structure of space which belongs to the Universe of Discourse in the contemplation of the Absolute. As man is the measure of all things, this space is sometimes referred to in the Upanishads as having a size proportionate to the thumb of each man (*angusthamatra*).

Percepts and Concepts Meet from Opposite Poles in the Universe of Discourse

Let us now think of a colour-solid along the lines we have elaborated in our writings. The achromatic colours could be located in a vertical axis, the top plus pole representing the fully brilliant white or lesser tints, while the bottom is its opposite, grading to the shade of fully dark black. The gray occupies the centre of the solid consisting of two cones stuck together on their bases. On the surface of the cones we can think of all shades or tints of different saturation or brilliance graded upwards, spiraling centrally, peripherally or downward through each of the specific areas giving room to each possible colour in graded fashion, and merging between the colours of the spectrum at the peripheral circumference of the bases.

Now percepts, being related to the senses stimulated by actual objects seen or otherwise sensed, would refer to the lower cone, and all possible shades would be representable there. The lighter tints could be represented on the top cone in a similar spiral succession, grading finally into the brilliance of the white apex of the cone. Where the horizontal surfaces of the bases of the two cones juxtaposed cuts the vertical line joining the two apexes of the cones, we can imagine a point of origin where the grey colour is to be located. Being achromatic it has no status as a surface but only an inner quality like pure thought or apperception, while the chromatic colours like red or green are more actual or practical in their status in the structure, being also most peripherally removed from the origin marked by the grey point at the core of the total structural situation.

Now in order to give definiteness of structure to the Universe of Contemplative Discourse, we should think of the white point or apex of the top cone as representing the conceptual aspect of thought, while the perceptual is the corresponding point at the bottom of the dark cone. Concepts as well as percepts grade into mere names or pure intuitions of actuality, respectively in the plus and minus sides of the total situation. The Universe of Discourse thus gets a structural schematic, subjective and selected frame of reference, which has its existence in the core of the normative notion of the Absolute. The justifications for all these statements have been made already in our allied writings elsewhere.

From the neutral point of origin or reference we can imagine innumerable specificatory rays of cognition as emanating from the centre of what we can think of as the core of the human power of understanding, just in the same way as we can visualize rays from a central Sun, whether we should think of such a Sun within us or without us, schematically, nominally or both. This distinction of inside and outside should not arise in respect of pure consciousness strictly speaking, although we by habit sometimes speak of consciousness as being inner or outer.

All we have to distinguish here is that the pure immanent-cum-transcendental world of Existence, Subsistence and Value ranges from the bottom of the vertical axis to the top, and that the practical relativistic horizontal factors range peripherally in sets in graded saturation, tint, shade or brilliance. The horizontal reference is to actual objects, whether thought of as universal concretes or discrete individual entities given to the senses. The one-and-the-many dialectics can alone resolve this final vestige of paradox.

Dualities Merge in the Neutrality of the Absolute Consciousness

All semiotic processes take place within the consciousness of man. Communicability of language presupposes at least this truth. Thoughts and the language that expresses them, correspond with a one-to-one parity between them, thoughts being more definite than words, which can be arbitrary and may differ with each vernacular. One name can refer to many discrete objective entities, and many discrete entities given to the senses objectively can all be inclusively thought of as having the form of one meaning content which would include all the particulars together.

In the world of Contemplative Discourse and the thoughts that underlie all possible discourses, we have thus the possibility of all percepts and concepts, names and forms being inclusively comprised schematically and nominalistically, at least in the general consciousness of the Absolute Contemplative Self. This is a high secret which the Guru philosophy has underlined. Without recognizing this, most of the verses under review will remain a closed book to students of the philosophy intended by the Guru.

At the risk of possible repetition let us quote here two significant verses which underline this basic verity that all events that belong to the world of contemplative thought and its resultant discourse have their basis in the common ground or amorphous matrix of contemplative consciousness, which itself can remain formless or even crypto-crystalline in respect of the thought elements contained in the matrix.

> As out of knowledge sparks of fire innumerable arise
> Asserting the being of non-being so as to make the world
> emerge;
> Know that outside of knowledge not a thing exists;
> Such knowing unitive awareness yields.
>
> (Verse 89)

Even anterior to this the Guru has gone so far as to say that this is a secret most people cannot get:

> Of one thing there can be many as in many objects
> One single meaning can reside; by such knowledge we
> can know
> Consciousness as comprising all, differencelessly without
> any remainder;
> This ultimate secret, however, is not given for all to
> know.
>
> (Verse 73)

After thus locating all semantic events or relation-relata consciousness within the matrix or common ground of general consciousness, which itself knows no specificity, the Guru masterfully elaborates the content and structural peculiarities of the Universe of Contemplative Discourse in a sequence of verses from 36 to 42.

This is perhaps the longest section of the series in which a single philosophical aspect is consistently developed by the Guru. The Guru's major contribution to Vedanta may be said to consist of this analysis of the content of the Universe of Contemplative or Absolutist Discourse which gives equal place to the pure and the practical, the phenomenal and the noumenal, and a due place to the relative and the absolute, in a globally, unitively and neutrally conceived normative notion of the Absolute.

When studied side by side with a similar series found in the Guru's more mature and more systematically conceived work, the *Garland of Visions of the Absolute* (*Darshana Mala*), we can see how this analysis is one of the major contributions made by the Guru to Advaita Vedantic speculation. What Jaimini and Badarayana and after them Shankara tacitly took for granted in their grand visions, Narayana Guru has here laid bare more explicitly, both in its analytical and synthetic implications at once. The position this discussion occupies in this later work, near the most central position of the symmetrically conceived series, further guarantees that the Guru meant it as a kind of keystone to the whole of the speculative superstructure that he had in mind in the monumental vision implied in his work as a whole.

Consciousness itself has a subjective and an objective aspect. The most intimate equation between them is established in that most central of verses, the 50th, of the

Guru's *Darshana Mala.*[2] This circumstance must be noted by the careful and critical student to help him to view the secret alluded to here with all the importance that the Guru himself meant to give it.

It is also to be noted that a one-to-one correspondence is implied here between the Self and the non-Self aspects. In our study of the *Darshana Mala,* these implications have been made clearer. In Chapter V of this work, the broad lines of the structure of the Universe of Contemplative Discourse are kept in mind by the Guru. It gives to speculation that scientific status so desirable to Vedanta, which at present is so much steeped in a *lingua mystica* of its own, both esoteric and cryptic in its secrecy.

Turning to the series of verses, Verse 36 of the *Atmopadesha Shatakam* distinguishes the two structural reference axes which we called the vertical and the horizontal as corresponding to the "same" and the "other" respectively. The point of intersection marks the origin of these mutually exclusive aspects that diverge as we go farther from their common point of junction within the neutral contemplative Self, here referred to as "other-sameness." Except for the Cartesian coordinates that we have introduced for the sake of precise mathematical reference, the implications of the two axes and their common point of participation in the Self are quite evident. The verse reads:

> The powers of understanding are many; all of them under
> two sets,
> The "same" and the "other" conclusively can be brought.
> Merging into that form of "other-sameness"; of these,

2. *yad bhashyate tad adhyastam anadhyastam na bhashyate yad adhyastam tad asad apy anadhyastam sad eva tat.*

   What is object of consciousness, that is conditioned;
   What is unconditioned, that is not object of consciousness.
   What is conditioned is non-existent;
   But what is unconditioned, itself THE EXISTENT IS THAT.

To clarity of vision one should awake. (Verse 36)

In Verse 37 the contemplative implications of these two axes of reference are indicated for the guidance of the spiritual aspirant or the contemplative who seeks full Self-realization. The horizontal world of values is not favourable to spirituality or contemplative progress because of the ignorance of which it is the product. The rest of the verse is sufficiently clear:

> To subdue even somewhat the obduracy of the "other"
> Is hard indeed without understanding's infinite power;
> Even by such should one gain mastery over it and thus attain
> Close access to Her who is discrimination's anti-sensuous one. (Verse 37)

In Verse 38 the Guru gives very precise definitions distinguishing the horizontal with its multiplicity, and the vertical which is unitive in outlook. In any set of entities, whether perceptually or conceptually understood, the central verity is one and its semantic implications on the side of the peripheral are many. Unitive factors are ranged along the vertical axis of the total knowledge situation, and the multiple aspects along the horizontal. To take an example dear to the context of Platonism, beautiful things are horizontal while Beauty with a capital letter is vertical. The same with values such as Truth, Justice, etc. God is one and creation many. The verse reads:

> What appraises manifold variety the "other" that is;
> And the "same" is whatever unitively shines on:
> Thus grasping the situation above, into that state
> Which yields "sameness," melt and mix and erect sit.
> (Verse 38)

In Verse 39 the implications of the two main references or correlates are further elaborated into their respective plus and minus aspects, the more virtual and universal remaining negative and the more actual and particular being brought under the specific (*vishesha*). Each of the two main aspects thus become subdivided into two. In terms of the Cartesian correlates that we have been adopting to clarify linguistic complications, each of these axes can be understood to have its own plus and minus aspects, according to the convention already acceptable to mathematicians who deal with complex numbers. Except for the epithet "never-to-detachment-gains" applied to the horizontal plus aspect of the Universe of Contemplative Discourse, all else is clear in the verse which reads as follows:

> Following up further the said powers a further bifurcation there is,
> One of these is an attribute of the "same" while the other
> Qualifies the harsh "other" that never-to-detachment-gains;
> Thus making two kinds of each of these. (Verse 39)

In Verse 40 all predications possible in the manifested world of objects or in the thought world proper to metaphysics are inclusively and integrally brought under the purview of the two main references, along with the specificatory factors belonging to each of them. There could be a disproportionate blending of the four elements of the total situation by the constant alternating circulation to which all events in consciousness are subject. Consciousness is a sum-total emergent, the resultant of a process of alternating circulation of thought, whether such an alternation takes place within the span of a split second, or like the rhythm of a heartbeat or a respiratory cycle it has its own proper unit duration. There is also a subtle osmotic interchange of essences, substances, or existent factors, conforming to the fourfold pattern, in which different proportions come into play to determine the world that is measured out objectively, as opposed to the Self which is the measure of itself. This bold and sweeping generalization about the emergence of all phenomenal aspects of the world from the inner structural elements which have been analysed side by side, is perhaps a major contribution of the Guru to Vedantic speculation, never before so clearly analysed:

> On to the "same" and on to the "other," there constantly alight
> Their respective specifying factors; although not proportionate.
> Through the spinning phase of these two in all,
> All predications whatsoever there are do come to be.
> (Verse 40)

The remaining two verses of this section give clear definitions of the notions so far indicated in respect of the four divisions in all. We know that the Samkhya philosophy had a scheme based on the theory of the three *guna*s, with Nature and Spirit *(prakriti* and *purusha)* as its two poles. When the three *guna*s attained equilibrium, peace or equanimity would be attained. Improving on such a scheme, the two Mimamsakas had each their own scheme based more on the semantic polyvalence of the Word. Jaimini and Badarayana both relied on semantics for arriving at the notion of the Absolute, although in the former school this notion was only implicit to the context of the Vedic ritualism.

We have elsewhere[3] devoted whole chapters to this aspect, and referred to *vacyartha* (literal meaning) and *lakshanartha* (indirect figurative analogical meaning) on which Shankara himself, although an anti-ritualist Vedantin, largely relied. To analyse the Universe of Contemplative Discourse to reveal the structure of the Absolute, therefore, is not a new departure which the Guru here adopts for the first time in Vedantic speculation. To reject the extraneous and adopt the intrinsic in interpreting the great dicta of the Vedanta, such as *tat tvam asi* (That Thou Art), etc., by the method of *bhaga-tyaga* (rejection of parts), belongs properly to the methodology of Vedantic speculation. The Guru has definitely improved on

3. See *Vedanta Revalued and Restated*

these ancient methods by giving here a complete structural analysis of the Universe of Contemplative Discourse with every aspect fully defined. He gives indications also of how the contemplative should adapt or adjust his meditation in order to establish himself in the wisdom of the union with the Absolute for spiritual progress, liberation or salvation. These two remaining verses bear comparison with Verses 2, 3 and 4 of *Bhana Darshana* in Section V of the *Darshana Mala* of the Guru[4]:

In "This is pot" the initial "this" is the harsh
While the "pot" is what makes its specific attribute;
For the mind with its myriad Indra-magic to come,
Understand that "this" is the basis of functioning.
(Verse 41)

In "this is knowledge" the initial "this" is the "same"
While its specifying factor is the cognitive consciousness;

4. The verses in question are:

sthulam sukshmam karanam cha turyam chedi chaturvidham
bhanashrayam hi tannama bhanashya' pyupachary (2)

drishyatam iha kayo' ham ghatoyam iti drishyate
sthulam ashritya yad bhanam sthulam tad iti manyate (3)

atra kaya ghata iti bhānam yat tad vishishyate
tathaham ayam iti yat samanyam iti ca smritam (4)

As the concrete, the subtle, the causal and the Absolute,
Basic Consciousness (is) of four kinds
So these names even of basic Consciousness
Are also applicable to consciousness.

Lo here "I am the body, this is the pot"
Depending on the concrete
What looms as consciousness
That is known as the concrete.

Here what is the consciousness of the body
And the pot, that is the specific
Likewise too, what is (the consciousness) of "I" or "this"
Is known as the generic.

For the mind and all else to be effaced for the good path
to gain,
"This" it is that one shoud contemplate. (Verse 42)

It would be profitable to note here that the mind in the last verse belongs to the harsh or "other" aspect and is therefore one that is to be assigned to the limbo of the horizontal and the absurd in the Universe of Contemplation. Full contemplation is thus referred to with complete definitions of terms used and full directions are given to the contemplative for his guidance for the attainment of the goal of *atma-vidya* or the Science of the Self, which is the same as the Science of the Absolute. For purposes of the Universe of Contemplation, the Self, the Absolute and Supreme Felicity through contemplation are all here treated as interchangeable terms having reference to the same normative notion of the Absolute.

The Guru himself has underlined this interchangeability in Verse 5 of the 8th chapter on *bhakti* of his later work, the *Darshana Mala.*[5] The vertical minus zone thus stands revealed as the richest of the aspects of the Absolute known to contemplation according to the Universe of Discourse that has been structurally analysed above.

---

5. *ananda atma brahmeti namaitasyaiva tanyate*
iti nishchita dhiryasya sa bhakta iti vishrutah.

Bliss, the Self and the Absolute
Are said to be names of this alone.
In whom there is such awareness
He as a contemplative is well known.

7

The Methodology and Epistemology in Guru Philosophy

Guru Philosophy is not argumentative or polemical in its approach to its problems. It has a simplified way suited to its higher critical as well as intuitive speculation on contemplative values. It is full of precise definitions or definite intuitive personal experiences of the mystic contemplative.

At the same time a certain apodictic certitude is given to the statements made, as it were, from the side of the a priori by appeal to the common experience known to all men as general knowledge enshrined in the form of collective experience that can safely be taken for granted. Proverbs and common linguistic usage are seen to be employed to serve the purposes of proof in the arguments of Shankara and in the Upanishads, which are his models in this matter. Proverbially known truths have almost an experimental value in that they constitute the experience of mankind lasting through the test or correction possible through generations of usage.

When we say that the proof of the pudding is in the eating thereof, we rely on such a simple methodology that, instead of questioning such a statement, most people smile assentingly and remain silent. This is because there is nothing to be argumentative or polemical about. The certitude is like hitting the nail on the head, and is characterized as downright or apodictic. Two aspects of reality have merely to be juxtaposed to induce the conviction which silences further questioning or doubts. They tally or together become so evident, the one lending certitude to the other, that the point is made straightaway.

It is only where experience is weak that an elaborate experiment under laboratory conditions becomes necessary. Scientific problems, mostly in connection with the manufacture of articles of trade, may need such elaborate arrangements. But for the main problems of life which have to be faced by all men or women, young or old, particularly those of a general and abstract nature with which metaphysical speculation has most to do, there is a large available body of accepted opinion which, when rank superstitions are weeded out, will yield support to verities.

Just as grass need not be cultivated in a garden or nursery, there is common experience to support many philosophical truths which are significant for wise or intelligent living for man seeking his happiness freely. Eristic, sophistic, syllogistic or propositional calculi, in which induction and deduction move haltingly up or down the scale of generalities or particularities through middle terms and arbitrary premises, are only important when rival relativistic values tear man's mind this way or that at once, and even at that they are highly questionable. Often there are too many items to be taken into account, and it is possible sometimes that the opposite is possible by, as they say, "the same token." In the course of higher contemplative reasoning where such rival values of everyday life do not loom large, the polemics of logic or mere ratiocination do not have to play an important part.

As with Spinoza's approach to speculation, which resembles Euclid in its method of axioms, postulates, etc., proved through theorems or corollaries certified by apodictic verities, speculation with the Guru, when not directly based on the intuition of higher contemplation, is supported by the homeliest of analogies or examples which already exist and are available to any linguistic tradition.

That a child mistakes a mirror image to be real, or treats her doll as if it had life, are examples of such found in the *Darshana Mala* of the Guru, side by side with generalizations made directly from mystic experiences. Mistaking a rope for a snake or a post for a ghost are classical analogies of the same order used in Indian speculation.

Analogies certify definitions and vice versa. No more verification is called for nor is possible. One is meant to clarify, justify or lend whatever semblance of support it might be possible to give to the other. The certitude is not the effect exclusively of the one or the other but is a natural emergent resultant of both together as in the case of the theorem of Pythagoras which can be proved in two ways, i.e., by actually cutting and pasting the figures or algebraically by axioms and riders as the teacher will do on the blackboard.

Guru philosophy is critically convincing by the mere bringing together of the visible and the intelligible aspects. This is the secret of the methodology of the Guru, which necessarily presupposes an absolutist epistemology of its own which is inseparable from it. The axiomatic and the demonstrable aspects meet here. When we add to these two factors the final regulative requirement that any truth to be true must also have value significance in human life, the three factors required for scientific certitude of any vision of truth will be sufficiently guaranteed.

In the particular work we are presenting in this series of introductory essays, the *Atmopodesha Shatakam,* a strict academic treatment is still not respected by the Guru, and as he indicates in the very first verse, he is content to present his contemplative mystical experiences with either definitions or critical analysis of topics, in a manner of thinking aloud rather than in the style required for convincing any opponent. Instructions and hints to the contemplative are strewn throughout the text. His way is to take the disciple by the hand and lead him upward step by step, as Virgil did to Dante in the *Divine Comedy.* The work is primarily meant to be an aid to the contemplative aspirant in Self-knowledge rather than a regular textbook on the subject. It is, however, rich in Guru philosophy proper.

Usual Logic Falls Short of Paradox and Does Not Attain the Absolute

Intuition, and not logic, can attain the Absolute. Even within the scope of logic proper there are two main kinds, viz., one which recognizes contradiction and excludes the middle ground, and that which is dialectical in approach which proceeds by cancelling out thesis and antithesis into a central synthesis. The former moves horizontally, the latter vertically. Bain and Bradley represent these rival schools respectively. Aristotelian syllogistic logic has its place in the former kind of textbooks, where the forms of syllogisms reveal themselves with their four alternatives of logical form. Logical form opens the door to some mysterious element as the basis of all reasoning, whether inductive or deductive. That it falls within four groups, and four only, must have something to do with the structure of thought itself, fundamentally understood. Syllogisms ascend or descend through middle terms from major to minor premises, deductively to the more particular, or inductively to the more general judgements, in this fundamental fourfold fashion. By playing with premises and inferences of different kinds, endless alternatives or varieties of conclusions become possible.

The status of syllogistic reasoning is thus questionable. Its results do not yield any degree of firm ground of certitude but get lost in the maze of "ifs" and "buts," "either-or" or "neither-nor," "both" or "none," etc., all of which come within the range of the possibilities of the propositional calculus. The mechanistic structure of thinking in the world of necessities and contingencies with multiple and rival claims for Truth at any given time is the region or domain in which such reasoning is called upon to solve problems mostly of minor incidental significance in life. Fundamental questions lie outside its scope. Just as a mechanic has to decide which part of a machine has to be pressed down or raised up, or loosened or tightened in repairing it, these are intricate interdependent clusters of cause-effect propositions to be tackled alternatively or in graded steps, to set right relative aspects of a situation. The total situation itself is beyond the scope of such piecemeal reasonings. Intuition or dialectics deal with more important aspects of human understanding and help in problems of life and death significance.

In common with Vedantic methodology, Guru philosophy bypasses the usual piecemeal instruments of reasoning in favour of overall ones of a truly philosophical order. Some of the peculiarities of such a methodology which presupposes its own epistemology can be studied under the heads of: (1) non-being as a negative something (*abhava*), (2) primacy of cause over effect (*sat-karana*), (3) primacy of material cause over incidental or efficient cause (*upadana karana*), (4) the dialectical relation (*samanvaya* or *ubhayalinga*), (5) admitting the principle of indeterminism (*anirvachaniya*), (6) treating immanent and transcendent as belonging to a homogeneous epistemologically neutral context (*samanadhikaranatva*), (7) viewing reality without seeing subject, object and meaning disjunctly, i.e., without accepting *triputi*, and (8) including value (*priya*) as a final regulative reference for fact or truth as the third, along with *asti* (existing) and *bhati* (looming in consciousness). This is the same as viewing the Absolute in its entirety as Existence, Subsistence and Value, i.e., *sat, chit, ananda*. These several items of methodological and epistemological importance in Guru philosophy are common to Vedanta in general. Even a passing explanation of each of these would take us beyond the scope of our present enquiry.

The elements of pure reasoning employed in Guru philosophy are inseparable from their own presuppositions and implications in general epistemology and axiology, many of which we have already covered in the present series or in

Vedanta Revalued and Restated. A more systematic and complete discussion of these items may be found in *An Integrated Science of the Absolute,* based on the *Darshana Mala* (Garland of Visions of the Absolute) of the Guru. Here our object being limited to presenting preliminarily the kind of intuitive reasoning that the Guru adopts, which mainly consists of definitions and explicatory analogies, it will serve our purpose to show at least the kinds of reasoning he did not specialize in.

The Computability or Measurability of the Absolute is Summarily Rejected

The measures applied to the validity of truth in Vedanta, referred to as *pramana shastra* (the science of valid reasoning), are six: viz., *pratyaksha* (what is directly given to the senses); *anumana* (inference); *arthapatti* (hypothetical postulation); *anupalabdhi* (impossibility of a conclusion); *upamana* (analogy); and *shabda* or *agama* (scriptural assent). In his *Darshana Mala* the Guru mentions only three for the purposes of his methodology. These are perceptual (*pratyaksha*), inferential (*anumiti*), and knowing through analogy (*upamiti*). Subjective experience which is verified by the last mentioned measure of validity takes the place with him of *shabda* or authority of the scriptures accepted dogmatically. The hypothetical inductive approach is omitted by the Guru as ambiguous. All *pramanas* (measures of validity) which are ratiocinative in status are discredited as being of no use for the final means of knowing the Absolute, which is beyond the paradox of maya's uncertainty principle. He states this unequivocally in Verse 94 of the *Atmopadesha Shatakam,* which should be read with Verse 32 quoted at the end of this chapter:

> This which presents itself, as a mixture of the world
> And what is real; is a great iniquity indeed;
> Indeterminate and unknowable to word or thought,
> How could valid reasoning move therein? (Verse 94)

Shankara comes to a similar conclusion at the end of his commentary of the first four verses of the Brahma Sutras. We have to invert the course of philosophical speculation and take an inner view of flowing truth as a whole, as Bergson would put the same difficulty in *An Introduction to Metaphysics.* Christian mysticism also knows of the *via negationis,* which is the negative way of approach of *neti neti* recommended by the Upanishads and adopted by the methodology of Vedanta. The effect is false, and the cause which is, as it were, anterior to it, more real. This is the way of *sat-karana vada,* the method of giving primacy to cause over effect, and thus progressively canceling effects out backwards. Backward sublation of effects in reverse series till an epistemologically revised ontology arises, by double negation from the level of immanent realities to transcendent ones where general ideas prevail by double assertion, through dialectical intuition consisting of canceling counterparts into the unity of absolutist status — such is the complex and complete cycle that Vedantic methodology adopts in its reasoning process.

At the core of the total knowledge situation is the principle of pure apperception as known in Herbartian psychology, from which point the process of double assertion takes over and finally brings general concepts to refer to the core of the central normative apperceptive Self. Thought passes through grades of richness or indigence in such a course, sometimes more transparent, sometimes opaque, sometimes dark-splendid or at other times fully self-luminous, according to the position in the alternating process propagated like quantum pulsations in the atom or unit wave-particles. Mystic experience alone can confirm the verity on such matters, just the same way as the physicist has to rely on observation as the final arbiter. The experience of the mystic and experience of the physicist belong to opposite extremities of the same total knowledge situation. Possibilities and probabilities coexist on a neutral ground here, one lending certitude to the other.

Axiomatic and Experimental Certitude

Scientific certitude can reside with equal force at two poles of the total knowledge situation. Metaphysics fixes its faith on axiomatic a priori theoretical certitudes given to the experience of the race or at least what is given to rare philosophers who have fully benefitted from the heritage or experience of the contemplative philosophical insight of the race through eternal years. As *Homo sapiens* man is born with a right to be wise, if not perverted therefrom. General ideas thus forming the human heritage give us a frame of reference for the guidance of speculation. Just as it is difficult for a mariner to guide himself easily if latitudes and longitudes are omitted from a map, it will not be easy for the reader who might have some other loosely coherent scheme than the total knowledge situation with the two opposite poles that we have just referred to, to follow clearly the line of thought that the Guru develops in his writings.

Let us, for example, take Verse 90 from the *Atmopadesha Shatakam*, where reality, based on the experience of the race, theoretically vouches for a world order called *ritam* which, with its opposite *anritam*, are brought to bear upon the fundamental notion of existence in the observational sense, which is to be distinguished as coming under the general category of *sat* (existence). *Sat* may be said to be physical in origin and *ritam* is its metaphysical counterpart. *Sat* would be a kind of essential existence, while *ritam* would be an operationally valid existence. There is running through both these orders of truth or reality the same common principle of verity. The reader unfamiliar with the different connotations of these words *sat* and *ritam* would find it helpful to keep the structural plan of the total knowledge situation in mind in order to follow the two-sided implications of the scheme in the mind of the Guru. Verse 90 reads:

> What has no basis in reality (*anritam*) can never hide
> what exists,

Experience vouches for this; asserting the reality
Of what exists, at every step, by Existence (*sat*) all is here enveloped
The body and such effects have been made up of Existence. (Verse 90)

A block of marble rid of what is extra makes for its value as well as existence as a piece of sculpture. There is assertion of truth on one side of existence, and this is complemented on the other by the non-contradiction of what inheres in the world order. These together give us a vertical axis, in which at every level there is pure Existence, Subsistence and Value. The Bhagavad Gita too makes a similar assertion in XVI, 26. Vertically existence prevails and horizontally the breezes of phenomenal unreality, uncertainty or indeterminism blow, giving rise to an interplay of possibilities and probabilities. The general value-subsistent-and-existent content of *sat* is not in reality affected by the hierarchy of falsehood's waftings to abolish truth.

This same picture is brought out by the Guru in Verse 76 of the same series more graphically as a process by using the analogy of a well in which gusts of wind continuously waft in sand. Both ascending and descending dialectical reasonings meet from opposite poles of the total situation to give one and the same reality. The reality of the one is proved by the other. By full apperception one coincides with the other. Such are some of the methodological and epistemological secrets of a schematically unified Guru philosophy.

Apperception Resides at the Core

If for the purposes of clear visualization, schematically understood, we divide the totality of the content of knowledge at any time and place for any man into two halves by a horizontal line passing through the centre as a diameter dividing the circle representing such a knowledge situation, producing a top and a bottom half, we can visualize the content of consciousness into two distinct divisions.

The top half would contain "conceptual" relations or relata and the bottom half would contain the "perceptual" counterparts which have a one-to-one correspondence with the same conceptual elements. To give a familiar example, there is a rose that is conceptual and one that is perceptual. The latter is more directly related to the actual rose, while the concept of the rose has its reference to a nominal rose which resides in the pole of abstract imaginings of which the human mind is capable.

In other words concepts are nearer to "names" while percepts are nearer to "forms." These two divisions that cover all relations or relata possible of being contained in the human consciousness schematically generalized and understood for purposes of semantic clarity, interact in the form of apperceptions. There all conceptual or perceptual accentuations or slants in thought are cancelled out and absorbed in neutral terms. Apodicticity resides here. According to the methodology and epistemology of the reasoning employed in Guru philosophy, certitude results when this kind of union or fusing from opposite poles takes place. Although this way of looking at the result of contemplation is developed in different contexts of the writings of the Guru, it is in the following verse of the *Atmopadesha Shatakam* that this truth is clearly stated:

> This which is non-distinct from knowledge, than knowing which knowledge
> Straightaway, here there is none other to know
> As any ultimate knowing beyond; such the supreme secret
> Of the most informed of men; who is there to know?
>
> (Verse 63)

In the name of orthodoxy or heterodoxy men are used to treat the perceptual and the conceptual aspects of knowing as disjunct or dualistic. Both the alternative lopsided positions are wrong. At the core of the total knowledge situation, direct apperception makes it possible for knowledge to be known without ratiocinative effort or ascetic tortures. Knowing one aspect in terms of the other in the neutrality of unitive fusion between them, is the supreme secret pointed out. One of these aspects proves the other. Such is the secret of reasoning in the Guru philosophy.

When read together with another verse in the series where the same is referred to from the standpoint of a "thing-in-itself" rather than in terms of the apperception of two aspects coming together, we get a further clarification of the central unitive normative notion of the Absolute proper to Guru philosophy. This other verse refutes the possibility of separate realities in the world of the "intelligibles" as in Plato, as opposed to the world of "entelechies" originating in prime matter ontologically as in Aristotle. The central meeting point is the unitive factor where the notion of the Absolute is proved by itself:

> Another reality this world can have none; contrary
>   assertions
> Made by men in the world, lack understanding all;
> Although an ignoramus could mistake it for a reptile
> Could a flower garland beneficial ever a snake become?
> (Verse 20)

The "thing-in-itself" is known not by syllogistic ratiocination but is to be appraised directly by the tallying of its two possible epistemological counterparts, one perceptual agreeing with the one that is conceptual.

A Scientific Epistemology is Neutral to Scepticism and Belief

Guru philosophy accepts the broad outlines of Vedantic epistemology, inasmuch as it does not rely wholly on the *pramana shastra* (the science of valid measures of reason) while recognizing its findings in a general overall fashion. The man of *uhapoha* (dialectical intuition) is the proper *adhikari* (qualified or fit man) to unravel the secrets of *atma-vidya* or the Science of the Self, i.e., Vedanta. This is categorically stated by Shankara in his *Vivekachudamani* (Crest-Jewel of Discrimination) in Verse 16, which reads: "Superior man of wisdom, well versed and fully specialised in dialectical intuitive understanding (*uha poha*) where analogy and its subject are involved, is one qualified for Self-knowledge."

All the five *pramanas* (measures of what is valid) are respected only to bring into relief the uncertainty principle of maya or *anirvachaniya* hiding reality paradoxically at its very epistemological core. Shankara, while voting for the validity of the *pratyaksha* (observable evidence) tends to emphasize the *shabda pramana* (the validity of the a priori knowledge implicitly contained in the scriptures). He tends to think of the Hindu scriptures more particularly than any other scriptures and, to this extent, tends to be non-universal in his outlook, though with natural excuse.

The five *pramanas* are revised and restated for Vedantic purposes in the *Vedanta Paribhasha,* a recognized textbook for determining the accepted position of Vedanta in this respect. This work, attributed to Dharmaraja Adhvarin, goes into the matter thoroughly. It gives to the *pratyaksha* (observables) sufficient validity to let it remain consistently homogeneous with an overall epistemological scheme in which all such valid measures of reasoning enjoy equ .lity of status under the aegis of the master notion of the Absolute.

To a scientific epistemologist who tends to give more importance to observables than to mere scriptures, which only believers tend to extol, there is, in traditional Vedanta as it is actually handled by its protagonists at present, a touch of orthodoxy in favour of the believer in closed scriptures like the Hindu Vedas. Static and closed aspects tend to be treated more favourably by them than the fully open Upanishadic outlook, which does not support any static religious ideas.

In revising and correcting this asymmetry and giving to Advaita a fuller scientific status, the Guru replaces *arthapatti* (postulation) and *agama* (the Vedas and other *shastras* treated vaguely together) by the third *pramana* referred to in his *Darshana Mala* in Section VII, Verse 8, by an inclusive *pramana* based on analogy which he calls *upamiti* (knowing by analogy). The language of analogy, parables or protolinguistic representations is widely used in all the scriptures of the world for dealing with a priori aspects of truth. Mythology arises from the free use of such literary devices. Mathematics deals with the same a priori through axioms or their corollaries, supplemented by structural verifications when possible, as in the quantum and relativistic theories of the present day.

The mathematically revised use of such analogical language has not yet taken its full place in scientific epistemology, although thinkers like Eddington have initiated such an approach. Such attempts, however, remain still at a tentative stage. This will be sufficiently evident from what Eddington has written: "Even in relativity theory which deals with the Absolute (in a somewhat limited sense) we continually hark back to the relative to examine how our results will appear in the experience of an individual observer."[1] It goes without saying, therefore, that the selective subjectivism and structuralism that Eddington introduced into the philosophy of science needs more revision and adaptation to overcome its tentative status at present.

On the other side, Vedanta has to shed its tendency to adhere to closed, static, traditional scriptures and regain a normality *vis-a-vis* other scriptures of the world, to become universal, dynamic and open as a scientific epistemology would require. The revisions of the Guru and his neutrality between scepticism and belief or as between the a priori and

1. A.E. Eddington, *The Philosophy of Physical Science*, (Arbor Paperbacks, University of Michigan Press, 1958), p. 88.

the a posteriori gives to it that very normative scientific status that puts his metaphysical speculation on a par with that of physics.

As we cannot afford to elaborate these aspects except through a fuller treatise, we shall not linger here longer for the present. There are four of the hundred verses which we shall be content, in concluding this study, just to quote with hardly any comment. A careful scrutiny of these verses will reveal the neutral normative nature of the position that the Guru maintains in his attitude, which he intends to be fully universal and scientific, neither taking the side of the believer or of the sceptic, the orthodox or the heterodox, of any traditional context of any time or any part of the world. It is here that Guru philosophy excels in being fully scientific:

> The inert, no awareness can have, awareness no cogitation needs.
> Nor does it hold discourse; knowing this awareness to be all,
> And giving up all, transparency of spirit one gains,
> And in bodily bonds confined, one suffers never more indeed! (Verse 30)

> Without prior experiencing, no inference there could be
> As this has never before been experienced by the senses
> The existence of the operator
> Is never given to inferential thought. (Verse 31)

> It is not the operator but the operation that we know;
> The said operator being ever unseen, the world and all else
> Is nought, while lending it outer semblance of shape.
> It is awareness alone that really remains. (Verse 32)

The overall scheme into which such statements fit is seen from the very next verse:

> Knowledge in order to know itself
> The Earth and other manifestations became.
> In inverted manner thus, now mounting, now changing over

Like a circulating fire-faggot, it keeps turning round.
(Verse 33)

It is thus an integrated picture of the process of higher reasoning that emerges, instead of any piecemeal methodology as in unit judgements or other ratiocinative elements of thought.

8

Protolinguistic Imagery

The Unified Field Theory of Einstein was the attempt of a mastermind of our time to bring together under one scheme the gravitational and the electromagnetic versions of the universe, which were beginning to make the universe fall apart into two distinct worlds, one where gravitation operated and the other where electromagnetic waves were given the status of reality.

This theory is said to be of epoch-making importance in the world of physics. An equally necessary synthesis of the world of names and the world of forms, one referring to the intelligibles and the other belonging to the context of the visibles, has equally held out a challenge to speculators and metaphysicians through the ages, eluding their unified integration in one and the same context in the world of thought, whether physical or metaphysical.

Crystalline or Cryptic Language of Profound Philosophy

The limbs of any equation in mathematics or physics significantly bring together two aspects in the world of absolute discourse. Like mathematics, where the main task is to create certitude by bringing together two aspects of reality so that one throws light on the other, forming the limbs of an equation revealing a law, a rule of logic, or a truth of value, philosophy is obliged to use signs or symbols. The more profound the philosophy the more cryptic the language it is obliged to employ.

Experiments, as well as experiences treasured in language in the form of general ideas forming the heritage of humanity from antiquity spoken of as Wisdom in general, are all based on understanding one thing which is a "proper" element as known to modern algebraic geometry, in terms of another which is its own "improper" version. The interplay of proper and improper elements is a matter that mathematics has recently discovered, and when analysed it finally consists of the same principle as explaining a deep-seated truth with convenient picture language, analogies or parables.

The world of pure mathematics is the one that belongs to the richest zone of the Absolute, which comprises the objective universe just as a corollary is covered by a theorem, or as an axiom includes all possible postulates that are particular instances of the same generalized fact or principle.

If all men are mortal some must be necessarily so a priori. This is an epistemological verity which we shall not linger here to discuss in detail. We have had occasion to do so already in several contexts and we shall be doing so again more finally in pages to come in the next work, dedicated to the "Science of the Absolute." Here we want to indicate only that when thought attains to white heat it tends to become conceptualized into a compact correlated whole in a symbolic, cryptic or generalized language, which can be said to be the metalinguistic version of the truth expressed in the light of the fundamentals of algebra as a pure science.

When, on the contrary, thought descends negatively into itself, in and through the vertical axis wherein all thought must move up or down in its dialectical or semiotic process, it tends to become held together in a different way of globality or unity, resembling more a geometrical crystal. The crystal expresses the "form" of things mathematically, representing the axiomatic togetherness where, due to lack of contrast between general ideas, the obverse and converse of propositions imply or presuppose each other. Even when understood to be different classes of concepts as exist in the language of any philosophy or religion, we still have some notion like that of divinity where all attributes fuse into unity.

By whatever name known it means the same. If we called the Sun the source of heat or the focal point of all light rays, we mean only the Sun. All attributes can thus refer to the same object without inner contradiction between any two of them.

Hypostatic and Hierophantic Versions of Reality

There is thus a hypostatic version of truth or reality and a hierophantic version of the same at the other pole. The latter is solid while the former is pure radiance at its origin in the mind of man.

The 'I' in man is shared by all other men who use the first personal pronoun in any part of the world at any time. The 'I' thus viewed comes to have a status that is universal and eternal, which can be thought of positively and algebraically as belonging to a class of all classes. Alternatively it may be viewed more as a concrete Absolute given to the schematization of pure geometry where, like a crystal, it tends to be existent like a Monad of monads. Here the characteristics are visible rather than intelligible. The colour-solid thought of as a crystal independently of its bigness or smallness would mark the negative second pole. This is the existent ontological aspect of the same Absolute.

These matters cannot be finally discussed except in a work devoted to such aspects as a whole, and we therefore reserve the fuller elaboration of these ideas for a future work. All we want to do at present is to review the Absolute here summarily in the light of its structural, schematic, subjective and selective implications and possibilities as belonging together. We are interested here in just the "togetherness" of all possibilities and probabilities. These accord with a secret innate structure where all relations and relata meet with polarities, antinomies and contradictions, their middle grounds included or excluded as the case may be, in a correlated global whole. The human mind can think of or visualize this in its best of speculative or mystical moods. The

Guru Narayana was one of those fully capable of soaring to such philosophical heights and reaching such depths of mystical Self-awareness. The few examples from the *Atmopadesha Shatakam* below will throw light on the nature of the immanent and transcendent worlds that came within the scope of his meditations on the Absolute.

Examples of Verses with Structural Implications

(A) TRANSCENDING INITIAL PARADOX

As early as the eighth verse we meet with the complex structural figure of speech that is used by the Guru as a literary device with masterful advantage as in the Upanishads, to which we have made allusion elsewhere. Instead of establishing one analogy at a time, the Guru is here seen to treat a cluster of analogies together, as given to his global intuitive mystical vision. There is no evil of mixed metaphor here because of the organic togetherness implied.

Descartes makes use of the analogy of a complex mechanized fountain found in the Royal Palace where he lived in Sweden with the Princess of that country shortly before he died, to show the mechanistic nature of the human body, and how the spirit is like the pressure of water acting at different levels to produce the variety of phenomena called life. Instead of understanding this as a figure of speech, most critics of Descartes nicknamed him a dualist who believed "monstrously" that the body was a machine. The manner in which the bones are articulated unmistakably reveals the mechanical character of the body. The spirit is compared here to the vertical aspect of the mobility of water which has its horizontal counterpart in the body which is its *natura naturata*. The laws to which the body as such is submitted are mechanistic, but this does not apply to the spirit, which is like the water circulating inside the mechanized fountain in the park of the Swedish Princess. The water is meant to be the real, while body and its varied mechanical phenomena are horizontally derivable from it.

The *elan vital* of which Bergson spoke much later, uses another analogy. Philosophy has to rely either on the schematic language of mathematics or of analogy to express itself. When the Guru employs complex systems of organically conceived multiple analogies held together by a unitive epistemological or methodological or even axiological principle, this would not be considered as outside the scope of critical philosophy as understood in modern times. The mechanistic aspect of life here in the Guru's analogy of the gun is itself the means by which the contemplative has to figuratively transcend paradox and gain unitive vision. The duality inevitable to initiate a discussion is abolished by itself, as the gun is what shoots down its own peripheral counterpart, the birds:

> Eating of the fruits five, such as light
> Perched the while on a shot gun foul-smelling,
> Ever in wily change, what can bring down in shreds these five,
> Such a lucid inner form-wielding, the Self must brilliant become! (Verse 8)

The world of peripherally alluring values given to the five senses and their corresponding objects referred to as the five fruits is what is under reference here. The ends and the means of transcending this world of peripheral mechanistic values are here compared to a gun on which such sensual values are perched. Contemplative life can begin only by a radical attitude toward this world of puerile and evanescent values which are in a constant state of whimsical and fanciful change through vanity of interests. The tragic situation is pictured by making the birds sit on the gun, which is the same evil means to transcend all evil in life in the same way as a thorn could be used to remove a thorn in the leg. Paradox is to be transcended in and through itself. Such is the reasoning implied.

(B) THE DOUBLE DOMAIN OF CONCEPTS AND PERCEPTS

In Verse 17 we have equally complex imagery revealing the two-sided structural aspect of the content of the Absolute, thought of in terms of Self-consciousness. The analogy, belonging to the world of mechanics and sense pleasures as such, gives place here to that of a lamp, which suits contemplative life better for the next step in the direction of more non-dualistically conceived self-introspection. We read:

> Suffering (fire) filled, with petals five and tiers two,
> Rotating beginningless, such is the lamp hanging high
> Which is the Self burning on in shadow form, with past habits
> For oil, and function verily for wick.
>
> (Verse 17)

The Self has two stages which revolve, one as the shadow or reflection of the other. The conceptual world can be said to be made of light while the perceptual is made of shadow, though belonging together with the light coming from above, which is the world of the intelligibles. Apperception is the flames, each sense having its own, duplicated by afferent and efferent nervous energy circulating between subject and object or the Self and the non-Self.

(C) THE APPERCEPTIVE CORE OF CONSCIOUS BECOMING

In the next verse with structural implications, which we shall examine now, the core of the cosmo-psychological ground within the schematically understood structure of the Absolute is ably compared in terms of pure duration, as with Descartes and Bergson:

> Half-a-second is what is the prime hub
> Of the wheel of the car, mounted whereon, the universe rolls on;
> Know this to be the sport of that beginningless One,
> Ever growing on in the core of awareness pure.
>
> (Verse 34)

The wheel of phenomenal becoming, ever active but without motion, as the unmoved mover in a pure sense, is a paradox in its "pure act", here described as purposeless sport. All life activity is apperceptively situated at the core of consciousness, and is centrally understood as infinitesimally small while at the periphery it could be elaborated and multiplied to the limits of the expanding universe at the outermost of the galaxies. This process is beginningless and alternates with its complementary half of negative contraction as indicated elsewhere in the same series in Verse 72. Here the use of the analogy of the wheel with the location of pure consciousness at the core and the universe at the periphery, is mainly intended to explain the structure of the Self within which the universe itself is comprised. The theological, cosmological and psychological aspects of the Absolute are brought to refer to the same local neutral or central point of all apperceptions, whether of time or of space, in an eternal context of causality or absolute becoming.

(D) THE SPIRITUAL PROGRESS OF THE SELF

The same progression of a chariot mounted on a wheel of time is under reference in Verse 69, which elaborates the imagery further:

> With hearing and such as horses linked, while bearing within
> The image of the Self, and controlled by the master of faculties,
> Is the libido-chariot mounted whereon the ego rides
> Dealing unceasingly with each thing of beauty as it proceeds. (Verse 69)

The complexity of a mixed metaphor cannot be stretched further than in this verse, where every word refers conceptually or perceptually to the progress of the Self through the phenomenal universe in life. One is reminded of the analytical psychology of Freud and Jung as well as the

Upanishadic verses[1] where the horses and the charioteer have been used similarly. The tradition started there has only been completed here.

(E) THREE PERSPECTIVES OF THE SAME PROCESS

Then we have a beautiful series of three verses in sequence, but taking different structural perspectives of the Self in its cosmo-psychological setup. Complex graphical imagery which remains still dynamically true to the flux of life can find no more perfect expression than in these verses:

> Nature is water; the body, brine; the Self, the deep;
> The "I", "I" rumbling within, the magic of the waves that arise.
> Pearls they are each flowering of Wisdom within;
> And what one drinks of oneself, immortality, verily it is!
> (Verse 75)

> As with a well into which measureless sand is wafted
> By successive gusts, tier on tier, so too
> Exposed to the waftings of untruth's hierarchy
> The inner Self inwardly multitudinous forms it gains.
> (Verse 76)

> The ultimate is the sky; wind, that power expansive;
> Awareness, the fire; water represents the perceptive organs;
> What is given objectively to the senses, the earth;
> And what thus keeps as five principles burning has its secret in the One alone. (Verse 77)

Here schematic thinking of the relation-relata complex, with the psycho-cosmic core of the Absolute as its content, is treated in fully dynamic terms, not statically as with the rationalists of Europe beginning from Descartes and ending with Leibniz, but in fully living terms as revised by Bergson in terms of the *elan vital.*

---

1. Cf. *Katha Upanishad*, III. 3-9.

The central thinking substance here implies a *schema moteur* rather than merely a geometrically conceived static entity. The process of becoming finds its full place in the analogy of the well that is being gradually silted up as described in the central of the three verses. No aspect of life, abstract or concrete is omitted.

A Living Picture of the Contemplative Process

In order to extract correctly for philosophical purposes the implications of these culminating verses (75-77) bearing on structuralism, subjectivism and selectionism, revealing the process of being and becoming together within what constitutes the cosmological as well as psychological content of the Absolute, one has to keep in mind the following rules and peculiarities of the philosophy of the Guru:

(a) The subject and the object are treated unitively in terms of the same psycho-cosmic dynamism within consciousness. Whitehead spoke of the "togetherness" of all things and the "process" which was at the basis of his rather Platonic picture of the universe. The pre-Socratic hylozoists, however took another perspective of the totality of the structure of the universe in which the elementals like fire and water played their respective roles within the "megascopic" and "microscopic" structure of a Monad of monads. Both these rival perspectives, one hypostatic and the other hierophantic, are treated of in the first and last verses of this sequence of three verses. One has to place oneself within the total knowledge-situation without difference of subject or object before the implications here become clear to the student of contemplative metaphysics or of mystically understandable speculation.

(b) In all three verses together a normative notion of the Absolute is implied. One looks, as it were, upward from lying down on the earth when viewing the relation-relata complex revealed in the first of the three verses. Ascending dialectics leads one to the world of values like the Supreme Good which belongs to a universal class of all classes in notions such as that of God or of the attributes of divinity known in theologies such as that of St. Thomas Aquinas or Ramanuja of the Indian context. The same speculative process can descend into concrete universals of a material ontological status as represented by a crystal such as a dodecahedron or a tetrahedron. Reality when visualized existentially gives varied philosophies such as modern existentialism or phenomenologies of the mind.

(c) Pragmatic or social values hide in an intermediate zone from these extreme positions. Bergsonian instrumentalism and the social utilitarian and pragmatic values covered within the scope of the philosophy of a John Dewey or a William James, are comprised within this intermediate zone, where uncertain winds, some pluralistic or material in content and others more neutrally monistic in status, can alternately come into play, always implying a principle of inevitable uncertitude as with Heisenberg. Subject and object have to be fused into one generalized entity before ideas can be made to ascend again into the world of supreme or idealistic ultimate values. Utilitarian interests in social life are many at any given time. From the refrigerator to the television set, we can think of various utilities or luxuries between which a pragmatist can be torn every minute of his life by rival and multiple attractions and repulsions.

(d) When we think of philosophy in the West it is of course more usual to think in terms of the heritage of metaphysics or speculation as found in the legacy left to Europe by philosophers like Plato and metaphysicians like Aristotle. There is separation in modern Western Philosophy between ontology and teleology, and subjects that imply any judgement of value are often relegated to the sections that are separately treated as ethics or aesthetics. After Kant much confusion remains between what is analytic and synthetic, transcendental and immanent, a priori and a posteriori, and the phenomenal and the noumenal values in life. The divorce of theology and philosophy, which is to be directly laid at the door of the nightmare of the Inquisition and the burning at the stake of "unbelievers" like Bruno, has spoiled the structural unity of Western Philosophy for all time. A god in a theological or Christian sense is outside the scope of the best metaphysicians or methodic speculators like Descartes. The ontological proof of God became necessary because of the repugnance for the dogmatic a priorism or belief in a God as in the prophetic religions. The Guru philosophy remains whole and pure and untainted by the fissiparous trends of modernism. The total global situation is transparently revealed thus to his vision.

More of such implications could be derived endlessly from the notion of the Absolute contained in these verses. It is not our purpose here to treat all of them exhaustively. We are interested for the present only in pointing out that, when the core of the subject matter and the object matter of philosophy in general are understood unitively from a normative standpoint, such knowledge helps to put much desirable order into both metaphysics and speculation while minimizing mere verbosity.

9

Ethics, Aesthetics and Religion in Guru Philosophy

It is usual in Western philosophical tradition to treat of ethics and aesthetics, together with a way of life that can be said to be good and based on a right sense of values, as apart from philosophical speculation proper. This separation of all that involves any judgement of value into a kind of appendix to philosophy proper must have had its historical explanation in the fact that in the Middle Ages extreme theocratic power dominated life in the West, of which the horrors of the Inquisition have left an imprint on modern thought which still refuses to recognize or be reconciled with any value judgement or way of life which resembles religion.

Philosophers like Descartes had to recant, rewrite or at least suppress parts of their normal writing for fear of offending the Pope. Bruno was burnt at the stake for resembling a pantheist and is a martyr to the cause of modern science. Indian philosophical tradition however has remained innocent of these dark chapters of the ancient regime of Europe. In the interests of a global, integrated and complete world philosophy it would be a virtue for modern philosophy to incorporate matters of axiological (value) import more organically into the total corpus of correct and methodic speculation.

Guru philosophy, as we have seen hitherto, is of a global and synthetic order where mere rationalism sinks into the background, bringing intuition and dialectical reasoning to the fore. Values in life err by being treated separately as something strictly falling outside its scope. The analytical and the synthetic tendencies are more equally blended and refer to an overall scheme of the Absolute as a normative value-reference to guide all speculation, while criticism acts still as a corrective throughout.

When we come to the question of ethics and aesthetics, we have to remember that value considerations spread out everywhere in the writings evenly, and the meager space given to them should not be hastily interpreted to mean that such questions are considered unimportant. A spiritually sound sense of values and way of life, with value considerations regulating man's relations with God as well as relations with his fellow man, are held to be implicit within philosophy's scope.

Obligatory Injunctions Different from Free Ethical Principles

The Guru here therefore puts his finger not on conduct as such but on the fundamental principles on which human relations and conduct are based. According to Sanskrit tradition respected through the ages, and respected by the Guru too, in *jnana* (wisdom) and *karma* (action), which when dualistically conceived have to be kept apart, there is open a unitive way in which, without duplicating each other, they can have fundamental aspects that mutually presuppose each other.

The perennial sources of human goodness, relations or conduct are one thing, while changing standards of good behaviour subject to historical fluctuations are another. The latter are treated in *smriti*s or *dharma shastra*s, of inferior status to Wisdom texts such as the work before us.

A Dialectically Conceived Ethics

To derive ethics out of a speculative body of doctrines or truths has always been a delicate problem for philosophers. Thus the categorical imperative of Kant has to depend on the "thing-in-itself" or on a metaphysics that is both transcendental and immanent at once. When ends and means are treated dualistically, justifying each other, we have a Machiavellian brand of ethics. There are closed and static religious or ethical attitudes where relativism may be said to prevail, resulting in hedonism or getting lost in teleological aspects rather than stressing the ontological.

Aristotle's Nichomachean Ethics is the result of recognizing the specific forms of value whereby life is expressed through matter, through its potent possibilities or *entelechia*. The Golden Mean is goodness. Platonic ethics stresses the ability to appreciate the True, the Good and the Beautiful, at the level of ideas rather than things. Epicurean and Stoic ethics fall apart by their absence of or stress on austerity as a virtue. Vedism in the Indian context has a hedonist and relativist ethics, while Buddhism and Vedanta, err, if at all, on the side of the opposite tendency of severe austerity. Books like the Bhagavad Gita strike the balance between these opposing trends, and a subtle axiological interplay of dialectics may be seen to regulate aesthetics and ethics to save them from killing all joy in life. In them a balanced outlook is substituted, regulated by a neutral attitude and dictated by a wisdom of the Absolute understood in a unified perspective integrating into unity epistemological, methodological and axiological considerations.

The method proper to such an approach is not in ratiocinative reasoning but in an approach based on dialectical treatment together of counterparts. What is good for the king must by the same token be good for the subjects, and what is good for the servant must also be good for the master. Cause and effect must be capable of being interchanged as limbs in the dialectical reasoning process. If a wife is kept happy the husband has peace in the house, or when a son is famous the father shines too by his glory reflected on to him. Such are some handy examples of the dialectical approach. This can also be called the Yoga Ethics of the Gita.

Dialectical methodology is thus different from the simple syllogistic reasoning of Aristotle, which is in reality the domain of the incertitudes of *if, but, or, neither-nor, both, neither, only, when,* etc., full of hesitant puzzlements in thought. Direct intuitive or imperative certitude is apodictically given by the reasoning that the Guru adopts here, where the two limbs of the same equation lend certitude each to the other. In Biblical dictums such as "Love they neighbour as thyself," we have a tacit recognition of this variety of dialectical reasoning which is, in axiological matters, more direct and telling than the hesitant faltering steps of ratiocinative thinking, which by mistake some philosophers of the West still insist on assuming belongs to a more philosophical method.

The Socratic analytical approach that eliminates error by questioning the opponent employing the basis of *reductio ad absurdum,* and the Aristotelian approach through ascending or descending from the particular to the general or vice versa, using syllogisms where the excluded middle implies the principle of contradiction, are both inferior to the pre-Socratic approach of a Parmenides or a Zeno, who were the last of the real dialecticians.

Closely scrutinized, the Guru's method gives full recognition to this old time method of reasoning. It is by bringing together the counterparts of an ethical or religious situation that the Guru makes his conclusions apodictic, necessary or imperative, whether dealing with questions of ethics or of religion. As for aesthetics, the two counterparts are the self and the non-self in cosmo-psychological or spiritual progression through the phenomenal that we have to visualize imaginatively. Every vestige of cosmo-psychic duality becomes abolished here in the nonduality of the self and the non-self in the same Absolute Self.

How Aesthetics is Derived from Philosophy

At the end of the previous chapter we examined Verse 69

as an example of structural imagery. This verse pictures graphically the course of spiritual progress in any man, and it contains a significant sub-clause which we have now to notice. The self is said to be in constant relation with the world outside in a subtle subjective and dialectically understandable manner. There is a constant interchange of enjoyable essences, a kind of osmosis that everlastingly goes on between the two aspects of the self and the non-self. This dialectical interplay of value factors from subject to object and vice versa is, according to the Guru, the source of all joy, which covers the best instances of what we call the aesthetical appreciation of values. Of course, there are grades of joy ranging from pleasures comparable to small change to Absolute Bliss which is that of the gold coin. They are all, however, comprised under the same general law of all-aesthetical joy.

Kindness as the Common Basis of Religion and Ethics

The very first verse of another composition of the Guru dealing with kindness gives us the key to his method in all ethics. He starts with the most general of postulates of his absolutist outlook in life by stating that all belong to one common brotherhood in the Self. At the next step he asks how then we can kill living beings, knowing that they belong to the same content of universal joy that is the essence of this same Truth.

The Good, the True and the Beautiful are lasting values in the context of Absolutism. Hence the merciless killing and eating of animals is said by him to be untenable on the basis of a very direct reasoning belonging to an imperative order. By hurting another one hurts one's self in a dialectical context, though this aspect may not be so evidently clear in a mechanistic context. This verity is brought out in so many words in Verse 25 of the *Atmopadesha Shatakam* as follows:

What is favourable to one and for another trouble brings,
That conduct is what is against the Self.
That flame of fire that another's suffering great involves
Falls and burns its flame in the ocean of infernal flames.
(Verse 25)

In conversation the Guru has taken even the example of speaking ill of another as a factor that tended to make oneself spiritually weaker. This subtle law of reciprocity, dialectically and subjectively understood, reveals for us the basis of the ethics that the Guru derived from the first principles of his philosophy.

Ethics when implicitly understood in its mystical or religious form is found in almost all the verses of the series. The reader can look for them and find them explicitly or implicitly presupposed everywhere. All religious life presupposes kindness, as the Guru explicitly states in one of his compositions, *Jiva-Karunya-Panchakam* (Kindness to Life):

All are of one Self-fraternity,
Such being the dictum to avow;
In such a light how can we take life,
And devoid of least pity go on to eat?

The Nondual Basis of All Morality

Guru ethics can be reduced to its simplest form when we say that when one serves two masters or accepts a double standard of values, one is going wrong. Truth in life is to be found as existing in and through life for itself, and not as something to be discovered disjunctly in some place "elsewhere." This verity is a guiding principle of applied ethics, which the Guru addresses in Verses 21 to 24. The fundamental law of ethics is however implied in Verse 20, which introduces this section of ethics consisting of four verses:

Another reality this world can have none; contrary
assertions
Made by men in the world, lack understanding all;
Although an ignoramus could mistake it for a reptile
Could a flower garland beneficial ever a snake become?
(Verse 20)

Ethics has thus its origin in one's Self where the non-self is articulated with it or participates nondually with it.

The Ego as the Epicentre for All Conduct

The moral dictum that says one should do unto others as one should do unto oneself, is derived from the same dialectically absolutist ethics that the Guru adopts as seen in these verses. He puts it however in a form in which duality in the philosophical context is abolished at one and the same stroke. Verses 23 and 24 are nearer to the origin of morality than the other two, 21 and 22, derived more indirectly. When loving one's neighbour as oneself, one avoids the duality between egotistic interests by canceling out dialectical counterparts. These verses read:

For another's sake, day in and out
Unstinting strives the generous and kind man;
The niggard, lying prone, whatever frustration's toil
undertakes
Is for his own sake alone! (Verse 23)

What here we discriminate as this man or that
Is the prime form of the Self alone!
Conduct that for one self-happiness spells
Must another's well-being bring about at once.
(Verse 24)

The Formation of Closed Static Units in Society and their Unethical Status

Many kinds of relativistic preferences are possible in the group life into which man is born and ekes out his life necessarily as a gregarious animal. Each group can consider its own interests egocentrically. When a man, for example, wishes that his own caste, tribe, race, sex or nation must win over another, he is committing one of the fundamental errors or sins against the interests of humanity thought of as a unit in the absolutist context. The rival claims possible for relativist unilateral interests are many, while when the same situation is viewed dialectically and unitively, without duality or contradiction between the component units, whether of family or nation, peace and happiness become naturally spelt out.

When understood and applied correctly the dialectical approach acts as a universal solvent of problems of a competitive character, and makes for orderly cooperation. The ancient division in India of human society into four *varnas*, (social levels) according to the value world natural to each, as seen in the so-called "caste system" has proved a failure, though perhaps based on sociological principles fundamentally valid and well intentioned. The great mistake was that, instead of viewing the matter as fluid and as a process of dynamic formation or everlasting flux, static and closed hereditary caste, rigidly conceived on the basis of watertight groups, petrified the whole process and made of the experiment, otherwise theoretically bold, into a Himalayan blunder and monumental failure.

In spite of its failure, however, wise individuals can apply in their lives the dynamism of the open dialectical approach implicit therein in their personal lives, instead of attempting to erect any sociopolitical system thereon. The mechanistic leveling of personal values at the present day tends to make such a thought impossible. Trying the experiment again would cost India too much. The formation of closed static groups preferred by each member of society as against a rival one is fraught with great danger. In Verses 21 and 22 the Guru points out the origin of the confusion involved, as follows:

A certain group is dear, that to me is dear,
What is dear to me and what is to another, thus it is
That round each item of value-interest confusions
come; know, therefore,
That one's own preference must accord with another's
dear desire. (Verse 21)

What is dear to the other, that is mine and what I prefer
Accords with the preference of the other man, such is
the course
Of discreet conduct; therefore the act that aims the good
of a man,
In the love of fellow-man must its motive have.
(Verse 22)

Thus, the seal is put here in the last lines above on the dialectical basis of all human conduct involving relations between man and man. Such a scientifically thought out absolutist attitude can be seen to cover inclusively many features that schools of ethics from Machiavellianism to Nichomacheanism, in themselves all partial speculations in ethics, have left out of their purview. The Kantian "imperative" as well as the Bergsonian "creative" brands are all covered here by the Guru's dialectical absolutist approach.

The One Religion of the Guru

Of all closed static groupings in society the one most fraught with danger to man is the formation of rival religions on a relativist dualist basis. Conflicts become possible under such conditions. When what contributed to such a life of internal strife within men in the formation of wrongly motivated religious groups is once discovered and eliminated from religious life, all falls into unity, by analogous tendencies between groups becoming revealed as between each religious formation.

Moses and Jesus differ in their outlook, as also the Old Testament from the New Testament, through the value sets implied in each. Vedism likewise differs from Vedantism.

Analogously, on the other hand, the obligatory aspect represented by the Ten Commandments can be found in the Pentateuch as well as in the Bible. Taboos and bans prevail here and there, overtly or tacitly, in all religions, and exclusive fanaticisms are possible in every case where orthodoxies might clash against rival orthodoxies. The delicate way of Wisdom in this matter is discussed by the Guru in Verses 44 to 49, which we shall examine here.

In order to be able to lay bare the philosophical implications of the One Religion that is in the mind of the Guru, let us read this sequence of six verses in a selected order of our own. The topic covered by each can be enumerated as follows:

(A) ALL RELIGIONS HAVE THE OVERALL AIM OF HAPPINESS

All religions when viewed horizontally as different from each other in expression, reveal many features that make for contrast. When we take a verticalized, inclusive or contemplatively dialectical view of the same situation of all religions understood together, a mutual agreement or transparency of content reveals itself between them, because the overall aim and end of all religions, however diverse, is none other than Happiness in life, here or hereafter, or both. Verse 49 enunciates this unequivocally as follows:

> Every man at every time makes effort in every way,
> Self-Happiness to secure; thus in the world
> Know there is this One Religion alone; known thus and
> Avoiding evil, one should his inner self attune.
>
> (Verse 49)

(B) THE DEEP MUTUAL ADOPTION IMPLIED IN RELIGIOUS AFFILIATION

When a man accepts or adopts a certain religion as an ideology or a pattern of behaviour as the one he likes or calls his own, there is a deep-seated fusion of the self and the non-self factors which takes place within him. Egoism tends often to fan and exaggerate the disparity of religions, but when the relation is contemplatively bipolar and verticalized, wherein the true Self in man and not the ego participates, adoption does not result in conflict.

The possibility of adopting a religion as one's own is itself, as the Guru points out, only a recognition of the homogeneous parity in the participation of the self and the non-self factors involved. By itself this possibility belongs to the pure Self, and when understood in such a pure perspective, is fully dignified and conducive to Self-realization. The danger, however, is that this pure nature of bipolar adoption becomes misapplied. Then *adhyasa* or superimposition mutually of non-Self factors onto the Self and vice versa takes place. Herein alone danger lurks. We read:

> The dweller within the body, from its own status as pure being,
> In respect of each possible thing, treats all
> As "that is mine" or "this is mine" transcending bodily sense;
> All are in reality realized, when we think of what this means.
>
> (Verse 48)

The possibility of such mutual adoption already implies, in principle at least, a homogeneity between the two aspects of the Self and the non-Self.

(C) RIVAL RELIGIONS REALLY PLEAD FOR THE SAME VALUE

We see that the protagonists of any religion dream of uniting all humanity under one faith. Just as a member of a certain nation might want all nations to come under its sway, there is an error implied in zealots for any particular religious formation. Hindus might want all the world to become Hindu and so on. If each religious zealot only realized that, in this kind of plea, all sailed in the same boat, rival antagonisms could be minimized. This travesty implicit in the unwise rivalry between religious groups, such as Unitarians and Trinitarians, causing much trouble that can be avoided, is alluded to with telling effect in Verse 47:

> All plead but for one religion to prevail,
> Which the disputants fail to remember withal;
> Those wise ones freed from disadoption of another's
> faith
> Can know here wholly the secret of all this. (Verse 47)

(D) THE NATURE OF THE IRONY IMPLICIT IN RELIGIOUS RIVALRY

After understanding the secret mentioned above, the rest can be read and understood without much comment:

> Ignoring that in substance various religions are the same,
> Like the blind men in respect of an elephant, fools wander
> In this world; imitate not their way,
> And not agitated like them, one should calmly settle
> down! (Verse 44)

> One religion is not good enough for another and the
> doctrine cardinal
> Stated in one, according to another's calculations is found
> defective;
> Until that day the unitive secret herein is known
> with certitude
> There shall continue to be confusion prevailing
> in this world. (Verse 45)

> Victory by fight is impossible here; one as against one
> No religion by fighting gets exterminated; not
> knowing this
> The opponent of a stranger faith,
> His own doom shall be in vain fight for, beware!
> (Verse 46)

Verse 44 underlines the need for taking a global view of religious systems. Treated piecemeal one tends to compare, as it were, the leg of one with the hands of another. Comparative religion must tend to establish the points of affinity in corresponding structural aspects of religions, rather than stress differences based on aspects torn out of the proper context or perspective. The familiar analogy of the blind men and the elephant is used advantageously by the Guru here.

Verse 45 stresses the need to see the underlying unity of religions.

Verse 46 underlines the fact that persecution only makes unilateral faith firmer. The martyrs to any deep belief prove the irony of the situation in the history of any religion, and this is contrary to what might be expected by mechanistic reasoning. The apocalyptic touch of the last line above gives a prophetic touch to the Guru's philosophy of religion.

10

Guru Philosophy Summarized

1.0 Guru philosophy represents a total neutral and normative approach to what is philosophically significant or valuable to human life, from both the existential and the subsistential aspects of the Absolute to the context of which such a wholesale approach belongs.

1.01 Such an approach involves a regulative action for a way of life, as well as a way of understanding facts, truths or reality.

1.02 It calls for initial scepticism as well as full willingness to believe. In other words, the a priori and the a posteriori are equally respected in Guru philosophy.

1.03 Many other antinomies, polarities, dichotomies or ambivalent factors enter into the structure of the certitude that Guru philosophy seeks. Such precise and valid forms of speculation tend to make it a science rather than a mere verbose or wild speculation. In other words, there is implicit in it a unitive methodology, an epistemology and an axiology proper to it.

1.04 The phenomenal and the noumenal, the pure and the practical, the perceptual and the conceptual, the quantitative and the qualitative, action and understanding, are pairs of antinomies belonging to different zones or levels of consciousness, within which lie the visible or the intelligible universe given to the eye or to the mind. They belong either to the vertical or the horizontal value worlds.

1.05 What is given to the senses objectively is the horizontal, and what is given to the self as "I" or "my" or "mine" belongs to the vertical. To categorize the given contemplative data as belonging to these axes of reference is the first key to the easy understanding of the Guru's philosophy. The enjoyable nature of the spread-out universe is treated unitively with the Self, while the enjoyer is the vertical counterpart of the same paradoxical dialectical situation.

1.06 Both human nature and cosmological nature aspects participate herein by a sort of mathematical intersection rather than as a psychophysical parallelism.

1.07 The vertical component is that of the Self, and the horizontal that of the non-Self. The Self, which is not given to the senses, comprises all possible levels of value from the most immanent to the most transcendent.

1.1 There is a constant osmotic reciprocal exchange of knowledge as if through a retroactive exchange between the rich and fully transparent aspects of the Self and the non-Self, and this results in presenting value factors and interests that rise and circulate. They comprise psychological, cosmological and theological factors in a constant flux of change and becoming. This process goes on eternally between these two axes of reference.

1.2 This alternating play of inter-physical and trans-subjective factors tends to horizontal activity at a given moment when nescience prevails, and again gets absorbed into pure verticality of reason at another moment.

1.3 An absolutely and purely active principle of thinking substance lies beyond or behind the paradox of the plus and the minus in the many layers of life interests, belonging to the fourfold status of the actual, the perceptual, the conceptual and the nominal, which are integrally held together and envisaged in Guru philosophy.

1.4 Such an Existent-Subsistent-Value when understood in all its secondary implications gives satisfactory answers to major doubts and dissolves conflicts in life. Such knowledge makes one free and yields a peace that passes understanding. Banishing sin, decreasing suffering, being a pearl of great price, or a leaven that can permeate subtly the whole of life, are other known ways of stressing the value of the same science of the Absolute. Even a little of this can banish great fear, as the Gita would prefer to put this same verity.

1.5 Salvation and heaven mean only the same high value of Wisdom represented by this Science of all sciences.

1.6 Cosmogony, cosmology and psychology approached phenomenologically rather than merely objectively, ethics and aesthetics, with a chapter that corresponds to theology, together with an eschatology that covers questions pertaining to apocalyptic images of prophetic import of life here and hereafter, all treated unitively in terms of normalized human understanding — such are some of the branches covered in Guru philosophy.

1.7 It is an inside contemplative view that Guru philosophy takes. It covers the same ground as some of the world's great scriptures, but in a positive and less mythological, merely theistic or fable-like style of discourse.

1.8 Structural and schematic imagery as a precise protolinguistic device is seen to be retained in the Guru-literature in such a revised and modernized form that it becomes possible to erect a mathematically precise science on the foundations laid by the Guru in his philosophy.

1.9 A veritable Science of the Absolute is foreshadowed in his writings, of which the Darshana Mala marks a more culminating point of attainment.

2.0 Vedantic schematism, structuralism and selectionism are further boiled down to reveal the protolinguistic and the metalinguistic patterns underlying the world of discourse, and corresponding to the semiotic, syntactic and pragmatic processes of thought and tendencies within the informative cybernetics of consciousness. Axiomatic thinking reveals its utmost possibilities in the correct mathematical logistic of the Guru. It avoids mere mythology and theology except where he wishes to clarify some protolinguistic aspect.

3.0 Speculation attains apodictic, dialectical and rhetorical finality in the Guru's writings, so that by going one step further one is able to step on the firm land of a veritable Science of the Absolute, yet to be fully formulated in the light of modern knowledge.

4.0 By sight and sound our human intelligence inserts itself correctly and, as it were, cybernetically into a world of automatic and retroactive discourse or semantics, with a surprisingly uniform symmetry of structure that all theories or laws of nature seem to respect, where concepts and percepts equate themselves into circulating processes that are sometimes reversible and at other times not so.

5.0 The living organism fits itself into a universe which is both physical and metaphysical at one and the same time, and what formalism or mechanism belongs to it schematically has its range of extrapolated applicability in the microscopic and megascopic realities, without being limited by experiment or more than experimental experiences natural to the human race.

6.0 Science in its latest version lends support to Guru philosophy and vice versa, and their method and theory of knowledge are beginning to resemble each other. Some very bold flights of speculation in Guru philosophy seem now to gain a validity which they could not have had from science understood fifty years ago.

7.0 The physical and the metaphysical aspects of reality are beginning to be treated as belonging complementarily to each other, as the vision of the Guru clearly envisages. A whole hierarchy of classes that can rise perceptually, making for classes of classes analytically or synthetically, is not a matter any more of mere verbose or vain speculation, either in science or in philosophy.

8.0 Science now calls for bolder and bolder speculative flights, instead of the caution that it commended a few years ago. The task of bridging the wide gap in scientific thought that at present separates axiomatic from experimental thinking, calls for fuller freedom for the philosopher capable of flying very high in pure speculation. It is exactly herein that Guru philosophy excels and scores, where hesitant attitudes that fail to face the situation frontally fail miserably. Such efforts are neither philosophy nor science.

9.0 Instead of failing doubly it is thus that Guru philosophy succeeds doubly in laying the foundation of a science of all sciences, not merely remaining lukewarm as a philosophy of science or as a science of philosophy.

10.0 The philosophy of the Guru, like mathematical calculations, respects a formalism that it shares in common with all logical or correct thinking. Where common sense fails, a calculus strictly conceived, which makes allowance for tautology as well as contradiction within its scope, regulates its speculative procedures.

10.1 When the limits even of such empirical positivist reasoning have been passed, the Guru depends on a dialectical approach where double negation is employed with advantage, as when language makes one "yes" from two "nos" or when in algebra two minuses multiplied make a plus.

10.2 Such reasoning transcends paradox.

10.3 The hierarchy of classes, wherein propositions are true or false, whether logically or factually, gets neutrally absorbed in the class of all classes from both sides.

10.4 Instead of excluding the middle ground as in the syllogistic structure of thought, speculation can ascend or descend at will between alternative values in which subject and object become interchangeable terms.

10.5 In stating the implications of the second law of thermodynamics, we have in the heart of modern physics a bold generalization, which, if it could be thought of as a reversible process, would come nearest to this kind of dialectical ascent or descent in respect of factors of universal import, whether concerned with notions such as positive or negative entropy, or between heat and work, or any other pair of metaphysical or physical elements or factors, related through complementarity as understood by Niels Bohr or tending to indeterminism as in Heisenberg's theory.

11.0 What we wish to underline here is merely the fact that modern laws of physics when they speak of a physical universe, deal with abstractions and generalizations at least as vague as any that classical speculators dared to venture.

11.1 Metaphysics and physics are hardly distinguishable in the formalized language that they both use.

11.2 If parables and literal analogies are replaced by a precise mathematical language, one becomes as good or as bad as the other, according to the correctness or arbitrariness involved.

11.3 It is neither experiment nor calculus that should be considered the final arbiter, but both as belonging to a normative notion of the Absolute.

12.0 Knowledge seeks to know itself. All things rise and change into pure thought. Pure space would then remain self-radiant. The Self and its knowledge together make one reality. The pure thing-in-itself knows no dual alternative. There is no truth other than or dualistically apart from what is given here itself. All things are real in themselves but cancel out when examined as consisting of exclusive classes.

13.0 Semantically all diverse or discrete entities merge in the semiotic entity of the pure Meaning of all meanings.

14.0 Halting speculation that ratiocinates piecemeal with propositional "ifs" and "buts", is a weak instrument for the Guru in his bold unitive, wholesale, neutral, frontal and global approach and vision of the Absolute.

14.1 Although analysable into its own structural and schematic elements, the vision is one that is downright and totally convincing. Experienced normally as a wonder or a tremendous mystery, the understanding of this could even strike one down by its powerful onset within consciousness, prepared for by a harmony or transparency established between the Self and the non-Self.

14.2 In the correct and normal mystical state experimental truth is not degraded nor logical reason effaced, but both exist inclusively at a higher level of dialectical intuition.

14.3 The analysis and the wonder of the Absolute go hand in hand in Guru philosophy.

14.4 Instead of one gaining a symmetrical primacy over the other, the total knowledge situation envisaged in its perfectly symmetrical structure thus gives due place to the will to believe as also to the will for critical disposition or systematic doubting.

15.0 Guru speculation lives and moves in a vertical axis where the Self holds in unity the aspects of Existence (*sat*), Subsistence (*chit*) and Value (*ananda*).

15.1 The evidence of the eye, which is experimental, cancels here into the evidence of the name or the Word. The Logos thus meets the Nous of the Socratic and pre-Socratic contents of Western speculation.

15.2 There is a neutral stratum or zone in thought or consciousness of the absolutist context, which is the richest of the stuff that consists of pure human understanding or reason. It is transparent to this double aspect, giving wonder on one side and revealing the schematic structure at the core of the Absolute on the other.

15.3 Wonder may be said to refer to the positive aspect of the vertical axis, with schematic structuralism into which all mathematically understood elements of the physical world enter as components or ingredients constituting the negative aspect of the same.

15.4 Speculation is best, not when it is accentuated positively or negatively, but when both of these remain in the neutral ground between the two polarities. When metaphysics and physics are treated unitively without duality between mind and matter, we have two limbs of a universal equation. As with the notion of positive and negative entropy, speculation can proceed irrespective of their reversibility, that is, free from the mathematics that confines itself only to irreversibility, as in that of Carnot.

16.0 An extrapolated series of ensembles or classes can be subjected to an ascending or descending series of value factors, in the ascending order of Existence-Subsistence-Value (*sat-chit-ananda*) or as descending in a value significance first, merging into reverse series of subsistence next, and to spread out into manifold existences simultaneously manifest as in ordinary life. Contiguity or continuity can hold together thus the one and the many.

16.1 The books of nature, truth or value should be capable of being read both ways to abolish all partiality of points of view, so as to yield that neutral Absolute which is beyond all blemish of one-sided predications.

16.2 All values could be of Subsistence or Existence interchangeably, to yield one and the same unitive Self.

16.3 Maya, as understood in Guru philosophy, is the overall philosophical category of all possible errors, starting from simple optical illusions through eidetic representations of phenomenalism, to the noblest and subtlest forms of philosophical error that could vitiate wisdom even through such factors as science (*vidya*) and nescience (*avidya*) or nominalism and conceptualism.

16.4 All horizontal factors are meant to be covered by this omnibus term maya, and it stands equally for the negativitat of Hegel and the Uncertainty Principle of Heisenberg. It comprises all phenomenological, eidetic, ontological or psychological presentiments.

17.0 Even the faintest vestige of duality as between Self and non-Self, or subject and object, is repugnant to Guru philosophy.

17.1 Guru philosophy has a theology that avoids all equivocation in respect of the problem of evil, and instead of trying to explain it away by any solipcism or principle of "the best of all possible worlds" it lays it squarely at the feet of God Himself as part of the wondrous or tragic elements of

His own creation, which is neither meant to be good nor evil but beyond both.

17.2 God transcends paradox in His most high stature, rising without apology to the heights of proper absolutism.

17.3 Paradox can be transcended either frontally facing the fact of evil as a contradiction, or bypassing it by a dialectical approach of absorbing all middle grounds.

17.4 An immanent-transcendent absorption in the Self of all possible selves is involved here.

17.5 God then drinks His own poison, inevitable in creation.

17.6 To put the same in different rhetoric, evil is to be treated as a part of the game of creation, attributed to His sense of comedy or sport. Although evil is not explained away it is included in a larger scheme of reality where good and bad cancel into the sheer Glory of the Absolute. Then the horizontal evil given to human eyes would only crown them vertically with more enhanced goodness by its double negation.

17.7 The last vestiges of the negative taint of maya get abolished in the brave contemplative seeking absolute freedom or happiness through the negation of negation, until, passing through an ascending stage, it touches positive heights of the Value of values. Any name becomes good enough for each value, and when universally and expansively understood as the crowning glory of God instead of as the principle of Evil, maya purifies and perfects itself further by a descent into the levels of the universal concrete.

17.8 Both concrete and abstract reside as aspects of the Self that holds all possible antinomies together like a bundled sheaf of corn.

17.9 The paradoxical elements tending to duality in the Absolute might persist till the final vision of a supreme union between the vertical and the horizontal takes place in the contemplative who has correctly and clearly attained his term.

18.0 Then the atom refuses to be split further. Seeking its own perfection or plenitude from the other pole of the same total situation, Infinity gains its ultimate fullness of term. Both meet in the high neutral value of the Absolute, which involves neither positive effort nor negative passivity to attain. The knower of the Absolute is the Absolute.

18.1 When the paradox that life presents to a thinking man, whether a philosopher or a mystic, is transcended through a correct method and discipline combined, one being complementarily positive to the other in a complex four-limbed epistemological quaternion or frame of reference, a high value of happiness, peace, fearlessness and clarity of spirit is attained.

18.2 The hierarchy of men and gods and the alternation of birth and death are abolished for him. Being and becoming get merged into one inner Self-experience in which man attains Peace.

18.3 Horizontalism that yields errors drops its innermost veils, and man stands face to face with the universe in himself.

18.4 Eschatological value worlds hereafter and apocalyptic visions of a doomsday vanish, self-effaced.

18.5 A simple scientifically understandable cosmogony, a mathematically precise logistic guiding thought and conduct held unitively under the aegis of the overall regulative notion of the Absolute Value, an afterlife that leaves behind a corpus of good repute as real and valuable as any actual life lived here and now, a transparency and a perfectly detached equilibrium between rival interests or activities, and the boldness to identify oneself with the Absolute in full reverent non-egoist humility, always with an unlimited kindliness that is present as a corollary to fully sympathetic understanding of the unity of all life, with recognition of all normal values in life at their proper times and places, without any exaggerated unilateral outlook — such are some of the directive characteristics of Guru philosophy and the way of life it holds high.

18.6 The promise of peace, immortality and the joy of freedom, are all comprised in this attitude that knows no distinction of ends or means or disparity between ways of piety or wisdom.

18.7 Like the notion of a thermodynamic equilibrium with an overall independent autonomous cybernetic system, where action and retroaction cancel out into a zero state of sameness, in a fully reversible process of forward becoming and regression, contemplative life implies a principle of equality or equanimity where all osmotic interchange of factors in the grand respiration of life come to the pause of Self-identity.

18.8 This is the ultimate secret of the pundit, to which few can attain, as the Guru himself sadly deplores.

18.9 It is at this point alone that the many manifestations of the One, and the One Supreme Meaning that holds manifoldness in its unified semantic grasp of the Meaning of all meanings, can be realized. There is neither *that* nor *this*, nor Existence (*sat*) different from Subsistence (*chit*) or Value (*ananda*). All these aspects fuse to make the grand confection of great value called the Absolute within oneself. Such are some other bold conclusions of Guru philosophy which he himself underlines as difficult for all to grasp.

19.0 Axiomatic and experimental thinking meet in this wonder!

Appendix

One Hundred Verses of Self-Instruction
(Atmopadesha Shatakam by Narayana Guru)

1

Rising even above knowledge, what within the form
Of the one who knows, as equally without, radiant shines,
To that Core, with the eyes five restrained within,
Again and again prostrating in adoration, one should chant.

2

The inner organ, the senses, and counting from the body
The many worlds we know, are all, on thought, the sacred form
Of the supreme Sun risen in the void beyond;
By relentless cogitation one should attain to this.

3

These phenomenal aspects five such as the sky
Which as emergent from outside is here seen to be,
By contemplation one should bring to non-difference
As the sea is to the waves that rise in rows thereon.

4

Knowledge, its meaning known, and the personal knowledge
Subjective, together make but one primal glory;
Within the unrarified radiance of this great knowledge
One should merge and become that alone.

5

People here on earth, they sleep, wake and think
Various thoughts; watching over all of these with intent eye
There dawns a priceless light, which never shall dim again;
Led onward by this, one should forward wend.

6

One has to wake, then go to sleep, of food partake, or mate,

Thus do promptings dissipating keep coming round;
Whoever could there be, therefore to wake
Unto that reality's one and changeless form?

7

To wake never more, ever sleepless to remain, as awareness;
If for this today you are not fit, then in the service
Of those silent ones who ever dwell awake to AUM
Absolved from birth, steadily fix the form.

8

Eating of the fruits five, such as light
Perched the while on a shot-gun foul-smelling,
Ever in wily change, what can bring down in shreds these five,
Such a lucid inner form wielding, the Self must brilliant become!

9

He who dwells in contemplation beneath a tree
Whereon climbing, a creeper bears aloft on either side
The blossoms of the psychic states; mark, such a man,
By inferno unapproached ever remains.

10

"Who is sitting in the dark? Speak!" says one,
Whereupon the other, intent himself to know likewise,
On hearing the first, he asks; "Who may you even be?"
For both of these the word of response is One alone.

11

The repeated "I, I" contemplated from within
Is not many, but one; divergent egoity
Being multiple, in the totality of such
The Self-substance too, continuity assumes.

12

With skin and bone and refuse, and many an inner factor of evil end,
Lo, wielding these, one ego looms! This which passes,

Is the other; That greater Self which grows to perfection,
O, grant the boon, that it may not the ego swell !

13

Unto the Master who dons the ashes of the three modes,
Offering the flower of the inner self, inclining before him,
With all sense interests effaced, divest of all and cool,
Even from the grandeur of loneliness bereft, into glory sink!

14

That light, rid of three-fold view, that ever brighter burns
Upsurging and brimful beyond the bounds of the triple worlds,
Remember that it will never come within the reach
Of a hermit untrue, as Upanishadic secret lore declares.

15

Ten thousand years do a moment make to those favoured ones
Suckled in the milk of the pure transcendent; but when knowledge
Is within the power of the scope of relative immanent nature
Half-a-second would seem ten thousand years long.

16

If an arid desert most expansive should become overflooded
By river water all at once, such would be the rising symphony
Falling into the ears, to open then the eye; do therefore
Daily become the best of sages endowed with Self-control.

17

Suffering (fire) filled, with petals five and tiers two,
Rotating beginningless, such is the lamp hanging high
Which is the Self burning on in shadow form, with past habits
For oil, and function verily for wick.

18

The 'I' is not darkness; were it so blind
Unaware of this 'I, I' we should have remained;
Because of such awareness, the I-consciousness is not darkness
In order to know thus, to one and all declare.

19

"Bottom, top or tip, reality here, there or that" —
So do conflicts come: Prime Substance is all there is:
The inert here, all change and pass; how could a wave
Apart from the water's form, another reality have?

20

Another reality this world can have none; contrary assertions
Made by men in the world, lack understanding all;
Although an ignoramus could mistake it for a reptile,
Could a flower garland beneficial ever a snake become?

21

A certain kind is dear, that to me is dear,
What is dear to me and what is to another, thus it is
That round each item of value-interest confusions come; know,
therefore,
That one's own preference must accord with another's dear
desire.

22

What is dear to the other, that is mine and what I prefer
Accords with the preference of the other man, such is the course
Of discrete conduct; therefore the act that aims the good of a
man,
In the love of fellow-man must its motive have.

23

For another's sake, day in and out
Unstinting strives the generous and kind man;
The niggard, lying prone, whatever frustration's toil undertakes
Is for his own sake alone.

24

What here we discriminate as this man or that
Is the prime form of the Self alone!
Conduct that for one self-happiness spells
Must another's well-being bring about at once.

25

What is favourable to one and for another trouble brings,
That conduct is what is against the Self
One whose acts another's suffering great involve
Falls and burns in the ocean of infernal flames.

26

All limbs suppressing and standing as a bolt
The limb-owner mere vapour enshrouds within;
"This" man he takes different from "that" therefore
Owing to the weakness of unwisdom alone.

27

What in darkness remains aware, the Self indeed that is;
And knowledge that which as name and form,
As senses with inner organ, as actor and action,
Looms here as everything, like great Indra's magic, lo!

28

Bereft of bottom as of top, from bottom to the crest
What transparent awareness has, that is *turiya* consciousness;
The inert no knowledge has: what it cogitating tells
From in-between, is no knowledge at all, do mark!

29

The mind-blossom plucking, who offers to the Great Master,
No need has he, other works to perform;
Else, let him pluck blossom wild, or otherwise
The *maya*-spell let him repeat; the *maya* goes.

30

The inert, no awareness can have, awareness no cogitation needs;
Nor does it hold discourse; knowing this awareness to be all,
And giving up all, transparency of spirit one gains,
And in bodily bonds confined, one suffers never more indeed!

31

Without prior experiencing, no inference there could be
As this has never before been experienced by the senses

The existence of the operator
Is never given to inferential thought.

32

It is not the operator but the operation that we know;
The said operator being ever unseen, the world and all else
Is naught, while lending it outer semblance of shape;
It is awareness alone that really remains.

33

Knowledge in order to know itself
The earth and other manifestations became;
In inverted manner thus, now mounting, now changing over
Like a circulating fire-faggot, it keeps turning round.

34

Half-a-second is what is the prime hub
Of the wheel of the car, mounted whereon, the universe rolls on;
Know this to be the sport of that beginningless One,
Ever going on in the core of awareness pure.

35

Like the dawning altogether of ten thousand suns
Wisdom's function comes; such verily is what
Can tear asunder the knowledge hiding impermanent darkness of *maya* here,
And, as the primordial Sun on high, prevails.

36

The powers of understanding are many; all of them under two sets
Such as the "same" and the "other" inclusively can be brought;
Merging into that form of "other-sameness" of these,
To clarity of vision one should awake.

37

To subdue, even somewhat the obduracy of the "other"
Is hard indeed without understanding's limitless power;

Even by such should one gain mastery over it and thus attain
Close access to Her who is discrimination's anti-sensous One.

38

What appraises manifold variety, the "other" that is;
And the "same" is whatever unitively shines on;
Thus grasping the situation above, into that state
Which yields sameness, melt and mix and erect sit.

39

Following up further the said powers, a further bifurcation here is,
One of these is an attribute of the "same", while the other
Qualifies the harsh "other" that never detachment gains;
Thus making two kinds of each of these.

40

On to the *same* as on to the *other* there constantly alight
Their respective specifying factors; although not proportionate,
Through the spinning phase of these two in all,
All predications whatsoever there are do come to be.

41

In "This is a pot" the initial "this" is the harsh
While the "pot" is what makes its specific attribute;
For the mind with its myriad Indra-magic to come,
Understand that "this" is the basis of functioning.

42

In "This is knowledge" the initial "this" is the "same"
While its specifying factor is the cognitive consciousness;
For the mind and all else to be effaced for the good path to gain,
"This" it is that one should contemplate.

43

By Nature's action caught, and turned,
Men of good action too, alas, keep turning round!
Mis-action to counteract, non-action avails not.
Gain-motive bereft, Wisdom one should attain.

44

Ignoring that in substance various religions are the same,
Like the blind men in respect of an elephant, fools wander
In this world; imitate not their way,
And not agitated like them; one should calmly settle down.

45

One religion is not good enough for another and the doctrine cardinal
Stated in one, according to another's calculations is found defective;
Until that day the unitive secret herein is known with certitude
There shall continue to be confusion prevailing in this world.

46

Victory by fight is impossible here; one as against one,
No religion by fighting gets exterminated; not knowing this
The opponent of a stranger faith,
His own doom shall be in vain fight for, beware!

47

All plead but for one religion to prevail,
Which the disputants fail to remember withal;
Those wise ones freed from disadoption of another's faith
Can know here wholly the secret of all this.

48

The dweller within the body, from its own status as pure being
In respect of each possible thing, treats all
As "that is mine" or "this is mine" transcending bodily sense;
All are in reality realized when we think of what this means.

49

Every man at every time makes effort in every way,
Self-happiness to secure, thus in the world
Know there is this One Religion alone; known thus and
Avoiding evil, one should his inner self attune.

50

With earth and water, air and fire likewise,
Also the void, the ego, cognition and mind,
All worlds including the waves and ocean too
Do all arise and into awareness change.

51

From awareness the "I" sense first emerged;
Comes then with it "This"ness, as counterpart beside,
These, like creepers twain, do overcover entirely,
Hiding the whole of the *Maya* tree.

52

Filled with word-content, that day the firmament shall radiant blaze,
And into it shall be absorbed to extinction all the visionary magic,
Then, too, that small voice completing tri-basic cognition
Shall cease, and, lo! Self-radiance prevails!

53

That primordial potency that herein resides
Is the seed that gives birth to all here we see;
Merging the mind in that, never forgetting,
Maya-mind to end, ever do contemplation pursue.

54

The waking state, it obtains not in sleep
And sleep again does not attain consciousness
When awake; day by day these twain are born
Of *Maya's* womb and keep alternating on.

55

A long drawn out dream is this, and like sleep each day,
It gets extinguished; dream too likewise!
We can never see extinction thus to this; as it is
Hitched on to the pure aloneness, it goes round for ever.

56

Like waves instantly arising on the ocean
Each body one after one rises to subside again;
Where alas! is the term for this? Know this as action
Taking place perpetually in awareness-ocean's prime source.

57

Within the waveless ocean, there do abide
Endless *Maya*-traits which as potent configurations that assume
Bodies with such as water and taste remain
As beginningless effects forming various worlds upon worlds.

58

Thinking not in terms, ever new, of yesterday, today,
Tomorrow or even another day, never-endingly
Know, all things we count or measure
As of confusion's making; difference there is none at all!

59

Apart from awareness I have no being;
As distinct from me awareness cannot remain
As mere light; both knowledge and knower, contemplation
Reveals beyond doubt as of one substance alone.

60

Even when knowledge to egoism is subject in any predication
And one is unmindful of the ultimate verity of what is said
Yet as with the truth however ultimate, such knowledge
Can never fall outside the scope of the knowing self.

61

Outside objects hold the field each distinct from each
With the sense that measures, whose function is nescience,
And these in turn with many sets of names such as that of directions,
Or the sky, keep rising up and into awareness change.

62

Mere orthodoxy which keeps saying that one should not adopt
As one's own a doctrine belonging to another side, how can it
True knowledge bring? Lip service does not avail;
One has earnestly to contemplate the state supreme.

63

This which is non-distinct from knowledge, than knowing which
knowledge
Straightaway, here there is none other to know
As any ultimate knowing beyond; such the supreme secret
Of the most informed of men; who is there to know?

64

This which ever prevails, surmounting each interest-item,
One's proper retrospection alone can compromise:
By means of extremely lucid memory, however, the revealing
Of ultimate-wisdom-treasure is still not to be ruled out.

65

There is nothing here that we have not already once known;
Hidden by form, knowledge fails us; wakefully to know all this
There is none at all, limitless as it is,
Oh, who can there be at all to know this wonder dear!

66

Earthy factors shall come to be evermore;
One alone remains not subject to becoming;
What we know, what it is, what we are, are that same;
And all others too remain conforming to its form.

67

One that is beyond all count and the ordinary—
Besides these two what is of other form
In memory, in sleep, nor in any city on high
Could such have any existence, indeed!

68

As the ego-sense enters into the snake-rope forms
Now as knowledge, now as a limbed agent in alternating duality,
It becomes pure now and then again profane,
Thus should he understand, the intuitive man.

69

With hearing and such as horses linked, while bearing within
The image of the Self, and controlled by the master of faculties,
Is the libido-chariot mounted whereon the ego rides
Dealing unceasingly with each thing of beauty as it proceeds.

70

The one libido it is that as the "I" sense, the senses,
The inner instruments, the body and all these becomes
Unravelled; where is the term to this? The knower remains
Distinct only till knowledge becomes known.

71

Bereft of becoming none stays here on earth
In equalized state; a beginningless sport is all this!
In its global fullness, when, as a whole, one knows this
There comes to him unbounded happiness.

72

Now there is action which is nescience and again
There is the pure knowledge which is science
Ordained by *Maya* though these stay divided thus
The meta-dual attitude, the unitive *turiya* yields.

73

Of one thing there could be many, as in many objects
One single meaning could reside; by such knowing we can know
Consciousness as comprising all, differencelessly; without any remainder
This ultimate secret, however, is not given for all to know.

74

Particles there are innumerable in a world
As within such a particle a world too abides;
The inert merges thus in the mind-stuff, as the mind-stuff too
Within the body; thus, on thought they are One.

75

Nature is water; the body, foam; the Self, the deep;
The 'I', 'I' rumbling within, the magic of the waves that arise;
Pearls they are each flowering of Wisdom within;
And what one drinks of oneself, immortality verily it is!

76

As with a well into which measureless sand is wafted
By successive gusts, tier on tier, so too
Exposed to the waftings of untruth's hierarchy
The inner Self inwardly multitudinous forms it gains.

77

The ultimate is the sky; wind, that power expansive;
Awareness, the fire; water represents the perceptive organs;
What is given objectively to the senses, the earth;
And what thus keeps as five principles burning has its secret in
the One alone.

78

Neither is there death nor birth nor life duration here,
Nor men or gods nor others of that order; all name and form!
Like a mirage based on desert sands, is this thing that stands
Nor is it a thing at all with any content, note.

79

At birth-time being there is none
And the one born at another instant cannot be
How ever does this exist? Death too is even likewise;
All this but a flux and becoming of the mind-stuff pure!

80

Contraries like being and becoming, how can they
As creation endurance and dissolution, in one place co-exist?
For these three to pass into, there is nothing either;
Thus viewed, earth and other things are mere words alone.

81

Nature, dividing one time as the enjoyer,
As everything outside, immanent or transcendent in glory looms
At another time again, by "this-ness" expanded
It spreads out as the enjoyable universe.

82

Like the fire that emerges out of churning sticks
That boundless Wisdom that from within those who seek prevails
As the Sun ascendant in pure reason's firmament supreme
It stays burning and to its flames consuming, fuel everything becomes.

83

Breaking up, staying on, or rising again after a change over
To continue, such is the course of the bodily nature here;
Watchful of all the three from its position ultimate
The one cleftless Self, that free from all change remains.

84

Because of cognition, if one should say there is
Earthiness as a reality, that is not true; what there is, is sod;
Without stable content all the limitless entities that stand
Are but Nature-configurations abiding within awareness.

85

No shadow could exist without depending on a model original
Since the manifest world is seen to have no original model anywhere
Neither shadow nor actuality is this: all is seen
Like a snake that a gifted artist might cleverly sketch.

86

The body and other things all have no being one in another,
Thus the converse position becomes untenable;
As from day-to-day this remains without setting
It gains the status of verity emerging once again.

87

Each taken by itself all things here do exist; treated mutually
Each class excludes the other; considered in this way
The body and other things are neither real
Nor lacking in verity; they become unpredicable.

88

All things are real enough; the philosopher, however,
Grasps all things here as One; when not viewed
Through the inward eye, that great tribulation
Which is *Maya,* yields much puzzlement, indeed!

89

As out of knowledge, sparks of fire innumerable arise
Asserting the being of non-being so as to make the world emerge,
Know that outside of knowledge not a thing exists;
Such knowledge unitive awareness yields.

90

What has no basis in reality can never hide what exists;
Experience vouches for this; asserting the reality
Of what exists, at every step, by Existence all is here enveloped;
The body and such effects have been made up of Existence.

91

The effort that is made in view of something dear to one
As ordained too, remaining always constant and same
There is a dear value, unborn, unspent, unpredicable,
One and secondless, which ever endures as one's happiness.

92

As there is the law of energy remaining ever unspent
By outwardly directed action, there must needs be inwardly

A dear value that is inseparable from it, for which here
The action, is merely a symbol of outer recognition.

93

To one who has cut connection with the changeful body
There is nothing which surpasses in value his own Self;
As the interest that prevails in respect of oneself, as ordained also,
Never-ceasingly endures, the Self, eternal it is.

94

This which presents itself, as a mixture of the world
And what is real; is a great iniquity indeed;
Indeterminate and unknowable to word or thought,
How could valid reasoning move therein?

95

This expansive display of operative artifice as by *Maya* ordained
The shining creative principle of the universe is she;
And she, descending here, her limbs they are that become
The crust of the cosmic egg, in number ten million.

96

The atom and the infinite thus, as being and non-being,
Loom from either side; this experience too
Of being as well as non-being, shall thereafter extinction gain,
And devoid of any basis, shall forever cease to be!

97

Within the glory of pure knowing, the atom bereft of parts, shall extinct become.
And the infinite too, shall thereafter its own plenitude attain.
Direct experience can alone reveal this boundless
Stuff of intelligence pure, this silence-filled ocean of Immortal Bliss.

98

Till now, not a thing have we here known, as we have kept saying.

In every case, that there is something still of greater happiness;
Although the mind and other factors might vanish
The selfhood of the Soul (*Atman*) must be said to be Wisdom; ever unspent.

99

Knowledge and "I" are both one, for one divest of all veiling curtains;
Another might have reason to argue still;
If the "I" could be taken as other than knowledge
None there is to know knowledge here at all!

100

Neither that nor this, nor the content of existence am I
But existence, subsistence, joy-immortal; thus attaining clarity
Emboldened, discarding attachment to being and non-being,
One should gently, gently, merge in SAT-AUM.

Part III
The Search for a Norm in Western Thought

Introduction

As it emerged from the theological dogma of the Middle Ages, Western philosophy inherited the unresolved paradox that lay at the core of Greek tragedy, where the twin worlds of immanence and transcendence find themselves tantalizingly close yet never meshed. Greek drama gave voice to the problem: the alternately dynamic and faltering footsteps of humankind are out of synchronicity with the divine rhythm that gives them sustenance. Plato and his rebellious student Aristotle spoke of this conflict most clearly in the world of philosophical discourse. And though their voices were muffled for many centuries by the Church, the argument was re-awakened by the European Renaissance. The dialogue then was no longer phrased by choruses or defined by the ethos of tragedy. Rationality took the lead and the paradox was seen in the pull between a priori and a posteriori.

On this stage of conflict, Nataraja Guru begins to trace the search for certitude that has underlain the various philosophical schools. As a philosopher himself, Nataraja Guru is well versed in the different arguments as well as familiar with their historical backgrounds. His study begins with the nascent independence of scepticism that occurred following the decline of theological authority over philosophical speculation. Though initially liberating, scepticism had its own limitations — it cast its "lengthening shadow" — and Nataraja Guru examines how its definitions helped to determine the scope of inquiry in the West, what methodologies and axiologies were encouraged and which ones shunted aside. From the beginning note of scepticism grew the two major themes of idealism and rationalism. Nataraja Guru explores these developments and the specific ideas raised by Hume, Berkeley, Descartes, Leibniz and Kant through to Eddington and Bergson. As he does so, he continuously brings the focus back to the central problem that each philosopher is trying to elucidate: on what ground do we stand? The core paradox, whether or not it is acknowledged, centers around the duality of this world. Nataraja Guru shows how each philosopher's work is an attempt to resolve the contradictions implicit in this paradox and create a ground of certitude.

To establish certitude there has to be a framework within which to work, and this framework is erected on the "Norm" that Nataraja Guru refers to in his title. It is not a norm of averages or standard behaviour but a foundation that functions as a central reference point of understanding and clarity. The norm is both the meeting ground of different aspects of a given situation and the guide or rule by which these aspects are judged and regulated. To know the norm in each philosopher's thought it is necessary to examine his assumptions and their implications as well as his stated theses. This is the course Nataraja Guru follows throughout the book. He elucidates the reference that each particular norm has to an Absolute Norm, and how each particular certitude is a description of one aspect of the Absolute. For Hume this Norm was Human Understanding, for Hegel it was the Idea, for Bergson it was Intuition, and for Plato and Aristotle it was Mind and Time together.

Before he takes us through the step-by-step development of this study though, Nataraja Guru knows that we as contemporary readers must come to terms with the words themselves. Both "Absolute" and "Absolute Norm" are suspect concepts to the modern mind, implying a closed philosophical system. It is one of the ironies of history that what actually denotes the most inclusive framework has instead come to be considered a narrow philosophical attitude. This mistake has been made for a variety of reasons, the most significant of which being the placement of the Absolute in company with many other competing schools of thought, each vying for position and authority. The Absolute that Nataraja Guru reveals in this work is not a relativistic competitor. It is a ground of reference where particular possibilities find interrelation and complementarity. Here is where the original paradox of immanence and transcendence is resolved. The paradox exists because its opposing sides are in fact related. They are each other's complements. When the two aspects are seen separately, as divorced entities, we find ourselves in the well-known dilemma of modern philosophy: conflict adrift in a sea of doubt. But when the Absolute is seen as the ground where these polarities meet and give meaning to one another, then synthesis can take place. As Nataraja Guru himself writes, there is a "subtle reciprocity and mutual interdependence" between the specific constituents of the Absolute when seen in proper relation and position.

Nataraja Guru uses structural analysis as the key to clarify each individual philosopher's partial understandings. Rather than examining each idea in isolation, he is able to place them in a coherent pattern of development and relationship. One of Nataraja Guru's strengths is his grounding in two different systems of structural analysis. The first is the precise structuralism of modern mathematical thought. The definitions and positional placing of algebra and calculus and the further subtleties of modern physics are all employed by Nataraja Guru to trace the inner logic of philosophical argument. Supporting this mathematical structuralism is the more archaic framework that underlies traditional Indian philosophy and esoteric literature. In that structuralism, logic finds a key role, but so do intuition and metaphor. Nataraja Guru's skill is that he is able to wed these two structural approaches into a cohesive pattern.

A metaphoric desciiption of the Absolute Norm that is elucidated in this book is given in the *Mahābhārata*, in the story of the thirsty Brahmin. Traditionally each family had its own well from which it drew its water. A flood occurred and all the wells were submerged beneath one expanse of water. Yet the Brahmin, unable to accept the totality of water stretching in every direction, continued to paddle his canoe out to his own well and drop his bucket into it. In this series of essays which originally appeared in the magazine *Values* between January and November of 1966, Nataraja Guru uses a firm academic analysis to put us in the position where we can make the intuitive leap beyond the restricting limits of "our" well and "our" water to the all-encompassing Absolute which inundates and relates all points.

Deborah Buchanan

1

Some Background Aspects

Philosophy, which means "love of wisdom," refers to knowledge in general about ultimate truth, reality or value. Such knowledge must help man to lead an intelligent life. This consists of correct thinking, the cultivation of good taste and of acting in the best interests of one and all, for life here and hereafter.

Although the word philosophy only suggests "love" of wisdom, it is generally taken to cover the subject matter of wisdom itself as a whole.

Aristotle was known as "the Philosopher," and the word itself came into vogue in the West generally after Pythagoras, who called himself "a lover of wisdom."[1] In India, a philosopher is called a *jnanin,* one who knows, and not one who is merely interested in wisdom at secondhand, or who just loves it. The Sanskrit word *tattva-jnanin* (a knower of first principles) as referring to the Absolute or Ultimate Reality, would best correspond to the meaning of the word "philosopher" as used in the West.

Some branches of science such as biology used to be treated as Natural Philosophy, and only recently were annexed into the domain of science proper. Ethics and aesthetics were naturally taken to be within the scope of philosophy, although they refer to value-factors in life and thus must belong to axiology (the study of values) instead of

---

1. Pythagoras invented the term *philosophos* to distinguish himself as a dedicated follower of wisdom, from a mere sage or *sophos,* i.e., as one who lived the life of a wise man rather than a merely academic orator or lecturer on the subject.

having to do with logical reasoning or as a part of speculative metaphysics.

Aristotle was the first to use the word "metaphysics" which is even now treated as if it was interchangeable with philosophy. From its etymology in Aristotle's own writings, we can see that he put it after physics, and meant it to cover all aspects of thinking that refer to abstractions in reasoning.

Philosophy as we understand it here is not limited by any genetic or etymological considerations. We mean it to cover the whole field of speculation, omitting neither Existence, Subsistence nor Value.

Theology and Philosophy Part Company

Theology is considered to be outside the scope of philosophy in the West, but in the East theology and philosophy come closer together for treatment. Eschatology (speculation on what happens after death), too, enters into Indian Philosophy by right; but in Europe, after the Middle or Dark Ages when belief was given so much primacy, because of excesses practiced in its name, philosophers were compelled to part company with theologians and join hands rather with the speculative theorists of science and astronomy. Philosophy could not continue undivorced from theology or eschatology as in the ancient regime.[2]

---

2. We read (J.B. Bury, *A History of Freedom of Thought*, pp. 57 ff. Home University Library, London):

    The organized system of searching out heretics known as the Inquistion, was founded by Pope Gregory IX about AD 1233, and fully established by a Bull of Innocent IV (AD 1252), which regulated the machinery of persecution. . . . This powerful engine for the suppression of the freedom of men's religious opinions is unique in history.

    The Emperor Frederick II who was himself undoubtedly a free-thinker, made laws for his extensive domains in Italy and Germany between 1220 and 1235, enacting that all heretics should be outlawed and those who did not recant should be burnt, those who

India did not have to pass through such extreme periods in its history of thought, though it might have had other problems such as the primacy of ritual over reason, of Vedic orthodoxy over rationalism, etc. Although the status of a God in Europe after the Age of Scholasticism changed its position epistemologically from that of a teleological to an ontological God, theological dogma in India did not suffer any such abrupt change. Orthodoxy stressing Vedic ritualism and heterodoxy stressing reason without acts alternated, passing from one side of the road to the other many times during its history of three or four millennia rather than of centuries as in Europe.

Theology and dogma are found in both the philosophies of the East and the West, but differing aspects were stressed at different times in both regions, so that we cannot generalize and say that one was dogmatic and the other was not.

Upanishads Nearer to Modern Science

Oriental philosophy is not theological in the Scholastic sense. It admits of a large degree of belief in the authority of scriptures such as the Upanishads. These are more philosophical than theological in character. Such beliefs as they tacitly uphold do not detract from their fully philosophical status.

On the other hand, beliefs enhance philosophy by treating it more wholeheartedly and in a complete form by omitting none of its normal or natural branches. Philosophy has to cover all speculation about ultimate truth. It has common

---

recanted should be imprisoned, but if they relapsed should be executed; that their property should be confiscated, their houses destroyed, and their children to the second generation, ineligible to positions of emolument unless they had betrayed their father or some other heretic.

England. . . repressed heresy by the stake under a special statute (AD 1400); repealed 1533; revived under Mary; finally repealed AD 1676.

ground with science in its cosmological and psychological aspects, and when systematically presented with an ontology, epistemology and axiology, it may be said to include all knowledge or wisdom as a Science of sciences.

The natural curiosity of every thinker, as a member of the species *Homo sapiens,* to understand himself correctly in relation to the physical world may be said to cover the whole range of philosophy, whether in the East or the West. Understanding the Absolute in terms of the universe and the universe in terms of the Absolute is the supreme task of philosophy anywhere and for all time.

Among modern philosophers it was given to Giordano Bruno to state the case of post-Scholastic philosophy in this very way. Although Bruno believed in God in a more correctly philosophical rather than theological sense, he had to suffer martyrdom. His name remains, however, as one who gave to modern philosophy its new orientation and impetus after the Dark Ages.[3]

The Amplitude of Philosophical Speculation

A glance at the pages of any dictionary of philosophy will reveal the astonishing number of "isms" all comprised under the term "philosophy." Beginning from broad divisions such as Eastern or Western philosophies, one reads of Nordic or

---

3. Giordano Bruno (1548-1603) "A Dominican monk eventually burnt at the stake because of his opinions. He was converted from Christianity to a naturalistic and mystical pantheism by the Renaissance and particularly by the Copernican astronomy. For him God and the universe were two names for one and the same Reality. The culmination of the outgoing creative activity is reached in the human mind, whose rational philosophic search for the one in the many, simplicity in variety, and the changeless and the eternal in the changing and the temporal, marks also the reverse movement of the divine nature, re-entering itself and regaining its primordial unity, homogeneity and changelessness." B.A.G. Fuller. under Bruno in Runes' *Dictionary of Philosophy* (Jaico, Bombay, 1956).

Southern varieties. However, increased communications are abolishing such sharp distinctions, and East and West which, a century ago were supposed never to meet, are now believed, by some at least, to be coming closer together so as to yield finally what will be the integrated world philosophy of tomorrow.

Further, philosophies can vary in the problems they pose as most important and in the methods adopted to solve them. They can belong to different cultural contexts and have in their contents different aspects of reality presented as central subject matter. Some like to face philosophical problems piecemeal while others prefer to face problems generally in a wholesale manner. Bertrand Russell, for example, is for the piecemeal approach, and for excluding ethical considerations from philosophy and, in fact, anything which involves evolutionism or time.[4]

What is a Complete Scientific Philosophy?

Some philosophers give importance to the positive and the practical, while others emphasize the abstract and the implied aspects. A philosophy with an axe of special interest to grind can hardly be called philosophy. But nowadays it is normal to hear of officially accepted philosophies of countries with political motives behind them. Some put the limits of philosophizing in favour of actualities or the given data of an empirical nature, while others admit a great deal of a priorism into their speculations. Teleological and ontological approaches may each yield their own varieties in philosophizing. Between the extreme limits of materialism

4. Russell writes: "I believe that the elimination of ethical consideration from philosophy is both scientifically necessary and — though this may seem a paradox — an ethical advance" — *Mysticism and Logic* (Allen and Unwin, London) p. 29 and "Evolutionism . . . fails to be a truly scientific philosophy. A truly scientific philosophy will be more humble, more piecemeal." Ibid., p. 32.

and idealism we can imagine a series of possible philosophies which give primacy to bodily or mental aspects in their types of speculation. To prefer any one type to another is wrong.

In certain textbooks it is also usual to differentiate between races and to classify philosophy according to climatic or geographical conditions. For example, we read of a "robust" philosophy as opposed to a "passive" kind, of some that have an "active" as against a "dreamy sentimental" outlook, and of others that harmonize different elements to make philosophy perfect or beautiful.

If this kind of classification is to be accepted seriously, we have finally to concede one type of philosophy for each philosopher, making as many philosophies as there are philosophers.

Solipsism and syncretism give certain philosophies little value, and eclecticism and cyclopaedism do not face the problems but only give information about them. A metaphysics which is too axiomatic also fails at the other extreme.

What we wish to underline by listing the possible varieties of philosophy here, is that philosophy must be treated as a science of sciences with a central neutral normative notion for its reference. When a strictly conceived methodology, a complete epistemology and an axiology are all brought to bear upon the subject of philosophy, then and only then can it be called scientific. All its normal limbs must be left intact. The lopping of its main branches, which some modern thinkers propose, is disastrous to the whole prospect of the philosophy of the future, which has necessarily to rid itself of all parochialisms, cultural prejudices and confusion of tongues.

The emergence in modern times of a new branch of knowledge called the "Philosophy of Science" suggests already how the two branches are bound to overlap and encroach upon each other's domains as science becomes more theoretical and philosophy tends to adopt the strict methods of the positive sciences called "operational" or "demonstrable." In the process of such a *rapprochement* of the two disciplines from the poles of the a priori and the a posteriori we can even expect a Science of sciences to emerge. Philosophy, science and even theology can then be included under one integrated, normalized and re-normalized way of thinking in unified world terms and not from the babelized standpoint which prevails at present.

Occidental and Oriental Philosophies

In his Introduction to *A History of Philosophy,* John Edward Erdmann wrote as his opening sentence, "The task of apprehending his own nature in thought can only tempt the human mind and indeed it is only then equal to it when it is conscious of its intrinsic dignity — and as in the East, except among the Jews this point is not reached, we must not be induced to talk of a pre-Hellenic philosophy or worse still, of pre-Hellenic systems."

Frederik Uberweg also wrote in a similar strain in his *History of Philosophy*: "Philosophy as a science could originate neither among the people of the North, who were eminent for strength and courage, but devoid of culture, nor among the Orientals who, though susceptible to the elements of higher culture, were content simply to retain them in a spirit of passive resignation, — but only among the Hellenes who harmoniously combined the characteristics of both. . . . The so-called philosophy of the Orient lacks the tendency to strict demonstrations and hence in scientific character."[5]

Hegel, even in spite of the fact that his absolutist standpoint has much in common with Indian philosophy both in matter and method, reveals a more definite prejudice against Indian philosophy when he writes: "The Hindu mentality is pre-adolescent," and that its temperament is "sunk in childish dreaming," concluding his appraisal with the words, "All in all, the character of spirit in a state of dream is the generic principle of Hindu nature." He further refers to the "infantilism of China with its language like baby-talk," and after

5. Tr. G.S. Morris Scribner, (New York), pp. 14, 16.

admitting that Greek philosophy attained some maturity he goes as far as to say: "In the Germanic culture, the spirit at last becomes fully conscious of its freedom and freely wills the identification of the individual, the eternal and the universal."[6]

Such easy generalizations, when they hold high one's own culture or country, cannot be taken seriously, especially because we find on the other side, ranged against these very pro-European philosophers, others of such high standing as Schopenhauer not to mention scholars like Paul Deussen, Monier-Williams and Max Müller, who were disposed to speak of Indian Philosophy in another key of unstinted praise. On first reading the Upanishads in Latin translation, itself taken from a Persian translation, Arthur Schopenhauer considered it "the most rewarding and the most elevating reading which (with the exception of the original text) there can possibly be in the world. It has been the solace of my life and will be of my death."[7]

Dr. Paul Deussen visited India in 1893 and wrote of the high philosophical value of the Vedanta: "On my journey through India I have noticed with satisfaction, that in philosophy till now our brothers in the East have maintained a very good tradition, better perhaps than the more active but less contemplative branches of the great Indo-Aryan family in Europe, where Empiricism, Realism and their natural consequence, Materialism, grow from day-to-day more exuberantly, whilst metaphysics, the very centre of the heart of serious philosophy is supported only by a few, who have learnt to brave the spirit of the age."[8]

It can be argued that Deussen was favourably prejudiced toward Vedantism, but it cannot be denied that he was fully

6. B.G. Fuller, *History of Philosophy*, (Holt, New York) p. 325.

7. R.E. Hume, *The Thirteen Principal Upanishads*, (Oxford), pp. 3, 4.

8. Paul Deussen, *Elements of Metaphysics*, (Macmillan, London), p. 323.

informed about the nature and requirements of the philosophy of India or Europe. We are therefore tempted to quote further from his 1893 address at Bombay before he said farewell to India, when he made pointed reference to Western philosophers who had affinity with Indian thought, as he continued, "Eternal interests are higher than the temporary; and the system of the Vedanta as founded on the *Upanishad*s and the *Vedanta Sutra*s and accomplished by Sankara's commentaries on them — equal in rank to Plato and Kant — is one of the most valuable products of the genius of mankind in its search for the eternal truth."[9]

He concluded by saying that Vedanta was "the strongest support of pure morality and is the greatest consolation in the sufferings of life and death."[10]

Such recognition coming from a professor of a European university cannot be brushed aside as insignificant, especially when we remember that the original texts of the Vedanta were only beginning to be known in the West at that time.

In the opinions of Hegel and others who minimize the status of Indian philosophy, it is not hard to discern that most of what they said was due to ignorance combined with their own pan-Germanic or other personal loyalties. It cannot be gainsaid, however, that in the West there still lingers large body of ill-informed opinion amounting to prejudices against Oriental philosophy in general and in respect of Vedanta in particular. At the same time it must be admitted that there is also a growing body of persons who go in the opposite direction by being too ready to admire even some of its weak points. Max Müller and Josiah Royce were other philosophers who avoided any prejudices but who still valued Vedanta.

Prof. Müller, in admiring Vedanta wholeheartedly, first takes the precaution to shelter himself behind Schopenhauer, so as to be in good company, when he says: "Schopenhauer

9. Ibid., p. 324.

10. Ibid., p. 337.

was the last man to write at random, or to allow himself to go into ecstasies over so-called mystic or inarticulate thought. And I am neither afraid nor ashamed to say that I share his enthusiasm for the Vedanta, and feel indebted to it for much that has been helpful to me in my passage through life . . . for fitting men to lead contemplative or quiet lives, I know no better preparation than the Vedanta. A man may be a Platonist, and yet a good Christian, and I should say the same of a Vedantist."[11]

We have quoted philosophers and professors of the subject to set at rest once and for all the usual charges leveled at all Oriental philosophies. Some condemn it by a sort of faint praise, and when they do enumerate the charges they can be brought under the designations of sentimentalism, dogmatism, or of being mythological, theological or even mystical, as against being positive, demonstrable, operational, critical or rational.

These charges will seem quite natural when we look at philosophy as connected with its own history in the West, whose peculiarities we have referred to already. But once freed from prejudices, one is sure to see in Vedanta a noble monument of human speculation quite in keeping with the dignity and maturity of human understanding. Speculation about the Absolute cannot be expected to soar any higher.

The objection to a priorism in the West is a reaction due to the exaggeration of aspects of belief during the Middle Ages, as already pointed out. But pure philosophy when complete, cannot omit its normal speculative core nor favour a posteriorism against a priorism. Both have to be given their legitimate places in a common, whole or global epistemology and methodology.

Instead of belief and heresy as in Europe, India has been torn between rituals and reason, but the rivalry has lasted

---

11. Max Müller, *Indian Philosophy*, vol. II (Susil Gupta, Calcutta, 1952), p. 79.

uniformly throughout its history, extending three or four thousand years from the days of the heterodox Vedic Guru Brihaspati to the most orthodox of pontiffs of some of the existing Vedic *maths* (scholastic institutions) of the present day. Normalized philosophy has to be one integrated subject. One and the same humanity cannot afford to have more than one philosophy which is in keeping with its nature and dignity.

Modern Mistrust of Metaphysics

Modern philosophy starts with a general sceptical attitude towards beliefs of the ancient regime. The horrors of the Inquisition and the nightmare of a witch-hunting attitude of mind still haunted the minds of the people when the Age of Reason was ushered into existence by the Renaissance. Human nature demanded a life of truth, dignity and freedom. The invention of the telescope and what is called the Copernican Revolution mark the period wherein the wonder about God was displaced by the wonder about the physical universe. Facts took primacy over ideas at one stroke. With each triumph of scientific discovery in what was called "progress" men began to take their stand more confidently on facts and not on theories or beliefs. This tendency got accentuated by geometric progression through the decades after the Renaissance. Today, all a priorism and any speculation depending on it tend to be discredited more and more.

Scholastic speculation itself seemed to have gone beyond the limits of strict logical or empirical validity. The laws of rational validity and the use of intuition as an instrument of higher dialectical reasoning were matters ill-understood or only beginning to be understood after the days of the classical philosophers of pre-Christian Europe. They too depended for such matters on the philosophical tradition justly belonging to the pre-Socratic philosophers.

To engage in philosophical speculation became the preserve of the select few. Popular imagination took an interest only in whatever could be "proved" experimentally, or at least by the use of understandable, though conventional and arbitrary, mathematical operations. The French Revolution marks the period when the common man began to hold a central place in public life in a modern sense. And he preferred cyclopaedias to treatises, and information to speculation.

The combined influence of the vitriolic pen of Voltaire and the appeal to deeper contemplative ways of Rousseau won the masses over to the side of rationalism and natural spiritual values. But these individual writers could not stem the tide of "technocracy" and "progress" which flooded over to the detriment of deeper human values.

Modern Philosophy Begins with Scepticism

Descartes came out with a philosophy in which God still had a place; not, however, as a hypostatic entity, but as a power who had his being at the core of the phenomenal universe itself, ontologically, from whose new centre *occasionalism* could bring about the interaction of mind and matter.

Descartes had to present such a scientifically valid God with great caution because of fear to the Church. He is said to have revised one of his writings so as not to offend it. He still had to fear persecution.

So instead of a theological God, we come in sight of a cosmological deity to which a first-rate scientist like Newton in England and a first-rate philosopher like Descartes in France both contributed. These contributions were both philosophical and scientific at once, because speculation and science had observables and calculables implied in them. A priori or axiomatic calculations went hand in hand with a posteriori inferences. Astronomy was the science wherein the blending with philosophy could conveniently take place. The Newtonian-Cartesian cosmos had held the field up to our own time and still holds its ground despite the spread of the ideas of relativity.

On the other side, theology became more and more subtle from the time of Thomas Aquinas, slowly removing itself from the everyday life of the common man and his day-to-day problems. The natural reaction to this was the rise of Empiricism, particularly on the English soil.

The burning of Bruno at the stake in 1600 may be said to mark the point in time when new ideas, tending to be sceptical, empirical or scientific began to prevail in the West. Astronomy and the Renaissance had made Bruno a heretic in the eyes of the Church, but he believed in God and was essentially a religious man. It was only the approved theological God of the Church that he rejected and thereby suffered martyrdom.

Philosophical Scepticism had to wait till the days of the British Empiricists, Locke, Berkeley and Hume. Although David Hume (1711-1776) came later than John Locke (1632-1704), his Empiricism made it impossible for him to accept any innate ideas which were properly those of Locke. Locke's treatment of the mind as a *tabula rasa* (a blank tablet) was a reaction against the tendency of the Middle Ages to give primacy to such matters as the soul and sin, and thus implied the same Scepticism which Hume later was able to formulate more boldly and in fully philosophical terms.

Although George Berkeley, an Irish Protestant Bishop (1684-1753) comes under the definition of an Idealist by the primacy he gave to the mind over matter, he accepted the same epistemological frame of reference as Locke. He spoke of primary and secondary qualities, one more internal than the other, and because of his method of starting with perception, he is grouped with the British Empiricists in textbooks, to be treated together with both Locke and Hume.

If we do not think chronologically, the extreme sceptic of that period may be said to be Hume, whose Phenomenology and Scepticism gave the impetus to what we recognize now as the chief feature of modern Western philosophy. Even in the twentieth century, Hume's way of looking on reality is the same which the so-called Logical Positivists or Logicists of our own time have also to a large extent approved and adopted for themselves.

Hume wrote scathingly about the Scholastic theologians and the vain metaphysicians of his time, as follows: "Chased from the open country, these robbers fly to the forest, and lie in wait to break in upon every unguarded avenue of the mind, and overwhelm it with religious fears and prejudices. The stoutest antagonist, if he remit his watch a minute, is oppressed. And many, through cowardice and folly, open the gates to the enemies, and willingly receive them with reverence and submission as their legal sovereigns."[12]

Although Berkeley was an ecclesiastical dignitary, his philosophical starting point is empirical in character. Instead of distinguishing primary and secondary qualities in perceived objects given to the senses, he argued just at the point of generalizing that *esse est percipi* or *percipere* (nothing exists except perceiving or being perceived). In other words he traced the reality of sensations to the mind and no further. How far his idealism was carried beyond into the domain of the a priori, analytically or synthetically, is not clear, and whether he agreed with Duns Scotus or with Peter Abelard or went into further subtleties of the Christian doctrine, adopting a classical Platonic, Aristotelian or Neo-Platonic approach, like Augustine or Thomas Aquinas, is difficult to answer from his writings. All we can say is that he differed sufficiently from the sceptics and empiricists of Britain, but in method and in the epistemology that he accepted for his reasoning, he had enough in common with the other two philosophers to justify his being bracketted with them for our purposes. When we remember that Hume had great influence on Kant and others, it is not wrong to say that

12. *Hume's Essays* (Routledge, London), p. 313.

Hume's scepticism in particular and the empirical and objective standpoint which went with it was, in reality, the starting point and the initial impetus for what is distinguishable as modern philosophy ranging from Realism at one end and extending at least until the time of Hegel to Idealism at the other end.

2

The Characteristics of Modern Philosophy

Modern philosophers in the West claim to be critical, well-reasoned, positive and non-dogmatic. This means that they are not ready to believe too easily, as in the Middle Ages, that they are scientific in method, and free from mythological or theological trimmings and elaborations.

They claim their philosophy to be "objective" or to have "demonstrable" proofs, with an "operational" character. They tend to avoid too much reliance on the a priori, the imaginary or the "sentimental." Practical utility also characterizes this outlook.

These traits can be seen to be linked with technocracy and the expansion of power of the dominant nations of Europe and America. Great cities like London, Rotterdam and New York, which stand today as visible monuments of Western civilization, neither represent nor accentuate any contemplative value. We have already seen how pan-Germanic enthusiasms affected the outlook of even otherwise sound philosophers like Hegel, making them look down upon anything of the nature of quiet contemplation with mistrust and contempt.

It goes without saying that philosophy can thrive best on contemplative soil.

That all was not well with Western civilization at the time of Voltaire (1694-1778) is sufficiently reflected in his writings and in the literature of his time. Colonial expansion, money-worship and mercantilism characterized the age, none of which aims can be said to be favourable for that calm philosophical outlook which needs dispassionateness in inquiry. The East had it and still retains this mental climate. There is a certain irony, or even a touch of humour, when we come to think of it, when Westerners speak of Eastern philosophy with contempt.

Some Specific Traits of Modernism

The formative period of what we distinguish as "modernism" in philosophy extends from Bruno to Hume (or to Hegel). The sceptical starting point of this modernist tendency was accentuated by different distinguishing features such as "rational," "critical," "intuitive" or "pragmatic." These traits marked the outlook of those who followed in the trail of this modernist impetus.

It follows through Descartes (1596-1659), Spinoza (1632-1677), Leibniz (1646-1716) and Kant (1724-1804), culminating in the idealism of Hegel (1770-1831). This brought modernism, as it were, to a natural impasse which it could not overcome without changing, subdividing and dispersing in the different directions of Materialism and Spiritualism.

After Hegel, who placed the notion of the Absolute at the centre of his philosophy, which had a dialectical method and an epistemology both of them inseparable, as he himself said, from his Absolute, modernism in England and America went in the directions of Pragmatism, Instrumentalism, and other varieties of philosophizing, wherein the tendency was, as its philosophers said, "analytic," with the rejection of everything pertaining to the a priori domain such as the notion of the Absolute.

Thus, Materialism, Existentialism, Phenomenology, and that Philosophy of Science which concerns itself with the nature of the physical world rather than with the metaphysical world, and with percepts rather than concepts, came into vogue.

The strong group of modern philosophers in Western Europe and America whose voice rings dominantly above all others today consists of representatives of this broad "analytic" division in philosophy, as they prefer to call themselves, whatever might be the precise meaning to be attached to this term. Perhaps it is because they discard the a priori position and the absolutist synthetic approach of Kant. As against Kant they want to distinguish their approach as a posteriori and analytical.

Besides celebrating "the decline and fall of the Absolute," a slogan of this group is "metaphysics is nonsense." They insist on truth being demonstrable, which strictly speaking would mean that the axioms of mathematics are myths. This position is clearly untenable, and even reduces philosophy to absurdity. Such a lopsided approach to truth stems from the absence of any normative central notion for their philosophy.

The Vienna Circle of Scientific Empiricism founded by Moritz Schlick (1882-1936) and the Logical Empiricism group or Logical Postivism group, led by Bertrand Russell (1872-1970) and his articulate camp-followers like Prof. A.J. Ayer (1910-1989), see the future trend of scientific philosophizing as the discrediting of speculations which do not apply directly or indirectly to the visible or perceptual world of modern physics.

To accept this position would be tantamount to the suspension of all truly metaphysical speculation and rejecting it as belonging to the limbo of the merely verbose and absurd. This is too great a sacrifice to make in the name of science, especially during the present century, when even in science, as considered by Eddington (1882-1944) and others, physics is primarily concerned with "concepts" rather than "percepts."

We shall have occasion to return later to this subject of the conceptual character of science. Meanwhile, we consider the a priori approach to philosophy as legitimate as the a posteriori, and if the former is objected to in the name of modernism it is not only Oriental Philosophy which will have no future, but speculation itself will lose its significance and thus defeat the whole purpose of philosophy. Future speculation at one and the same time must answer to the requirements of mathematical calculations as well as a more direct intuition of truth.

Science and Speculation

Physics comes first to mind when the word science is mentioned. It is supposed to deal with hard facts. It often starts with the measurement of objects and the observation of properties. When we pass from such items as colour, size, and so on, to the weight of the object under study, we come upon a notion of a new order which is no longer as simple as those given to the senses.

In weight, which is due to gravity, another order of deeper reality becomes evident, where our five senses do not help us directly. When we lift an object from the ground our muscles resist the gravitational pull to the centre of the earth. We can shut our eyes and cut off the other senses from connection with the object, but still have left a kinesthetic sense by which we appreciate inwardly as if with the mind. The transition from the notion of weight to that of inertia seems natural enough, but in the notion of momentum resulting from the multiplication of mass by velocity, we come upon a notion depending for its reality on something which is not sensible at all to any of the five senses.

We attain in fact to the domain of the calculables in the metaphysical world, which are away from the domain of simple observables. We cannot see, smell, touch, hear or taste weight. We have to form a vague notion of it to be standardized by reference to something arbitrarily fixed by some outside scientific or civil authority as the unit of weight. We can also have an indirect notion of weight from specific gravity, which implies the logical formula of things equal to the same thing being equal to one another.

Thus by imperceptible gradations of procedure we move from the examinations of the properties of a simple object into the world of axioms, arbitrarily fixed standards and pure calculables such as $M = mv$ (Momentum is Mass times Velocity).

Where exactly the observables are left behind and the calculables enter into the strictest and simplest of methods involved in problems of physics is thus hard to fix. In fact, observable and calculable elements enter so intimately into the structure of scientific knowledge that it is impossible to think of one without the other being taken as integral part of such knowledge.

For proof that understanding the observable in terms of the calculable is of the very essence of scientific knowledge, we have only to look at any professor of physics teaching with his blackboard full of equations, using mostly the letters of the Greek alphabet intermixed with other relational signs of mathematics. All speculation may be seen to move between the limits of observables and calculables, between tautology and contradiction.

Let us examine the Law of Gravity and of Universal Gravitation. Both were implied by Newton in his observation of an apple falling in his orchard. The gap between this simple event and the universal law which he derived from it, was filled by a series of mathematical calculations following on the method of Kepler. As we know, mathematics in its turn is based on axioms which do not call for demonstration or proof. They are given or a priori in character. The falling of an individual apple as an isolated event is treated as being related to the whole situation involving the entire physical universe. What is true of the part is also to be treated as true of the whole. This is a metaphysical dictum attributed to Aristotle and is fully a priori and metaphysical in status.

Thus through the mathematical calculus, where much logic resides, we arrive at what is called speculation. When commonsense examples of less than experimental value are employed with a logic that is not strict but uses the analytical and synthetical judgements without any methodic doubt involved, we have a loose kind of metaphysics.

This, however, is not the fault of metaphysics itself, but rather of the person who handles this instrument of knowledge. There are good and bad rules to be kept in mind in speculations, and it is the task of correct methodologists to strictly sort them out. For science as well as philosophy a methodology is important, because common experience and experiment are not fundamentally different. The a priori and the a posteriori enter into both in inverse proportion, reciprocally, as it were, from opposite poles of a total knowledge situation.

Hume's scepticism which, we have said, marks the extreme position taken by modern philosophy in respect of speculation in general, is really directed against the Scholasticism and theology of the Middle Ages, and not against any methodic speculation as such. There is a valid speculation which is verifiable, demonstrable, or both, and there is a loose speculation which violates fundamental rules and always fails to convince the common man, even by experience.

Hume himself reduced all speculation to two categories which are the same as the "observables" and the "calculables" which we have introduced. He wrote: "When we run over libraries, persuaded of these principles, [distinguishing such subjects as Theology and Morals etc.] what havoc must we make? If we take in our hand any volume; of divinity or school metaphysics, for instance; let us ask, *Does it contain any abstract reasoning concerning quantity or number*? No. *Does it contain any experimental reasoning concerning matter of fact and existence?* No. Commit it then to the flames; for it can contain nothing but sophistry and illusion."[1]

---

1. David Hume *Enquiry Concerning Human Understanding*, Essay XXXIX (Routledge, London), pp. 384-85.

All speculation in philosophy, whether of the sceptic or the believer, is full of examples which are strictly neither of apodictic validity nor of the degree of certitude of common experience. When taking any philosopher seriously, it is a matter needing the greatest caution to see how strict he is in the use of his examples.

Varieties of Certitude

All science is a search for certitude. Metaphysics is also the same. What is the kind or degree of certitude that we should expect from the different branches of knowledge?

In the domain of values, dialectical reasonings yield overall axiomatic certitudes valid in the context of the wisdom of the Absolute. Experiments, on the other hand, yield another kind of certitude which might be called apodictic. In between these two limits, one pertaining to unseen values and the other referring to something that operates in the physical world, there are other logical and factual certitudes ranging between these limits, which yield mere tautology or sheer contradiction. Factual, logical and value certitudes may be said to comprise the three steps which man can take in the progress of his reasoning in order to have certitude about even the meanest of significant factors or interests in life, up to the highest ideals of goodness or beauty.

We admit that these statements, made here in passing, require a great deal of elaboration to be fully convincing. This we cannot do for the present. At this stage in our discussion we are interested only in showing that whatever the kind of certitude of which we might be speaking, it contains two regulative factors — an observable element and a calculable. Taken together, fact and intuition explain truth absolutely, yielding the maximum possible certitude.

Two Proofs for the Pythagorean Theorem

Every schoolboy knows that the truth of the Pythagorean theorem can be revealed or proved in two different ways. In the lower classes where pupils still think in concrete terms of the visible, there is the method of cutting out of paper and pasting the squares on the sides of triangles, that go to make up the square of the hypotenuse. Starting from geometrical axioms in the higher classes, we arrive at the same degree of certitude without physical measurements. If we think of the certitude arrived at by one method and the same certitude by the other method, we can get the notion of a central neutral certitude which is both apodictic and dialectically convincing.

There is thus a positive, a negative and a neutral certitude involved in the two proofs plus the neutral conviction. That the conceptual certitude arrived at by the Euclidean method and the perceptual certitude arrived at by practical geometry lead to a central neutral and normative certitude which is not wholly dependent either on the visible or the calculable only, is what we wish to underline here as an overall general rule applicable to both physics and metaphysics. There is no worthwhile certitude, whether practical, pure or intermediate (neutral), which does not combine these three elements proportionately or disproportionately, in its essential resultant composition.

Common Sense and Certitude

Let us take another everyday example. A man calls in a carpenter to make a stool for him. The carpenter asks him what kind of stool he means. Then the man shows him the wood with which it is to be made and gives the carpenter the measurements. Here the kind of wood to be used is of the visible or the observable order, whereas the measurements being arbitrary and based on units that we keep in the mind, belong to the order of calculables. All the further details that the carpenter would be likely to ask fall under one or the other of these two categories and it is only when these two categorical determinatives have been given that the agreement or certitude between the two men takes place, and not if one of the factors predominates over the other.

Allowing for personal variations, they both understand the same thing, and certitude results from both the observables and the calculables coming together into one central notion.

Thus, whether it is universal gravitation, the Pythagorean theorem or a stool about which we seek certitude, we have to approach the same central notion from two poles of an epistemological order from which, when they neutralize, absolute certitude results. It is neither induction nor deduction which gives the central or scientific certitude to physics or metaphysics. It is the meeting of the a priori and the a posteriori approaches. Speculative and experimental approaches to physics or metaphysics should be treated as complementary and not contradictory in yielding certitude in the context of an integrated or unified science of the future.

Logical and Mathematical Certitudes

Definitions and proofs which relate or equate two groups which are views of the same central truth, constitute the essence of certitude in mathematics and its sister discipline logic, or logistic as it is coming to be known.

All mathematical proofs become reduced also in terms of the two limbs of an equation. The answers to all problems in mathematics are capable of being completely stated in the form of an equation, and when such an equation is followed by the letters Q.E.D. the demonstration is supposed to be complete. Thus certitude resides within the pure perceptual-cum-conceptual domain of mathematics and the greater part of speculation consists of an effort to arrive at such equations.

The nature of mathematics as a science and its relation to metaphysical speculation have been the subject of much discussion in recent years. Although opinions still differ, it is just possible for us, even at present, to make some simple basic generalizations. M. Edward le Roi, an eminent professor and member of the French Academy, who has recently devoted a whole volume on the subject of the philosophical status of pure mathematical thinking, sums up his position as follows:

> Finally, and perhaps above all, mathematics taken in itself, independently of its applications is, at the highest point to which we are permitted to attain, a work of pure thought, an invention of the spirit left to its own resources. If there exists a science which proceeds a priori by reason alone and which all the same shows itself to be solid, consistent, positive, capable of indefinite extension — that it certainly is. One calls it *science of reasoning* for signifying that it presents itself as a creation of the rational faculty operated, if not *ex nihilo*, at least after the first impetus, without ultimate recourse to any exercise at all of the perceptive faculties.[2]

To avoid going into the merits of such a claim we must be content to merely state that the science of mathematics, by grouping and juxtaposing, whether for defining or proving in its search for speculative metaphysical or pure certitude, relies on equating groups of realities or facts of two distinct or different orders. Thus it is that mathematicians arrive at certitude from two poles of reality.

Professor le Roi whom we have just quoted relies on his predecessor Poincare for two further important generalizations which are relevant to what we have said above. Each definition according to Poincare is a classification: "It separates the objects that satisfy the definition and those that do not satisfy and it ranges them in two distinct classes."[3]

Poincare makes another generalized statement about mathematics which also depends on relating two different classes when he writes: "Mathematics is the art of giving the same name to different things."[4]

---

2. Edward le Roi, *La Pensee Mathematique Pure* (Presses Universitaire de France, Paris, 1960), translated, p. 3.

3. Ibid., p. 97.

4. Ibid., p. 85.

The equation of classes of things or the operational to the purely conceptual levels in physics or metaphysics is the function of mathematics, and metaphysical speculation is fundamentally no other than this.

While it is true that speculation without a strict method and which violates laws of the theory of knowledge would give us questionable speculations, nevertheless, when there is a normative regulative principle and when the aims of philosophy are properly defined, a speculation which gives room equally for scepticism as for belief will result.

Eastern philosophy excels in the a priori aspects of speculation, while Western science gives primacy to the a posteriori approach. Both can be used correctly in the name of an integrated science or philosophy. After the Middle Ages, Western philosophy started its history anew with scepticism as its keynote. Rationalism and Criticism are only milder versions of the initial scepticism, and from Bruno to Hume and Hegel we have the "unbelievers" standpoint influencing the course of Western thought. Scepticism has as much wisdom to give as belief, and the contributions made by the rationalists and the idealists here are equally significant.

3

The Lengthening Shadow of Scepticism

For two hundred years, from the time of David Hume to Bertrand Russell among British philosophers, we are able to see one and the same sceptical attitude, like a lengthening shadow, influencing the history of modern thought in the West.

At the start, such a scepticism had a legitimate cause, but whether it is justified forever is another question. The same influence prevailed also on the Continent, but in a less evident form, as the spirit of the experimental sciences became established. Only those problems which were capable of being demonstrated in the laboratory, at least on a small scale — in other words, what "worked" — were considered to be certain or proved.

The educational system has given an experimental or mechanistic bias to knowledge at the expense of the study of the humanistic aspects. The three features of the scientific method, namely experiment, observation and inference, were given prominence in valid thinking. The calculable aspects of thinking were only tacitly taken for granted. For anything to have the flavour of dogma was enough for it to be discredited.

But by a strange nemesis the objection to dogmatism reached a degree of rigidity as great as the insistence on the side of belief of the days of the Inquisition. It is enough to say that an idea belongs to or savours of the Middle Ages to have it condemned. Neither Hume nor Russell have been able to shake off the nightmarish memory of the Inquisition altogether from their attitudes.

In Russell we see a confirmed sceptic and empiricist who admits into his methods only such elements of logistic and mathematical principles which are derived plainly without any element of wonder or mystery. In spite of this fact, he lays down categorically that, "A philosopher who uses professional competence for anything except a disinterested search for truth is guilty of a kind of treachery."[1] But at the end of the same chapter in his book in which this statement occurs, he contradicts himself without admitting it when he refers to "the philosophical school of which I am a member."[2]

A member of a particular school cannot be fully open-minded. He cannot treat rival schools as the same as his own. There is sure to be a closing of frontiers against some rival point of view, and this is against the spirit of an open-minded scientific attitude. There can be the orthodoxy of a believer and also the orthodoxy of a sceptic. Both can be over-emphasized, with equally disastrous results for the future of philosophy as a whole.

Russell's writings show that he was against theology and dogmatism, and thought philosophy should not include a "higher" way of knowing. By this he would exclude most of the fundamental questions of philosophy, shutting out anything a priori or what is based on intuitive or axiomatic truth. He would have philosophy advance piecemeal, i.e., "by successive approximations to truth."

In other words, if we are to be convinced that $A = A$ we must have a method by which the conviction will grow within us stage by stage and not immediately or all together at once. A deep-seated prejudice against anything of the nature of the a priori seems to persist in making Russell a sceptic for scepticism's own sake, in just the same way as some dogmatic

1. Morton White *The Age of Analysis*, (Mentor, New York), p. 202.

2. Ibid., p. 203.

and orthodox people insist on their own belief as being the most important. They forget that axiomatic certitude at one pole and the apodictic character of simple experiments which work with a certain amount of inductive certitude at the other pole, are both complementary aspects of an epistemological and methodological frame of reference in which speculation, whether called physical or metaphysical, has necessarily to live and move. That such a prejudice against a priorism is entertained by serious thinkers is astonishing to impartial observers who are themselves not influenced by its historical and geographical causes.

Russell states his position regarding what he considers scientific philosophy as follows:

> A scientific philosophy such as I wish to recommend will be piecemeal and tentative like other sciences; above all it will be able to invent hypotheses, which even if they are not wholly true, will yet remain fruitful after the necessary corrections have been made. This possibility of successive approximations to the truth is more than anything else the source of the triumph of science, and to transfer this possibility to philosophy is to ensure a progress in method whose importance it would almost be impossible to exaggerate.[3]

The axioms and postulates of mathematics are not hypothetical approximations to truth, and yet they are widely employed in the methods of arriving at certitude in the simplest of scientific investigations. To exclude the axiomatic and the a priori would be to limit the scope of philosophy very drastically indeed.

Inadequacy of Analytic Approach

Bertrand Russell is one of a large group of present day philosophers who are sceptics in their general outlook. They believe in experimental proof. What savours of the a priori is

3. Bertrand Russell, *Mysticism and Logic* (Allen and Unwin, London, 1959), p. 113.

wholly repugnant to them. They are for a piecemeal approach to truth through successive hypotheses which are only approximations to truth, but which they think will one day be established as empiricism and logic gain ground. They also distinguish and limit themselves by labeling their philosophical attitude "analytic." It is not clear what precise meaning this term has. It is probably because they oppose Kant's a priori *synthetic* approach, that they call themselves analytic. Russell continues the quotation above as follows:

> The essence of philosophy as thus conceived is analysis not synthesis. To build up systems of the world is not, I believe, any more reasonable than the discovery of the philosopher's stone. What is feasible is the understanding of general forms, and the division of traditional problems into a number of separate and less baffling questions. "Divide and conquer" is the maxim of success here as elsewhere.[4]

A careful study of the above paragraph reveals that, in spite of his love of dividing philosophy into bits, Russell does refer to something which he does not explain but only vaguely alludes to as "general forms." This seems to provide a safety valve for him through which he can escape the charge of limiting the method, scope and content of philosophy altogether as generally understood in the world. By "general forms" he must be alluding to some structural overall peculiarity of truth, whether factual, logical, or both. This overall structural peculiarity referred to as "general forms," whatever they may be, cannot be anything within reach of the empirical and analytical approach. That this might be of a logical order is to be surmised from an article by Russell entitled "On the Importance of Logical Form" in which he says:

> The importance of logical form may be illustrated by what may be called the principle of the dictionary: given

4. Bertrand Russell, *Mysticism and Logic* (Allen and Unwin, London, 1959), p. 113.

> two sets of propositions such that by a suitable dictionary, any proposition of either set can be translated into a proposition of the other set, there is no effective difference between the two sets. Suppose — to take a hypothesis that I neither affirm nor deny — that all scientific propositions can be tested in terms of physics and can also be stated in Berkeleian principles, in terms of psychology; then the question as to which of these forms of statement is more correct has no meaning, since both or neither must be correct. Such dictionaries which can, as a rule, only be constructed by the help of modern logic, suffice to dispose of a large number of metaphysical questions, and thus facilitate concentration upon genuine scientific problems.[5]

For the first time we find Bertrand Russell, the strict empiricist, using approvingly expressions like "the principle of the dictionary," which must consist of propositions or predications with a one-to-one correspondence between them. They belong to two distinct domains, one of them physical and the other psychological or mental. One of these can be understood in terms of the other, whichever it may be that will finally be considered valid.

Such a structural form, based on logic or thought, will yield some kind of certitude which will help us to distinguish the scientific from the unscientific aspects of what at present passes for metaphysics. The simple question that naturally arises in the mind of anyone after reading and taking seriously such vague statements, is whether the whole of this problem treated together is of a physical or of a metaphysical order. The Berkeleian world at least, being mental, must be fully metaphysical in status. In the parenthetical clause above we can see the unwillingness of a confirmed sceptic and empiricist to commit himself in giving primacy to the mind or to matter. But in spite of this hesitation, it is not hard to see that the

5. *The International Encyclopedia of Unified Science*, vol. 1, part 1 (Chicago University, U.S.A., 1955), p. 41.

whole or the double-sided structure has its basis in something which is not of a physical order merely, and that the only context into which both can be fitted is that of a notion of the Absolute, where the two aspects can exist without contradiction.

How this view can be tenable in itself requires a more detailed epistemological discussion to prove. We shall not now enter into such a discussion, because aspects of the same problem will become clear as we go on with the present line of inquiry, step by step. Further on we shall come to a fuller discussion of the implications of subjective-selective structuralism in the light of the modern philosophy of science. What we want to underline at present is that even strict empiricists and sceptics are being led inevitably by the developments of modern science to accept more than what is analytical and a posteriori. They are beginning to admit metaphysics again into their thought by the back door. A priorism and absolutism thus come to find a place, though still unofficially, in the writings of modern sceptical empiricists. Thus they begin to resemble the believers against their own declared intentions.

The analytic approach for which Russell stands becomes evident in his writings. What he is really up against is the synthetic a priorism of Kant. But Kant takes care to explain in great detail the "Division of General Logic into Analytic and Dialectic."[6] He also has an overall epistemological scheme into which all his philosophy fits consistently. In spite of all this trouble by Kant, Russell finds no difficulty in calling him confused. When we look for justification for this in Russell, we find he relies on a favourite phrase only (which we have italicised in the quotation below), which is enough to show how a priorism can be employed by philosophers quite casually and unconsciously. The relevant paragraph reads:

6. Immanuel Kant, *The Critique of Pure Reason*, tr. by F. Max Müller (Doubleday and Co. New York, 1959) pp. 58-60.

> Suppose we are confronted with the problem of space as presented in Kant's Transcendental Aesthetic, and suppose we wish to discover what are the elements of the problem and what hope there is for obtaining a solution for them? It will *soon appear* that three entirely distinct problems, belonging to different studies, and requiring different methods for their solution, have been confusedly combined in the supposed single problem with which Kant in concerned. There is a problem of logic, a problem of physics and a problem of theory of knowledge. Of these three the problem of logic can be solved exactly and perfectly; the problem of physics can probably be solved with as great a degree of certainty and as great an approach to exactness as can be hoped in an empirical region; the problem of theory of knowledge, however, remains very obscure and very difficult to deal with. . . .[7]

It will be seen from these citations from the writings of the dean of the sceptical and empirical school which persists to the present, that he wishes to curtail drastically the scope, content and methods of philosophy to suit his own partial pet notions of what it should be. His final position on philosophical method or theory of knowledge remains exceedingly vague and questionable. How far mental factors are to enter his analytical domain of a demonstrable or visible world remains a mystery.

If unified science, which is the dream even of Russell and his followers of the Vienna Circle, is to be realized, the synthetic approach through the a priori of Kant and the analytic approach which discredits the a priori, must be integrated on the basis of an absolutist norm for all thought or speculation as two complementary standpoints. The "principle of the dictionary" or rather two dictionaries with a one-to-one correspondence between them, seems to us to suggest in a distant way only the lines of such an integration

7. Russell, *Mysticism and Logic*, p. 114.

of physics and metaphysics. Russell and his followers cannot accept such principles and still remain empiricists.

Philosophy Must Rise Above Slogans and Isms

A scientific philosophy must have a normalized reference with a strictly conceived methodology, a correct epistemology and a scale of values which must be capable of referring to such a norm implicitly or explicitly conceived. At the present time such a norm does not prevail. Instead, as in politics, the philosophical domain is torn into rival camps. We hear slogans such as "metaphysics is nonsense"[8] with which a London professor kicks off the ball, as it were, in his recent book, and in a volume called *The Age of Analysis*, *The Twentieth Century Philosophers*, the title of the opening article is "The Decline and Fall of the Absolute."[9]

To celebrate the fall of the notion of the Absolute has become a fashion, because even in the domain of science, relativism has come into prominence. There is also a repugnance to absolutism of any kind in politics in the post-Hitlerian mentality of Europe. Whatever the reasons, political or scientific, they are continuations of the same long shadow of scepticism to which we have already referred.

The Vienna School of philosophers dreams of a unified science as well as of a language through logistic. They stand for analysis as against synthesis, for the a posteriori against the a priori. They further support a variety of logic of their own which they claim to be positive, demonstrable or "operational." This is based on observations and experiments with a scientific method which admits of hypothetical approximations to truth, rather than any wholesale approach to absolute truth given a priori.

Such a limitation of the scope of philosophy and its methods too, they believe would be conducive to philosophical

---

8. A.J. Ayer *Language, Truth and Logic*, (Gollancz, London 1946), p. 1.

9. Morton White, op. cit., p. 13.

progress. If a group of sportsmen preferred outdoor games, that would not mean that indoor games were not legitimate. In a unified body of knowledge of which such philosophers dream, it is unthinkable why they should limit the scope of philosophy itself in this manner. Analysis and synthesis, the a posteriori and the a priori must be given their legitimate places in philosophical speculation. All that anyone can insist on is to ask philosophers to conform to a stricter methodology, a more correct epistemology, and have some normative principles to regulate the axiological (value) aspects of speculation. Even if we should think of the philosophical attitude of the West as a whole, it cannot be considered as anything more or less than a variety of world philosophy in which we have to see the coexistence of all possible "isms" that distinguish individual schools.

If, instead of including all under an overall scheme of integration, some insist on excluding others, the dream of a unified science or philosophy will never be realized. To make statements about Oriental philosophy as being no philosophy at all, or that Kant is not a philosopher in the true sense of the term, as some are doing, can only be attributed to parochialism and closed loyalties. Actually philosophy, whether of the East or the West, should be looked upon as one of the basic consolations of human beings anywhere in the world at any time.

The scope, contents and methods of philosophy need to be properly defined and delimited. It is in this respect that it is important to determine a normative central notion for philosophy. Whether called truth, fact, reality or highest good, some regulative central notion must be understood before we begin the task of integrating branches of knowledge, irrespective of their belonging to the physical or the metaphysical order. In short, philosophy must rise above the stage of partial loyalties expressed by slogans and "isms," however justified they might happen to be in their respective limited spheres.

4

The Absolute as the Normative Reference for Philosophy

As a department of knowledge, philosophy must refer to something definite. All branches of science which have been systematized or formulated with any precision have implied in them a central unit or norm. The notion of the living cell is central in biology. Heat is thought of in terms of calories, and each kind of electrical energy has its own unit by which that particular kind is fixed and normalized for purposes of discussion, definition or measurement.

In philosophy we find that each school or individual system is distinguishable by a central notion round which it is built. Existentialism is built around the notion of existence and not around the notion of essence. In the philosophy of Spinoza the notion of substance occupies a central and normative position. In theology God occupies a similar position. Whether in science or philosophy, we are required to have some central notion for reference both for normalization or re-normalization of speculations or inferences. They must go neither too far in a plus or a minus direction from the norm.

When we think of philosophy as a whole there is the notion of the Absolute. This can be defined and normalized for the purpose of serving as a regulative principle around which all speculation can turn as its pivot or locus. Such a notion has to be necessarily of the nature of an extreme abstraction and generalization. A certain amount of arbitrariness must attach to it in the same way as the arbitrarily chosen name "rose" refers to the real on one side and on the other side to the idea of the rose. Similarly the notion of the Absolute must have the capacity of referring to the actual or visible physical world on the one hand and on the other hand to the conceptual aspect of the same as found in the terms of a dictionary.

When one of these aspects is equated to the other a neutral notion results. This neutral Absolute, at least for purposes of language and semantics, must be considered as the normative reference for all speculation, philosophical, scientific, or both.

When we approach the notion of the Absolute from the side of the notion of the relative on which it must depend for meaning, we have to make some allowances for structural, subjective and selective details which correspond to the categories of philosophy.

From the side of the Absolute, which is self-sufficient and does not depend on any relativistic notion at all, we require a pure notion of the same Absolute treated in itself.

Broadly, it is in these terms that we must think of an integrated philosophy or of a unified science. The further implications of such a normative notion, with its structural peculiarities, based on the categories of thinking, will be developed stage by stage in the present study, and particularly in the next part, where it will be re-examined from the standpoint of the Vedanta philosophy.

The Content of the Term "Absolute"

When Kant says that we cannot know the thing-in-itself he refers to the purest ultimate which does not depend for its meaning on any other notion that we already know. If its meaning should depend even to a faint degree on another notion, as for example in the way the notion of light depends on darkness, it cannot strictly be called the Absolute. A notion of the Absolute which is empty of all content would signify nothing to the human mind. In spite of this difficulty the human mind is able to give some meaning to the term Absolute, and tries to fill it with a content which depends on the various contexts in which thought concerning the Absolute becomes necessary.

In conversations we often hear the expression "absolutely" when a person wants to affirm or deny something with the fullest possible emphasis. Other uses of the word as in absolute zero temperature and so on, point to an ultimate quality limit of some kind. When we use the word as a noun with a definite article and speak of "The Absolute" we find that it becomes a fully philosophical notion and is actually used in this sense by various great thinkers both in the East as well as in the West, modern and ancient. The wide range of the use of this term is itself sufficient reason for us to adopt it, even with its varied connotations, as the one word which can conveniently refer to a central normative notion for all philosophy.

We have only to glance at the paragraphs under which the notion has already been examined, for example in any modern philosophical reference book, to be convinced of the suitability of the use of the term "The Absolute" as the central norm of all philosophy. Except in the case of those leaders of schools already referred to, who have set their minds against anything savouring of the notion of the a priori for their partially conceived reasons, we find that there is a general acceptance of the term among representative philosophers the world over. We read the following extracts from Wilbur Long's article on "The Absolute":[1]

> ABSOLUTE, THE: (In Metaphysics) Most broadly, the terminus or ultimate referent of thought. The Unconditioned. The opposite of the Relative (Absolute).

There is a singular and a generic use of the term. Under the singular usage he states:

---

1. The quotations that follow are from the article "The Absolute" in *The Dictionary of Philosophy*, ed. Dagobert D. Runes (Jaico, Bombay 1956).

> While Nicholas of Cusa referred to God as "the absolute" the noun form of this term came into common use through the writings of Schelling and Hegel. Its adoption spread in France through Cousin and in Britain through Hamilton. According to Kant, the Ideas of Reason seek both the absolute totality of conditions and their absolutely unconditioned Ground. . . . For Hegel . . . the Absolute is the All conceived as a timeless, perfect, organic whole of Self-thinking Thought. In England the Absolute has occasionally been identified with the Real. The specific emphasis given to this all inclusive perfection varies considerably, i.e., logical wholeness or concreteness (Hegel), metaphysical completeness (Hamilton), mystical feeling (Bradley), aesthetic completeness (Bosanquet), moral perfection (Royce). . . .

As the years pass, we note that the connotation of the term gathers to itself more and more aspects of philosophical verities, realities or values. It should be noted here that Kant uses the notion of the Absolute for a double reference both from the relative as well as from the fully absolutist side. We shall have more to say on this later. Here we shall note the growing use of the term in various senses and in various countries as an indication for us to show that when the notion has been properly determined with its double aspect, both structurally and non-structurally, we have already available the possibility of finding a central normative reference for all philosophy.

The inclusive nature of the notion is sufficiently clear from the following further remarks by the same writer:

> More recently the term has been extended to mean also (a) the All or totality of the Real however understood, and (b) the World Ground whether conceived idealistically or materialistically, whether pantheistically, theistically or dualistically. It thus stands for a variety of metaphysical conceptions that have appeared widely and under various names in the history of philosophy.

As regards the notion as it prevails in different regions of the globe, we read further:

> In China the *Wu-Chi* (non-Being), *Tai Chi* (Being), and on occasion, *Tao*. In India, the Vedantic *Ātman* (Self) and Brahman (the Real), the Buddhist *Bhūtatathatā* (indeterminate Thatness), *Vijñaptimātra* (the One, pure, changeless eternal consciousness, grounding all appearances) and the Void of Nāgārjuna; in Greece the cosmic matrix of the Ionians, the one of the Eleatics, the Being or Good of Plato, the World Reason of Stoicism, and the One of Neo-Platonism. In patristic and scholastic Christianity, the creator God; the Ens Realissimum, Ens Perfectissimum, Sui Causa, and the God of mysticism generally. (Erigena, Hugo of St. Victor, Cusa, Boehme, Bruno.) In modern thought: the Substance of Descartes and Spinoza, the God of Malebranche and Berkeley, the Energy of materialism, the Space-Time of realism, the Pure Experience of phenomenalism and the *ding-an-sich* of Kant.

We have quoted at length here because this article brings together all aspects of the content of the term "The Absolute" from as wide a range as could be expected, both regionally and ideologically, omitting neither modern nor ancient philosophical and cultural growths. Even mysticism and religion are covered, and the void (*shunya*) of the Madhyamika School of Buddhism is also included under the category of the Absolute.

It is true that as presented in a dictionary this review of the content of the term "The Absolute" requires to be further revised, corrected and coordinated to yield a fully normalized notion for our purposes. Some of the additions or subtractions will be found in the further remarks we shall have to make. In the meantime a rough idea of what to expect for inclusion within the wide range of connotations of the term can be gathered from the above extracts. We must add here, though in passing only, that the Absolute can be approached from the side of the Relative Absolute or from the side of the Absolute Absolute. This is due to innate epistemological limitations of the human understanding. We must look for the clarification of such a double-sided approach in the next and following sections.

The Implied Paradox in the Absolute

Modern scientists after Einstein are never tired of saying that Newton and Euclid were absolutists in their outlook, while they themselves, on the contrary, are relativists. This relativism is not just relativism in the ordinary context, but a Relativism with a capital letter, having a rival status with the Absolutism which it opposes. Both of these rival terms have to be written with a capital first letter. In other words, one of these depends for its meaning on the other, so that there is a paradox implied as between the two notions.

This brings us face to face with one of the most knotty epistemological problems in the domain of pure speculative philosophy. Transcending paradox is the same as the problem of rejecting the principle of the excluded middle and of contradiction. Like the thesis and antithesis of Hegel resulting in a synthesis, we have to imagine that "the Relative" which depends on its own Absolute counterpart, and "the Absolute" which depends on its own counterpart "the Relative," cancel each other out into the neutrality of a central Absolute that knows no second.

In Shankara's Vedanta, as we shall see, the same problem of having to resolve the two *Brahman*s, the higher and the lower, the qualified and the unqualified, into the unity of the final Absolute, presents itself again and again in his commentaries, although the arguments remain at least baffling and unconvincing. A delicate form of dialectical methodology is implied here which we shall not discuss at present. In the domain of modern relativistic theories this same difficulty appears in a very acute form, as evidenced in the following quotation from a Professor Temple:

> The paradox of the situation is this. On the one hand Newton professes a doctrine of absolute space and time, but in his doctrine of dynamics there is implicit a principle of relativity. On the other hand the nineteenth century physicists, of whom we may take Maxwell as a shining example, professed a sort of relativity, but Maxwell's electromagnetic theory employs an absolute space and time. Here we have a paradox on paradox, and the purpose of the special theory of relativity is their resolution.[2]

How the special theory of relativity of Einstein resolves this paradox is not easy to follow without full training in the mathematical and other technicalities of modern physics. All that we are able to say is that the notion of the Absolute which must be implicit in the solution of the paradox, is viewed unilaterally, not from the philosophical side, but strictly from the operational or behaviouristic aspect only. Temple explains this operational principle further:

> The second thing which I think is worthy of consideration (concluding the special theory of relativity) is the operational principle, that we, as physicists, are not concerned with philosophical discussions of the nature of space and time, but the behaviour of measuring rods and clocks.[3]

Thus it is to an Absolute of a relativistic order that Einstein as a physicist limits himself. For further light on the question, we have to turn to Eddington, who does not hesitate to call himself a philosopher and a scientist at the same time. In his book *Space, Time and Gravitation* he has the following remarks to make on the relation between the Absolute and the Relative:

> All physical knowledge is relative to space and time partitions; and to gain an understanding of the Absolute,

2. *Turning Points in Physics — From the Relative to the Absolute*, Lecture by G. Temple (Harper Bros, New York, 1961), p. 70.

3. Ibid., p. 82.

> it is necessary to approach it through the relative. The Absolute may be defined as a relative which is always the same no matter what it is relative to. Although we think of it as self-existing, we cannot give it a place in our knowledge without setting up some dummy to relate it to. And similarly the absolute differences of space always appear to be related to some mesh-system, although the mesh-system is only a dummy and has nothing to do with the problem.[4]

Here we find a new development. Instead of confining himself to the physical absolute of space and time, Eddington admits a pure Absolute which is the subject matter of philosophical speculation. He uses one as a corrective to the other. A neutral Absolute would be the resultant of the two factors, the dummy and the original canceling each other out into a central notion of the Absolute. In order to justify fully this last statement, we must approach the same paradoxical problem of the relation between the Relative and the Absolute in greater detail. Suffice it here to sum up and say that there are three positions which it is possible to take: first, there is the Relative Absolute which is that of the dummy of Eddington in the quotation above; second, there is the pure Absolute given to philosophy; and third, there is the neutral Absolute which knows no second.

The Relational Structure of the Absolute

The Absolute would be an empty word if we did not fill it with some content derived from the relative aspect of Reality, from which our experiences and thoughts have their starting point. The content of Reality as understood in the context of the Absolute has to contain both abstraction and concrete objects. They can be referred to broadly as predicables. All predicable entities will have something that stands for them in the dictionary. This is the domain of the nominal or that of

4. A.S. Eddington, *Space, Time and Gravitation*, (Harper, New York, 1959), p. 82.

the word. The word must have as its counterpart, what corresponds to its meaning.

Generally, if we say a "chair" or "rose," we have the word on one side and the object on the other. Words like "knowledge" and "love" will also have these two sides, so that we can generalize and say that Reality is filled with names and forms. These predicables are causes or effects, substances or attributes, generic or specific entities or, in most generalized terms, they represent some relation or relata.

The human mind is capable of thinking of all these predicables as particulars or universals, or in different groups, classes or sets, serially in contiguity or in continuity. Analytic and synthetic thought can move among these predicables in a priori or a posteriori fashion, linking them into ramified clusters of various kinds of togetherness or separateness. There can be a one-to-one correspondence between them, and some might by association or habit suggest others as antonyms or synonyms.

Without elaborating this, we can stop here with an initial generalization about such a system of predicables as being a complex of relations and relata. When the time factor is introduced into this the idea of order of succession is added to the static picture of relations and relata, and thus a process or a flux characterizes the resulting phenomenological picture. Thought circulates between the poles of analysis and synthesis within the limits of a priori and the a posteriori. There is a rhythmic alternation according to life interests, and consequent attention to some items of greater interest at one given time than to other items at other times, as life unravels in individuals.

The actual world becomes supplemented by dream or imaginary worlds and possible worlds that depend on mere hearsay. If we give primacy to the subject or the observing self we witness a passing show, but if we fix our attention on each predicable individually, our field of consciousness may be pictured as being filled merely with relation-relata complexes.

When we open our eyes we see the relata, and when we think with closed eyes we have the relations given to the mind. All relations and relata refer to existents. These can be subjected to reasoning of a logical order, and since they must have some human significance or value, they must come under the category of the Good. Existence, subsistence and value factors enter into the predicables. Sometimes the conceptual may dominate and at other times perceptual aspects.

When all these are made to fit into one scheme it tends to become too complicated, and therefore our aim should be to eliminate the extraneous. When this is done systematically we arrive at the fundamental remaining categories constituting a residue which cannot be further eliminated without the pure Absolute, as the substratum of the structure, showing itself transparently through the relativist mesh or dummy. When the bare categories of thought, such as time, space or causation are retained, the structure becomes more convenient as a reference in our discussion of the Absolute and its content, than if we were to elaborate and fit all sorts of details, however legitimate, into the picture. We are therefore obliged to apply the principle of Occam's Razor and cut down to the minimum the items we want to include. Thus the pure Absolute and the Absolute with the structural aspects included in it may help each other in throwing light on the normative Absolute, which we have to delimit and fix as clearly as possible.

We find to our advantage here that Eddington himself has tried to present a simplified picture of the relation-structure of the totality of reality, which is not other than the Absolute. This happens to be sufficiently suitable for our purposes, although as Eddington himself admits, some of the assumptions are arbitrary and adopted only in the name of simplicity. He says:

> *Relation structure*: We take as building material *relations* and *relata*. The relations unite the relata; the relata are the meeting points of the relations. The one is

> unthinkable apart from the other. I do not think that a more general starting point of structure could be conceived.
>
> To distinguish the relata from one another we assign them *monomarks*. The monomarks consist of four numbers ultimately to be called "co-ordinates." But co-ordinates suggest space and geometry and as yet there is no such thing in our scheme; hence for the present we shall regard the four identification numbers as no more than an arbitrary monomark. Why *four* numbers? We use four because it turns out that ultimately the structure can be brought to better order that way; but we do not know why this should be so. We have got so far as to understand if the relations insisted on a three-fold or a five-fold ordering it would be much more difficult to build anything interesting out of them; but that this is perhaps an insufficient excuse for the special assumption of the four-fold order in the primitive material.[5]

Coming from such a well known scientist and philosopher, the above relation structure built on what he calls "the primitive material" (which cannot be anything other than the Absolute) affords for our purposes in this study a sufficiently firm springboard for arriving at the normalized notion that we are seeking to establish. From other aspects derived from other philosophers like Kant and Spinoza, we shall have more to add later regarding the structural aspects of the content of the Absolute, so as to make it philosophically as well as scientifically self-consistent and complete.

But before we pass from the structure as presented by Eddington, we must add the remark that all relations and relata are not to be looked upon as static and fixed for all time, or to be the same with all persons anywhere, irrespective of their interests or temperaments. Depending on our

5. A.S. Eddington, *The Nature of the Physical World,* (Dent, London, 1947), pp. 225-26.

axiological goal certain interests prevail which accentuate certain relations or relata aspects as more important than others. In spite of this and also because of this personal element of the thinker or observer, whatever is of interest to the individual self gains primacy over merely objective or mathematical aspects. There is a vertical relation which links the self and the non-self aspects of a relation-relata complex organically and dialectically, giving primacy alternately and in living terms to one or other interest at a given time.

Reserving such further considerations for future discussion and elaboration, Eddington's structure may be considered acceptable as far as it goes for our present purposes, as a basis for discussion. We have to add that Eddington's hesitation to speak in terms of the coordinates of analytical geometry for the reason that this would suggest space, need not be respected in the light of modern developments in the relationship between geometry and algebra and of the contributions of topology and vectorial and projective geometry (inclusive of the Euclidean as a particular instance among them). Herein Hilbert's contributions are noteworthy.

Space can be treated as gross as well as intuitioned, as space spatialized and as space spatializing. These are further considerations in whose light we shall have to revise and supplement the relation-structure presented by Eddington. The physical, mathematical, logical, personal, ethical and phenomenological versions of the Absolute are bound to differ in structural details of a specific kind suitable for each context, but the overall features of the structure will remain the same in all cases. Eddington himself admits that the scheme offered by physicists is still of a relativistic order, and that an absolute scheme which would satisfy the requirements of both physicists and metaphysicians has still to be worked out: "The relativity of the current scheme of physics invites us to search deeper and find the absolute scheme underlying it, so that we may see the world in a truer perspective."[6]

6. Ibid., p. 43.

In a later work Eddington refers to his "selective subjectivism and structuralism" which is more philosophical, as the title of the book, *The Philosophy of Physical Science*, indicates. Here he improves on the relation-structure, and boldly sums up as follows: "In our view the physical universe is neither wholly subjective nor wholly objective — nor a simple mixture of subjective and objective entities or attributes."[7]

A Normalized Epistemology Needs Structure to be Recognized

There are three aspects of speculation or investigation which must be kept in mind if philosophy is to become more scientific, or if science is to admit a more correct philosophy as its inevitable counterpart. Our last quotation from Eddington points to the fact that even the physical world is not wholly objective, but is also subjective. How much then should metaphysics be more subjective than physics, although in its turn metaphysics cannot be without an objective reference? The total knowledge situation understood unitively or in an all-inclusive self-sufficient or absolutist context, has thus to be considered as being both subjective and objective at once.

We should not just think of a promiscuous mixture of subjectivity and objectivity. These have a subtle reciprocity of one-to-one correspondence. The categories of the one enter into relation with schematic aspects of the other in the pure domain of what is called human understanding. Certain innate or fundamental laws, rules, or necessities prevail in the domain of causes and effects, relations and relata, calculables and observables, facts and logical validities, which refer to the epistemological, methodological or axiological considerations, thus making of philosophy a complicated field in which problems have to be solved by thought or research

7. A.S. Eddington, *The Philosophy of Physical Science* (University Michigan Press, 1958), p. 27.

to secure the best human interests in matters big or small. Each tree has its seed from which alone there is the possibility of its growing, and not from any other.

Thus a subtle law of necessity or possibility links certain causes with their effects, and there is also a world of chance or probability where certain results predominate and not others. We are therefore obliged to think of a fundamental structure of the total knowledge situation which in reality is none other than the normative notion of the Absolute implied in what is vaguely referred to by sceptic philosophers as human understanding. Empirical, logical, dialectical and purely mathematical or axiomatic ways of thinking refer to different aspects of what this vague term "human understanding" implies. There are different levels of abstraction or generalization possible within the overall domain of understanding.

How a perceptual, an actual, a conceptual and a nominal entity such as the word "chair" can all coexist in one common human understanding, without contradiction and with or without an excluded middle ground, and how what is "fact-true" need not be logically so, and how a philosophy which has utility as a goal, and how the self and the non-self enter into the structure of the normative notion of philosophy that we are seeking, are all problems requiring separate and careful elaboration. Ontology, teleology, realism and other "isms" too numerous to mention, have all to be accommodated within such an integrated normative notion. At the end of our studies in these essays we hope to be in a better position to undertake this task.

The epistemological structure or the limitations of knowledge requires recognition of rules, laws or necessities belonging intrinsically to categories and schematic structural peculiarities to which all thinking or speculation has to be subjected. Methodology too has to follow the lines or axes of reference, frames or forms implicit in such a scheme. Where axiology prevails in philosophical speculations higher intuitive and value-factors must be dialectically treated. Thus, whether philosophical or scientific, subjectivism and structuralism count in speculation. In the integration of thought this kind of schematism or structuralism plays an important part. It is in recognition of such a necessity that we shall follow in these pages the implications of this aspect which have been hitherto neglected or given inadequate attention in the domain of philosophical speculation.

Vertical and Horizontal Aspects of the Absolute

Now, after grasping the significance of the relation-structure as presented by a scientist — Eddington — and the schematization as presented by a philosopher — Kant — if we keep in mind that modern geometrical postulates have, corresponding to them, valid algebraic axioms or theorems, which are making for an exact discipline now known as the algebra of geometry, we shall be sufficiently justified here in taking one step beyond what both the above eminent authorities have suggested. This is to say that the total knowledge situation, which is the subject matter and the object matter at the same time, has always two complementary sides, which are related to each other in the form of a one-to-one structural and complementary relationship.

Whether we call them reality and appearance, noumenon and phenomenon, quality and quantity, time and space, the conceptual and the perceptual, the self and the non-self, cause and effect, etc., these two aspects are always present. They constitute the central problem that philosophy in general is called upon to solve.

With a little practice in scrutinizing these and other such pairs, which different philosophers employ in stating their positions clearly, we shall soon be enabled to see that where the principle of contradiction and excluded middle are admitted, and on the other hand where all is included, we have yet another aspect of such a dual pair.

Two things or bodies cannot occupy the same space, or in other words, matter in space has the property of impenetrability. Conceptually, however, one circle can be contained in another. This latter we can appreciate with the eyes shut, while the former needs the eye to be kept open. The visible and the intelligible worlds referring to the body and the mind, belong therefore to these distinct twin orders which coexist in the common substance of the Absolute. Space and time, one objective and the other subjective, coexist in the pure being of the substance of the Absolute.

This participation and separation implies a structure which can be represented by two intersecting lines like Cartesian coordinates, with four limbs. The point of intersection is where the two aspects have common ground in the Absolute. If we think of relations and relata we have to put relations of contiguity in the horizontal and those of continuity in the vertical. At each point of intersection we have to relate schematically and structurally a plurality of relata with their component limbs. Each of these complexes can pass for a monad.

This representation offers us the barest skeleton of the schematic structure with whose help the normative notion of the Absolute required for the integration of knowledge can tentatively be arrived at even at the present stage of our inquiry. Further justification and elaboration will be found in the light of other authoritative writings such as those of Spinoza, which resemble this scheme as we have once mentioned.

Further, such a scheme offers us a nuclear notion combining characteristics of thought processes which should enable us to build round it a language common to all sciences and free from local or traditional limitations of linguistic frontiers. This itself would be a great advantage, by the mere de-babelization which would result.

5

A Normative Methodology for All Philosophy

Speculative philosophy and experimental science have each their methods proper to the problems that they have to solve and belonging to whichever aspect of total or absolute reality is their proper domain.

In each case the method must depend on the kind of knowledge and its structure in each branch of knowledge. Methodology thus depends on epistemology and vice versa. Hegel's methodology is especially suited to the extremely idealistic position that he takes, but in the domain of the physical sciences Hegelianism or even Socratic methods would have no applicability because those sciences give primacy to empirical aspects of reality and not to any subtle essence of it.

Bacon pointed out that scientific method depends on experiment, observation and inference. Inference in science is inductive in character. The truths of science are the laws that are tentatively and hypothetically arrived at within the limits of the empirical world of so-called positive realities. When we go beyond the limits of the empirical we leave laws of nature and turn inwards into the world of cogitations, reasoning, logical or mathematical calculations and the like, so as to arrive at solutions, convictions or certitudes in respect of problems of truth.

Fact truth is not the same as logic truth. Here again we could confine ourselves to a form of syllogistic reasoning which would admit of the principle of contradiction and of the excluded middle, or we could use still higher reasoning called the dialectical. This consists of equating counterparts, which give us certitude by revealing that one set of facts, truths or realities are the same as another, thus disclosing some fundamental relational aspect having significance in human life.

Between a posteriori inferences from experimental data, we pass thus into the domain of such propositions as the famous Cartesian dictum, *cogito ergo sum*, and build rational or theoretical speculations upwards till we touch a region in pure higher reasoning which employs dialectics, called by Plato the highest instrument of reasoning, independent of all visible or sensible facts.

This kind of reasoning, the dialectical, which takes us to the threshold of higher idealistic values in life is the third and the last step in philosophical methodology taken as a whole. The laws of nature refer to the world of existence. Rules of thought, whether axiomatic or based on postulates, refer to the world of subsistence. The third step of reasoning lives and has its being in the pure domain of human values, those referring to the True, the Good or the Beautiful, which are values in life and thus belong to the domain of axiology.

The visible, the intelligible and the value worlds which we can mark out on a vertical line represent levels of higher and higher reasonings culminating in the dialectical. It is like soaring, or resorting to ascending dialectics as spoken of in certain circles. This level has, just inferior to it, the world of formal or syllogistic reasonings admitting of the limits of contradictions at its lower limit and of tautology at its higher limit, where logistic and propositional calculi are employed.

At the lowest level in this vertical axis, where empirical or at least ontological factors prevail, referring to existent aspects of the physical world actually, perceptually or even conceptually understood, we have a region where certitudes naturally take the form of laws such as that of gravitation, or the conservation of matter and energy. Electromagnetic and thermodynamic laws belong to the Einsteinian physical world, whether treated epistemologically as real or ideal.

Thus existential, subsistential and value aspects of the Absolute have three different methodological approaches, one proper to and compatible with each.

A normal methodology applicable to integrated knowledge whether philosophical or scientific has to accommodate within its scope these three kinds of approaches to certitude, each in its proper domain. The experimental method suits existential aspects of the Absolute, the logical suits the subsistential and the dialectical suits the value aspects of the Absolute. Interest in the physical world gives place in the second stage of ascent to logical psychology or phenomenology, where ratiocination plays its part. Finally we ascend higher into the third aspect of the Absolute where value relations hold good and the instrument or methodology used is that of dialectics.

When the observer and the observed, the operator and the operated, are treated together, we have the method of modern relativism. Otherwise stated, these are methods which are more absolutist in outlook. In fact, these terms seem to be used interchangeably at present, being used against each other as between Newtonians and Euclidians on the one side and Einsteinians on the other. Relativism must presuppose absolutism, as everyone can guess independently.

As in mathematical equations where the terms are interchangeable, the dialectical counterparts in the context of the Absolute refer to the Self or the non-Self aspects and cancel each other out in favour of the Absolute Self, where we reach the terminus of all speculation or reflexive contemplation. The so-called Socratic or the synthetic, the ascetic or the mystical, the psychological, the critical or the transcendental, the dialectical or the intuitive, the reflexive or the eclectic, axiomatic, inductive or the deductive methods could all be given their legitimate places in a total overall schematic view of the normative notion that we should keep in mind here.

An Overall Epistemology

Epistemology is a Greek word often translated into English as "theory of knowledge." It is a fairly recent branch of philosophy. Epistemology may be said to be a more global and conceptualized view of reality. Instead of saying "I know," we seem to take a step backwards here and say "I know that I know." The subject matter and the object matter of knowledge are both comprised within it.

Now if we put the questions of "how," "why" and "what" to the person who claims to "know that I know" we arrive roughly at the understanding of the scope and limits of this new way of philosophy. When we consider the status of this department of philosophy we see that it belongs to the order of self-introspection. Thus it belongs to the contemplative context. As epistemology examines the Self in terms of the non-Self, and vice versa, covering not only the origin, methods and validity of knowledge, but also the structure of knowledge, which can exist only on something which is behind as a basis of the structure, we come nearer than ever in epistemology to the norm of the Absolute neutrally conceived, with its plus and minus sides treated together. The structure needs grounding on some *tabula rasa,* which can only be human understanding in its most ultimate, abstract or general sense.

The normative Absolute must be accepted here again as a regulative notion. The rival claims of other branches or other divisions of epistemology should not distort or minimize the importance of this overall view of the knowledge situation. Both the Self and the non-Self have to be within the scope of the epistemological view. Whether we call these aspects of the Self and the non-Self subjective or objective, observer or observed, operator or operand, psychological or cosmological, a balance has to be struck between them to avoid the egocentric or extreme forms of solipsism. The a priori and the a posteriori aspects also have to be correctly equalized in a normalized epistemological outlook proper to philosophy as a whole.

When epistemology becomes thus properly normalized and renormalized from both the poles of the total knowledge situation it can easily become the foundation of a Science of all sciences, including both the physical and the metaphysical.

The Revised Philosophy of Science

Among philosophers of science it is Eddington again who has recognized the need for normalization through epistemological revision of the status given to scientific knowledge. He paves the way for an integrated or unitive science which is neither subjective nor objective, nor a mere promiscuous mixture of the two, but a science having a correct neutral epistemological status of its own, normalized and renormalized as between the a priori and the a posteriori. The following extract from Eddington's writings will show how even physicists resort to epistemological revisions in respect of the reality which is their subject:

> Selective subjectivism, which is the modern scientific philosophy, has little affinity with Berkeleian subjectivism, which if I understand rightly, denies all objectivity to the external world. In our view the physical universe is neither wholly subjective nor wholly objective — nor a simple mixture of subjective and objective entities or attributes.[1]

Striking the norm between the subjective and the objective is a problem for absolutist epistemology. It depends on the fact that both these counterparts have a common structural correspondence. The thesis and the antithesis, the microcosm and the macrocosm, and the Self and the non-Self have between them a relationship which, when subjected to a dialectical treatment as counterparts, as both true or

1. A.S. Eddington, *The Philosophy of Physical Science*, (University of Michigan Press, U.S.A., 1958), p. 27.

both false, yields, by cancellation of numerator and denominator, or by plus and minus annihilation, the neutral Absolute, which is the common central reference for both. This is an overall epistemological law which both physicists and idealists are beginning to formulate, though not as yet in finalized terms.

In Indian Vedanta, as we have already seen, there is again the ever-unsettled question of unity or duality between the *saguna Brahman* (the relative Absolute) and *nirguna Brahman* (the absolute Absolute). The reduction of this duality in terms of the unitive central neutral Absolute is even there, as in the domain of the philosophy of science, still an unresolved problem. A fully absolutist approach with a more consciously developed dialectical methodology inevitable and inseparable from it, can alone be expected to clear the way for the integrated knowledge of unified science. How Hegelian dialectics and the absolutism that went with it lost its way in the sands of extraneous political fervour is what we have already seen. As for Eddington's attempts to bring about a drastic epistemological revision, he unfortunately died before he could fully establish his case, and even when living he was conscious of the odds against which he had to fight. This is evident from what he wrote:

> I expect I shall be accused of exaggerating the epistemological element in modern physical theory . . . . From the time of Newton until recently the epistemology of science was stationary; for two hundred years the extending and ordering of our knowledge of the physical universe continued without modifying it. . . .
>
> Generally, he (the physicist) prided himself on being a plain matter of fact person. . . .
>
> Thus, although scientific epistemology has always been part of the domain of physics, the physicist has left it so long uncultivated that, when at last he turned attention to it, his right-of-way was questioned. My impression is

that the general attitude (among leading physicists) might be described as *grudging acceptance*.[2]

The three epistemological features that Eddington wishes to apply to the theory of physics are put in the words "subjectivism," "selectionism" and "structuralism," to which he has devoted a whole book with many chapters. It is not easy for us to form a complete idea of what he wished to say. For our purpose it is not necessary to go into the technical details of the physicist. All that we can do is to take a peep into his study through a door left ajar, as it were, so that we might have at least a rough idea of what normalization and renormalization from the a priori and the a posteriori aspects of the Absolute mean, so that we can in such a light follow more intelligently modern trends in thought.

In order to clarify what we might have to say later and in the comments on the *One Hundred Verses of Self-Instruction* of the Guru Narayana, for which this is an introduction, we shall extract from the writings of Eddington just a few more lines on this topic of epistemology:

> The epistemological method of investigation leads us to the study of the nature of the frame of thought, and so be forewarned to its impress on the knowledge that will be forced into it. We may foresee *a priori* certain characteristics which any knowledge contained in the frame will have simply because it is contained in the frame. These characteristics will be discovered *a posteriori* by physicists who employ that frame of thought, when they come to examine that knowledge they have forced into it. Procrustes again.[3]

Normalization and Re-normalization of the Absolute

The allusion to Procrustes in the above quotation brings

2. Ibid., pp. 52, 53.

3. Ibid., p. 109.

us to the question of the norm and how it is the resultant of the correction of the experimental in the light of the theoretical, and the theoretical in the light of the experimental, so that what agrees from the side of both at once is the neutrally or absolutely right in the final sense. Eddington calls this double process of correction for requirements of epistemology "the Procrustean treatment."[4] Procrustes was a giant of Greek fable who was said to have stretched out or chopped down his guests to fit the bed he had constructed, to which story Eddington added a supplement to say that "He measured them up before they left next morning, and wrote a learned paper 'On the Uniformity of Stature of Travellers' for the Anthropological Society of Attica."

What Eddington did not explain by reference to the fable was left for Sir Edmund Whittaker to clarify further, giving the name "Re-normalization" to the treatment. He explained it thus:

> The development of quantum electro-dynamics has in fact shown the necessity for what is called *re-normalization* which is precisely a recognition of the difference between the observed and the theoretical values of *e* and *m*. . . . Although Eddington did not live to see the development of the modern practice of re-nomalizing *e* and *m*, he saw that a situation of the kind must arise, and he uttered a warning against expecting too close an agreement between his theoretically calculated values and those obtained by measurement.[5]

Those who came after Eddington, including Prof. S.R. Milner and others, have made further progress on the same lines and shown beyond doubt that predictions made through theory have been verified by practice. This fact is enough to

4. Ibid., p. 116.
5. Sir Edmund Whittaker "Eddington's Principle" in *The Philosophy of Science*, (Cambridge University Press, New York, 1951), p. 25.

prove that there is a norm in the domain of science common to theory and practice which has a neutral or central status of its own. In other words, it is absolute in its status in the context of science conceived as a whole, experimentally or non-experimentally, which is the same as saying quantitatively or qualitatively. If we extrapolate and apply this principle to the domain of thought in general, whether called physical or metaphysical in a unified sense, we have the same absolute norm emerging into our view quite clearly and unequivocally.

Normative Axiology

Methodology and epistemology are natural and necessary pre-suppositions to an absolutist or normative axiology for all philosophy or unified science. The word 'method' naturally suggests scientific method first and perhaps dialectical method last. Epistemology moves within the limits of reasoning where metaphysics resides, and only by extended or extrapolated application does it refer to the ontological aspect of reality. Science gives primacy to existence and reason to subsistence, and what is existent and substantial must needs have a value significance for man, for whom all knowledge may be said to have significance.

The True, the Good and the Beautiful refer to the world of values, preferences or desirables. God, the final cause, is also most good according to Aristotle, and the *summum bonum* of classical philosophy is also a value factor. Hedonistic, pragmatic and utilitarian values, besides aesthetic and religious values, and science itself as a means as well as an end in axiology, are familiarly known to different philosophies. The Self and the non-Self equated yield absolute value in the normative Self. All knowledge of the Self being for the sake of the Self, and the Self itself being of the nature of consciousness, which is essentially of the stuff of knowledge, there is no duality of ends and means when axiology is conceived unitively. Vedanta recognizes this verity in the great dictums, the *maha-vakyas*, representing the final doctrine of that kind of thinking. A scale of values from the most earthy to the most pure, ranging between the dark and the bright poles of personal life, which fits in with its corresponding cosmology, is also permissible in the context of absolutist axiology.

When knowledge and the self meet and cancel each other out in the neutrality of the experience of the Absolute in the Self, we have the terminus or the goal of all axiology. The Absolute becomes the adorable or the most loveable or dearest value. A hierarchy of values resulting from the dialectical cancellation of lower and higher values is also legitimate in the context of the normative or absolutist principle in which we can examine all possible values significant to human life.

There is a cosmological wonder about the physical world and about God who is thought to be its origin and source. The former belongs to the visible and the latter to the intelligible. A series of wonders could be ranged, graded from terra firma to the subtlest of mental abstractions, containing the same element of wonder. The sense of wonder is the basis of adoration or poetic ecstasy. Thus value verges on the mystical.

Science and Wonder

Scientists, like the matter-of-fact people they want to be considered, never display attitudes of wonder and its allied feelings about truth or reality. Usually they tend to dismiss such matters as sentimental. This axiological factor against which orthodox scientists shut their front doors, seems however, to be entering the strict preserves of the scientific house by the back door when we find Sir Edmund Whittaker exclaiming:

> We stand in awe before the thought that the intellectual frame-work of Nature is prior to Nature herself — that it existed before the material universe began its history

> — that the cosmos revealed to us by science is only one fragment in the plan of the Eternal.[6]

Such language is not unlike that of the pulpit which one may hear any Sunday, but this time it refers to the nature of the physical world and not to God. The word "Eternal" which must refer to the Absolute, scientifically understood, is the common integrating normative link between theology and science, though perhaps not consciously employed by the eminent scientist here. Even if so used, there would be a number of more orthodox scientists who might, as Eddington has put it, "question his right-of-way."

Science Resembles Vedanta

Prof. Erwin Schrodinger is another eminent scientist who is heterodox enough to refer to Vedantic doctrines, such as *atma = brahman*. In the epilogue of *What is Life*? he writes:

> i) My body functions as a pure mechanism according to the Laws of Nature.
>
> ii) Yet I know, by incontrovertible direct experience that I am directing all motions, of which I foresee the effects that may be fateful and all important in which case I feel and take full responsibility for them.
>
> The only possible inference from these two facts is, I think that I — I in the widest meaning of the word, that is to say, every conscious mind that has ever said or felt 'I' — am the person, if any, who controls the motion of the atoms according to the Laws of Nature.[7]

Further remarks on similar lines but more elaborate can be found in Schrodinger's later book, *My View of the World* (Cambridge University Press, 1964).

---

6. Sir Edmund Whittaker "Eddington's Principle" in *The Philosophy of Science*, (Cambridge University Press, New York, 1951), p. 31.
7. A.S. Eddington, *What is Life*? (Cambridge University Press, New York, 1951), p. 89.

This quotation from an up-to-date scientist resembles the text of the Bhagavad Gita (XVIII, 61) where it is stated:

> The Lord dwells in the heart region of all beings, O Arjuna, causing all beings to revolve through the principle of appearance (*maya*) (as if) mounted on a machine.[8]

Even Dr. Robert Oppenheimer is reported to have remembered his studies of the Gita and was forced to exclaim about the terrific white light produced by the first atomic explosion, repeating the words of Arjuna "It was as if it were the glory of a thousand suns" (compare the Bhagavad Gita XI, 12 which reads — "If the splendour of a thousand suns were to rise together in the sky, that might resemble the splendour of that great Self.")

The wonder of Absolute Reality evidenced in nature or in God can thus claim equally the admiration of the mystic as well as the greatest of scientists without detracting from their proper status or dignity as fully intelligent humans.

Wholesale wonder about life or the nature of the split atom thus brings open-minded scientists near to the value aspects of science such as the wonder of the Absolute when they approach it from the side of the relative. A normalized version of the same value factor will bring us as near as possible to the notion of the neutral Absolute as an existent, a subsistent and a high value. In a scale of values it will occupy the top position as the *summum bonum*. Ends and means meet in all values viewed under the aegis of the Absolute.

8. See Prof. O.F. Reiser of the University of Pittsburg, USA, in his project, *Prometheus and Krishna*.

6

The Search for the Absolute

Implicitly or explicitly all philosophy must refer to the Absolute. Although the open recognition and use of the term has been of recent origin, we have already seen how, ranging from theology to science, many schools of philosophy have had the Absolute implied in their systems.

A cosmological, a psychological and a theological Absolute, besides a scientific one, have all been in vogue for some time, and the distinction between what is a relativistic and an absolutist approach has come to the forefront of thought ever since Einstein's relativism began to be talked about.

But even before Einstein, philosophers such as Hegel and Bergson have stood for their own kind of absolutist approach, different though their definitions of the Absolute might be. Philosophy needs a revised epistemology and methodology before we can say which of the definitions is the more correct.

Even when philosophy and science have been standardized or normalized, there is another more important presupposition which both of these subserve. This is, that unless we have an idea of the purpose of life, and give to the least and the greatest of values in life a graded position in an absolute scheme, mere absolutism can easily carry us to explosive extremes when applied to group life.

Pan-Germanism, Marxism and various forms of Fascism in politics, or charlatanism in spiritual walks of life are not unknown dangers to modern generations. Of those who openly called themselves absolutists in philosophy, whether it was an approach or an "ism" to which their philosophies may be justly said to conform, two names stand out: Hegel and Bergson. So before we pass on to see how even those who were not labeled absolutists openly were still tacitly or unconsciously absolutists, we shall examine here briefly these two philosophers. They were the first to be bold enough to recognize openly the absolutism in their respective outlooks.

Hegel's Absolute Idea

In Hegel's *Encyclopedia of Philosophy,* Gustav Emil Müller, the translator, annotating Section 5 of the preliminary note on *The Theories of Knowledge*, explains correctly the usual mistake of calling Hegel's philosophy a form of idealism. It is true that when we stress the notion of his Idea those who call Hegel an "absolute idealist" might at first seem to be right; but the epistemologically understood Idea of Hegel is characterized by a certain comprehensiveness which is an absolutist quality by virtue of which the label "idealism" would not be justified. Dr. Müller explains this clearly as follows:

> Historians have labeled Hegel's philosophy 'absolute idealism' — this is just as pointless as any other 'ism,' even though the 'idea' is a central term, equivalent to and exchangeable with 'reality as such,' 'world itself,' 'universe,' 'comprehensiveness,' the 'Absolute.' His 'absolute idealism' might just as well be called 'absolute realism' but is neither, because any standpoint which has an opposite is not the Absolute.[1]

If we add a few words from Hegel himself where he underlines the all-comprehensive epistemological nature of the notion of the Absolute as he intended it to be, we shall have, for the present enough of an idea of Hegelian absolutism for our purposes:

> S 160 . . . *Intelligent objectivity* and *objective intelligibility* in process are particular expressions of the idea.

---

1. G.W.F. Hegel, *Encyclopedia of Philosophy*, tr. Gustav Emil Müller, (Philosophical Library, New York, 1952), p. 71.

> S 161. All previous determinations of the Absolute are absorbed in this definition: *The Absolute is Idea.* They all participate in its truth and are true only as far as they participate in it. . . .
>
> The Absolute Idea is not the idea of something or other, rather it differentiates itself in many concrete systems of life and remains the One all-embracing process and activity in all of them. . . .
>
> The idea is freedom: The Absolute determines itself and is determined by nothing outside itself. Its eternal presence is one with its restless creativity. It never stands still; it leaves standing no seemingly finished manifestations of its life.[2]

Here the notion of the Absolute has an essentially epistemological status, and its methodological aspect is supplied by the dialectical approach. The all-comprehensiveness of the Idea is seen to be dialectically conceived when he refers to it above as being both "intelligible objectivity" and "objective intelligibility" at one and the same time. It is like saying "this is the son of the father" and "this is the father of the son," both of which refer centrally to one and the same reality.

The process that is stressed above covers the same ground as the Absolute to be comprehended by Bergson, whose ideas also we shall examine presently. When Hegel says the Absolute's "eternal *presence* is one with its restless *creativity*" (our italics), we have two aspects of the Absolute brought very close together. One of them may be said to refer to "being" and the other to "becoming." Between them, being and becoming present a paradox. How they can coexist is an enigma that has not been fully examined either by Hegel or Bergson. Even Shankara, the Vedanta philosopher, as we shall see, is hard put to resolve the implied paradox between

---

2. G.W.F. Hegel, *Encyclopedia of Philosophy*, tr. Gustav Emil Müller, (Philosophical Library, New York, 1952), pp. 152-53.

what he called the qualified or affected Absolute (*saguna Brahman*), and the Absolute that is fully real (*nirguna Brahman*) according to him. "Transcending duality" as they say in India presents the same problem as "resolving paradox" in the linguistic context of Western philosophy.

Although Hegel and Shankara come very close to each other in discovering the norm of thought in philosophy, there is some retouching still necessary in methodology, epistemology and axiology if the normative notion that we are seeking in this study is to emerge fully into view.

By stressing merely the epistemological or idea aspect at the expense of the two others, Hegel falls short of what is required for that complete notion of the Absolute. Moreover, he underscores the aspect of restless activity of the Absolute as he conceives it when he says above that "It never stands still; it leaves standing no seemingly finished manifestations of its life." Here his pan-Germanic "will to power" becomes already evident. This is the factor that warped and distorted his approach to absolutism, as we have already said. His approach needs axiological reorientation so that the pure creativity of the Absolute may not give justification for partial egoistic distortions of the will and its miscarriage into undesirable and disastrous channels, which it did, as later history records. The ego in man is an ever-present danger which will distort any normative notion and bend it to its own prejudices. Only on the soil of absolute detachment and dispassionateness can the right kind of absolutism flourish, as history and individual lives have amply shown.

The Bergsonian Absolute of Change and Becoming

The Hegelian notion of the Absolute more or less ended in a blind alley, losing itself in politics and sociology, where some action or conquest was the dominant consideration. But Bergson broke off from both his Classical and Relationist predecessors in philosophy, to whose line, starting from Descartes, even Hegel may be said to belong.

Bergson gave fresh impetus to philosophical speculation based, not on conceptualization, even in such grand outlines as the Hegelian Idea, but in living and experienced terms stemming out of biology rather than geometry and physics. According to Bergson the latter were mechanistic non-living stills or moulds in which the molten liquid of thought was solidified. The mechanistic intelligence can attain only the relative, but man needs the intuitive approach to questions about time, duration or motion from *inside* the situation instead of from *outside*, so that thought can attain the Absolute.

Bergson was thus not interested in the Absolute directly, but found a method by which one could attain it from the relative. For him, intuition was the instrument by which man is able to attain the Absolute in actual living experience and not as a mere Idea, however metaphysically or mathematically sound it might be. He explains:

> From the overlooking of this intuition proceeds all that has been said by philosophers and by men of science themselves about the "relativity" of scientific knowledge. What is relative is the symbolic knowledge by pre-existing concepts, which proceeds from the fixed to the moving, and not the intuitive knowledge which installs itself in that which is moving and adopts the very life of things. *This intuition attains the absolute.*[3] (our italics)

The relative and the Absolute are two aspects of reality, one given to mechanistic and the other to intuitive thinking. The world of mechanistic thinking is only a machine, but when the mind works properly, Bergson says, it produces men of intuition who will resemble gods. This idea of the Absolute as opposed to the relative has a structural secret enshrined within it (which we shall examine later) by which paradoxes like that of Zeno are transcended by the capacity

---

3. Henry Bergson, *Introduction to Metaphysics* tr. T.E. Hulme, Library of Liberal Arts, (Bobbs-Merrill Co., New York, 1955), p. 53.

to think intuitively and by overcoming the natural tendency to conceive processes mechanistically.

Absolutism Suffers a Setback

Where Bergson found an instrument of thought which could attain the Absolute, Hegel went into the content of the Idea of the Absolute and worked out its conceptual implications. Bergson's approach was methodological while Hegel's was epistemological. The axiological implications were not properly worked out by either of them, and to that extent their notions of the Absolute were incomplete. Hegel's Absolute was a culmination of the original sceptical impetus in modern thought which began with Descartes and continued with Hume as a philosopher and with Newton as a scientist. Because Hegelianism caught up again with the idea of God, which had been discarded at least in its classical, Scholastic or theological sense with the dawn of the age of Reason, Hegelian Absolutism ended in a blind alley.

Modern minds still fought shy of anything that sounded like dogmatism or belief. Hegel's absolutism could find a place for belief in God, and so may be said to have completed the cycle which began with the extreme of the absolute belief in the idea of a World Spirit and its affinities with a theological idea of God as representing the Absolute. The Father, the Son and the Holy Spirit were all capable to being fitted into the notion of the Absolute of Hegel. Thus theology entered the domain of philosophy by the back door after the front door had been slammed against it by sceptics like Hume.

No wonder, then, that a reaction set in at the very heart of modern philosophy after it had become developed as far as the Absolute of Hegel. Empiricists and sceptics such as Bertrand Russell, who in many cases began as admirers of Hegel, finally turned their faces against him. They called themselves Positivists, Empiricists or Analytical Philosophers, and there is at present a whole line of them who stand for something far different from the absolutism implied in Hegel.

Moore, Croce, Santayana, Whitehead, Jaspers, Heidegger, Sartre, James, Dewey, Ayer and Russell bring up a long line of modern thinkers who are considered as ranged against absolutism as a philosophical doctrine. Morton White examines their philosophies in a volume called *The Age of Analysis*. In his very first essay called "The Decline and Fall of the Absolute" we have an opening paragraph which states the case against the idea of the Absolute:

> It is a remarkable tribute to an enormously muddled but brilliant German professor of the nineteenth century that almost every important philosophical movement of the twentieth century begins with an attack on his views. I have in mind Hegel . . . without whom we cannot begin a discussion of the twentieth century. Not only did he influence the originators of Marxism, Existentialism and Instrumentalism — now three of the most popular philosophies of the world — but at one time or other he dominated the founders of the more technical movements, Logical Positivism, Realism and Analytic Philosophy. The point is that Karl Marx, Kierkegaard the Existentialist, John Dewey, Bertrand Russell and G. Moore were at one time or other close students of Hegel's thought and some of their most distinctive doctrines reveal the imprint or the scars of previous contact or struggle with this strange genius.[4]

Analytical Philosophers are those who direct their minds away from the general a priori to the particular that can be verified either by measurement or experimentally by scientific inferences or methods. If Hegel gives us a notion of the one Ultimate Absolute, the Analytical Philosophers lead us to the discovery of the pluralistic atomic reality by thinking of the particulars implied in the general.

That analysis and synthesis are two processes that have to be combined in any absolutely conceived or unified

4. Morton White, *The Age of Analysis* Mentor Paperback, New York, 1955, p. 13.

epistemology or methodology is sufficiently evident to impartial philosophers who have no axe of their own to grind. To raise slogans such as implied in the attitude quoted above would not therefore be in keeping with a correct philosophical spirit. The excesses of the Middle Ages, as we have pointed out, cast lengthy shadows which made modern philosophy travel from Hume's Absolute Scepticism to Hegel's form of Absolute Belief.

In between in the total scheme one must place in a graded order the Rationalists, Descartes, Leibniz, Spinoza and Kant, each of whom wrote respectively in terms of Occasionalism, Monadism, Substance and the Thing-in-itself. Their positions contained elements of both scepticism and belief, the former often yielding place to the latter. The totality on which this Rationalism traced its impress was called Human Understanding, the Thinking Substance, the Pure Critical Reason, or the Principle of Sufficient Reason, etc. All of these implied elements of the Absolute from the side of the subjective agent of reasoning. If Bergson was able to write of "attaining the Absolute" through intuition, and Hegel was able to put the notion of the Absolute at the very centre of his philosophy, the other philosophers may be seen tacitly to place the Absolute in the fore or aft of the knowledge situation implied between the subject and the object. Some recognition of the Absolute was tacitly or overtly given by all those philosophers, whether they said it in so many words or not. How this was so, we shall show in the next section.

Although absolutist philosophy suffered a setback during the Age of Reason it still had prominent adherents. The names of eminent philosophers such as Hamilton, Bradley, Bosanquet and Royce can be included among those who have taken their stand on some aspect or other of the absolutist position, whether in the context of metaphysics, mystical feeling, aesthetic completeness or moral perfection. Presently we shall also see how Empiricists and Rationalists have absolutist notions whether in the background or foreground of their schemes. Both analysis and synthesis have to find their respective places in the absolutist methodology. The introduction into philosophy of value factors and of moral perfection as an ideal makes absolutism an inevitable part of any philosophy claiming completeness or comprehensibility. Some may be described as methodological absolutists, others as epistemological absolutists, with a third group, who treat of value factors, who are the most complete philosophers, being axiological absolutists. When we include all these partial absolutisms into a unitary plan we begin to have a full view of the normative notion which we seek.

The various extant modes in which philosophers of the West have made efforts to fix the notion of the Absolute have been masterfully reviewed by Sir William Hamilton. The following extract from his writing shows exactly how far speculation in the West a century ago had gone in this respect. In a letter to H. Calderwood, who attacked Hamilton's idea of the Infinite, which is a notion allied to that of the Absolute, there are three points that Hamilton takes care to underline which are also of great value to us to remember in this present inquiry. The three points are:

1) The Infinite that I contemplate is only as in thought.

2) If I deny the Infinite can by us be *known*, I am far from denying that by us it is, must, and ought to be believed.

3) . . . there is a fundamental difference between *the Infinite* and a relation to which we might apply the term infinite.[5]

After stressing thus the purely conceptual, contemplative and independent status of the notion, Hamilton gives a list under six heads in which Western philosophers absorbed the Absolute, as follows:

1) Some carry the Absolute by assault — by a single leap — place themselves at once in the Absolute —

5. Sir William Hamilton, *Lectures on Metaphysics* (Appendix, vol. II) Blackwood, Edinburgh, 1877, pp. 530-31.

take it as a datum; others climb to it by degrees — mount to the Absolute from the conditioned, — as a result. Former — Plotinus, Schelling; latter — Hegel, Cousin are examples.

2) Some place cognition of the Absolute above condition or limitation (Plotinus, Schelling). Others reach . . . it through contrast, difference . . . giving when sifted a cognition of identity (absolute) (Hegel, Cousin).

3) Some . . . abolish the logical laws of Contradiction and Excluded Middle (as Cusa, Schelling, Hegel). Plotinus is not explicit. Others do not (as Cousin).

4) Some hold that to know the Absolute is to be the Absolute — to know the Absolute is to be God . . . others hold the impersonality of reason in holding that we are conscious of eternal truths as in the divine mind (St. Augustine, Malebranche, Price and Cousin).

5) Some carry up man into the Deity (as Schelling); others bring down the Deity to man. . . .

6) Some think the Absolute can be known as an object of knowledge . . . others that to know the Absolute we must be the Absolute (Schelling, Plotinus).[6]

When we remember here that Schelling influenced Hegel and figures in more than one context in the above analysis by Hamilton, and that in Germany at that time Vedantic ideas prevailed, it might not be too far-fetched to suppose that the Upanishadic notion of the Absolute has influenced European thought.

The great Orientalist Max Müller studied under the Sanskritist Prof. Bopp in Berlin about 1845. Schopenhaur's admiration of the philosophy of the Upanishads is well known, and the affinities of Kantian a priorism in respect of categories of time, space and causality which helped Schopenhauer to treat the world as will and presentiment, are all aspects of absolutism quite familiar in the context of Advaita Vedanta.

6. Ibid.

The thing-in-itself touches the absolute reality, although it was left at that and not developed into its own status as the Absolute, which it was given to Hegel to formulate. This was a concession of Kant to the spirit of scepticism which was the initial impetus for modern philosophy, which had passed through Cartesian Rationalism and reached a more mature form under the label of critical reason instead of merely methodic doubt.

How the Absolute of Vedanta resembles modern notions of the Absolute is seen also in writers and thinkers of more recent years, like Royce (1855-1916). We shall see this clearer when the position of Vedanta has been discussed in the next section. We can state here, however, that in Royce the notion of the Absolute receives more finished concreteness or transfiniteness (as Royce himself would prefer to say) than in Hegel, and comes nearest to the notion of the Absolute which is implied in the Upanishads themselves.

7

The Absolute Implied in Empiricism

In textbooks of philosophy, Locke, Hume and Berkeley are usually labeled empiricists, sceptics, or both. But Berkeley at least must be included among idealists, since he gave primacy to mind over matter. Locke himself believed in a God, and could be called a God believer, but he did give primacy to perceptual over innate aspects. Hume was a more thoroughgoing sceptic who was willing, most uncompromisingly, to put all Scholastic ideas into the melting pot.

Although thus classified as sceptics in superficial textbooks, the British trio of philosophers, who like Voltaire and Rousseau of the European mainland were the forerunners of the Age of Enlightenment, can be seen, on closer scrutiny, to hide their own absolutism and variety of what might be called belief. An examination of their position will help us to fix the normative notion that we are trying to define.

As a dignitary of the Church and at the same time a philosopher of the Age of Reason, Berkeley built his views round the formula *esse* = *percipi* and was not so much of a sceptic as to offend the Church. Locke too was a believer in God, but his God was part and parcel of his own philosophy rather than a God who conformed strictly to the theological or Scholastic standards of the age that he was leaving behind. Hume was more uncompromising, and even modern empiricists and sceptics look to him for some leadership in their own ways of thinking. Because of his extreme or absolute scepticism and phenomenalism, we shall discard chronological order and examine his position first, to see if he had any tacit absolutism hiding behind his front of total disbelief.

The Absolutist Background to Hume's Scepticism

In the religious and theological sense Hume is known as an extreme sceptic who did not believe in any deity as a necessary source of phenomenal reality. Did he believe in anything at all? That would then be the natural question for us to put if we want to find the absolutist element which must lurk at the core of any philosophy worth the name, and to which Hume cannot be an exception.

That he himself kept an open mind in this matter is evident from the conclusion of his *Dialogues of Natural Religion*, where he says, "To be a philosophical sceptic, is in a man of letters the first and most essential step towards being a sound believing Christian." This reveals an open mind. It is the Scholastic notion of deity which did not appeal to him. When, in spite of such disbelief, Hume still thinks in terms of such a factor as "Human Understanding," we arrive at a notion where he touches, consciously or unconsciously, on some factor of an absolutist status.

No one has experienced human understanding as such. It is a total or generalized supposition which Hume accepts as a priori, that all humans treated collectively have this common faculty or quality of consciousness in general, which he prefers to call "Understanding." He goes further than just referring to this understanding, which is a kind of ultimate reference of an epistemological order, and fills it with two items or final categories of content. He categorically states that either "quantity or number" or "experimental reasoning" are the only two items of significance in any book one might pick up in any library. If a book does not contain one or other of these items, he asks us "to commit it then to the flames."

It is legitimate to ask how he arrived at these two final categories which have significance in the context of human understanding. By so doing it is not difficult to see how even

Hume gives some a priori content to what he calls "Human Understanding," which to him is an ultimate reference in the background of his system, tacitly taken for granted. Such a notion touches the Absolute, whether expressly stated as such or not.

The content of such a notion perhaps requires to be further elaborated, and when Kant, who was influenced by Hume, actually did this in terms of space, time and causality, those Kantian categories in fact contained similar elements to the thing-in-itself which could not be known, and as such represented the Absolute of Kant. It was not different from the *tabula rasa* of Locke either, or from the mind of God of Berkeley, where primary and secondary qualities of perception and the powers attached to them reside.

We shall see later that these very same absolutist elements came to be recognized as observables and calculables by scientists. Whatever the name given to these categorical items in the ultimate absolutist background notion, they conform to the visible or to the intelligible elements contained in the core of the Absolute, the visible referring to the practical and the intelligible to the pure. In order to avoid getting lost in the different names that different philosophers might give to these two factors, for taxonomic purposes we are going to adopt for the convenience of generalized and abstracted reference, the terms *vertical* for pure and *horizontal* for practical or visible, reserving the further clarification or justification of such a choice to be developed stage by stage in this work as a whole. As Cartesian correlates are not altogether unknown to modern scientific and mathematical thought, this way of nomenclature should not be considered altogether strange.

Locke's "*Tabula Rasa*" as the Absolute

Like the thing-in-itself of Kant and the emptiness of the phenomenalism of Hume, we find Locke insisting on a clean slate as the basis of consciousness. He could not have arrived at this notion by purely empirical reasoning. He must have felt it intuitively within him. On such a clean slate, which he calls "Human Understanding" he, like Hume, has to find room not only for primary and secondary qualities arising objectively from the material world, but also for that vague category which he calls "powers" which neither belongs to the objective nor to the subjective sides, but occupies a neutral position between them. Even Hume went so far as to indicate, "Every simple idea has a simple impression that resembles it."[1] Thus there is room within the Human Nature of Hume for a sort of one-to-one correspondence between ideas and impressions. Locke's *tabula rasa* is also likewise filled with these so-called "powers" of the understanding, which have a neutral and central status which he describes as follows:

> *Three sorts of Qualities in bodies*:
>
> *First*, the bulk, figure, number, situation and motion or rest of their solid parts: these are in them, whether we perceive them or not. These I call *primary qualities*.
>
> *Secondly*, the power that is in any body, by reason of its insensible primary qualities, to operate after a peculiar manner on any of our senses, and thereby produce on us the different ideas of several colours, sounds, smells, tastes, etc.
>
> *Thirdly*, the power that is in any body, by reason of the peculiar constitution of its primary qualities to make such change in the bulk, figure, texture and motion of another body, as to make it operate on our senses differently from what it did before. Thus the sun has power to make wax white and fire to make lead fluid. (These are usually called *powers*).[2]

---

1. David Hume, *Treatise on Human Nature*, (Selby Briggs, London, 1896), p. 1.
2. *The English Philosophers,* (Modern Library, New York, 1939), pp. 269-70.

We have to note here that these powers are within *any body* subjectively and only the primary qualities are real and in the objects themselves. The secondary qualities, Locke is careful to make it clear in the same essay as being "such qualities which in truth are nothing in the objects themselves but powers to produce various sensations in us by their primary qualities."[3]

A careful scrutiny of the status of primary and secondary qualities and those powers which Locke says are not objective but "in us," must necessarily refer to something within the collective mind of humanity, belonging to human understanding and conceived in generalized terms. It is well known that when Locke describes the consciousness of man as a *tabula rasa*, he means to say that it is without innate content. On the other hand, these secondary powers not residing in the objective side, have necessarily to be subjective. How they are present in all men without being objective is an enigma which can be satisfactorily explained only by thinking that secondary qualities are virtualities within individual consciousness and that the so-called "powers" refer deeper to some special energy like that of the sun or fire in the physical world which is still inside, as it were, (not being objective even according to Locke) in the collective consciousness of man, lodged at the core of human understanding, which itself is a clean slate.

Here we have the same enigma of the relative and the Absolute which we have discussed already. There are certain categories to be structurally fitted into the relative or minus side of the shield called the Absolute, and there are other categories on the other or plus side which is the fully absolute aspect of the same Absolute. The *tabula rasa* can be placed between these two rival aspects of the Absolute.

Although Locke himself avoids such names as "innate ideas" or the Absolute, he tells us enough about the nature

3. Ibid., p. 265.

of reality to compel us to fit his ideas into a scheme of the Absolute on the lines we have discussed. The "powers" have to reside in the Absolute subjectively as they refer to human understanding in general. Here, starting from the empirical, Locke attains the Absolute. Reason, which abides in human understanding, and revelation are, according to Locke, of divine origin, forming two poles in the absolute Human Understanding. Although both are important and equally dignified in epistemological status, Locke would rely on reason primarily and on revelation only secondarily. He himself explains the relations between the two as follows:

> *Reason and revelation*: Reason is natural revelation, whereby the eternal Father of light and fountain of all knowledge communicates to mankind that portion of truth which he has laid within the reach of his natural faculties: revelation is natural reason enlarged by a new set of discoveries communicated by God immediately, which reason vouches the truth of, by the testimony and proofs it gives, that they come from God. So that he takes away reason to make way for revelation, puts out the light of both and does much-what the same, as if he would persuade a man to put out his eye, the better to receive the remote light of an invisible star by telescope.[4]

Far from denying innate ideas he raises them thus to the status of being two aspects of truth that come from God. The eye and the telescope however, look outside and not into the soul. The *tabula rasa* thus remains unaffected by these remarks of Locke about a God who is viewed here more cosmologically than psychologically. The God, however, being the author of both the aspects of human understanding, must needs have an absolutist status, neither inside nor outside.

---

4. *The English Philosophers,* (Modern Library, New York, 1939), p. 397.

The Theological and Philosophical Absolute in Berkeley

Bishop Berkeley was a philosopher and a theologian at the same time. In his essay entitled *Of the Principles of Human Knowledge*, his main effort was to refute the idea that unthinking objects could exist outside the mind. He was opposing Locke here. His tendency was to substitute a cosmological Absolute outside, as the notion of God who was not merely outside but could be known as mind, spirit, soul or oneself. The formula *esse* = *percipi* sums up the Berkeleian position *vis-a-vis* the prevailing forms of scepticism and empiricism of his time.

It is not here in his refutation of Locke that we have to look for the Absolute as implied in the philosophy of Berkeley. The very fact that he continued to be a dignitary of the Church suggests that a Christian God was at the back of his mind even when he argues with the sceptics of his time in a fully philosophical language. God may be said to have been his philosophical Absolute, but the theological notion of spirit was used interchangeably by Berkeley with the same as understood in the philosophical context. There is no serious problem for us therefore to show that the notion of the Absolute as the Most High God was acceptable to Berkeley although he is always seen bracketed with British Empiricists in textbooks of philosophy. This must be because of his epistemological frame of reference, which belongs to the context of giving primacy to sensation and perception and such matters in which he had to develop his argument against other empiricists of his time. Thus he may be said to belong to an empirical context rather than being an empiricist pure and simple. The position of Berkeley is summed up in his own words as follows:

> Besides all that endless variety of ideas or objects of knowledge there is likewise something that knows or perceives them, and exercises diverse operations, as willing, imagining, remembering, about them. This

> perceiving active being is what I call *mind, spirit, soul* or *myself.* By which words I do not denote any one of my ideas, but a thing entirely distinct from them wherein they exist, or which is the same thing whereby they are perceived, for the existence of an idea consists in being perceived.[5]

Although thus giving an absolute status to the mind, Berkeley takes care to remain a pious Christian speaking the language of theology and degrading philosophical speculations when he concludes by saying:

> So shall I esteem them [my labours] altogether useless and ineffectual if, by what I have said I cannot inspire my readers with a pious sense of the presence of God; and having shown the falseness and vanity of those barren speculations which make the chief employment of learned men, the better to dispose them to reverence and embrace the salutary truths of the Gospel, which to know and practise is the highest perfection of human nature.[6]

The two tasks which Berkeley was called upon to fulfil by his labours at one and the same time were loyalty to the Church and to present sound arguments in speculative philosophy. The Absolute of the Gospels and the Absolute which gave the mind a central position were supposed by him to be without any mutual contradiction. It would take a separate study to verify if this can actually be so. We shall therefore close this review with the remark that even in their philosophies which referred in all three cases to human understanding, reason or knowledge, in most general terms, the so-called empiricists of Britain had some elements of unmistakable absolutist status. They were all implicit absolutists who had, as it were the normative notion of the Absolute as a private reference at the back of their minds.

5. *The English Philosophers,* (Modern Library, New York, 1939), p. 523.

6. Ibid., pp. 578-79.

8

The Absolute as Implied in Rationalism

From the empiricists, who went as far as the dictum *esse* = *percipi,* beginning with absolute scepticism about the content of consciousness in the so-called rationalists, (who too had their own version of the Absolute implied in their thought), we reach the domain where the famous statement of Descartes, *cogito ergo sum* (I think, therefore I am) holds a fundamental position.

In this transition the accent shifts from the outer world of values or realities to the inner. The curiosity of the sceptic based on the nature of perception turns to the study of the reasoning faculty. Among the items with which final dogmas or reasoned findings by systematic doubt in speculation are reached, terms are used such as method, criticism, clarity of certitude, and even intuitive awareness.

The transition may be said to be from the wonder about the outer world to the wonder about the inner. This is the same as saying from the cosmological to the psychological. In both these broad divisions, however, there are many overlapping aspects. Our aim here is not to go into detail, but just to discover where the contribution of the rationalists towards the gradual building up of a normative notion of the Absolute, each in his own domain, is to be found.

Cartesian Rationalism

Descartes may be seen to have given mind, God, duration and substance absolutist status in his writings. As a rationalist Descartes gave primacy to the mind, about which he said that in the "consciousness of seeing or walking, the knowledge is manifestly certain, because it is then referred to the mind which alone perceives or is conscious that it sees or walks."[1] The mind thus attains to a central status in Descartes' epistemology. God is also a theological aspect of the centre of Cartesianism as will be evident from the following:

> It is impossible we can have an idea of representation of anything whatever, unless there be somewhere, either in us or out of us, an original which comprises in reality, all the perfections that are thus represented to us; but, as we do not in any way find in ourselves those absolute perfections of which we have the idea, we must conclude that they exist in some nature different from ours, that is, in God, or at least they were once in him; and it most manifestly follows (from their infinity) that they are still there.[2]

Duration is another notion of great dignity and eminence in the context of Cartesianism, so that we can say that it belongs also to his conception of the Absolute. About duration he says:

> The duration alone of our life is sufficient to demonstrate the existence of God.
>
> For we easily understand that there is no power in us by which we can conserve ourselves, and that the being who has so much power as to conserve us out of himself, must also by so much the greater reason conserve himself, on rather stand in need of being conserved by no one whatever and, in fine, be God.[3]

There is also the notion of substance in Descartes. It may be said to take a more central position in the context of the Absolute than the term God or mind:

---

1. Rene Descartes, *A Discourse on Method,* tr. L. Veitch, (Dutton & Co., New York, 1951), p. 168.
2. Ibid., p. 172.
3. Ibid., p. 173.

> By substance we can conceive nothing else than a thing which exists in such a way as to stand in need of nothing beyond itself in order to have its existence. And, in truth there can be conceived but one substance which is absolutely independent, and that is God. . . . And, accordingly, the substance does not apply to God and the creatures *univocally*, to adopt a term familiar to the schools; that is, no signification of this word can be distinctly understood which is common to God and them.[4]

Mind, substance, God, duration and the possibility of interaction through God of mind with body, are all notions found in Cartesian philosophy. But they are not put together under one schematic unitive absolute factor. As we shall see presently, his successors Spinoza, Leibniz and Kant, each in their own fashion, accomplished this task. They merely worked on the framework presented by Descartes, the father of modern philosophy, and if the normative notion that we seek is to be found in the Rationalists, the greater part of the credit goes to Descartes. Scepticism and belief, body and mind, and many such pairs are brought into relation with the central notion of substance or God through which or in whom interaction becomes possible. Things as we see them or sense them have their reality only in the mind. Such are some of the features of the Absolute, the outlines of which emerge clearly in his *Principles of Philosophy* and *Principles of Material Things* which two aspects of human knowledge in general, Descartes treated methodically.

Further, what we have elsewhere tried to distinguish as the vertical and the horizontal aspects of the normative or Absolute consciousness, are strikingly referred to by Descartes as follows:

> There are only two modes of thinking in us, viz., the perception of the understanding and the action of the will.

4. Ibid., pp. 184-85.

> For, all the modes of thinking of which we are conscious may be referred to two general classes, the one of which is the perception or the operation of the understanding, and the other the volition or operation of the will. Thus, to perceive, by the senses (*sentire*), to imagine, and to conceive things purely intelligible, are only different modes of perceiving (*percipiendi*); but to desire to be averse from, to affirm, to deny, to doubt, are different modes of willing.[5]

The distinction drawn here between two aspects of thinking which meet in a central consciousness, although not quite clear even from the notes given by the translator which make them more vague, may at least be recognized by us as representing passive and active aspects which other rationalist philosophers after Descartes will also be seen to adopt in their own ways. An absolute thinking substance with a structure not unlike the correlates in mathematics (of which Descartes himself was the originator) is thus seen to come here into view.

The Absolute Norm Implicit in Spinoza

We have noticed that the philosophers of the Age of Reason or Enlightenment spoke in the name of Human Understanding or Knowledge, as the very titles of their works have sufficiently revealed. The nature of this understanding was mostly taken for granted by each of them, and, except in the case of Bishop Berkeley whose Christian background was deliberately retained in the name of duty to the Church to which he was indebted, all the others left the background factor of human understanding as something vaguely assumed.

In Descartes, it is easy to see how, through the transparency and simplicity of his ideas, which he arrived at through methodic doubting, there is still visible the broad outlines of the idea of God restated and presented in a

5. Rene Descartes, *A Discourse on Method,* tr. L. Veitch, (Dutton & Co., New York, 1951), pp. 177-78.

revalued form. The background of Spinoza was Jewish and not Gentile, but in spite of this he too followed closely on the lines of Descartes, improving on what Descartes had begun to say, in a form that resembled Euclid, based on axioms, postulates, corollaries, theorems and lemmas, and not troubling himself to go into the details of the mechanisms of sensation or perception.

Spinoza treated nature more realistically than Descartes, for whom nature tended to be absorbed in the mind. For this reason Spinoza has been mistaken for a pantheist, although the notion of the Absolute and of God were more fully and specifically treated by him than by Descartes. In Spinoza precision attains to a mathematical status, and having risen to the heights of a priorism he is able to descend into ethics, and even into discussions based on the Christian Gospel and into the domain of politics in his famous *Tractatus Politicus*. Although the notion of the Absolute is thus more explicitly present in the writings of Spinoza, the main outlines of the notion remain almost the same as with Descartes.

In Spinoza's system the notion of substance is central. Such a central notion is valid in the context of nature to which the positive sciences also belong. It is also valid in the context of the idealism of Plato and others of the classical context, and it is lodged in the core of ethics, natural theology and politics. Spinoza defined this central notion as follows:

> By substance, I mean that which is in itself, and is conceived through itself: in other words, that of which a conception can be formed independently of any other conception.
>
> By attributes, I mean that which the intellect perceives as constituting the essence of substance.
>
> By God, I mean a being absolutely infinite — that is, a substance consisting of infinite attributes, of which each expresses eternal and infinite essentiality.[6]

6. Baruch Spinoza *Ethics,* Vol. II tr. Elwes, (Dover Publications, New York, 1951), p. 45.

It is not hard to notice here some improvement in the content of what has been tacitly referred to as human understanding, which with the sceptics like Hume had to be guessed at, and which emerged only in mathematical outline form in Descartes. In Spinoza it stands out in better relief, being correctly balanced between the background aspects and the overt foreground aspects of reality, which according to Spinoza must have correct human and scientific significance. We have to notice here that in the last quotation, God and substance are treated as coming univocally under the same term, and this cannot be any other than the Absolute. A being who is absolutely infinite and which is a substance at the same time cannot but be univocally related as the meaning of one normative notion.

After we have arrived at the notion of substance there are two other modalities under which the substance can be viewed. These give us the two axes of reference at the core of the absolute substance, as related to active or passive nature. As a note to Proposition XXIX of his *Ethics*, Spinoza explains this as follows:

> Before going further, I wish here to explain what we should understand by nature viewed as active (*natura naturans*) and nature viewed as passive (*natura naturata*). I say to explain, or rather call attention to it; for I think that, from what has been said, it is sufficiently clear, that by nature viewed as active we should understand that which is in itself, and is conceived through itself, or those attributes of substance which express eternal infinite essence, in other words God, in so far as he is considered as a free cause.
>
> By nature viewed as passive I understand all that which follows from the necessity of the nature of God, or of any of the attributes of God, that is, all the modes of the attributes of God, in so far as they are considered as things which are in God, and which without God cannot

exist or be conceived.[7]

The all-important question of how body and mind interact, how one is inserted into the other or is articulated therewith, has puzzled both idealist and materialist philosophers for ages in the East and in the West. There must be a homogeneity for purposes of one order of realities acting on another, which is called in Sanskrit *samanadhikaranatva*. This problem is ably bypassed by Spinoza when he lays down: "The order and connection of ideas is the same as the order and connection of things."[8]

The rival theories of psychophysical interaction, parallelism, and occasionalism that philosophers in Europe, brought up in the tradition of Scholastic thinking like what Descartes and Malebranche had advanced as an explanation for this problem of the participation of mind and matter, found in Spinoza's attitude something new which belonged to the Jewish background, as he himself stated elsewhere: "This truth seems to have been dimly recognized by those Jews who maintained that God, God's intellect, and things understood by God are identical."[9]

In trying to explain more clearly this relation between particular things or modes and the infinite idea of God, Spinoza, though with some apologetic hesitation, indulges in a schematic representation which was a partial improvement, it being left for Kant to present properly and more precisely, as we shall see. Here it is interesting to note that already both the relativistic plan of the Absolute and the Absolute which is fully so are brought together. The following note to Spinoza's Proposition VIII under the heading *Of the Nature and Origin of the Mind*, speaks for itself:

---

7. Baruch Spinoza *Ethics,* Vol. II tr. Elwes, (Dover Publications, New York, 1951), pp. 68-69.

8. Ibid., p. 86. (Part II, Proposition VIII).

9. Ibid., p. 86. (note).

> If anyone desires an example to throw more light on this question, I shall, I fear, not be able to give him any which adequately explains the thing of which I here speak inasmuch as it is unique; however, I will endeavour to illustrate it as far as possible. The nature of a circle is such that if any number of straight lines intersect within it, the rectangles formed by their segments, will be equal to one another; thus infinite equal rectangles are contained in a circle. Yet none of these rectangles can be said to exist, except in so far as the circle exists, except in so far as they are comprehended in the idea of the circle. Let us grant that, from this infinite number of rectangles, two only exist. The ideas of these two not only exist, in so far as they are contained in the idea of the circle, but also as they involve the existence of those rectangles; wherefore they are distinguished from the remaining ideas of the remaining rectangles.[10]

The subtle reciprocity and mutual interdependence which is implied between a pair of concrete individuals holds good in a general sense, irrespective of the generality or particularity, abstractness or concreteness, in the overall context of the Absolute. Under the aegis of the Absolute, big and small, the one and the many, part and whole, the abstract and the concrete, the general and the particular, are all reciprocally or mutually interrelated. Such must be the nature of the subtlety that Spinoza here wishes to drive home with the use of the mathematical language of geometry as supplementary to his propositional or axiomatic statements in theoretical abstraction elsewhere in his work.

We shall have occasion to see the affinity of this with Leibnizian monadology and the schematization employed by Kant as we proceed, and also how later on even Eddingtonian subjectivism and structuralism develop the same theme on scientific as well as philosophical lines. Thus theoretically at

---

10. Baruch Spinoza *Ethics,* Vol. II tr. Elwes, (Dover Publications, New York, 1951), pp. 87-88.

least, through a form of mathematical thinking, the knotty problem of participation of mind and matter, its insertion or articulation that must be presupposed in various ways by different philosophers, is here transcended in terms of an overall substance which is God or the Absolute, with two modes and endless attributes, existences and essences, all having between them a transparency or homogeneity between the relative parts and the totality. All is univocally conceived as a sort of transfinite entity given to the mind of one who doubts or wonders about the nature of reality. The *turiya* state in Vedanta will be seen to resemble this.

Monadology and the Normative Absolute

Scepticism, the starting impetus in modern philosophy, gave room to methodic doubting in Descartes, who like Locke and Newton, was interested in cosmology and allied aspects of the "object matter" of philosophy, rather than in its subject matter. Descartes, it is true, brought in mental cogitation as equally important. He was the originator of analytical geometry, and the geometrical precision that he introduced into philosophical thinking was continued in the thinking of Spinoza too. Human understanding was a background notion left vague and undefined by all these rationally-minded and empirically inclined philosophers.

Leibniz becomes a little more definite. Instead of thinking of a whole and its infinite parts as distinct, we find him improving upon the position arrived at by Spinoza, who in his turn, was improving upon the understanding of Descartes. Mathematics was responsible for the improvements, and Leibniz was the philosopher who shared with Newton (though controversially), the glories of the discovery of the infinitesimal calculus which did not stop merely with the static notion of infinity, but helped to enter into the core, dynamically, of the real in both its aspects of being and becoming at once.

Leibniz' monadology thus became his lasting contribution to the philosophic thinking of his age. Although the pluralistic and atomic monad might seem, at first, to have nothing in common with an overall notion of the Absolute, and in spite of the fact that monadology was not given the necessary finishing touches by its author which would have made it fully satisfying as a completely worked out notion, yet there are many absolutist features of the monad which are of special interest to us because many of the obscurities of previous philosophers have been masterfully clarified by him.

The atomic entity called the monad has one member at least of its many species which is distinguished by the term *monas monadum*. This is a version of monad which crowns all other monads, however numerous. This forms the model for all the variations of possible structural factors. As the notion of the Absolute norm that we seek need not depend on the number of varieties possible under its genus, we need not be prejudiced in our search for the Absolute as a norm, even in and through the complications of what Leibniz presents in his monadology. It would therefore be interesting to scan the main features of the notion of the monad before saying whether it satisfies the requirements of a normative notion or not.

Monads are the only real existences, infinite in number, forming an infinite series, created and annihilated all at once, and not generated and imperishable, with qualities of perception and appetition, but having no parts and not situated in space, incapable of being perceived by the senses. Each monad is spontaneously self-active like incorporeal automata, containing the future with which, in the present, it could be "big" (or impregnated), all its ideas being innate with a dynamic self-identity continually unfolding or enfolding itself. Monads have no windows and are mutually exclusive, each independent and as if existing with God alone besides itself. They are natural substances and metaphysical atoms or metaphysical points, centres or concentrations of the world, capable of certain changes in correlated grades, implicitly containing the whole universe, variously represented, while each represents its own body distinctly. Each monad combines body and soul as its elements, being both active and passive and influencing one another ideally. There is a mutual agreement between them, not to be realized by sense or imagination (though not so simple as the clocks with perfect mechanisms, one striking while the other is showing the hour, which oversimplified example has caught the popular imagination). The degrees of perception of monads make for the possible differences between one monad and another. There are three grades of created monads, each higher grade having the characteristics of the lower: the unconscious, conscious and self-conscious. The monads progress towards perfection individually and not merely as all monads together. The dominant monad, called by Bruno and Leibniz *Monas Monadum* is synonymous with God.[11]

Like Bruno, Leibniz is more of a believer than a sceptic. This is revealed by his mistrust of the methodic doubt of Descartes, which he attributes to some kind of quack pose to catch the public eye.[12] He differs from Fichte and Hegel as also from the realism of Herbart so that the question of placing Leibniz in his correct perspective in modern thought is not an easy task. To the extent infinitesimals are univocal with the notion of the Absolute, Leibniz may be called an absolutist, but otherwise he is just a philosopher who introduced the differential calculus into his thought. The above summary which we have gleaned from Robert Latta's work requires much more elaboration to make full meaning, but we can safely generalize and say that for our purposes

---

11. This summary adheres closely to what is fully elaborated in *Leibniz' Monadology and Other Philosophical Writings,* tr. Robert Latta, (Oxford, 1951).

12. Ibid., p. 54, where Leibniz says that Descartes' method of doubt is as "trappings to appeal to the people" (*phaleras ad populum*).

here, it amounts to a view of the Absolute from the side of the relative.

Leibniz' mathematical intuition may be said to have attained the status of the Absolute, but being inclined to appreciate quantities rather than qualities, existences rather than essences, his elaborate and highly interesting picture of reality, dynamically conceived, needs further finishing touches by way of renormalization in some respects and normalization in others. His principle of sufficient reason and of *petites perceptions* and many of the paradoxes as between the rival claims of contradiction and identity that enter into the structure and dynamism of the monad, which is a thing and not a thing, leaves us gasping and wondering rather than in open disagreement. This is due to the fact that monadology is neither fully scientific nor merely a mystical vision.

Both Hegel and Bergson may be said to have gone further, but even they did not go far enough to fix the notion once and for all. We should agree with most of what Leibniz said, except for the binding factor of the overall notion of the Absolute as such, which is rather weakly developed in monadology. That absolutism has two approaches, one to attain the Absolute through possibilities of the a priori, and the other through the probabilities of the a posteriori, is the essence of the position we take here. It involves normalization and renormalization of the notion from two epistemological poles, without giving primacy to one or the other. In the light of such a neutral position, the monadology of Leibniz may be said to be slightly asymmetrically placed in favour of existence at the expense of essence, although substance is given full recognition in his absolutism. We shall deal with this more fully when we come to Kant.

As a philosopher who was sometimes interested in Rosicrucianism, the variety of belief that Leibniz represented is not altogether of the usual type, and perhaps this too explains his tendency to over-accentuate some of his speculative conclusions in graphic form. We cannot help feeling that we are concerned here with a metaphysical story or parable, or a mathematical conundrum, or both.

The contribution of monadology to philosophical thought in general, as it stood in his time, is ably summed up as follows:

> With the concept of the monad, Leibniz feels that he has overcome the Cartesian dualism of mind and body, refuted the psycho-physical parallelism and pantheism of Spinoza, destroyed atomic materialism, reconciled the Scholastic nominalistic view that the individual alone is real with the realistic contention that universals also have real existence, and combined Plato and Aristotle. For the monad, besides being the least common denominator of mind and matter, is individual and concrete but also possesses a Form and exemplifies an Idea, of which being unique, it is in itself the only example and instance.[13]

Although we do not consider Descartes dualistic nor Spinoza pantheistic, the above summary of the contribution of monadology helps us to see at a glance how far Leibniz was able to give concreteness and consistency to the implied absolutism of his predecessors. What interests us primarily here is the analysis of the content of the Absolute, which becomes filled with more structural, concrete and dynamic features and given a unique and unitive form and an idea compatible with it. Except for some epistemological and methodological normalization and appraisal of its value or significance, we have, in the contribution of Leibniz, something definite to work upon in our search for a fully normative notion. Leibniz seems to us to stop short at a serial hierarchy of values rather than arriving at one Supreme

---

13. B.A.G. Fuller, *A History of Philosophy*, Book II, (Holt and Co., New York, 1949), p. 109.

Absolute Value.[14] This last step is made possible by the schematization of Kant, whose contribution to the normative notion of the Absolute we shall examine presently.

Monadic and Schematic Thought Distinguished

Speculation aided by mathematics may be said to have reached its full term in the monadology of Leibniz. Descartes as the discoverer of the correlates and Leibniz as the inventor of the infinitesimal calculus have made full use of their geniuses, not only in those domains, but in the service of speculations about truth or certitude. Spinoza too, derived from his own background, as we have seen, a way of abstracting and generalizing, which we have quoted already and which amounts to the same kind of abstraction which mathematicians employ, although in his case he got it from the context of Jewish wisdom. He put it in the form of a postulate or axiom when he said, "God's intellect and things understood by God are identical." Here we have a subtle epistemological verity stated in theological language. A thing thought by God is more actual than the content of the intellect of God. God himself as the basis of his intellect is removed two degrees negatively in the direction of abstraction and generalization.

As two parallel mirrors can reflect the original and its image as many times as one can stretch one's imagination, so the power of the human mind to abstract from one abstraction and to generalize from one generalization is endless. This endless process of the mind for analysis or

14. Latta, *op. cit.*, p. 350. Cf. the extract from a letter of Leibniz to Princess Sophie: "And as there is reason to think that the universe itself develops from more to more and that all tends to some end, since all comes from an Author whose wisdom is perfect, we may similarly believe that souls, which last as long as the universe, go also from better to better, at least naturally (*phisiquement*) and that their perfections go on increasing, although most often this takes place imperceptibly and sometimes after great circuits backwards."

synthesis does not annihilate the resultant central notion common to the image and the original, the plus and the minus of the possible notions. Analysis and synthesis, a priorism and a posteriorism, immanence and transcendence, necessity and contingency are basic epistemological factors belonging to the absolute consciousness of man. Infinity of regression or progression does not abolish but rather confirms, at least in schematic outline, and at least nominally, the notion of the Absolute. As the Vedanta philosophy expresses it, the final categories are *name* and *form,* of which the latter would represent the schematic and the former the nominalistic aspect. When we abolish name and form, the plus and minus sides, the notion of the Absolute emerges in all its neutral glory. It is in such a neutral verity that we have to seek to place the normative notion.

9

The Absolute from Kant to Eddington

Just as it is possible in mathematics to deal with an inconceivable quantity such as the square root of minus one, so it is possible for pure thought to reach a notion which will satisfy any thinkable condition.

Modern mathematics has its transfinite numbers. Projective and vectorial geometrical spaces have also introduced into the formal domain of visibles many abstractions of abstractions. Thus we can have a class of quantities in brackets or under a vinculum. If this is possible in algebra, then it must be possible in philosophy too to think of a vinculum applied to the notion of infinite substance.

The absolutism of Josiah Royce arrives at such a generalized possibility in respect of infinites. Actual and epistemological infinites are two different things, but one is not less real than the other as a notion. Such a pure notion attains the Absolute and gives the norm for all thought. All becomes abolished in its favour. Subject and object cancel each other out in the neutrality of such a notion of the Absolute.

The peculiarities of the schematized version of reality, which we shall now consider, attains to such a neutral status in the notion of the Absolute. A schematic notion can belong equally to the conceptual as to the perceptual, the former tending to be algebraic and the latter tending to be geometrical in status. If we keep these basic epistemological features in our minds it will be possible to appreciate better the Kantian *schematismus* as Kant himself explains it in the quotations below. Before quoting Kant, however, it may not be out of place here to see how this tendency to think in schematic form or image is nothing new, but is one which Kant received, handed down even from the classical times of Plato and Aristotle.

Pre-Kantian and Post-Kantian Schematismus

To enumerate categories and to put them together as a whole in a schematized form in the context of the ultimate truth has been the universal concern of all philosophy, and a persistent habit throughout the history of human thought. The immanent and the transcendent aspects of truth must seek neutral ground with a double reference, facing the a priori and the a posteriori at once. Plato himself gives to the notion of time such a central status. Time is that mysterious and elusive category which is most suitable for schematic treatment, with all the dynamism which belongs to it naturally in the actual experience of everyone. Plato calls time "the moving likeness of eternity" and writes:

> When the father who had begotten it saw it set in motion and alive, a shrine brought into being for the everlasting gods, he rejoiced and being well pleased he took thought to make it yet more like its pattern. So as that pattern is the Living Being that is for ever existent, he sought to make this universe also like it, so far as might be, in that respect. Now the nature of that Living Being was eternal, and this character it was impossible to confer in full completeness on the generated thing. But he took thought to make, as it were a moving likeness of eternity; and at the same time that he ordered the Heaven, he made of eternity that abides in unity, an everlasting likeness, moving accord to number — that to which we have given the name Time.[1]

---

1. Plato, *Timaeus* tr. F.M. Cornford, (Library of Liberal Arts, New York, 1959), p. 20.

Although expressed in antique quasi-mythological and theological language, Plato's object here evidently is to schematize eternity and time while retaining its dynamic status. The expression "the moving likeness of eternity" is sufficiently suggestive here. Instead of Plato's central category of time, Aristotle schematizes and gives structural and concrete form to the mind, which he takes as the central notion. In *De Anima* (Book III, Chapter 5) we read:

> In fact, mind as we have described it, is what it is by virtue of becoming all things, while there is another which is what it is by virtue of making all things: this is a sort of positive state like light: for in a sense light makes potential colours into actual colours.
>
> Mind in this sense of it is separable, impassible, unmixed, since it is in its essential nature activity (for always the active is superior to the passive factor, the originating force to the matter which it forms).
>
> Actual knowledge is identical with its object; in the individual, potential knowledge is in time prior to actual knowledge, but in the universe as a whole it is not prior even in time. Mind is not at one time knowledge and at another not. When mind is set free from its present conditions it appears as just what it is and nothing more: this alone is immortal and eternal.[2]

Although the language in Aristotle is different from that of Plato, his teacher, there is an implicit kinship between time and mind that each places on a pedestal, as it were, to give it full absolute status, and in bringing out the subtle mechanism of mobile process and the structural divisions according to the functions of time or mind or Living Being and its Eternal Image respectively. The attempt made by both is to give a concrete form to something very abstract and general. Herein lies the schematization. Plato may be

2. E. McKeon, *Introduction to Aristotle,* (Random House, New York, 1947), pp. 220-21.

said to give primacy to the vertical and Aristotle to the horizontal aspects of the same schematic notion of the Absolute.

After Kant, Hegel too wrote of the Concrete in respect of his Absolute Idea. An Idea can be "concrete" only because of its schematized version. Reminiscent of Plato, Hegel also calls dialectic "the moving soul of the world-as-process"[3] and defines it as follows:

> There are three aspects in every thought which is logically real or true; the abstract or rational form, which says that something is; the dialectical negation, which says that something is not; the speculative-concrete comprehension: A is also that which is not, A is non-A. These three aspects do not constitute three parts of logic, but are moments of everything that is logically real or true. They belong to every philosophical concept. Every concept is rational, is absolutely opposed to another, and is united in comprehension together with its, opposites. *This is the definition of dialectic.*[4]

Whether dialectic is called the soul of the world process by Hegel, or the moving likeness of eternity by Plato, or by Aristotle conceived as mind which is free from the present conditionings and becomes released as the immortal or the eternal, there is a common implicit *schema* to which all of them seem to adhere and which is made more explicit by Kant. Schematization as such was properly discussed only by this philosopher of modern philosophers. Kant's *Critique* thus contains elements of the philosophy of philosophy itself.

Whether considered mobile or concrete, as being, becoming or both, it is to the credit of Kant to have clarified a type of two-sided thinking that neutralizes into a *schema.* In a whole section devoted to what he elaborately calls *The*

---

3. G.W.F. Hegel, *Encyclopedia of Philosophy,* tr. Gustav Emil Müller, (Wisdom Library, New York, 1959), p. 83.

4. Ibid., p. 82.

Transcendental Doctrine of the Faculty of Judgement or Analytic of Principles, in the chapter which in turn is described as "The Schematism of the Pure Concepts of the Understanding," Kant states that the pure concepts of the understanding can be applied to phenomena represented in *concrete,* schematically. He explains this as follows:

> In our case there must be some third thing homogeneous on the one side with the category, and on the other with the phenomenon, to render the application of the latter possible. This intermediate representation must be pure (free from all that is empirical) and yet intelligible on the one side, and sensuous on the other. Such a representation is the *transcendental schema.*[5]

He further clarifies his nomenclature of the factors of these pure concepts of understanding when he says:

> We shall call this formal and pure condition of sensibility, to which the concept of the understanding is restricted in its application, its *schema;* and the function of this understanding in these *schemata*, the *schematism of the pure understanding.*[6]

Again, he says:

> This representation of a general procedure of the imagination by which a concept receives its image, I call the *schema* of such a concept.[7]

What we should extract from the above citations from Kant are: firstly, that he assumes a possibility of thinking of absolute reality conceptually under categories and also perceptually as a *schema*, and when there is a homogeneity between them established by the understanding we get, by the employment of intuition (which abstracts and generalizes from both poles, as it were, the phenomenal and noumenal),

---

5. Immanuel Kant, *Critique of Pure Reason,* tr. Max Müller, (Doubleday, New York, 1961), p. 104-05.

6. Ibid., p. 105.

7. Ibid., p. 106.

a schematism which is a function of the understanding referring both ways. Secondly, by his idea of transparency as between conceptual and perceptual aspects or by the participation on neutral ground of what is mental with what is material, he assumes a homogeneous medium of some sort of an absolute thinking substance. This is one of the most delicate philosophical problems which, as we have seen, has been pictured or described in various ways by Plato, Aristotle and others. Hegel's resultant of a synthetic concrete idea has its plus and minus sides in the thesis and the antithesis to be dialectically treated. In the Vedantic context we have the same homogeneity referred to by the term *samanadhi-karanatva* (the character of belonging to the same order).

Although we shall see that the notion of a *schema* as understood by Kant undergoes further elaboration at the hands of Bergson, who conceived it as a dynamic *schema moteur*[8] instead of just a *schema* that might appear static in the eyes of the philosopher of the flux of the *elan vital* (vital urge), the broad lines in which this schema-making faculty of the human understanding has been examined by Kant and Bergson remains one of the major triumphs of modern thought.

From Bergson's Schema to Eddington's Structure

Between Bergson and Eddington we have two ways of philosophizing, each of which may be said to be modern as well as scientific. If one may be called a scientific philosopher the other might be called a philosopher of science. Physics and metaphysics, experiment and speculation, observables and calculables enter into the domain of both, though with different proportional combination, to give us apparently differing schematic or structural representations for their references. At least in the order of semantics they have the same status and serve each philosopher in transmitting to

8. Cf. Henry Bergson, *Oeuvres Matiere et Memoire,* (Presse Universitaire de France, Paris, 1959), p. 254.

the reader precise notions of what they wish to convey about the nature of life or of the physical world. The scheme is also a semantic reference using signs of algebra as well as the correlates of geometry. Experimental findings can be verified by calculus, while geometrical representations can confirm what might be uncertain or vague as stated in algebraic signs. Just as a map can help with certitude in relation to a gazetteer of names and places and vice versa, so the schematization is for normalization and renormalization of findings. This process cannot take place in any other medium than the Absolute, where the visible forms and the calculable names have their common centre.

Thus all becomes comprised under either name or form as the final categories in consciousness as understood in Vedanta. The reference common to name and form may not have an existence, subsistence or a value in itself, except for serving as a central reference for purposes of language. It may be a mathematical abstraction but its absolutist content cannot be denied, whether fixed in the subject or the object of the thinking mind, without which even language would be of no purpose.

Like the *Logos* and the *Nous* of the Greek and the *vak* of Sanskrit, the Absolute Norm requires an extremely formal or merely nominal status, but its use in integration and normalizing language as well as in formal thought, to which every entity, abstract or concrete, must finally conform and be inclusively comprised under its aegis, is a matter which is beyond all possibility of doubt.

Eddington's Conceptual View of Physics

Observational aspects have often held primacy over calculations in the world of the physical sciences. What was seen to work on a small scale in a laboratory was given more importance for scientific certitude than anything of the nature of the a priori. Although, on final analysis, mathematical demonstrations were based on a priori presuppositions, this kind of demonstrability was taken for granted and, until the day Eddington subjected the whole position to a thorough revision, it was not given its full place in the epistemology of physics. We have already made note of some of the broad outline features of Eddingtonian structuralism in relation to the notion of the Absolute.

Now we have to take a closer view of its implications so as to bring both physics and metaphysics under the same integrated view. In this connection it is important and significant to note that Eddington took a firm stand on the primacy of concepts and assertions over brute facts as such treated in their actuality and first hand objectivity. The epistemological revision to which he subjected science will be amply evident from his posthumously published book, *Fundamental Theory* where he writes: "The evaluation of the cosmic number: The cosmic number $N = 3/2\ (136.2)^{256}$ is most picturesquely described as the number of protons and electrons in the universe."[9] He explains this as follows:

> The whole calculation of N is an essay in the representation of conceptions by symbolic algebra. *It is the conceptions that matter.* We have to express in mathematical symbolism what we think we are doing when we measure things: for if we had no conception of what we were doing, the result of the measurements would not persuade us to believe anything in particular.[10]

This emphasis on the conceptual aspect in Eddington is not, however, a one-sided epistemological approach. Elsewhere he states categorically, "For the truth of the conclusions of physical science, observation is the Supreme Court of Appeal."[11] It is not by the sacrifice of observation

9. A.S. Eddington, *Fundamental Theory,* (Cambridge University Press, 1946), pp. 265-66.

10. Ibid., p.266.

11. A.S. Eddington, *The Philosophy of Physical Science,* (University of Michigan Press, 1958), p. 9.

that Eddington stands for a form of thought in which concepts have primacy, for he also says, "whatever we have to apprehend must be apprehended in a way for which our intellectual equipment has made provision."[12] And again he adds, "Every item of physical knowledge must therefore be an assertion of what has been or would be the result of carrying out a specified observational procedure."[13]

The implications of the theoretical considerations on which Eddington takes his stand are not easy to discuss here fully. For our purposes, however, it is not difficult to see from the above citations that he has a form or frame of reference which is of a conceptual or subjective order, but which appeals to observational and theoretical aspects at the same time from a sort of neutral ground which is of somewhat the same order as the schematization of Kant which we have already examined, in that it has epistemological reference to the observational and the conceptual at one and the same time. Observed facts as such have to be treated in an abstract way as descriptions or assertions, so that they can fit into the frame or form that he speaks of. Thus the frame is of a schematic or a semantic order.

Eddington points out that the physical universe is to be distinguished from the universe of physics, the latter being more conceptual than perceptual. The subtle schematic homogeneity as between conceptual, perceptual or actual aspects, which have always to be matched correspondingly when describing actions of everyday life, such as that of a man sitting in a chair, is strikingly brought out by Eddington when he questions the statement sometimes heard from theoretical physicists that they are not concerned with actual chairs, etc. They are concerned with chairs as well as with all the corresponding abstractions possible about chairs when

---

12. A.S. Eddington, *The Philosophy of Physical Science,* (University of Michigan Press, 1958), p. 115.

13. Ibid., p. 115.

the chair and the person who sits on it are both fitted into a common epistemological frame or form of reference. Explaining this, he says:

> Let us first notice that the phrase, "chairs we sit upon" adds nothing to the term "chair". For what sits on the chair is the body, and if we have to discriminate the scientific chair, i.e., the object, not really the chair which the physicist describes, from the familiar chair, we must also discriminate the scientific body i.e., the object, not really a body, which the physicist describes from the familiar body. So when we sit on a chair, the familiar body sits on a familiar chair, and the scientific body sits on a scientific chair. And if there is an abstract body it doubtless performs an abstraction of sitting on an abstract chair.[14]

It is neither easy nor possible for us to enter into the merits of Eddingtonianism. For our purposes it is enough to grasp that thought situations have an intrinsic consistency and sequence, and that the promiscuous mixing up of grades of thinking is not scientific. Inner structure has to be respected. The conceptual aspect in which scientific descriptions are possible, and fitting thought into its proper frames or forms, are all-important in the Eddingtonian philosophy of science. He writes in terms of structuralism, subjectivism and selection of certain impressions as against others, all of which suggest to us the same schematization not different from the norm that we are seeking to define. We shall now take one step further in the same direction of Eddingtonianism.

Selective Subjectivism and Structuralism

In summing up his final position in respect of his philosophy of science, Eddington writes:

---

14. Ibid., p. 159.

> Neither the scientific advances of the last decade nor the years of reflection have altered the general trend of my philosophy. I say, 'my philosophy' not as claiming authorship of ideas which are widely diffused in modern thought, but because the ultimate selection and synthesis must be a personal responsibility. If it is necessary to give a short name to this philosophy, I should hesitate between 'Selective Subjectivism' and 'Structuralism'.[15]

What Eddington calls subjectivism would correspond to what Kant might call an a priori synthetic aspect of reality. The selection results from our minds acting like a sieve with a special kind of mesh which Eddington explains as follows:

> There is a big gap between this and the passive reception of sensory impressions; and in this gap the selective influences of our intellectual equipment have their opportunity. If we consider the sequence, objective event–perception–physical knowledge, there is a double shifting, firstly by our sensory equipment, secondly by our intellectual equipment.
>
> In analysing this intellectual activity I shall make use of the phrase 'form of thought'; or, when the form is in some degree elaborated, 'frame of thought.' This may be regarded as a predetermined form or frame into which the knowledge we acquire observationally is fitted.[16]

Aided by mathematical calculations, Eddington is able to travel into much subtler explanations and generalizations, whose considerations here would be inconsistent with our main aims. Kant might use the terms a priori and "synthetic" where Eddington would use "subjective" and "structural." Hegelian terminology may be "dialectical." Plato presents the same picture with time and eternity as his basis, and Aristotle relies on mind. These differences should not confuse us. We

15. A.S. Eddington, *The Philosophy of Physical Science,* (University of Michigan Press, 1958), p. viii.

16. Ibid., p. 115.

must try to see how in each case there is a double reference, one pure and the other practical, or as with calculables or observables, between which a neutral notion has been outlined by each of these great philosophers. The time-space continuum of modern relativity can be viewed in the light of the frame that Eddington outlines as follows:

> When knowledge is formulated in a frame which compels us to separate a time dimension from the fourfold order to which it belongs, a component called the mass is correspondingly separated from the fourfold vector to which it belongs; and it requires no profound study of the conditions of separation to see how the separated component is related to the rest of the vector which prescribes the velocity. It is this relation which is rediscovered when we determine experimentally the change of mass with velocity.[17]

The increase of mass with velocity is a law established experimentally by many famous scientists before Eddington. This experimental result is seen from the a priori side by Eddington in the light of the frame or form of thought already present subjectively. When one is matched with the other we have by mutual normalization a notion that is neutral and understood schematically or structurally.

What Eddington wants to convey is best done in the language of higher mathematics. This is shown by his generalized definition of existence as a structural concept when he writes: "The structural concept of existence is represented by an idempotent symbol."[18]

This idempotent symbol belongs to the context of complex numbers. The letter J, when it satisfies the formula $J^2 - J = O$, is called idempotent. The idea of the quaternion, of the coordinates of Descartes, the quadrature numbers and vectorial space are all involved here, into whose

17. Ibid., p. 116.

18. Ibid., p. 162.

intricacies we do not wish to enter at present. At this stage, all that we wish to underline is that both algebra and geometry enter here as partners in revealing the structure of reality, existence or truth. These basic notions must live, move and have their being only in an overall normative notion of the Absolute. There is no other possibility suggested by anyone so far. Thus it is in the language of mathematics that we find final answers to some important questions of philosophy proper. Thought, logic, mathematics, the propositional calculus and semantics have much common ground between them. All possibilities and probabilities reside in the heart of the Absolute, which is the normalizing factor of reference for all science, whether understood as physics or metaphysics.

10

The Bergsonian Schema and the Absolute

The kind of absolutism that Bergson attains through his intuition of creative becoming has been examined by us generally, already. Without reopening the discussion of his philosophy let us see whether he had some schematic or structural ideas adopted from his predecessors in Western philosophy.

The Schema Moteur

Any kind of statically fixed mathematical concept is, we know, repugnant to Bergson's point of view. He thought that such statically finalized ideas were due to the weakness of the human mind when not endowed with that penetrating intuition by means of which the philosopher enters into the heart of a knowledge situation and is able to take an inside view, which is ever in the process of becoming.

It is therefore not normally to be expected that Bergson would think in terms of a schema, so it is strange to notice that he too resorts to schematic thinking in respect of his analysis of factors, matter and memory, thought and movement, and other aspects of consciousness of body and mind. Without admitting them to be understood in the same manner as Kant, who, according to him, was too conceptual or static, he adopts the same term "schema" and refers to it as a *schema moteur,* bringing into the Kantian schematization an element of vital movement.

Epistemologically considered, the distinction is very thin indeed, but being a vitalist rather than a rationalist, perhaps he felt he had to underline the aspect of flux as against the bias of the intellect, which might give a partial or lopsided picture of the Absolute when viewed schematically. The general background of Bergsonian metaphysics, which is the culmination of modern Western thought through its stages of extreme scepticism, empiricism, rationalism, dialectical approach, and finally through the use of direct intuition as an instrument of thought, is ably summarized by Bergson in a special study called *An Introduction to Metaphysics.*

There, after boldly generalizing about the very nature of metaphysics, by stating categorically, as a starting dictum that "Metaphysics, then, is the science which claims to dispense with symbols,"[1] he arranges, under nine items numerically, the special features of his approach to the subject. Under item VIII he says that intuition attains the Absolute. The basic parts of the nine items are given here for ready reference:

I. There is a reality that is external and yet given immediately to the mind.

II. All reality, therefore, is tendency, if we agree to mean by tendency an incipient change of direction.

III. Our intellect, when it follows its natural bent, proceeds, on the one hand, by solid perceptions, and on the other by stable conceptions.

IV. It is clear that fixed concepts may be extracted by our thought from mobile reality; but there are no means of reconstruction of the mobility of the real with fixed concepts.

V. The demonstrations which have been given of the relativity of our knowledge are therefore tainted with an original vice; they imply, like the dogmatism that they attack, that all knowledge must necessarily start

1. Henri Bergson, *An Introduction to Metaphysics,* tr. T.E. Hulme, (The Library of Arts, New York, 1955), p. 24.

from concepts with fixed outlines, in order to clasp with them the reality which flows.

VI. To philosophize, therefore, is to invert the habitual direction of the work of thought.

VII. The object of metaphysics is to perform qualitative differentiations and integrations.

VIII. What is relative is the symbolic knowledge by pre-existing concepts, which proceeds from the fixed to the moving, and not the intuitive knowledge which installs itself in that which is moving and adopts the very life of things. **This intuition attains the Absolute.**

IX. The whole *Critique of Pure Reason* ends in establishing that Platonism, illegitimate if ideas are things, becomes legitimate if ideas are relations, and that the ready-made idea, once brought down in this way from heaven to earth, is in fact, as Plato held, the common basis alike of thought and of nature. **But the whole of the Critique of Pure Reason also rests on the postulate that our intellect is incapable of anything but Platonizing — that is, of pouring all possible experience into pre-existing moulds.**[2]

The reader will have to seek fuller clarification about the generalized conclusions of Bergsonian metaphysics from his writings, but it is not difficult to see from this summary that he himself has prepared and presented to us under italics in serially numbered form, what exactly the peculiarities are of his way of philosophizing. Intuition can attain the Absolute and philosophers from Plato to Kant have not taken care to respect the fluid nature of reality, which they tend to conceptualize statically.

These are the two main objections or special points that Bergson wishes to underline, which we must especially note

2. Ibid., pp. 49-59.

for our purposes in the above extract. It is strange that the last parts of items VIII and IX are left without italics, whether purposely or by mere omission by Bergson, for it is exactly in these phrases that we see some occasion to supplement his thoughts which, in other respects, call for no modification. We have put these lines in bold type: "This intuition attains the Absolute" and "The Critique of Pure Reason also rests on the postulate . . . of pouring all possible experience into pre-existing moulds."

Bergson's objections or amendments to the Kantian schematic version, are made a little more explicit in another context where he writes:

> He (Kant) affirmed, against his immediate predecessors that knowledge is not entirely resolvable into terms of intelligence. He brought back into philosophy . . . that essential element of the philosophy of Descartes which had been abandoned by the Cartesians.
>
> Thereby he prepared the way for a new philosophy, which might have established itself in the extra-intellectual matter of knowledge by a higher effort of intuition. Coinciding with this matter, adopting the same rhythm and the same movement, might not consciousness, by two efforts of opposite direction, raising itself and lowering itself by turns, become able to grasp from within, and no longer perceive only from without, the two forms of reality, body and mind? Would not this two-fold effort make us, as far as that is possible, relive the absolute?[3]

The "two efforts of opposite direction" which Bergson refers to in this quotation suggest the schema which, according to him, has to be dynamic and non-intellectual, and is given to the intuition, which can identify itself with the double movement referred to. The process and the becoming stressed

3. Henri Bergson, *Creative Evolution*, tr. Arthus Mitchell, (Random House, New York, 1944), p. 389.

by the dynamism here has already been noticed by us in the Platonic image of time as "the moving likeness of eternity," and Aristotle's image of the "mind set free from present conditions."

If we examine Kant more closely, we find that the schematization he writes about is neither an intellectual concept nor a static thing as would be suggested by the Bergsonian mould. Kant takes care to say that it is a "formal and pure condition of the understanding." Schematism is not the schema itself but "a function of the understanding." The difference between what Bergson would call a *schema moteur* and the function of the understanding called schematism will be a thin one if the dynamism that Kant omits is added to the elements of the schema. On his part, Bergson does not fill the schema with any definite and detailed structural content to the extent that Kant was able to do with his categories or Eddington with his selective structural factors or relations and relata.

What is given to the Bergsonian intuition is the life tendency or the creative *elan* expressed in biological rather than in mechanistic terms. The points of contact and of difference between the schema in both cases is a matter requiring too much of our attention to show completely here. Bergson as a pragmatist and instrumentalist is able to bring to view pure aspects of movement in reality, while Kant may be said to confine himself to thought in a more conceptual sense. Both however, have somewhat the same scheme in their minds.

The bare outlines of the Bergsonian *schema moteur* are discernible in another context where he goes into the question of the subtle and intricate subject of defects in speech such as aphaxia (lack of the power of speech), apraxis (lack of the power of reading) and dylexis (inhibition after a few words). He examines thereby the psychophysical mechanism in minute detail, basing himself on the medical evidence of various experts. When a new language is heard and spoken we are not able to appreciate anything more than just sounds. The deafness or the muteness involved in the situation arises from the lack of coordination of the motor tendencies of the muscles of the voice to the impressions received by the ear. As this coordination is developed, the sensory-motor mechanism comes into more and more perfected working order. Advancing this explanation, Bergson says: "Thus will take place in our consciousness, in the form of nascent muscular sensations, that which we shall call the *schema moteur* of the speech that is heard."[4]

This *schema moteur* is something that reveals the tendencies in human consciousness, and must be either a concept or some thought-pattern. It must have its being dynamically understood as moving up or down where memory aspects meet motor aspects. It is intuition which is able to enter into the situation in consciousness and understand it as if from inside. As it is also intuition that can attain the Absolute, the schema traces itself on the basis of the Absolute, without merely living in the world of the intelligibles of Plato.

The *schema moteur* is as far as Bergson goes in accepting anything like the schematization of Kant. Platonizing with intelligible ideas may raise our thoughts to the world where symbols become inevitable. By its very definition, Bergsonian metaphysics dispenses with symbols altogether. Pure movement may not be capable of being expressed in symbols conceptually, but there might be a perceptual way through which it could be represented, as in quantum mechanics where vectorial space is subjected to analytical or projective treatment. Geometry, moreover, can be supplemented by algebra, and both together may be utilized categorically and schematically, the one lending certitude to the other so as to make a normalized notion emerge into view. Such are some of the possibilities that suggest themselves to us, although only in vague outline yet at the present stage in our

4. Henri Bergson, *Oeuvres: Matiere et Memoire*, (Presses Universitaire de France, Paris, 1959), p. 55. Our translation.

discussion. A separate study will have to be devoted to this question of a language wherein algebra and geometry can come together to complete an integrated normalizing basis for scientific thinking and expression. Such a language will use both symbols and schematic representations where symbols alone are not applicable, and both together will help to give content to the Absolute that philosophy as well as science is seeking. The moulds, which are objectionable when considered to be static, would then have a revised fluid and dynamic status without losing the schematically subjective structure given to an inner intuitive vision of reality.

Bergson Employs His Own Schematic Language

If metaphysics is a science dispensing with symbols and attaining the Absolute directly through the unitive approach, what is its means of communication? This question should naturally occur to anyone. Grasping incipient movements or tendencies might have to depend on some sort of mute language of its own, free from symbols which might fix it conceptually. Is Bergson himself able to say what he wants to say without anything that is symbolic or schematic? For linguistic purposes at least, one is obliged to resort to some means of expression, and this necessity binds even the philosopher who wishes to avoid every kind of error or ambiguity arising from linguistic limitations. What is not spoken in a drama is expressed in gestures or poses, and words and gestures together make it real through hearing and seeing taking place together. Graphs and maps are in wide use in the scientific world as also plans or blueprints of various projects where visible schemes or sketches form part of precise linguistic expression. Even road signs speak with arrows and circles what cannot be expressed by words or symbols. Thus the possibilities of visual aspects of language, which avoid symbols of an intellectual order are endless in variety and scope. The content of the *schema moteur* can use analytic, projective or vectorial geometry, and there is a great future for schematization as the basis for all such "languages."

In trying to give some content to the *schema moteur* that Bergson has thus arrived at, we find that he adopts two different approaches. In the first place he relies largely on pre-Socratic philosophers, as well as on Plato and Aristotle, and gives us insight into what they meant by providing us with concrete ideas corresponding to the mobile scheme he had in mind. His other approach is through the use of geometrical language, which he just begins to use, without going into all those aspects like projective or topological geometry which are of more recent development. As an example of the first kind we shall content ourselves with one citation. After explaining how Platonic ideas and the *nous* of Aristotle were blended together in the notion of *nous poetikos* in the Alexandrian philosophers, Bergson explains:

> There is then within us, or rather behind us, a possible vision of God as the Alexandrians said, a vision always virtual, never actually realised by the conscious intellect. In this intuition we should see God expand in Ideas. That it is that 'does everything', playing in relation to the discursive intellect, which moves in time, the same role as the motionless Mover himself plays in relation to the movement of the heavens and the course of things.[5]

After indicating thus the virtual status of a vision in the language of theosophy, we find him elsewhere analysing the content of the schema into its component parts. The idea of pure mobility as given to intuition is the main aspect of the dynamism of the scheme of thought which Bergson brings into evidence. In isolating this pure mobility, which has its ascending and descending aspects between matter and mind, the intelligence is like "a lantern glimmering in a tunnel," imparting reality to static aspects of life. Pure becoming is not given to intelligence in this way. One has to enter into it to know it. Thus Bergson wishes to lay down here a subjective

5. Bergson, *Creative Evolution*, p. 350.

process of becoming. In so doing, he adopts at times the schematic language of geometry. His success should indicate to us the lines on which the same could be developed further.

We shall focus our attention briefly on three schematic representations which Bergson employs successively in bringing out the sensory-motor mechanism of our psychological life. He first divides it into two distinct elements which he says the associationist psychologists did not do correctly because of their ignorance of the total structure of consciousness as he describes it. Let us examine the first of the three figures and study its implications in Bergson's own words:

> We have distinguished three forms, pure memory, image-memory and perception, of which none is produced in fact, in isolation. Perception is never a mere contact of the mind with an object that is present: it is entirely impregnated with image-memory which completes in interpreting it. The image-memory in its turn, participates with 'pure memory' which it starts to materialize and with the perception where it tends to incarnate itself: envisaged from this last point of view, it defines itself as a nascent perception. Finally, pure memory, independent by right, does not manifest itself normally except in images that are vivid and coloured, which reveal it. In symbolizing these three terms, by consecutive segments AB, BC, CD of the same straight

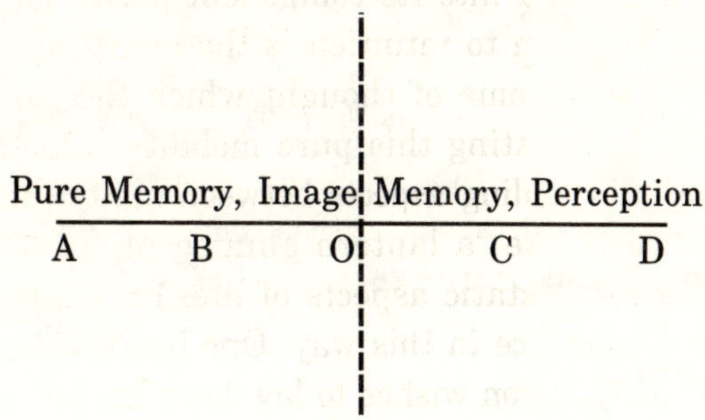

Figure 1

> line AD, one can say that our thought describes this line in a continous movement which goes from A to D and that it is impossible to say with precision where one of the terms finishes and where the other commences.[6]

Here in Figure 1, Bergson gives content schematically to the horizontal aspect of psychological consciousness. Later on he supplements the same scheme with Figure 2, adding:

> Our perceptions, actual and virtual, extend along two lines, one that is horizontal, AB, which contains all the objects given simultaneously, and the other vertical, CI, which gathers to itself a scale of successive memories in time. The point I, which is the intersection of the two lines, is the only one that is given actually to our consciousness. . . . In the first place, the objects spreading in graded fashion along the line AB represent to our eyes that which we are going to see, while, the line CI contains nothing but what we have already seen.[7]

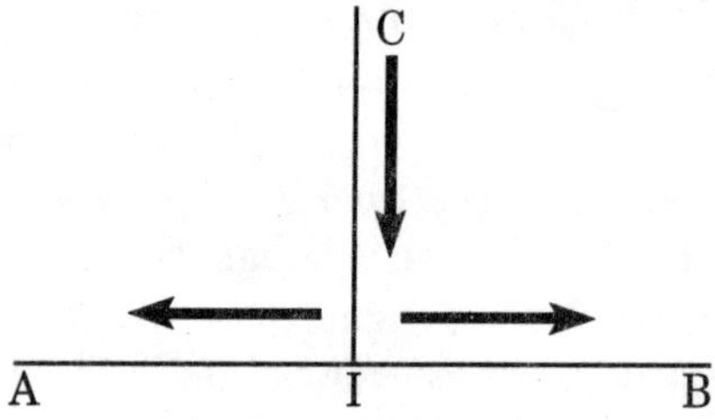

Figure 2

In Figure 2, Bergson brings into the same schematic representation both the horizontal and the vertical factors in the structure of consciousness. Referring to Figure 3, he says:

> If I represent by a cone SAB the totality of souvenirs accumulated in my memory, the base AB founded on the past, remains immobile, while the summit S, which figures at each moment of the present, advances

7. Bergson, *Oeuvres,* p. 285.

8. Ibid., p. 293.

ceaselessly, and also ceaselessly touches the mobile plane P of my actual representation of the universe. In S is concentrated the image of the body; and forming part of the plane P, the image limits itself to receiving or to giving that action which emanates from all the images of which the plane is composed.[8]

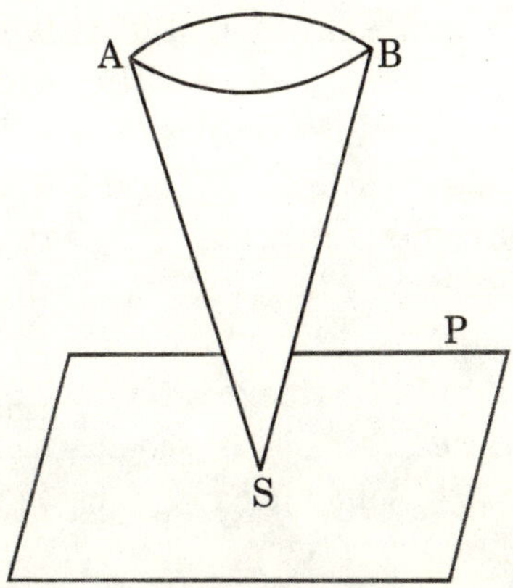

Figure 3

The *schema moteur* which Bergson refers to as taking place within consciousness when two people communicate through language, could also be elaborated into figures on the lines that Bergson has employed above. It would involve, however, trans-physical and intra-subjective events and would have to be worked out in a more complex and elaborate manner to make any meaning. Even the figures given here are vague and incomplete in many respects. This mobile event, further must have an ascending and descending mobility.

Eddington too, we can see, has resorted to such a schematization in his book. *The Nature of the Physical World.*[9] All professors using blackboards indulge in such schematic

9. A.S. Eddington, *The Nature of the Physical World*, (Dent, London, 1947), pp. 54 and 57.

language to supplement their verbal lectures. A proper attempt at schematic representation in a normalized manner is still to be presented.

Concluding Remarks

The notion of the Absolute is implicit. It is at once the subject matter as well as the object matter of all human speculation. It is also the function of what is sometimes called by empirically minded philosophers "Human Understanding." This notion of the Absolute can be viewed from the side of percepts in a fluid mobile form of becoming within consciousness through intuition. The same intuition can penetrate into the Platonic levels of the intelligibles and reveal to us a world of concepts nearer to ideas than to things. There is a constant exchange of thought tendencies understood in pure terms which we can think of schematically as consisting of intuitive semantic tendencies or processes taking place, osmotically exchanging essences through a kind of cosmo-psychologic respiration. The Bergsonian intuition specializes in such motor aspects schematically, while Kant, when subjected to and brought under the same intuitive dynamism and rid of static conceptualism, can also be made to fit into a common scheme. Both together make a plan combining dynamically, as living processes, the world of conceptual becoming as also its perceptual counterpart, to form a common total knowledge situation.

Such a common *schema* so combined into one, can exist only on a basis of general semantics, where semiotic processes are neither of the stuff of mind nor of matter, but occur in a homogeneous matrix of the stuff of which the human soul or psyche is made. This is like the neutral stuff that William James and later Bertrand Russell and others refer to in their doctrines of neutral monism. The thinking substance of Spinoza and the unmoved mover of Aristotle, as also the idea of the moving image of eternity mentioned by Plato in *Timaeus* to which we have alluded, with the *nous poetikos* of the Neo-Platonists, are all supposed to be entities that are neither mind nor matter. Even empirically minded logical positivists like Bertrand Russell are seen to rely upon this same neutral monism. Thoroughgoing sceptics like Hume also rely upon a phenomenology empty of any theological spirit, soul or God. They tacitly accept, as the basis for their scepticism, a Human Understanding which in reality takes the place of the absolute consciousness of the Self. The Self thus tacitly recognized gets a further increase of life in the history of Western speculation with Descartes, whose starting point is the famous dictum *cogito ergo sum*. Here again the Self comes back to the central position, even in the framework of rationalist speculation, to be further clarified and elaborated through Leibniz and Spinoza to Kant.

The "observer" of Einstein and the indeterministic particle physics regulated by quantum mechanics reveal the presence of mind or matter or both in the unified theories of the present day. The hylozoism of the pre-Socratic philosophers thus becomes once again fashionable in modern thought and claims our respect and attention today. Susan K. Langer, writing in *Philosophical Sketches* observes:

> But the greatest of all philosophical insights, the first generative ideas begetting any science at all, lies near the beginning of our whole intellectual culture — the concept of transformation of matter, which we meet first in the physical doctrines of the early Ionians. It has become such a basic assumption in our scientific thought, and has been so highly corroborated by experience, that we no longer recognize it as a philosophical notion. We have extended it from 'matter' to 'energy' and all other conceptions of physical reality. But it really was a bold metaphysical conception; some of Thales' contemporaries could still say, "The sun is new every day."

Modern Phenomenology and Existentialism have helped to revise the contributions of modern methodology, epistemology and axiology, and are also making speculation today more whole or complete. A normative notion of the Absolute, recognized as the regulating integrated unified reference for all correct or scientific schools of thought, anytime or anywhere valid, has to emerge into view soon if speculation is not to be lost in mere verbosity, and if science is not merely to be limited to supplying modern comforts or amenities even when we forget war weapons and their accessories, which give science only negative credit, if any at all.

Science needs normalization from the side of concepts, and speculation has to be regulated or re-normalized from the side of percepts. Thus between normalization and re-normalization lies the nature of precise thinking, based on correct human understanding.

Such are the general lines on which our thoughts have run in concluding this series of essays on the search for a norm in Western philosophy.

11

Summarized Elements of the Absolute Norm

Based on the Upanishads, which are known for their bold flights of pure speculation, the ancient traditional thought known as Vedanta affords us some valuable hints about an integrated unified notion of speculation under the aegis of the same normative notion of the Absolute which is the direct concern of the Upanishads.

In concluding this work, we have to refer to *Vedanta Revalued and Restated*, where we dealt with the notion of the Absolute as implied in the Vedanta of India. In that series on Vedanta, chapters such as "The Double Domain of the Word" and "Semantic Polyvalence in Vedantic Thought" gave us a firm basis on which to build our own finalized version of a dynamic structural scheme.

We have also already covered much ground in *The Philosophy of a Guru,* which might have been titled "The Normative Notion as the Key." Those two works, along with the present one which is concluding here, form an introduction to the text with commentary of the *One Hundred Verses of Self-Instruction (Atmopadesa Satakam)* by the Guru Narayana. It should be clear that the intention of these essays is to present the Guru's philosophy in its proper context, that is to say, in the light of modern thought as well as Indian Vedanta.

It will be noticed that speculation in Guru philosophy has attained to further integration and normalization than in the Vedanta itself. Vedanta marks in this respect the culminating limit to which earlier Vedantists like Shankara,

Ramanuja and Madhva could take it. Perfection of the same tradition on stricter lines of method, epistemology and axiology has resulted in that rare product called Guru philosophy. It is in presenting this in its proper setting that we have traveled so far in time and space. Speculation in Guru philosophy attains to a degree of apodictic certitude which raises it at once to the status of a science. These pages have been written only to justify what might appear to the general reader to be a seemingly tall claim in favour of a Guru philosophy by one so prejudiced.

Advance Outline of the Normalized Scheme

It would not be fair to keep the reader any more in suspense about the terminus of all this seemingly circumlocutious course of speculation. Philosophical speculation can be of two kinds: one concerning the Philosophy of Science and the other the Science of Philosophy. With Eddington and Bergson, referred to in the present series of essays, we have roughly covered the ground of the Philosophy of Science. The Science of Philosophy has to be approached through semantics, logistic, mathematical principles and allied scientific disciplines developed in recent years. Many people are not familiar with the laboratory equipment, the techniques, new logistic and mathematical principles, as also semantics, that go together to clarify the new field of unified science or integrated wisdom, with a proto-language or a metalanguage of its own.

So that the reader may not be troubled with technical details of the less familiar kind, we have relegated such discussion in the form of a monograph. This monograph has received the seal of the Academie Royale de Belgique of Brussels, and has been written in a fully academic style, so that its quality and claims may be above suspicion. This monograph will help the reader to see the justification for some other of the points of the normative scheme which will be given a preview presently. Then we must also refer to many other articles we have written, in which aspects of this scheme and justifications for it have been kept in mind consistently and persistently through three decades or more, as applied to departments of knowledge such as education, economics, etc.

Our thoughts have a plan on which they live and move. This plan is linguistically or mathematically analysable, but is not to be treated as a reality in itself. Further, it has to be thought of in double or duplicated form, one side that is protolinguistic in status and the other that is metalinguistic. One of these lends certitude to the other, just as in human experience the name "rose" supports the rose that is visible and has perfume. Finally one proves the other as simply as in the saying, "the proof of the pudding is in the eating thereof." Geometry can supplement algebra and vice versa, as modern mathematicians agree. Of these algebra is more arbitrary than geometry, which is more earthy and less ideological or symbolic. Schematically speaking both have the same status in an absolutist theory of knowledge. These statements have been justified in various ways in the present study as well as in companion writings elsewhere, to which the critical student is referred.

The Guru Position Summarized

Philosophical speculation must have a norm and a frame of reference to regulate and limit its findings. Full-fledged philosophizing cannot be based on piecemeal methods or on a halting trial-and-error approach where mere opinions come into play. To make speculation scientific this norm must first be precisely defined. It is the structural aspect of the Absolute which can give this precision to all or any speculation, and speculation must at the same time refer, explicitly or implicitly, to the notion of the Absolute.

In the present book we have reviewed the whole range of modern thought to justify this conclusion, and we have not omitted to refer to older philosophers of the West like

Aristotle and Plato, wherever their views could confirm our findings.

The norm has to be understood both in the concrete terms of a structural scheme geometrically understood, and in terms of the more conceptual metalanguage of logistic or mathematics such as is more natural to algebra. Combining unitively perceptual and conceptual factors as the content of the Absolute, after all that we have had to say so far, we can perhaps venture to put down schematically the gist of the conclusion we have arrived at.

Just as the name "rose" given to the actual flower has necessarily to be arbitrary and different for each of the many vernaculars of the world, there has necessarily to be an element of arbitrariness involved in the schematization employed below. Further it should be remembered that the schema is only a linguistic device for reference and can be thought of intuitively with its own fluid dynamism as Bergson would insist upon, as well as by the pure thought of Kant's *schematismos* as understood by him. The semantic status of the scheme must anyhow absolve it from being considered a reality or a fetish in itself belonging to the imagination. If vector or tensorial analysis is useful in modern geometrical algebra, the scheme recommended here cannot be considered altogether without validity, at least as a frame of linguistic reference to normalize speculation in general. The practical or beneficial service to which the scheme could be put by thinkers or writers is finally the only criterion of its validity.

Summing up thus our position in respect of this proto-cum-metalinguistic scheme, we give below the bare outlines of some of the elements which make it up, leaving further elaborations and explanations in the pages of the other two books to which we have referred. Valuable applications kept in mind in departments of thought such as educational theory, economics, Indian myth, Greek tragedy, not omitting the Upanishads, etc., will also be found in the numerous essays we have already contributed.

By way of further apologetics for presenting here a simplified structural scheme for regulating and normalizing correct scientific or metaphysical speculation, we make reference here in ten summarily numbered items to some of the most fundamental peculiarities or secrets which have been recognized by keen thinkers the world over. These should be kept in mind to justify the scheme in the eyes of well-informed and intelligent thinkers or critics.

1°. *The Principle of orthogonality* runs through all the plans of nature. Thinking of such concepts as the Good, the Beautiful and the True implies this *rightness* which is the same as the orthogonality so important in the growth of trees or in building pyramids or skyscrapers. The vertical and the horizontal lines of reference become thus basic and fundamental to thought as well as to language.

2°. *The principle of the quaternion* in the structure of complex numbers and affording the justification for the acceptance, generally, of the Cartesian coordinates in tensorial, vectorial, projective and topological geometries, besides the analytical, is also a second basic law, rule or secret principle running through nature as well as through all thinkable worlds of intentions, rational or value systems (or worlds of classes), sets or ensembles. If we add to these schematic and semantic aspects a dynamism belonging to the circulation of thought, or semiotic processes, we shall have touched upon three of the most important aspects of the scheme.

3°. *Names refer to forms and forms to names*, and, in the strict epistemology in the *universe of discourse* in Boolean algebra, one is arbitrary in terms of the other. Both cancel each other out into the neutral notion of the Absolute. The name aspect may be said to refer to the world of the intelligibles of Plato and the form to the visibles. These could also be named calculables and observables, pure and practical, appearance and reality, the phenomenal and the noumenal, or primary and secondary qualities as in Locke. The Understanding, which is the basis of empirically secondary qualities or phenomenologically of *epoches* or events in consciousness, refers to the vertical and the horizontal aspects respectively. By using these terms, which can be variously referred to as mental and material, mundane and spiritual, etc., as used loosely in languages and in their more numerous vernaculars, one only gives to these various couples of antinomies used by different philosophers a nomenclature independent of particular actual entities.

Here we only follow the precise way of mathematical nomenclature, which consists of abstraction and generalization of all particular cases that are extant now or might become extant hereafter. Like the coordinates of Descartes with the *X* and *Y* axes, which are useful in all kinds of convariations, reciprocities and relationships in time or space whether held together in nature or within forms of reasoning or thought, the scheme is meant only as a reference. Matter and form in Aristotle should be understood to apply, according to what we have said, to the vertical and horizontal respectively, instead of conversely as it might at first seem when compared with Platonic divisions of visibles and intelligibles. The primary qualities of Locke will be vertical as against the horizontal secondary ones, and in Descartes *perception* will be horizontal and *will* vertical. This distinction takes some time to recognize correctly, if not carefully practised in advance.

4°. *The paradox of the one and the many* has to be resolved, as in Leibnizian monadology, where they coexist in a dialectical relation as in Zeno and Parmenides. The *Monad of monads* and the *individual monads* have a pre-established overall absolute regulating reference. The small and the big, the one and the many, the part and the whole, do not affect the structuralism as we understand it here as applicable to the Absolute or its content.

5°. *There is an ambivalent law of alternation* to which the dynamism at the core of the Absolute, structurally understood, is subject. This could be compared to the systole and diastole of the heart. Organisms that grow and divide have the same alternating rhythm to be understood through centripetal and centrifugal influences on the *absolute substance* or the *unmoved mover* at the core of all pure dynamics or processes in the context of the Absolute. The implications of the logarithmic spiral solid of Archimedes is suggestive of a structural scheme for thought processes. We shall bring this forward more completely later. A figure of eight alternation in two vectorial or tensorial spaces, with a one-to-one correspondence between them, as in the heartbeat with its systole and diastole, is as far as we can confidently put forward a formulated structuralism at present.

6°. *The kind of space* that we must keep in mind is one wherein geometry can meet with as much abstraction and generalization as in its sister discipline algebra. Both disciplines must have a homogeneous ground or matrix, neither mental nor material, but neutral, so that the *schema moteur* such as that of Bergson to be understood here can function within its own vertical and horizontal amplitudes or limitations, although with certain asymmetries or disproportions as between one or the other of these two aspects represented by the axes of reference. The space is not limited to Euclidean space only, but is multidimensional. We are satisfied in using a two-dimensional space for the present, for convenience in the simplest of cases of schematic representations, with which alone we are at present concerned at this stage of our study.

7°. *The geometric mind of nature* that designs the varieties of forms through which it wishes to express itself, includes in some corner of its being a regular solid like an inclination or tendency. This is sufficiently clear from the crystallographic shapes seen in minerals such as pyrites and even in snowflakes or in the simple cubical crystals of common salt. The disc of the sunflower reveals designs and proportionate numbers, showing the logarithmic spiral and the sense of proportion of the Golden Number. To make a scheme which is valid geometrically and algebraically at once, therefore, would not be against what nature itself keeps in mind in its creative urge for manifestation.

8°. *There is a double domain of the Word* where, in terms of pure consciousness, there is a darker negative and a brighter positive half. This is the word of the two dictionaries, one that is Berkeleian and the other Lockean. *Relation* and *relata* are the stuff which is all comprehensively included within the scope of these two domains of the Word, where they can coexist when unitively viewed on a homogeneous matrix or neutral ground in Absolute Self-Consciousness.

9°. *The alternating circulation of thought,* in search, as it were, of its own other pole, takes place creatively along the vertical axis, or along the more material or mechanistic horizontal axis, as with a growing ammonite, with right and left hand twists. To visualize this way of evolution requires multidimensional mathematical thought involving logarithmic spirals, etc. We are not yet venturing here into its intricacies.

10°. *The combined or unified field theory,* suited to quantum mechanics, particle physics, and relativity, where gravitational and electromagnetic forces coexist in a general expanding, contracting or mysterious universe hitherto matter-of-fact, which physicists too are now engaged in unravelling, whose wonder grows as they succeed, will afford us further confidence in presenting a more elaborate scheme than we are at present bold enough to outline. The *lingua mystica* of the Upanishads too, understood in the light of a language of unified science, will suggest many valuable leads here.

Index